L'Ecriture et le Reste

"Les saintes et adorables paroles de l'Ecriture"; frontispiece, Sacy Bible, 1702 (Service photographique, Bibliothèque Nationale)

L'Ecriture et le Reste

The *Pensées* of Pascal in the Exegetical
Tradition of Port-Royal

David Wetsel

With a Foreword by Philippe Sellier

" 'N'y a-t-il point moyen de voir le dessous du jeu?'
'—Oui, l'Ecriture, et le reste.' "—"Le Pari" (680/418)

Ohio State University Press
Columbus

Copyright © 1981 by the Ohio State University Press
All Rights Reserved.

Library of Congress Cataloguing in Publication Data

Wetsel, David, 1949–
  L'Ecriture et le reste.

  Bibliography: p.
  Includes index.
  1. Pascal, Blaise, 1623–1662. Pensées. 2. Apologetics—17th century. 3. Catholic Church—Doctrinal and controversial works—Catholic authors. I. Title.
B1901.P43W47   230'.2   81-9610
ISBN: 978-0-8142-5359-5   AACR2

Contents

Acknowledgments — ix
Foreword, by Philippe Sellier — xi
Introduction — xv

PART ONE: THE BIBLE IN THE THEOLOGY OF PORT-ROYAL

I Le Chemin aux Granges: Pascal's "Entretiens" with Le Maistre de Sacy — 3

Pascal and Sacy: Critical Intuition versus the Hard Facts 3 Pascal's "Conversion" and the First Retreat at Port-Royal-des-Champs 4 The *Entretien avec M. de Saci*: A Problematic Text and Its Sources 7 The Evolution of Pascal's Apologetic Vocation 17 The Bible at Port-Royal 20 An Analysis of the *Entretien*: The Uses of Profane Philosophy 24 Subsequent Meetings of Pascal and Sacy: The "Conférences" at Vaumurier 36

II Monsieur de Sacy and His Bible — 45

Sacy's Role at Port-Royal 45 The *Nouveau Testament de Mons* and Arnauld's Defense of Vernacular Translations of the Bible 48 Sacy's Translation of the Old Testament: "Le Langage obscur du Saint Esprit" 53 The Bible and *la libre pensée* 56 Sacy's Apologetic Counteroffensive: A Defense of the Literal Inspiration of Scripture 61

III Sacy's *Préface à la Genèse*: Exegesis in the Service of Apology — 71

The Significance of the *Préface* 71 Moses and the New Testament 73 "Nécessité de prouver aux Chrestiens la divinité de Jésus-Christ comme les saints l'ont prouvée aux payens" 76 Proofs of Christianity Drawn from outside Revelation 79 Sacy's Exposition of his Exegetical Principles 84 On Reading the Bible 92

PART TWO: THE BIBLE IN THE ARGUMENT OF THE *PENSEES*

IV Pascal's Biblicism: The Apologetic Consequences of a Literal View of the Fall   99

The Centrality of the Fall in the Argument of the *Apology* 99 "Un Lieu effectif": Sacy's Presentation of the Fall as a Historical Event 102 Parallels in the *Pensées*: The Specificity of Revelation and the Paradox of the Doctrine of Original Sin 108 "L'Ordre du monde": The Fall Translated into the Language of *expérience* 114 The Absence of a Scriptural Exposition of the Fall in Pascal's Argument 119

V From *Expérience* to Revelation: The Role of the Fall in Pascal's Apologetic Strategy   125

Ordering Pascal's Argument: The *Copies* and the "liasse table de 1658" 125 "Misère"/"Grandeur": The Fall Presented as Philosophical Hypothesis 130 "A.P.R.": The Transition to Revelation 139 The "Conférence" of 1658: The Testimony of Etienne Périer and Filleau de la Chaise 145 Pascal's *libertin* 152 "Preuves convaincantes": Toward a Historical Proof of Revelation 159

VI "L'Ecriture et le Reste": Pascal's Historical Demonstration of the Credibility of Christianity   165

"La plus grande des preuves" 165 "Soumission et usage de la raison" 166 "Le Dieu qui se cache": The Hidden Character of Revelation 170 "Les deux sens de l'Ecriture" 173 Pascal's Vision of Sacred History: The "témoignage" of the Jews 182 "Preuves de Jésus-Christ": The Obscurity of the Historical Jesus 189 "Prophéties": The Definitive Argument of the *Apology* Reconstructed with the Aid of the Sacy Bible 193

Conclusion   211
Bibliography   223
Indexes   227

Illustrations

	"Les saintes et adorables paroles de l'Ecriture"; frontispiece, Sacy Bible	Frontispiece
1	The *Memorial*	6
2	Chronological Table from Sacy's *Préface à la Genèse*	63
3	Title page, *La Genèse*	72
4	"Le Serpent d'airain"; illuminated chapter title, *Les Nombres*, Sacy Bible	75
5	*La Terre sainte*; engraving, Préface, Sacy Bible	90
6	The "Liasse-Table" of 1658, as reproduced in the *Première Copie*	128
7	Passage suppressed in the dossier "Contrariétés" in the *Recueil original*	134
8	Scriptural citations crossed out in the dossier "Contrariétés" in the *Recueil original*	137
9	First page of "A.P.R." in the *Recueil original*	141
10	"Prosopopée" from "A.P.R."	144
11	Moses parting the Red Sea; illuminated chapter title, *L'Exode*, Sacy Bible	186
12	The divine inspiration of Isaiah; illuminated chapter title, *Isaie*, Sacy Bible	195
13	Page documenting a projected argument of "Prophéties": "La Sincérité des Juifs," in the *Recueil original*	201
14	The exaltation of the Divine Name; illuminated title, Préface, Sacy Bible	205

Acknowledgments

My research in France would have proved almost impossible to carry out without the guidance and encouragement of Professeur Jean Mesnard (Université Paris IV), Professeur Philippe Sellier (Université Paris V), and M. André Gazier, bibliothécaire de la Société de Port-Royal. My special thanks are also due my teachers at Brandeis University, particularly Professor Murray Sachs and Professor Erica Harth, without whose patience and help this project never could have been undertaken and finished. I would also like to thank other advisers and friends whose help proved invaluable: Professor Edward Engleberg (Brandeis University); Professor Paul Bénichou (Harvard University); Professeur Bernard Dorival; M. and Mme J.-F. Pelletier; Mlle Agnès Pelletier; Mlle Cécile Drouilly; Agnès and Maurice Comtet; M. François Buresi; the Reverend John M. Livingstone; the Reverend John R. Purnell; Professor Anthony Pugh (University of New Brunswick); Mr. Bradley Berke; and Mr. Robert Sevensky.

The following institutions provided financial and other assistance without which my work could not have been undertaken: the Sachar Foundation, Brandeis University; the American Council of Learned Societies; the Institut Français de Washington; the Andrew W. Mellon Foundation, University of Pittsburgh; and St. George's Anglican Church, Paris.

Avant-Propos

La Bible de Port-Royal, connue sous le nom de son maître d'oeuvre et principal artisan, Lemaistre de Sacy, demeure aujourd'hui encore la plus belle traduction jamais donné en langue française. Ce monument littéraire, érigé peu à peu, au cours du dernier tiers du dix-septième siècle, a nourri la méditation de nombreux chrétiens de France pendant deux cents ans. Plusieurs des meilleurs écrivains français y ont puisé idées de récit, rythmes et images, comme Lamartine ou Hugo. Ce sont les progrès rapides de l'exégèse biblique à l'époque de Wellhausen (1844–1918) qui ont conduit à l'éclipse de la traduction des port-royalistes, vers la fin du dix-neuvième siècle. Dès lors se sont succédé les Bibles de Crampon, de l'Ecole de Jérusalem, d'Osty-Trinquet, et la Traduction oecuménique, pour ne citer que les plus répandues.

Mais une telle éclipse ne saurait être que provisoire. Maintenant que personne ne songe plus à contester la supériorité de l'exégèse moderne, les ambiguïtés sont levées : il devient possible de rouvrir la splendide traduction de Port-Royal, en ne s'attachant qu'à sa beauté littéraire, ou à sa grandeur religieuse.

Passionnante pour le lecteur moderne, la Bible de Sacy l'est encore davantage si ce lecteur est de ceux qu'aiguillonne le désir de comprendre les mentalités du dix-septième siècle. L'univers mental d'un homme cultivé, entre 1650 et 1700, abonde pour nous en zones d'ombre. Ne faut-il pas se faire quelque peu ethnologue pour dialoguer avec des écrivains ou des penseurs qui datent la Création du monde de l'an 4004, croient connaître le jour où Abel fut tué par Caïn? Si les contemporains de Louis XIV s'ouvrent à l'idée d'un espace infini, combien fini demeure le temps de leur histoire! Combien erronée, ou lacunaire, leur connaissance des peuples! Impossible donc de comprendre pleinement un Pascal ou un Bossuet sans s'être familiarisé avec leur vision du monde, une vision à laquelle la Bible sert non seulement de centre, mais aussi de cadre.

C'est ici que le livre de M. David Wetsel, *L'Ecriture et le Reste : The "Pensées" of Pascal in the Exegetical Tradition of Port-Royal*, frappe, dès son titre, par la pertinence de la question qu'il pose. Oui, il est fondamental de situer l'*Apologie* projetée par Pascal au sein des travaux bibliques des port-royalistes. Et la plus aisée des voies d'accès à l'univers biblique des théologiens et des écrivains de Port-Royal, ce sont les amples commentaires qui accompagnent la traduction de l'Ecriture, tout au long des trente-deux volumes publiés par Sacy ou ses amis entre 1672 et 1696.

M. Wetsel entreprend l'exploration de textes aussi riches que peu étudiés. Certes Jean Steinmann, dans son *Pascal* (1954), avait compris à quel point l'écrivain partageait les conceptions de Sacy, et combien les développements du prestigieux traducteur pouvaient aider à comprendre les fragments parfois énigmatiques des *Pensées*. Mais il n'avait guère poussé l'enquête. Ce qui chez Steinmann n'était qu'esquissé acquiert dans les chapitres de M. Wetsel la fermeté du dessin. Comme on sait que Pascal a participé avec Sacy en 1656–57 aux discussions de Vaumurier sur la façon de traduire le Nouveau Testament, et comme d'étranges ressemblances existent entre certaines traductions bibliques des *Pensées* et la version de Sacy, il aurait été acceptable d'entreprendre presque d'emblée l'éclaircissement de Pascal par Sacy. M. Wetsel s'est voulu plus rigoureux, ce qui nous vaut un excellent "état présent" des apports de la recherche sur les rencontres entre Pascal et Sacy. Projetant de réaliser une édition critique des *Mémoires* rédigés par le secrétaire de ce dernier, Fontaine, l'auteur était bien placé pour faire le point sur la controverse autour du fameux *Entretien avec M. de Sacy sur Epictète et Montaigne*. Au même esprit de rigueur nous devons le second chapitre, "Monsieur de Sacy et sa Bible": le lecteur se trouve ainsi insensiblement préparé à entrer dans le coeur du sujet.

Car le centre du livre, c'est la découverte que la *Préface à la Genèse* de Sacy constitue une clé qui ouvre toute une part de l'apologétique pascalienne. On ne tarde pas à être frappé par la fécondité des rapprochements, et on comprend la légitime fierté de M. Wetsel, introducteur à "a document long ignored by, or unknown to, commentators and editors of the *Pensées*" [p. 71]. Au seuil du *Pentateuque*, et de l'ensemble des Ecritures, la *Préface à la Genèse* met en lumière l'unité des deux Testaments, la théorie des figures, l'autorité de Moïse (opposé à Mahomet), la présence cachée du Christ dans tous les textes... Que tous ces thèmes se trouvent aussi chez Pascal ne doit pas conduire à s'interroger de façon classique sur d'hypothétiques influences. Une fois de plus, on s'aperçoit qu'en dépit de l'indépendance de chacun d'eux, les écrivains-théologiens de Port-Royal forment véritablement un "groupe", où circulent et s'échangent les textes-clés et les formules de la Tradition catholique, et où se révèlent communs bien des principes de base. Cherchant à identifier telle citation inconnue des *Pensées*, j'en ai souvent trouvé la référence dans l'index si précieux des *Oeuvres complètes* du... grand Arnauld. M. Wetsel obtient des résultats non moins positifs, et de plus longue portée, en partant de Sacy.

AVANT-PROPOS

Ainsi armé, l'interprète pénètre dans les *Pensées*. Les développements de Sacy lui permettent de faire apparaître en pleine clarté les lignes de force de l'argumentation, foncièrement biblique, de l'*Apologie*: rôle central de la Chute originelle (misère et grandeur); importance exceptionnelle, sinon unique, des prophéties, c'est-à-dire du lien entre les deux Testaments, qui regardent Jésus-Christ comme leur centre...

Assuré dans sa démarche grâce aux apports de Sacy, M. Wetsel—qui utilise maintenant les introductions aux prophètes—sait ne pas prolonger des rapprochements qui ne tarderaient pas à être ressentis comme fastidieux, et dont se contentent quelquefois les érudits, au détriment d'une réflexion serrée. Dans les derniers chapitres de son livre, il *repense* le cheminement pascalien; il reconstitue une "chronologie" de l'histoire et élucide des calculs sur l'avènement du Messie qui déconcertent le lecteur moderne, mais sans lesquels l'argumentation est incompréhensible.

Enrichi de gravures tirées de la Bible de Sacy, l'ouvrage de M. Wetsel fait plus qu'améliorer notre connaissance de Pascal, il contribue à l'ouverture d'un champ. Les interférences entre les recherches bibliques du Grand Siècle (elles-mêmes peu explorées, si l'on excepte Richard Simon et Spinoza) et la création littéraire n'ont qu'insuffisamment retenu l'attention. A l'intérieur de ce champ, la Bible de Sacy demeure assez riche pour que d'autres questions lui soient posées, par exemple en matière de symbolique, de rhétorique, de théorie du langage ou de la littérature... Car nous ne sommes plus tentés d'oublier, aujourd'hui, qu'à Port-Royal la théologie ne se séparait pas d'une intense méditation sur "l'universelle analogie" et sur les pouvoirs de l'écriture.

Philippe Sellier
Professeur à l'Université Paris V

Introduction

"Le progrès des études sur Pascal et son temps," Jean Mesnard writes in the preface to his long-awaited study of the *Pensées*, "a obligé à modifier, par tout un apport nouveau, les positions de la critique."[1] This study seeks to contribute to this reassessment of the meaning of the *Pensées* by examining a context that has heretofore received little attention: scriptural exegesis as practiced by the neo-Augustinian theologians of Port-Royal.

Modern critical approaches to the *Pensées* often have been profoundly, though perhaps unconsciously, influenced by an interpretive principle inherited from the Enlightenment. According to this idea, Pascal's notes for his projected *Apology* for Christianity may be conveniently divided into two categories: the "pensées philosophiques" and the "pensées religieuses." This distinction, whose origins might be traced to Voltaire's *Remarques sur les Pensées de Pascal* (1734) and to Condorcet's edition of the *Pensées* (1776), has had a twofold influence on both modern critics and readers. On the one hand, this artificial dichotomy has obscured the apologetic character of the work by inviting critics to elucidate its purely "philosophical" meaning. At the same time, the distinction has engendered a kind of neglect on the part of readers of the *Pensées* of those passages that the critics deem as but of "theological" interest.

By examining the role of the Bible in Pascal's overall argument, this study seeks to point up the significance and interest of parts of the *Pensées* away from which modern readers and critics have seemed so willingly to turn. It is perhaps easy enough to understand why the typical reader of the *Pensées* has hesitated to make his way through an often difficult maze of historical and theological arguments. The kinds of proofs envisaged by Pascal run very much against the grain of the modern religious sensibility. They appear to violate the sacred modern idea that religious ideas are not subject to rational proofs. They are founded upon a view of history that has long since been transcended and presuppose a system of biblical science that has left but few traces in the modern imagination.

A series of influential critics have, for a somewhat different reason, relegated the theological and historical arguments of the *Pensées* to a place of secondary importance. They have not done so because they questioned the importance Pascal himself attributed to such arguments. Rather, assuming that the specifically Christian context of the *Pensées* has been exhausted as a means of reaching a deeper level of meaning in the work, they seek to transcend the drudgery of historical research and penetrate Pascal's deeper vision of things. Lucien Goldmann, for instance, argued that the unfinished state of the *Pensées* reflects an existential dimension inherent in Pascal's thought: "La seule forme adéquate au contenu des *Pensées* est le fragment."[2] Goldmann did not mean to deny the fact that Pascal's death prevented him from organizing the *Pensées* into a finished *Apology*. Rather, he sought to transcend a historical or biographical understanding of Pascal's use of the fragment form:

> Chercher le "vrai" plan des *Pensées* nous paraît ainsi une entreprise antipascalienne par excellence . . . il n'y a, pour une oeuvre tragique, qu'une seule forme d'ordre valable, celui du fragment, qui est recherche d'ordre, mais recherche qui n'a pas réussi, et ne peut pas réussir, à l'approcher.[3]

Goldmann's search for a "vision tragique" lying beneath the surface of the *Pensées* has influenced a whole generation of readers of Pascal. Goldmann's statement of what he is looking for in the *Pensées* helps us understand the spirit that has animated the modern attempt to find in the work a "philosophical" level of meaning that transcends the specifically Christian vision of things:

> Partant du principe fondamental de la pensée dialectique, que la connaissance des faits empiriques reste abstraite et superficielle, tant qu'elle n'a pas été concrétisée par son intégration à l'ensemble qui seule permet de dépasser le phénomène partiel et abstrait pour arriver à son *essence concrète*, et implicitement à sa signification, nous ne croyons pas que la pensée et l'oeuvre d'un auteur puissent se comprendre par elles-mêmes en restant sur le plan des écrits et même sur celui des lectures et des influences.[4]

The aim of this study is a good deal more modest. Because I am attempting to reconstitute Pascal's vision of sacred history and account for the importance of biblical exegesis in his *Apology*, my search is very much limited to what Goldmann calls "le plan des écrits . . . des lectures et des influences." I examine scriptural exegesis as practiced at Port-Royal in order to point up how very alien Pascal's vision of the infallibility of the Bible is likely to be to the modern reader of the *Pensées*. There is a danger in this approach. Historical research can fall into the same narrowness of vision as a purely literal reading of Scripture.

In seeking to understand the meaning of the *Pensées*, it may be well to keep in mind Pascal's own admonition to the student of the Bible: "Deux erreurs: 1. Prendre tout littéralement. 2. Prendre tout spirituellement"

(284/252). In attempting to penetrate and clarify Pascal's own vision of things, we should not imagine that we are really able to transport ourselves to the Port-Royal of 1658 and enter totally into a historical and religious point of view that is not our own. On the other hand, historical research can serve to prevent us from constructing private interpretations that deform the whole character of Pascal's justly celebrated defense of Christianity.

What might be called the *sens littéral* of the *Pensées* has troubled more than one modern critic. The work is a difficult one to read dispassionately. The reader who feels unable to participate personally in the dialogue between the religious and secular points of view finds himself in the position of having to construct a scenario that permits him to find a seat in the audience. Henri Lefebvre, for instance, solves the problem by confusing Pascal himself with the unbeliever to whom the *Pensées* are addressed:

> Pascal . . . s'engage dans un vaste dialogue avec lui-même . . . dialogue qui est en même temps un monologue intérieur . . . lui-même devient le théâtre et la pièce et l'acteur principal de la tragédie dans laquelle se déploie la conscience tragique.[5]

The unfinished state in which Pascal left his manuscript long served to obscure the apologetic character of the *Pensées*. For the same reason, the so-called "pensées religieuses" suffered considerable neglect. Their role in Pascal's larger argument was simply far from clear. Many editors of the *Pensées* attempted to reconstitute Pascal's apologetic scheme on the basis of evidence internal to the *Pensées*. Such "regroupements," Mesnard points out, "obéissaient généralement à des présupposés fort simples et fournissaient aux lecteurs des idées directrices dont la clarté était souvent obtenue par la réduction à une seule des multiples dimensions des textes."[6]

Only with the discovery of a general order established by Pascal himself has the true character of Pascal's *Apology* emerged. The editions of the *Pensées* of Lafuma (1950) and Sellier (1976) are based upon texts that reflect the extent to which Pascal had ordered and classified his arguments before the onset of his final illness. These editions, based upon the *Copies* of Pascal's papers made by the Périer family, reveal that the "philosophical" sections of the *Pensées* were but a provisional stage in Pascal's apologetic itinerary. These editions present a defense of Christianity that takes its definitive arguments from the realm of sacred history and whose ultimate objective is bound up with a proof of the credibility of the Bible.

The fragments that make up the second stage of Pascal's projected *Apology* have proved particularly inaccessible to readers and critics alike. They have found themselves confronted with cryptic arguments that have no discernible order and with long catalogues of scriptural citations whose documentary function is far from obvious. Moreover, the whole second stage of Pascal's arguments is founded upon a system of biblical science that is essentially foreign to a modern understanding of the two Testaments. Pascal's expertise in this science is derived from the teachings of the neo-Augustinian theologians of Port-Royal. Modern biblical commentaries are of little help in understanding Pascal's interpretation of most scriptural texts. Nor can we take classical medieval exegesis to represent Pascal's interpretive model. Port-Royal sought to circumvent the abuses of the Middle Ages and to initiate a return to the primitive models of Saint Paul and Saint Augustine.

Pascal's perspective on the entire Christian exegetical tradition is focused through the optic of neo-Augustinian theology. The theologians of Port-Royal are his principal means of access to interpretive principles as old as Christianity itself. Fortunately, we have at our disposal a paradigm of biblical exegesis as practiced at Port-Royal: a thirty-two-volume commentary on the entire Bible composed by Isaac Le Maistre de Sacy. Sacy was the recognized authority of Port-Royal on questions of scriptural interpretation. His commentaries on the Bible greatly simplify our task of making sense of Pascal's proofs of the authority and authenticity of Scripture.

There exist significant parallels between the major themes of Sacy's biblical commentaries and ideas that are central to the argument of the *Pensées*. In chapter four, I will examine a view of the Fall that Sacy and Pascal hold in common. That both exegetes elevate this doctrine to the status of a major interpretive principle is not all that surprising. The formula "Adam"/"Jésus-Christ" stands at the heart of neo-Augustinian theology. Of greater significance is their mutual emphasis on the Fall as historical fact. Pascal's entire argument in the *Pensées* hinges upon the same literalist interpretation of Genesis that Sacy spells out in his *Préface à la Genèse*.

Sacy and Pascal both emphasize the apologetic implications of the doctrine of Original Sin. In strikingly similar arguments, they elucidate the practical consequences of the corruption of human reason in Adam's fall from grace. Metaphysical proofs, both insist, are beyond the grasp of man's fallen powers of reason. Apology, both argue, can do no more than exploit proofs that God has already built into the fabric of Revelation. In Sacy's view, the Fall itself is one such potential proof: "Cette vérité est comme un flambeau qui éclaircit ce qu'il y a de plus inexplicable dans l'état présent où la nature humaine est réduite."[7] This same principle stands at the heart of Pascal's strategy in the first part of the *Apology*. The doctrine of the Fall, temporarily stripped of its Christian context and presented as pure hypothesis, serves to convince the unbeliever that the Christian Revelation merits his attention.

In chapter six, I will argue that Pascal's ultimate proof of the truth of Christianity was to have been based on an exposition of the fulfillment of the Old Testament prophecies. In order to be able to interpret these prophecies, Pascal will insist, "il faut les entendre" (305/274). The system of scriptural exegesis that Pascal develops in order to carry out such an interpretation is greatly clarified by the commentaries of Sacy, which shed particular light on Pascal's theory of "figures." Sacy teaches that the "sens spirituel" of a given biblical text never invalidates its literal and historical meaning. In its passion for allegory, medieval exegesis had relegated the "sens historique" of Scripture to a place of relative unimportance. Port-Royal's restoration of the primacy of the literal level of meaning in the Bible is crucial to the ultimate aim of Pascal's *Apology*: proving that Christianity is not of human invention by establishing its historical roots in the religion of the Old Testament.

Protestant exegesis all but abolished the traditional exegetical category of the "sens allégorique." Sacy's approach could hardly be more different. While defending a literal interpretation of every person and event in Holy Writ, Sacy at the same time carries allegorization to a new extreme. He finds "figures" of Christianity in almost every verse of the Old Testament. Sacy's very criticism of Protestant exegesis is that it reverses "l'ordre du temps." While abolishing the "figures" of the Old Testament, Sacy charges, the Protestants make the mistake of allegorizing the New Testament by their purely symbolic interpretation of Christ's institution of the Eucharist.[8]

Sacy's most fundamental exegetical principle—that the key level of meaning in the Old Testament is typological but that the New Testament must always be interpreted literally—is everywhere reflected in Pascal's analysis of specific biblical texts. Sacy's vision of the unity of the two Testaments is the cornerstone of Pascal's Christocentric view of the Bible: "Jésus-Christ que les deux *Testaments* regardent, l'*Ancien* comme son attente, le *Nouveau* comme son modèle, tous deux comme leur centre" (7/388).

Sacy and Pascal hold in common a carefully worked out theological rationale for the existence of "figures." Both exegetes elevate an idea implicit in the Augustinian tradition, the notion of *Deus absconditus*, to the rank of dogma. In both their systems, "figures" are a mechanism of divine predestination, serving to "aveugler les uns et éclaircir les autres" (264/232). When they set about proving the existence of two levels of meaning in the Old Testament, both rely upon a proof "par l'Ecriture même," basing their arguments upon (1) contradictions in the literal meaning of the Old Testament itself and (2) exegetical models found in the Gospels and the Pauline Epistles.

Throughout my study of Pascal's historical demonstrations, I will make use of arguments found in Sacy's *Préface à la Genèse*. Sacy's "Preuve de la prophétie par les Juifs" serves to clarify the role of Pascal's proof of the

Pentateuch in the larger argument of the *Apology*. Pascal's proof of the Mosaic authorship of the Pentateuch reproduces in almost exactly the same form Sacy's arguments concerning the longevity of the Patriarchs. His research into the "état des Juifs" mirrors a constant theme in the Sacy Bible: the centrality of the Jews to any proof of Christianity. Pascal's assertion that the "perpétuité" of the Jewish people "n'a point d'exemple dans le monde ni sa racine dans la nature" (736/492) finds its theological rationale in Sacy's explanation of why Israel's rejection of Christ was a historical necessity.

The definitive argument of the *Apology* is founded on an assumption often restated in the Sacy Bible: the Old Testament prophecies constitute "la preuve la plus assurée" of the Christian religion. Sacy's judgment that any argument in favor of the credibility of miracles must be founded upon the prophecies recalls a critical juncture in Pascal's formulation of his apologetic strategy. Abandoning the idea of an *Apology* constructed around a defense of biblical miracles, Pascal forged the notion that the Old Testament prophecies themselves constitute a "miracle subsistant" (211/180). Both Sacy and Pascal offer an explanation as to why the prophecies are superior to any proof founded upon "raisons naturelles." And both insist that God has built this proof into the very fabric of the Christian Revelation.

Our examination of Pascal's "plus grande des preuves" will suggest the need for a critical reassessment of the whole meaning of the *Apology* sketched by the *Pensées*. Neglect of Pascal's historical demonstrations has led many readers and more than one critic to conclude that the apologist's fundamental though unstated position is that of fideism. Faith alone, or so concludes a prevailing view of the *Pensées*, is the only source of certain knowledge about God. Though perhaps an accurate description of the *Essais* of Montaigne, fideism is far from the ultimate solution offered by Pascal's *Apology*.

Pascal's dissection of certain fundamental assumptions about human reason has definite parallels in the *Essais*. In the *Entretien avec M. de Saci*, Pascal lauds Montaigne's method. "Je vous avoue," he tells Sacy, "que je ne puis voir sans joie dans cet auteur la superbe raison si invinciblement froissée par ses propres armes."[9] The image of reason being brought to its knees "par ses propres armes" is an excellent description of Pascal's strategy in the first half of the *Pensées*. At that stage, however, Pascal's proof of Christianity has only begun to unfold. The *Apology* pushes on to a demonstration of the credibility of Christianity that is founded upon a proof of the credibility of the Bible. Reason is rehabilitated to serve the purposes of apologetics. The prophecies are proofs that are "solides et palpables" (221/189). Reason may act upon them without exceeding its inherent limits.

INTRODUCTION   xxi

In the last analysis, Pascal's proof of the credibility of Christianity is meant to be empirical. Pascal's contemporaries seemed to have grasped this fundamental principle. Writing in the preface to the Edition de Port-Royal of the *Pensées* (1670), Pascal's nephew Etienne Périer reminds the reader that his uncle's principal aim was to demonstrate "que la religion chrétienne avait autant de marques de certitude et d'évidence que les choses reçues dans le monde pour les plus indubitables."[10]

Such a view of the *Pensées* is totally at odds with the position of those who take the famous argument of the *pari* to be the key to the meaning of Pascal's whole *Apology* and conclude that the work is of a fundamentally "existential" character. Nothing could be further from the existential point of view than Pascal's assertion that God has built convincing proofs of the truth of Revelation into the fabric of sacred history. The prophecies are for Pascal "marques visibles" of the reality of a hidden God. They are powerful enough to convince reason that it must abdicate in the face of the case built for the credibility of Christianity. "Il n'y a rien de si conforme à la raison que ce désaveu de la raison" (213/182).

Footnote references are to three editions of the *Oeuvres complètes*. With the exception of the *Pensées*, Pascal's writings are cited from Louis Lafuma's edition (Collection l'Intégrale, Editions du Seuil, 1963). Historical documents not reproduced by Lafuma are cited from Brunschvicg's edition (Collection des Grands Ecrivains de la France). Additional references are to the as yet incomplete edition of Jean Mesnard (Bibliothèque Européenne). References to the *Pensées* appear in the body of the text. Two fragment numbers are given: the first refers to the edition of Philippe Sellier; the second to the text reproduced in Lafuma's *Oeuvres complètes*. Sellier's edition was chosen as a working text because it reproduces the *Seconde Copie*, the most accurate record of the state in which Pascal left his manuscript.

1. *Les Pensées de Pascal*, p. 10.
2. *Le Dieu caché: étude sur la vision tragique dans les Pensées de Pascal et dans le théâtre de Racine*, p. 225.
3. *Le Dieu caché*, p. 220.
4. *Le Dieu caché*, p. 16.
5. *Pascal*, 2:20.
6. *Les Pensées de Pascal*, p. 10.
7. *La Genèse: traduite en françois avec l'explication du sens littéral et du sens spirituel*, p. 253.
8. *Les Pseaumes de David*, Préface, p. 14.
9. Brunschvicg, 4:48.
10. Lafuma, p. 495.

Part One

The Bible
in the Theology of Port-Royal

I

Le Chemin aux Granges:
Pascal's "Entretiens" with Le Maistre de Sacy

PASCAL AND SACY: CRITICAL INTUITION VERSUS THE HARD FACTS

At least one among the first readers of the *Pensées* in the Edition de Port-Royal (1670) did not hesitate to offer the opinion that the apologist was not an expert in biblical science. "M. Pascal ne savait de l'Ecriture," observed a certain M. Manessier of the Sorbonne, "que ce que *les autres* lui apprenaient. On a trop loué ses *Pensées* . . . il n'était pas savant. C'était un bel esprit."[1]

Pascalian scholarship has not seemed overly concerned with the question of the sources of Pascal's biblical science. If "les autres" have traditionally been assumed to be the theologians of Port-Royal, few scholars have chosen to elaborate on the matter. In a sense, this is surprising. Since the eighteenth century, a tradition surrounding the famous *Entretien de Pascal avec M. de Saci* has repeatedly brought the name of Isaac Le Maistre de Sacy, the preeminent biblical expert at Port-Royal, into juxtaposition with that of Pascal himself. Yet only three scholars, none of them in what might be called the mainstream of Pascalian research, have ever attempted to argue that Pascal was closely allied with Sacy.

In his monumental if somewhat dated *Pascal et la Bible* (1930), J. Lhermet did not hesitate to draw the conclusion that Pascal did much of the research for his projected *Apology* at Port-Royal-des-Champs, "où il pouvait imiter M. de Sacy et suivre sa méthode de travail."[2] Geneviève Delassault, Sacy's only modern biographer, reached the same conclusion. "Si l'on considère l'influence que Sacy exerça sur la pensée de Pascal," she argued in 1957, "il est évident que le philosophe a pris . . . souvent le chemin des Granges."[3] André Gounelle, who thought he could detect in the *Entretien* the very genesis of Pascal's apologetic vocation, reached an even more enthusiastic point of view: "Si nous avons les *Pensées*, c'est un peu à Sacy que nous le devons."[4]

If only because scholars are by no means in agreement concerning Pascal's alleged "Jansenist" point of view, the idea that Sacy exercised a major influence on the thought of the author of the *Pensées* is an intriguing one.

However, when we look more carefully at the sources upon which Lhermet, Delassault, and Gounelle base their opinions, it is clear that the three researchers arrive at a hypothesis based more upon intuition than upon hard fact. The facts go something like this. Two brief references in letters of Pascal's sister Jacqueline permit us to establish with certainty not only that Pascal and Sacy knew one another but that Sacy briefly served as Pascal's *directeur de conscience* during his first retreat at Port-Royal-des-Champs in 1655. Another reference in a document left by Pascal's niece Marguerite Périer places Pascal at a meeting at which Sacy presented his translation of the New Testament to his colleagues at Port-Royal.[5]

These references are admittedly suggestive. Pascal's first meeting with Sacy took place just after his conversion experience, an event that almost all scholars underline as central to the writing of the *Pensées*. The second meeting concerned a subject, the Bible, that is central to the argument of the *Pensées*. However, only these two historical references permit us to document with complete certainty even the fact that Pascal and Sacy ever met one another. Nowhere in the works of Pascal is there a verifiable reference to Sacy or a direct citation from his writings. Sacy, who survived Pascal by more than twenty years, refers to Pascal or cites the *Pensées* only two or three times in the course of his vast writings.[6]

We will consider all these references in detail. First, we should not fail to note that there exists a tradition linking Sacy and Pascal that has persisted for nearly three centuries altogether apart from the reliable historical facts. The focus of this tradition, the document known as the *Entretien de Pascal avec M. de Saci*, bears many of the marks of an apocryphal account. If careful recent scholarship has proved beyond a doubt that parts of the *Entretien*, because they can be shown to be based upon discernible written sources, do in fact document an exchange of ideas between Sacy and Pascal, the same scholarship has thrown particular doubt on those very elements in the text that might lend weight to the theories of Lhermet, Delassault, and Gounelle. As a philosophical text, the *Entretien* is a document of the first order. As a historical or biographical document, it is a Pandora's box of textual and critical difficulties.

PASCAL'S "CONVERSION" AND FIRST RETREAT AT PORT-ROYAL-DES-CHAMPS

Composed by Sacy's secretary Nicolas Fontaine in the 1690s, the *Entretien avec M. de Saci* purports to be a transcription of a conversation between Pascal and Sacy that took place some forty years earlier. Fontaine prefaces his account of this conversation with a kind of mise-en-scène whose historicity we must attempt to verify:

> M. Pascal vint aussi, en ce temps-là, demeurer à Port-Royal-des-Champs. . . . Cet homme admirable, enfin étant touché de Dieu, soumit cet esprit si

élevé au doux joug de Jésus-Christ, et ce coeur si noble et si grand embrassa avec humilité la pénitence. Il vint à Paris se jeter entre les bras de M. Singlin, résolu de faire tout ce qu'il lui ordonnerait. M. Singlin crut, en voyant ce grande génie, qu'il ferait bien de l'envoyer à Port-Royal-des-Champs. . . . Il vint donc demeurer à Port-Royal. M. de Saci ne put se dispenser de le voir par honnêteté, surtout en ayant été prié par M. Singlin.[7]

Two sets of historical documents attest to the general credibility of Fontaine's account. The religious conversion to which Fontaine refers is recorded by the *Mémorial* (see fig. 1), Pascal's own account of being touched by divine grace on the night of 23 November 1654. In this document, sewn into the lining of his cloak and carried with him for the rest of his life, Pascal vows a "soumission totale" to his "directeur."[8] Given the fact that Monsieur de Sacy was to become, at least for a time, Pascal's *directeur*, we should perhaps take special note of this vow.

Fontaine's account of how Pascal came to meet Sacy is confirmed by letters written by Pascal's sister Jacqueline, a nun at Port-Royal in Paris. Writing to another sister, Gilberte Périer, Jacqueline never mentions the date 23 November 1654. Instead, she presents their brother's conversion as having taken place over a period of several months. When he visited her in late September of 1654, Jacqueline recalls, Pascal was in a state of great depression. "Au milieu de ses occupations qui estoient grandes . . . il se trouvoit détaché de toutes choses d'une telle manière qu'il ne l'avoit jamais ésté de la sorte." Pascal's feeling of detachment from the world was accompanied by a sentiment of "un si grand abandonnement du costé de Dieu, qu'il ne sentoit aucun attrait de ce costé-là."[9]

In the Jansenist scheme of conversion, the coming of a genuine conversion is often signaled by a feeling of complete separation from God. Jacqueline reports to her sister that she recognized this sign: "Je conçus des espérances que je n'avais jamais eues." In the course of her brother's subsequent visits, "si fréquentes et si longues," Jacqueline did not attempt to interfere with the work of the Holy Spirit. Her role, she reports, was simply to monitor Pascal's progress, "sans user d'aucune sorte de persuasion." Pascal's chief difficulty was persuading himself to accept the guidance of a "directeur." Jacqueline had recommended M. Singlin, the sisters' confessor at Port-Royal-de-Paris. For weeks, however, her brother had hesitated to go and see Singlin. Jacqueline dates Pascal's conversion from the moment of his decision, late in November 1654, to seek an interview with Singlin. "Je ne le connoissois plus . . . en l'humilité, en la soumission, en la défiance et au mépris de soy-mesme et au désir d'estre anéanti dans l'estime et la mémoire des hommes."[10]

Pascal was prevented from acting immediately upon his resolution to put himself under Singlin's direction. Singlin was away at Port-Royal-des-Champs. Moreover, he was hesitant to take on any more "personnes de

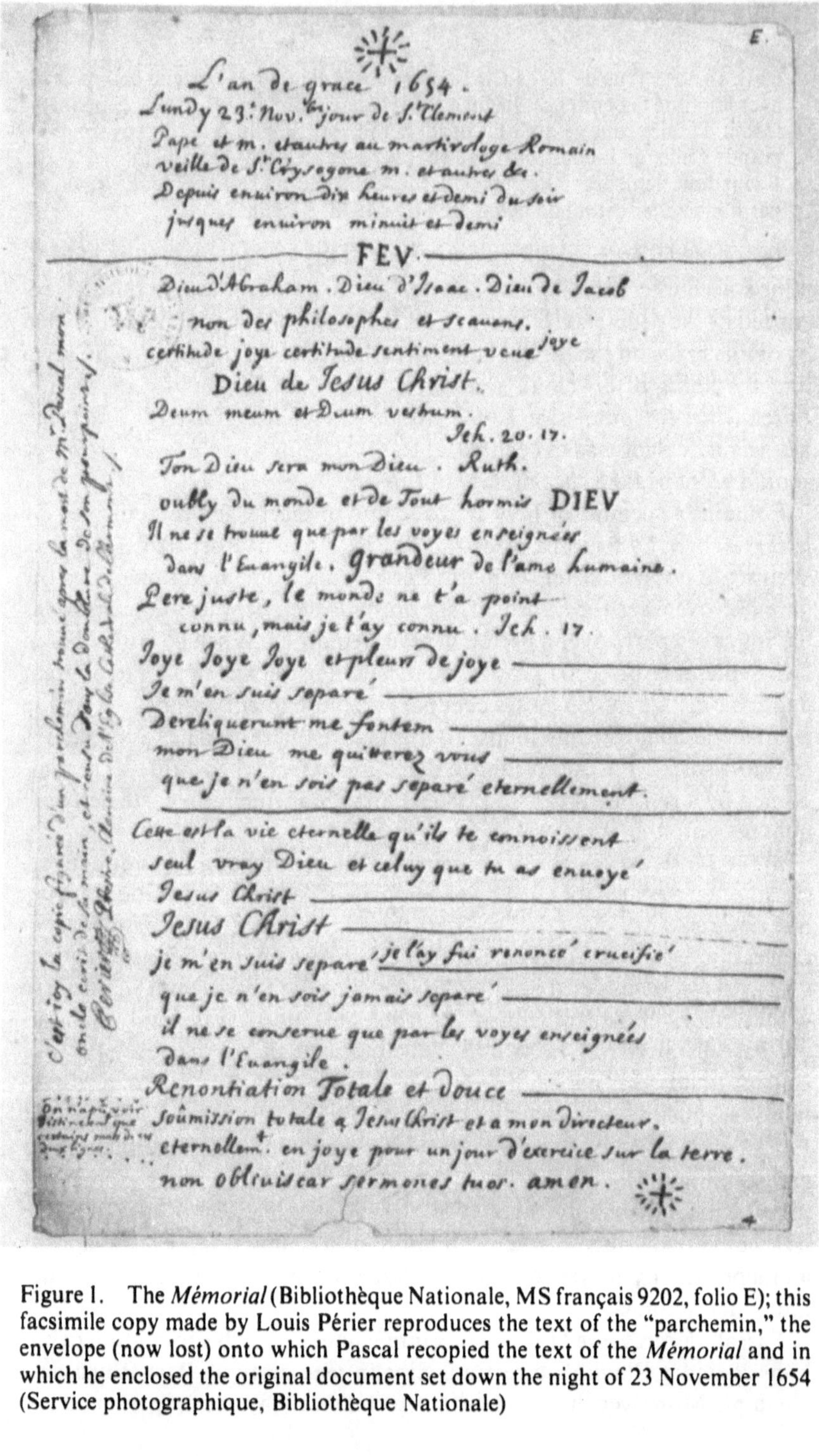

☨

L'an de grace 1654.
Lundy 23.º Nov.ᵉ jour de S.ᵗ Clement
Pape et m. et autres au martirologe Romain
veille de S.ᵗ Chrysogone m. et autres &c.
Depuis environ dix heures et demi du soir
jusques environ minuit et demi

———————— FEV ————————

Dieu d'Abraham. Dieu d'Isaac. Dieu de Jacob
non des philosophes et scavans.
certitude joye certitude sentiment veue joye
    Dieu de Jesus Christ.
Deum meum et Deum vestrum.
                        Jeh. 20. 17.
Ton Dieu sera mon Dieu. Ruth.
Oubly du monde et de tout hormis DIEV
Il ne se trouve que par les voyes enseignées
dans l'Euangile. grandeur de l'ame humaine.
Pere juste, le monde ne t'a point
connu, mais je t'ay connu. Jeh. 17.
Joye Joye Joye et pleurs de joye —————
Je m'en suis separé —————
Dereliquerunt me fontem —————
mon Dieu me quitterez vous —————
que je n'en sois pas separé eternellement.

Cette est la vie eternelle qu'ils te connoissent
seul vray Dieu et celuy que tu as envoyé
Jesus Christ —————
Jesus Christ —————
je m'en suis separé, je l'ay fui renoncé crucifié
que je n'en sois jamais separé —————
il ne se conserve que par les voyes enseignées
dans l'Euangile.
Renontiation Totale et douce —————
Soûmission totale a Jesus Christ et a mon directeur.
eternellem.ᵗ en joye pour un jour d'exercice sur la terre.
non obliviscar sermones tuos. amen.

☨

Figure 1. The *Mémorial* (Bibliothèque Nationale, MS français 9202, folio E); this facsimile copy made by Louis Périer reproduces the text of the "parchemin," the envelope (now lost) onto which Pascal recopied the text of the *Mémorial* and in which he enclosed the original document set down the night of 23 November 1654 (Service photographique, Bibliothèque Nationale)

condition" as penitents. Pascal proposed to his sister that he would change his name, leave his servants in a nearby village, and go on foot to see Singlin at Port-Royal-des-Champs. Jacqueline reports that she counseled her brother against such a rash course and promised to arrange an interview for him with Singlin. She tells Madame Périer that Singlin met briefly with their brother late in 1654 and sent him off at once for a retreat at Port-Royal-des-Champs. Pascal left Paris on 7 January 1655 and stayed for a few days with his friend the duc de Luynes at Vaumurier. A few days later he obtained "une cellule" at the Granges, the retreat house of the Solitaires of Port-Royal-des-Champs.[11]

In 1655, there were fifteen or sixteen Solitaires living at Port-Royal-des-Champs, most of them members of the Arnauld family. The Solitaires had given up wordly careers and devoted themselves to a life of prayer and penitence. Though they did not take vows, they observed a common monastic rule. The first of them, Antoine Le Maistre—whom the Jesuits accused of having read Scripture "avec trop de soin"[12]—had renounced a brilliant law career to live in solitude with his four brothers. Le Maistre's youngest brother, Isaac Le Maistre de Sacy, had taken orders so that he could serve as their confessor and spiritual director.

During his retreat at Port-Royal-des-Champs, Pascal attended the monastic offices and shared the fasts and vigils of the Solitaires. Nor did he lack a confessor. "M. S[inglin]," Jacqueline tells Madame Périer, "luy a pourvu d'un directeur dont il n'avait nulle connoissance, qui est un homme incomparable dont il est tout ravi."[13] There can be no doubt that this "directeur" was Monsieur de Sacy. Jacqueline, in a letter to Pascal himself during his retreat, mentions Sacy by name: "J'ay autant de joye de vous trouver gay dans la solitude que j'avois de douleur quand vous l'étiez dans le monde. Je ne sçay néanmoins comment M. de Sacy s'accommode d'un pénitent si réjouy."[14]

The letters of Pascal's sister serve to substantiate the general outline of Fontaine's mise-en-scène. Yet they tell us nothing at all about the nature of Pascal's first conversations with the *directeur* of his retreat. Since no other records exist that might permit us to corroborate the conversation recorded in the *Entretien*, our analysis of the reliability of Fontaine's account must be based upon an examination of the text itself.

THE *ENTRETIEN AVEC M. DE SACI*: A PROBLEMATIC TEXT AND ITS SOURCES

Shortly after Sacy's death in 1684, Mère Angelique de Saint Jean asked Fontaine to prepare a biography of Sacy based upon his own years as Sacy's secretary. Fontaine spent twelve years assembling his documentation. Only in 1696 did he begin to write his *Histoire des Solitaires de Port-Royal*, which he completed in 1700. Fontaine's manuscript remained unpublished until 1736, when Tronchai brought out a highly edited version of his work under the title *Mémoires pour servir à l'histoire de Port-Royal*. The dialogue that has come to be called the *Entretien de Pascal avec M. de Saci* figures in the second volume of Tronchai's edition of Fontaine's reminiscences.

In 1727, nine years before the appearance of Fontaine's *Mémoires*, a version of the *Entretien* was published by P. Desmolets in his *Continuation des Mémoires de littérature et d'histoire*. Shortly after its publication, Pascal's niece Marguerite Périer, living at Clermont at the age of eighty-four, set about tracing the origins of this document. Since it figured in none of the dossiers of Pascal's papers established by the Périer family after his death, its sudden appearance more than sixty years later seemed to her suspect. She addressed an inquiry to the Abbé d'Etémare, a priest who had frequented Port-Royal in the years before its dissolution.

The response of the Abbé Etémare, who writes to reassure Marguerite Périer concerning the authenticity of the account published by P. Desmolets, merits our attention:

> L'entretien de M. Pascal et de M. de Sacy sur Epictète et Montaigne est tiré (quoique cela ne soit pas marqué) des mémoires de M. Fontaine, secrétaire de M. de Sacy. . . . Il faut que cet entretien de M. Pascal avec M. de Sacy ait été mis par écrit sur-le-champ par M. Fontaine. Il est indubitablement de M. Fontaine pour le style, mais il porte pour le fond le caractère de M. Pascal, à un point qu'il est bien certain que M. Fontaine ne pouvait inventer rien de pareil.[15]

The judgment of the Abbé d'Etémare persisted unchallenged right through until the end of the nineteenth century. Sainte-Beuve detected in the *Entretien* not only the character of Pascal's thought but the style of the author of the *Pensées*: "l'accent original perce à chaque instant et domine." He reaches the conclusion that Fontaine's dialogue is a transcription of a historical conversation: "Qui donc a recueilli sur le temps ces vives paroles? Est-ce Fontaine, secrétaire fidèle? ne serait-ce pas plutôt M. Le Maître, auditeur muet? Dans tous les cas, elles tranchent avec tout ce qui les entoure; le propre de la parole de Pascal était de se graver ainsi et de faire empreinte."[16] Ernest Havet, reaching the same conclusions, offered an explanation of how Fontaine was able to reproduce Pascal's very words: "Il se peut qu'après l'entretien M. de Saci lui-même ait ordonné à Pascal de rédiger ce qu'il avait dit, et de fournir des notes à Fontaine."[17]

In 1655, Fontaine had been at Port-Royal-des-Champs for ten years. However, he was not yet Sacy's secretary, and no one would have dreamed that he would be the one to survive almost everyone else and write the history of Port-Royal. Moreover, as Jean Mesnard points out, Fontaine almost always signals his presence at the other "entretiens" he recounts during the course of his *Mémoires*.[18] In this instance, therefore, we are probably right to assume that he does not even wish to imply that he was present during the conversation he reports.

Only with Fortunat Strowski's *Pascal et son temps* (1907) did critics begin to doubt that the *Entretien* records a historical conversation. Strowski demonstrated that the citations in the *Entretien* from Epictetus and Montaigne are too precise to have been reproduced from memory, not only by Fontaine, but by the participants in the *Entretien* itself. Strowski went on to establish that Pascal cites Epictetus from a specific translation, that of the Dominican Jean de Saint-François Goulu (1607).[19]

Subsequent criticism moved in the direction of casting complete doubt on the historicity of the conversation reported by Fontaine. In 1951, Couchoud demonstrated that another "entretien" in the *Mémoires*, one purporting to reproduce a conversation between Saint-Cyran and Singlin, was pieced together from fragments of letters. Extending the implications of his demonstration to the *Entretien*, Couchoud concluded: "Au sens propre, concret du mot, le célèbre entretien n'a pas eu lieu."[20] Following Couchoud's lead, Geneviève Delassault undertook a more exhaustive study of the various "entretiens" recounted by Fontaine. Of the thirty-six she examined, Delassault managed to discredit the historicity of eighteen: four can be shown to have been pieced together from letters; seven take place before Fontaine's arrival at Port-Royal-des-Champs; another seven "présentent un caractère trop intime pour que l'on puisse supposer la présence d'une tierce personne." Delassault concluded that the *Entretien* must have been fabricated from an exchange of letters: "Fontaine aurait eu vraisemblablement entre les mains la correspondance que le philosophe et le théologien aurait échangée, après leur première rencontre aux Granges, en 1655, si nous pouvons toutefois nous fier à la chronologie donnée par l'auteur des *Mémoires*."[21] However, nowhere in the considerable body of Sacy's extant correspondence was Delassault able to discern even a single reference to Pascal.[22]

Recent scholarship has focused less on the question of whether or not the *Entretien* represents a historical conversation and more on trying to determine the character of Fontaine's sources. As Henri Gouhier observes, once one abandons the traditional notion that the *Entretien* represents a stenographic account, the question of whether such a conversation actually took place becomes much less difficult: "Du moment où personne ne voit plus dans le texte de Fontaine la reproduction fidèle de ce que Pascal et Sacy auraient dit, les principales objections à l'existence de l'entretien disparaissent."[23]

The most illuminating of all the studies of the *Entretien* is Pierre Courcelle's *L'Entretien de Pascal et Sacy: ses sources et ses énigmes*. Before turning to this landmark in the critical history of the text, we must pause to introduce another complicating factor. The difficulty of determining the sources of Fontaine's account is compounded by the fact that we do not possess an accurate text of the *Mémoires* of which it forms but one episode. A digression to this larger problem seems merited, if only because a complete account of the problems surrounding the various versions of the *Mémoires* does not exist elsewhere.

The *Entretien* exists in seven extant versions. Five of these figure in separate texts of the *Mémoires*; the other two, which we will consider first, are versions that reproduce only the *Entretien*. The first of these two is text D, first reproduced by Père Desmolets in 1727 in his *Continuation des Mémoires de littérature et d'histoire* (book 5, part 2) and the subject of the inquiry initiated by Pascal's niece Marguerite Périer. Reproduced in Lafuma's edition of the *Oeuvres complètes*, text D is probably the most widely known version of the *Entretien*. The Abbé d'Etémare reported to Marguerite Périer that the account had been "tiré . . . des mémoires de M. Fontaine, secrétaire de M. de Sacy."[24] However, important differences exist between this text and the version that appeared nine years later (1736) in Tronchai's edition of the *Mémoires*. In his analysis of the *Entretien*, J. Bédier conclusively proves that text D does not derive from Tronchai's edition but goes back to an anterior text. Moreover, Bédier shows that Tronchai's text (T) occasionally makes use of text D to correct faulty readings.[25] As far as the reader is concerned, text D presents one major failing: it omits a key bridge passage in which Fontaine sets up the context of the dialogue he is about to present.

Text G, discovered by Auguste Gazier at the end of the nineteenth century, has been the subject of scant but very divided critical opinion. Copied out in a volume entitled *Recueil de dissertations sur divers sujets théologiques et de morale*, this text bears the title *Jugement d'Epictète et de Montaigne par M. Pascal*.[26] Gazier believed the text to be the oldest extant version of the *Entretien*. This manuscript omits Fontaine's mise-en-scène and reduces Sacy's role in the dialogue to a bare minimum. Gazier therefore concluded that the manuscript represents a copy of the text that Fontaine himself used when composing the *Entretien*. "Fontaine, secrétaire et ami de M. de Saci," Gazier suggests, "ne sera pas résigné à lui assigner un rôle aussi effacé." For Gazier, what Sacy has to say in the other manuscripts represents interpolations on the part of Fontaine. Moreover, the manuscript, in Gazier's opinion, gives the impression of being the earliest extant version: "Papier, reliure, caractère de l'écriture, orthographe, tout concourt à démontrer que ce recueil remonte aux premières années du XVIIIe siècle."[27]

In a note recorded inside the cover of the volume containing text G, l'Abbé L. Cognet also suggests that the *Jugement* was Fontaine's immediate source:

> Je suis pour ma part, enclin à penser que ce n'est pas là une copie du texte de Fontaine, mais une copie du mémoire qui a servi à Fontaine à établir son propre texte. Je ne considérerais pas comme invraisemblable l'attribution de ce mémoire à M. Le Maître, qui a bien pu être présent à l'entretien et qui avait la manie précieuse d'écrire les conversations qu'il avait entendues. Cependant, l'attribution à Fontaine lui-même, qui a si longtemps servi de secrétaire à M. de Saci, paraît aussi assez naturelle.[28]

Comparing the *leçons* of the various manuscripts, Bédier reaches the conclusion that texts D and G, "unis par la communauté de l'erreur," form a family of texts that is separate from the family formed by the five versions of the *Mémoires*. However, Bédier is by no means convinced that text G can be taken to be anything resembling the original source used by Fontaine. His study of the other manuscripts leads him to believe that the *propos* attributed to Sacy hold considerable "titres d'authenticité": "le manuscrit publié par M. Gazier les a supprimés vainement; . . . ce manuscrit n'étant qu'un dérivé des *Mémoires* de Fontaine, et rien qu'un membre d'une famille connue par ailleurs [i.e., text D], ses remaniements isolés sont dépourvus d'autorité."[29]

Text T figures in Tronchai's edition of the *Mémoires* (1736). The inaccuracy of this text is largely a function of the way in which Tronchai, who had known Fontaine, thought it necessary to cut (sometimes extensively), revise, and embellish the whole manuscript of the *Mémoires*. Sainte-Beuve cites a letter of 1731 in which Tronchai evaluates the manuscript (probably a lost version of which text F is a copy) on which he will base his edition:

> On m'a envoyé à revoir . . . *l'Histoire des Solitaires de Port-Royal* par M. Fontaine que j'ai connu. Ce n'est rien moins qu'une histoire qui n'a ni ordre, ni chronologie, ni narration suivie. Ce sont des épanchements du coeur de ce bonhomme. En un mot, c'est un lambeau de ses vies des saints, farci de réflexions ennuyeuses et de prières répétées jusqu'à la nausée. J'en change le titre . . . j'abrégerai ses réflexions, et j'en ôterai entièrement quelques-unes.[30]

Bédier demonstrates that text T forms a close subfamily with two other manuscripts: F and J. Manuscript F, an incomplete version of the *Mémoires* now housed at the Bibliothèque Mazarine (MS. 4555), was found among the papers of Prosper Faugère. A version of the *Entretien* based upon this manuscript was appended to a posthumous edition (1897) of Faugère's edition of the *Pensées*. Manuscript J, an undated but complete manuscript of the *Mémoires*, belonged to Auguste Gazier and now remains in the hands of the Bibliothèque de la Société de Port-Royal (rue St. Jacques). Described by Jean Mesnard as "l'un des plus médiocres de la série,"[31] manuscript J is certainly one of the most difficult to decipher.

Bédier postulates the existence of a lost manuscript "z" that was the common source of J, F (through another lost manuscript "w"), and T. Manuscript "z," in turn, forms, together with another extant manuscript, B, a family that Bédier calls "y."[32]

Manuscript B, which belonged to Sainte-Beuve, may now be consulted at the Bibliothèque de la Société de l'Histoire du Protestantisme. The script in which this version is copied out is very easy to transcribe. Unfortunately, this manuscript extends only to about three-quarters of the text of the entire *Mémoires*. In a note inside the back cover, Sainte-Beuve observes: "Ce manuscript renferme des différences de texte qui . . . montrent quel a été le genre de corrections qu'y a apportées l'éditeur, M. Tronchai. Ces variantes, d'ordinaire peu importantes, prennent surtout de l'intérêt dans le récit de la conversation de Pascal avec M. de Sacy, p. 427–440. On y voit très au net combien le fond est bien de Pascal, mais combien la rédaction et la diction ont été retouchées."[33]

In the judgment of both Mesnard[34] and Bédier,[35] the most accurate extant version of the *Mémoires* is text M: manuscripts 2465 and 2466 at the Bibliothèque Mazarine. This manuscript, which runs to 1,155 pages, contains a preface that is of great help in establishing its authenticity:

> Ce fut à Melun que M. Fontaine composa cet ouvrage: il chercha, pour éviter la persécution, une retraite dans cette ville où il a passé les douze dernières années de sa vie dans une solitude aussi profonde que s'il eût été dans une prison. . . . Comme il n'écrivait que pour sa propre édification et uniquement pour rappeler dans son esprit ce qu'il avait vu et entendu de plus touchant et de plus admirable . . . il marquait simplement les choses selon que la mémoire les lui fournissait, sans observer autrement la chronologie et l'ordre des années. . . . Ce précieux manuscrit, que M. Fontaine laissa en mourant à son hôte et à son hôtesse en reconnaissance des bons offices qu'il en avait reçus, fut communiqué à une dame religieuse de la ville qui, étant capable d'en juger par ses propres lumières et par sa solide piété, le trouva si beau et si intéressant qu'elle s'appliqua tout entière à le transcrire, aux dépens même de sa santé. Cette dame, qui m'est proche parente, et dont le Seigneur a couronné depuis peu les mérites par la mort des justes, a eu la bonté de me le confier, et m'a laissé tout le temps nécessaire pour le faire copier. La Providence a voulu qu'il se soit trouvé des personnes assez zélées pour me prêter le secours de leurs plumes, et j'ai maintenant la joie et la consolation de voir fini un ouvrage qui était commencé depuis plus de quinze mois.[36]

Manuscript M, which is indeed copied out in a dozen or more hands, represents a copy, not of Fontaine's original manuscript (O), but of the copy transcribed by the "dame religieuse" of Melun (x). A family tree (see p. 13) of the various extant and missing versions of the *Entretien* established by Bédier[37] clarifies his understanding of the interrelationship of these texts:

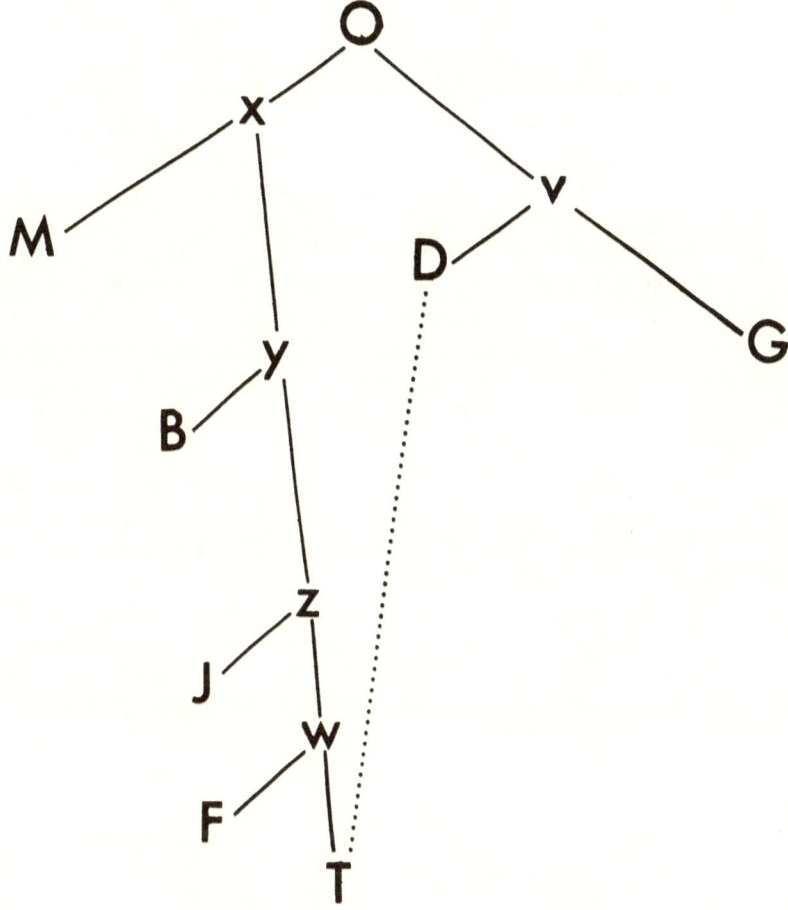

Extant manuscripts of the *Mémoires*:

M Bibliothèque Mazarine, no. 2465, 2466
B Sainte-Beuve (Bibliothèque de l'Histoire du Protestantisme, no. 113)
J Bibliothèque de la Société de Port-Royal, no. 22, 23, 24
F Faugère (Bibliothèque Mazarine, no. 4555)

Printed edition of the *Mémoires*:

T Tronchai, ed., *Mémoires pour servir à l'histoire de Port-Royal* (Utrecht, 1736)

Extant manuscripts of the *Entretien*:

D Desmolets (text in the Lafuma *Oeuvres complètes*)
G Gazier (Bibliothèque de la Société de Port-Royal, no. 128 bis)

Lost manuscripts:

O "ce précieux manuscrit que M. Fontaine laissa en mourant"
x copy made by the "dame religieuse" of Melun
v, y, z, w

If text M represents the most reliable version of the *Mémoires* as a whole, it nonetheless reproduces a less than totally correct version of the *Entretien*. Text D, and even some of the other manuscripts, indicate variant readings that seem more probable than those given by M. Bédier attempts to resolve this problem by comparing all the available texts of the *Entretien* and attempting to eliminate revisions, mistakes, and embellishments attributable to the various copyists. The "archétype" he comes up with[38] represents the most reliable text of the *Entretien* now available and will be the principal text of reference in this chapter.

Bédier's most important contribution to the study of the *Entretien* was to establish that all the extant texts derive from "un même original, O, *déjà fautif*."[39] Bédier insists that though it is possible to reconstitute the text written by Fontaine, this does not mean that we possess anything like the text of the original "entretien" between Pascal and Sacy: "Nous n'atteignons qu'un archétype fautif, sans doute parce que ni Pascal ni Fontaine n'avaient entièrement arrêté leur rédaction."[40]

Courcelle's entire study of the *Entretien* is in a sense founded upon Bédier's conclusion that Fontaine himself was not working with finished texts. "Divers copistes, puis Tronchai, puis les éditeurs modernes," Courcelle observes, "se sont ingéniés à donner à l'*Entretien*, par corrections conjecturales, une syntaxe régulière, un tour logique, un style coulant. Le mérite de Fontaine est, au contraire, de nous avoir préservé presque à l'état brut—si l'on excepte ses fâcheux raccords et ses transpositions au style indirect—les documents dont il disposait."[41] Courcelle admits that the text that we possess is indeed, "une fabrication de Fontaine." As he did for his other "entretiens," Fontaine made use of documentation at his disposal in his personal archives, stitching various fragments together as best he could. The "points de suture," Courcelle demonstrates, are easily recognizable "à leur maladresse, au style diffus, et aux formules de politesse." However, Fontaine's role ends there. The "propos prêtés à Pascal et à Sacy" correspond to the thought and style of each. Moreover, the "discours" attributed to the two are demonstrably not an artificial mosaic of passages taken from manuscript or printed works of either.[42]

If the "discours" of Pascal and Sacy were not fabricated by Fontaine, what then was their source? Courcelle disputes Mlle Delassault's hypothesis that Fontaine's immediate source was an exchange of letters between Pascal and Sacy. According to the epistolary rules of the seventeenth century, such letters would have been characterized by "une rédaction achevée," "une grande clarté," and "une forme élégante." The *Entretien*, on the contrary, is obviously based upon "notes personnelles, jetées hâtivement sur le papier, souvent sous forme de schémas en 'style télégraphique.' "[43]

Courcelle postulates the existence of two sets of "recueils de *Testimonia*" that Fontaine used to construct the *propos* attributed to Pascal and Sacy. These "recueils," obviously "destinés à étayer une démonstration," took the form of concise notes, "nullement destinées à la publicité," that had been set down by Pascal and Sacy themselves.[44] The primitive and fundamental "recueil" was that of Pascal: "Il sous-tend l'*Entretien* d'un bout à l'autre, et il est antérieur aux *Pensées*."[45] Courcelle is willing to entertain the possibility that Pascal prepared these notes in preparation for a discussion with Sacy. On the other hand, he finds it plausible that Pascal "ait constitué son recueil, non spécialement à la demande de Sacy ou en vue de le lui soumettre, mais simplement pour son plaisir ou son utilité personnels. Ce pouvait être un excellent moyen de mettre au net ses propres idées sur les *autorités* de ses amis libertins."[46]

Courcelle goes on to establish with complete certainty that the speeches of Pascal and Sacy in Fontaine's dialogue are based upon written sources. He finds twenty or more citations from Dom Goulu's translation of the *Propos* and *Manuel* of Epictetus and fifty-three explicit references to the *Essais* of Montaigne. Moreover, in the lines attributed to Sacy he finds twenty citations from the *Confessions* of Saint Augustine. The "discours" of both participants in the *Entretien*, he concludes, presuppose a rigorous preparation in which a whole series of precise citations have been selected, ordered, and sometimes modified. Such a process, he adds, could hardly be attributed to Fontaine himself.[47]

Though he lauds the way in which Courcelle has established an inventory of the sources of the *Entretien*, Jean Mesnard suggests the need to modify Courcelle's hypothesis concerning two separate sets of "recueils." The "unité rigoureuse du texte pascalien" leads Mesnard to believe that Fontaine cannot have been working with two separate sets of written arguments. If so, he asks, would Fontaine have presented Pascal as ignoring almost completely the *propos* of Sacy? Moreover, would not Fontaine have had great difficulty constructing a dialogue from "deux répertoires d'arguments séparés"? "Enfin et surtout," Mesnard wonders, "comment les deux recueils seraient-ils venus à la fois aux mains de Fontaine?" Mesnard postulates another hypothesis that takes all these problems into account:

> A notre avis, ce que Fontaine a eu en main, c'est un document d'un type extrêmement répandu, un écrit de Pascal dans les marges duquel Sacy avait porté ses observations. Celles-ci, particulièrement nombreuses au moment où, présentant Montaigne, Pascal expose des doctrines propres à scandaliser un chrétien sévère, ont procuré à Fontaine la matière d'un petit discours de Sacy. . . . Cette hypothèse . . . explique l'unité, la riguer logique et la fermeté des propos de Pascal: ceux-ci nous restituent en effet un écrit authen-

tique. Elle explique pourquoi les paroles de Sacy gardent l'empreinte de sa personnalité. . . . Enfin il est désormais très facile de comprendre pourquoi ce document, dont l'unité est ainsi préservée, parvint aux mains de Fontaine: il figurait parmi les papiers de Sacy.[48]

Mesnard and Courcelle certainly convince us that Fontaine made use of written sources attributable to Pascal and Sacy themselves. But what of the historicity of the conversation supposedly recalled by the *Entretien*? Is Fontaine's mise-en-scène completely fictitious? Philippe Sellier, who has dismissed the *Entretien* as a piece of "fiction rhétorique,"[49] tells me that he thinks the materials underlying the dialogue might date from as late as 1658. Indeed, if we suppose that the *Entretien* does recall the genesis of Pascal's apologetic vocation, the date suggested by Fontaine's mise-en-scène is quite problematic. For why would Pascal have prepared a study on Epictetus and Montaigne for a "directeur" of whom, as Jacqueline Pascal reminds us, "il n'avait nulle connoissance"?[50]

Jean Mesnard argues that critics have perhaps put too much emphasis on the apologetic implications of the *Entretien*. By viewing the dialogue from another perspective, he lends unexpected credibility to the date suggested by Fontaine's account:

> Le problème soulevé dans cet écrit relève au fond de la pédagogie: c'est le vieux problème de l'utilité des lectures profanes. . . . Que la pédagogie fasse insensiblement place à l'apologétique n'empêche pas de reconnaître le dessein primitif de l'étude. Or en 1655, à une époque où toutes les forces ne sont pas encore tournées vers la polémique, Pascal et Port-Royal se soucient beaucoup de pédagogie. C'est à cette époque que remonte la méthode de lecture exposée plus tard dans la *Grammaire générale*. . . . Mis en rapports avec Sacy, Pascal, sollicité ou non, lui aura remis le fruit de ses réflexions sur un problème qui les intéressait l'un et l'autre. Entre les nombreux éléments de réalité qui subsistent dans l'*Entretien* fabriqué par Fontaine, il faut donc compter la date qu'il lui assigne.[51]

Mesnard recalls that Jacqueline Pascal, writing to her brother during his first retreat at Port-Royal-des-Champs, makes a curious reference, in connection with M. de Sacy, to "des jeux d'esprit plus permis": "Je ne sais comment M. de Sacy s'accommode d'un pénitent si réjoui, et qui prétend satisfaire aux vaines joies et aux divertissements du monde par des joies un peu plus raisonnables et par des jeux d'esprit plus permis, au lieu de les expier par des larmes continuelles."[52] "Ne faut-il pas mettre au nombre des 'jeux d'esprit permis,' " Mesnard concludes, "les propos tenus au cours du fameux *Entretien*?"[53] Courcelle as well finds himself unwilling to dismiss completely the historicity of Fontaine's account: "Malgré les raccords factices de Fontaine, malgré le caractère écrit des deux recueils qui sont la base même de l'*Entretien*, quelques indices m'empêchent de récuser comme totalement fictive la mise en scène du rédacteur. . . . Je suis disposé à croire que les deux recueils . . . servirent de canevas à leurs discussions des jours durant, les nombreuses formules du type '*etc* . . .' fournissant l'amorce d'autant de développements oraux. L'artifice de Fontaine . . . a consisté surtout à styliser et à nous présenter—après ces lignes d'introduction mentionnant *plusieurs* entretiens—un entretien *unique*."[54]

If Courcelle is right and the *Entretien* represents a relic of a whole series of conversations between Pascal and M. de Sacy in January 1655, another important question remains to be explored. It is a question that Pascalian scholarship has too often neglected: Did Pascal's encounter with M. de Sacy play a role in the development of his thought or influence the shape of his future *Apology*? The conversion experience that led Pascal to Port-Royal-des-Champs and to M. de Sacy included a pledge of "soumission totale" to those who would direct the course of his spiritual life. Pascal's very arrival at Port-Royal-des-Champs signals his decision to commit himself to specific religious principles, principles of which Sacy was one of the chief exponents. Nor must we let the tone set by Fontaine's *Entretien* obscure the fact that Pascal has come to Sacy as a "pénitent." Before turning to examine the *Entretien* directly, I will attempt to place the text in two essential contexts. First I will examine the evolution of Pascal's theological ideas and apologetic vocation prior to his first encounter with Sacy. Then, through a discussion of Sacy's view of the Bible, I will attempt to suggest why the Sacy of the *Entretien* is so hostile to profane philosophy.

THE EVOLUTION OF PASCAL'S APOLOGETIC VOCATION

The *Entretien avec M. de Saci* does not represent the first time that a subject relevant to Christian apologetics surfaced in a conversation between Pascal and one of Port-Royal's *directeurs de conscience*. Six years earlier, in another series of conversations, he had offered his services to M. Rebours, confessor to the sisters at Port-Royal in Paris. In a letter dated 6 January 1648, Pascal reports the substance of his first encounter with Rebours to his sister Mme Périer: "Je lui dis avec ma franchise et ma naïveté ordinaires que nous avions lu leurs livres et ceux de leurs adversaires; c'était assez pour lui faire entendre que nous étions de leurs sentiments."[55]

In 1648, Pascal had been acquainted with the teachings of the Jansenists for two years. He had first come into contact with the writings of Saint-Cyran when two disciples of the master came to Rouen to tend his disabled father. Impressed by their teachings, Pascal underwent what is now called his "first conversion," persuading the rest of the family to follow his example. Pascal's "conversion" was marked by a fervor for orthodoxy of doctrine. "Ce qui l'a séduit" in the teachings of Saint-Cyran, Lhermet observes, "c'est cette méthode sûre et lumineuse qui prévient toute déviation et toute défaillance dans l'enquête théologique; ce qui l'a charmé, c'est la rigidité de ces dogmes soigneusement purifiés de tout alliage; ce qui l'a satisfait, c'est cette morale pure, parfaite et sans compromission."[56]

The fervor of Pascal's passion for orthodoxy of doctrine is perhaps best illustrated by "l'affaire Saint-Ange."[57] In the first flush of his "conversion," Pascal had chanced to meet Jacques Forton, a defrocked Capuchin who was expounding a curious refashioning of the Pelagian heresy of free will. Saint-Ange's approach to theology was essentially rationalist. He taught that with the aid of reason man might penetrate the realm of revealed mysteries. His theories seem almost a parody of scholastic theology. He claimed to be able to discover the mystery of the Trinity by rational demonstration. From this doctrine, he then deduced the Incarnation, the Eucharist, and a curious doctrine of his own by which he held that the physical bodies of Christ and the Virgin had been created from matter set aside by God at the Creation.[58]

Pascal arrived on the scene as Saint-Ange was discussing a somewhat less than orthodox view of the transmission of Original Sin. He immediately took the friar to task over his departure from Holy Scripture and the authority of the Fathers. In her *Vie de Monsieur Pascal*, Gilberte Périer cites the episode as proof that her brother had always opposed theological innovations and "hérésies inventées par la subtilité de l'esprit":

> Il y avait en ce temps-là un homme qui enseignait une nouvelle philosophie qui attirait tous les curieux. Mon frère ayant été pressé par deux jeunes hommes de ses amis il fut avec eux; mais ils furent bien surpris, dans l'entretien qu'ils eurent avec cet homme, de voir qu'en leur débitant les principes de sa philosophie, il en tirait des conséquences sur des points de la foi contraires aux décisions de l'Eglise. . . . Ils voulurent le contredire, mais il demeura ferme dans ses sentiments. De sorte qu'ayant considéré entre eux le danger de laisser la liberté d'instruire la jeunesse à un homme qui était dans des sentiments erronés, ils résolurent de l'avertir premièrement et de le dénoncer s'il résistait à leurs avis. La chose arriva ainsi car il méprisa cet avis; de sorte qu'ils crurent qu'il était leur devoir de le dénoncer à Mgr. du Bellay, qui faisait pour lors les fonctions épiscopales dans le diocèse de Rouen.[59]

It was a Pascal confident in the orthodoxy of his own opinions who in 1648 approached M. Rebours and offered his services to Port-Royal. "Je lui dis," Pascal reports to his sister, "que je pensais que l'on pouvait, *suivant les principes mêmes du sens commun, démontrer beaucoup de choses que les adversaires disent lui être contraires* [au sens commun], et que *le raisonnement bien conduit portait à les croire*, quoiqu'il les faille croire sans l'aide du raisonnement." Rebours was inflexibly opposed to any such proof of the truths of Christian doctrine. The Solitaire knew of Pascal's reputation as a mathematician and warned that his proposal of a scientific demonstration of religious truth "pouvait procéder d'un principe de vanité et de confiance dans le raisonnement."[60]

M. Rebours's coldness must have diminished Pascal's fervor. Six more years would pass before he once again offered his services in the Jansenist cause. In the intervening years, Pascal seems to have taken increasing care to distinguish between the respective roles of science and Revelation. Even before his conversations with M. Rebours, Pascal had tended to relegate reason and faith to separate spheres. Rome's condemnation of Galileo had produced a tremendous reaction in the scientific circles frequented by the young mathemetician and his father. It was argued that the church had interfered in a domain in which it had no authority.[61] Pascal's own position is reflected in his exchange of views with Père Noel concerning the possibility of a vacuum in nature.

Père Noel rejected the results of Pascal's "expériences touchant le vide" on the grounds that since God fills all things, no vacuum is possible in nature. In an attempt to deny the validity of Pascal's experiments, he subsequently invoked the doctrine of the Eucharist. Pascal replied that the authority of science must be separated completely from that of theology. "Les mystères qui concernent la Divinité," he admonishes P. Noel, "sont trop saints pour les profaner par nos disputes; nous devons en faire l'objet de nos adorations, et non pas le sujet de nos entretiens: si bien que, sans en discourir en aucune sorte, je me soumets entièrement à ce qu'en décideront ceux qui ont droit de le faire."[62]

"Je me soumets entièrement à ce qu'en décideront ceux qui ont droit de le faire." In other words, Pascal maintains, the church holds final authority in a matter of faith like the Eucharist. "Nous réservons pour les mystères de la foi, que le Saint-Esprit a lui-même révélés," he tells P. Noel, "cette soumission d'esprit qui porte notre croyance à des mystères cachés *aux sens et à la raison*."[63] In scientific investigations of natural laws, however, it is empirical evidence that is the ultimate arbiter.

In the *Préface sur le traité du vide*, Pascal elaborates this dichotomy between science and theology, opposing "l'autorité" to "le raisonnement." "Où cette autorité a la principale force, c'est dans la théologie, parce qu'elle y est inséparable de la vérité, et nous ne la connaissons que par elle." In order to establish complete certainty in matters "incompréhensibles à la raison," it is enough to "les faire voir *dans les livres sacrés*." These principles are "*au-dessus* de la nature et de la raison."[64] In theology there is no continuing revelation. All truths can be verified in Scripture.

Unlike theology, the natural sciences are open-ended. They are enriched by discoveries and slowly progress toward perfection. It would be "inutile," Pascal argues, to invoke "autorité" in the sciences. "La raison seule a lieu d'en connaître." Geometry, physics, music, medicine, and "toutes les sciences qui sont *soumises à l'expérience et au raisonnement, doivent être augmentées pour devenir parfaites.*"[65] Whereas theology inhabits a realm of closed revelation whose bounds are traced by Scripture, the natural sciences are subject to ongoing scientific investigation.

When he formulates the idea that scientific and religious truths are not of the same order, Pascal seeks to counter the abuses of both Saint-Ange and Père Noel:

> L'éclaircissement de cette différence doit nous faire plaindre l'aveuglement de ceux qui apportent la seule autorité pour preuve dans les matières physiques, au lieu du raisonnement ou des expériences, et nous donner de l'horreur pour la malice des autres, qui emploient le raisonnement seul dans la théologie au lieu de l'autorité de l'Ecriture et des Péres. Il faut relever le courage de ces timides qui n'osent rien inventer en physique, et confondre l'insolence de ces téméraires qui produisent des nouveautés en théologie.[66]

This partition of the authority of science and Revelation by no means represents Pascal's final resolution of the problem of the conflict between reason and faith. The issue surfaces again in the *Provinciales*. "La parole de Dieu étant infaillible dans les faits mêmes, et le rapport des sens et de la raison agissant dans leur étendue étant certain aussi, il faut que ces deux vérités s'accordent." Whereas, "le rapport des sens est unique," the text of Scripture lends itself to various interpretations. The problem, Pascal concludes, is one of arriving at an interpretation of the Bible "qui convient au rapport fidèle des sens."[67]

The fact that Pascal formulates the problem of faith versus reason in terms of scriptural exegesis is significant. By the time of the writing of the *Provinciales*, he had placed himself under the tutelage of theologians whose whole approach to theology was dominated by the Bible. If we are to understand the theological atmosphere in which Pascal's renewed apologetic vocation was nurtured and formed, we must understand the place of the Bible in the life and thought of Port-Royal. Here, too, we will discover the source of M. de Sacy's hostility to profane philosophy. For what is considered "profane" is necessarily defined in terms of what is held most sacred.

THE BIBLE AT PORT-ROYAL

The Port-Royal known and frequented by Pascal, Lhermet observes, might well be called "la terre classique de la Bible."[68] Scripture was constantly cited in the everyday conversations of the Solitaires and always consulted in difficult circumstances. Saint-Beuve cites a striking example of the special relationship that those at Port-Royal felt they had with the Bible. In 1664, on the eve of the royal dispersal of the nuns at Port-Royal-de-Paris, Mère Agnès opened the Bible at random, in a kind of "sort sacré," hoping to find "une parole d'à-propos."

The Bible fell open to a passage from the prophecy of Jeremiah, a passage that seemed so appropriate to the sisters' dilemma "que le prophète leur parut avoir bien pu de si loin penser à elles et les voir en esprit":

> *Vae pastoribus qui disperdunt*: Malheur aux pasteurs qui détruisent le troupeau de mon pâturage. . . . Vous les avez chassés dehors . . . mais moi, je visiterai sur vous la malice de vos desseins, dit le Seigneur, et je rassemblerai les restes de mon troupeau . . . et je les ferai retourner *à leur maison de campagne.*[69]

The sisters indeed regrouped and took refuge during the coming years at Port-Royal-des-Champs, their "maison de campagne." The episode was always looked back to as an example of the way in which God, speaking through Scripture, had especially favored his children at Port-Royal.

The Bible held such a place of honor at Port-Royal because it represented the purity of primitive Christianity. From start to finish, those at Port-Royal always conceived their enemies to be those who sought to introduce theological innovations into what was for them a closed Revelation. Attempting to sum up Port-Royal's accomplishments, the Jansenist historian Dom Clémencet observed:

> Ils ont possédé la science des Ecritures et nous l'ont apprise. Ils ont cherché dans tous les âges le dépôt de notre foi, et ils l'ont mis dans nos mains. . . . Qui a plus contribué que Port-Royal à épurer la Théologie en la dégageant d'un langage barbare et d'une infinité de questions inutiles et impertinentes, et en apprenant à la puiser dans les véritables sources, qui sont l'Ecriture et la Tradition?[70]

Port-Royal's devotion to the Bible radiated beyond the confines of the monastery itself and inspired a number of literary and artistic works of enduring importance. In addition to the *Pensées* of Pascal, we have only to think of Racine's sacred dramas *Esther* and *Athalie* and of the gospel scenes painted by Philippe de Champaigne. Of particular interest is Champaigne's *La Cène*, for which the Solitaires served as models for the faces of the Apostles.[71]

Monsieur de Sacy, "l'esprit même de Port-Royal" (Sainte-Beuve), was the prime mover of devotion to Scripture at Port-Royal. Recalling Jansenius' maxim "qu'il iroit jusqu'au bout du monde avec saint Augustin," Sacy would invariably add: "Et moi, j'irois avec ma Bible."[72] Everyone at Port-Royal had his particular vocation. Sacy's was twofold: confessor and biblical exegete. As confessor, Sacy never failed to direct his penitents to the study of Holy Scripture. "Dans la direction des Solitaires et en général dans la conduite des âmes," Fontaine insists, "le grand recours de M. de Saci, le remède auquel il renvoyait surtout et toujours, était la lecture et la méditation de l'Ecriture Sainte."[73]

Only the Bible, Sacy explained to penitents, can lead one to theological certainty. "L'expérience nous contraindra toujours d'avouer qu'il n'y a point d'autre voie pour acquérir cette lumière divine, et que ceux qui voudront y parvenir autrement, perdront leurs peines et seront toujours dans des ténèbres dont ils ne pourront jamais sortir."[74] Fontaine recounts that by the time Sacy was appointed confessor to the Solitaires, he had "retranché de ses études tout ce qui ne regardait pas la piété." "[Il] ne quittait qu'avec peine l'Ecriture et saint Augustin pour lire autre chose."[75] Sacy's devotion to the Bible must not be confused with the Protestant doctrine of "sola scriptura." To the authority of Holy Writ, Sacy always appended that of the Fathers of the church.

Sacy had little use for profane philosophy. "On parlait sans cesse," Fontaine recounts, "du nouveau système du monde selon M. Descartes et on l'admirait." When asked that he thought of Descartes, Sacy would say that he could but wonder at "la conduite de Dieu dans ces nouvelles opinions." Aristotle, Sacy observed, having usurped the rightful place of Scripture in the formulation of doctrine, "était enfin devenu le maître des ministres de l'Eglise." Sacy likened Descartes's role in overthrowing the philosophy of Aristotle to that of "un voleur qui venait tuer un autre voleur et lui enlever ses dépouilles." "Tant mieux, plus de morts, moins d'ennemis," Sacy would add, "il en arrivera peut-être autant de M. Descartes."[76]

In his study of Scripture, Sacy sought first of all to "concevoir une grande idee de Dieu."[77] God made the world, he tells Fontaine, for two reasons. "L'une pour donner une grande idée de lui-[même], l'autre pour peindre les choses invisibles dans les visibles. M. Descartes détruit l'une et l'autre." Suppose one said to Descartes that the sun is a "bel ouvrage." "Point du tout," the philosopher would reply, "c'est un amas de rognures." "Quelle nouvelle idée me donne-t-on de la grandeur de Dieu," Sacy asks, "en me venant dire que le soleil est un amas de rognures?"[78]

According to Sacy, Descartes is incapable of recognizing "les choses invisibles dans les visibles." For instance, instead of seeing in the sun, "et en tout ce qu'il produit dans les plantes l'image de la Grâce," the philosopher only attempts to explain superficial physical appearances. Those philosophers who dissect particulars rather than trying to understand the meaning behind the physical world, Sacy laments, "cherchent la vérité à tâtons":

> Je les compare à des ignorans qui verroient un admirable tableau, et qui au lieu d'admirer un tel ouvrage, s'arrêteroient à chaque couleur en particulier, et diroient: "Qu'est-ce rouge là? De quoy est-il composé?" . . . Au lieu de contempler tout le dessein du tableau dont la beauté charme les sages qui le considèrent.[79]

Sacy was unalterably opposed to a Cartesian view of natural laws. As far as he was concerned, fixed and immutable natural laws could only imply the God of the deists. This position brought Sacy into conflict with Nicole and Arnauld, partisans of "l'automatisme des bêtes." Descartes, by establishing a radical dualism between matter and thought, had rendered matter incapable of thought or feeling. Animals, exponents of this principle concluded, must be relegated unequivocally to the category of *res extensa* and treated as automatons.

Fontaine reports that Sacy was profoundly shocked by the practical consequences of Arnauld's enthusiasm for this new theory:

> On ne se faisoit plus une affaire de battre un chien; on luy donnoit fort indifféremment des coups de bâton, et on se mocquoit de ceux qui plaignoient ces bestes comme si elles eussent senti de la douleur. On disoit que c'estoit des horloges; que ces cris qu'elles faisoient quand on les frappoit, n'estoient que le bruit d'un petit ressort qui avoit esté remué, mais que tout cela estoit sans sentiment. On clouoit de pauvres animaux sur des planches par les quatre pattes, pour les ouvrir tout en vie, et voir la circulation du sang qui estoit une grande matière d'entretien.[80]

Sacy can only have put all his authority as spiritual director of the Solitaires into an effort to stamp out such practices at Port-Royal.

Sacy's disdain for human sciences and philosophy is reflected in his approach to the Bible. Purely human curiosity, he maintains, can have no role in any study of the sacred texts. "Libido sciendi" is one of the three "concupiscences" engendered by the Fall. "La passion de savoir qui s'attache à la science pour elle-même," Saint-Cyran had written, "nuit plutot qu'elle ne sert . . . pour la connaissance de la pure vérité."[81] Sacy stresses this idea in his letters to penitents, telling them that they must "mortifier la curiosité dans les choses saintes":

> J'ay des livres pleins de questions . . . sur l'Ecriture que je ferois conscience d'ouvrir s'il n'y avoit quelque nécessité qui m'y obligeast. Il faut laisser aux Docteurs à s'informer de ces choses. Et souvent même ils feroient bien de les négliger pour s'occuper entièrement à ce qui peut servir à leur édification et à celle des autres. . . . Mais pour tous ceux qui n'ont qu'à penser à leur propre salut, ils n'y doivent apprendre . . . qu'à connoître Dieu, non en examinant la vérité avec un esprit de curiosité, mais en l'adorant dans la simplicité de leur coeur. J'aimerois mieux considérer Eve tombée . . . et me la représenter comme un admirable modelle des pénitens, que m'enquérir comment elle ne trouva point à redire qu'une bête parlât.[82]

For Sacy, the Bible can never be the subject of purely intellectual inquiry. Rather, like the sacraments, it is a channel by which divine grace adapts itself to the needs of each reader. "Les eaux sacrées ont cela de particulier, qu'elles se proportionnent et s'accommodent à chacun: un agneau y marche, et elles sont en même temps assez profondes pour qu'un éléphant y puisse nager."[83] Sacy so often warned the Solitaires about the dangers of *libido sciendi* that we should not be surprised to find him giving a similar admonition to Pascal in the *Entretien*. The *directeur* to whom Singlin entrusted the new convert could express extreme hostility concerning the affairs of the secular world. To travel, he liked to say, was but to go and see "le Diable habillé en toutes sortes de façons: à l'allemande, à l'italienne, à l'espagnole, et à l'anglaise." The world, he often told penitents, is an inverted image of the Eucharist: "partout le Démon caché veut qu'on l'adore."[84]

Fontaine tells us, however, that Sacy's essentially monastic point of view never interfered with his spiritual direction. He presents Sacy as an extremely gifted *directeur* who is able to address himself to the individual interests of each penitent:

> La conduite ordinaire de M. de Saci, en entretenant les gens, était de proportionner ses entretiens à ceux à qui il parlait. S'il voyait, par exemple, M. Champaigne, il parlait avec lui de la peinture. S'il voyait M. Hamon, il l'entretenait de la médecine. S'il voyait le chirurgien du lieu, il le questionnait sur la chirurgie. Ceux qui cultivaient la vigne, ou les arbres, ou les grains, lui disaient tout ce qu'il y fallait observer. Tout lui servait pour passer aussitôt à Dieu, et pour y faire passer les autres.[85]

"Tout lui servait pour passer aussitôt à Dieu, et pour y faire passer les autres." It is in the context of Sacy's particular method of spiritual direction that we will begin to examine the *Entretien de Pascal avec M. de Saci sur Epictète et Montaigne*.

AN ANALYSIS OF THE *ENTRETIEN*: THE USES OF PROFANE PHILOSOPHY

As a record of an actual conversation between Pascal and Sacy at Port-Royal-des-Champs in January 1655, the *Entretien* would at first appear to make little sense. If this text really is a relic of Pascal's first encounter with his new *directeur*, does it not seem odd that the subject of their conversation is profane philosophy? In the first place, Sacy deemed the study of philosophy useless in spiritual matters. And why would Pascal, whose very conversion involved a rejection of the God "des philosophes et des savants,"[86] have prepared a series of notes on the subject of Epictetus and Montaigne?

Fontaine seems to anticipate this very question. Sacy, he tells us, was acutely aware of Pascal's reputation as a *savant*: "Les lumières qu'il [Saci] trouvait dans l'Ecriture . . . lui firent espérer qu'il ne serait point ébloui de tout le brillant de M. Pascal, qui charmait néanmoins et enlevait tout le monde." It is Sacy himself who, in the same way he might have begun to question Philippe de Champaigne about painting, initiates the conversation about philosophy:

> [Saci] crut donc devoir mettre M. Pascal sur son fonds, et lui parler des lectures de philosophie dont il s'occupait le plus. Il le mit sur ce sujet aux premiers entretiens qu'ils eurent ensemble. M. Pascal lui dit que ses livres les plus ordinaires avaient été Epictète et Montaigne, et il lui fit de grands éloges de ces deux esprits. M. de Saci, qui avait toujours cru devoir peu lire ces auteurs, pria M. Pascal de lui en parler à fond.[87]

Though set down by Fontaine in the form of a classical dialogue, the *Entretien* recalls, not a debate, but an instance of spiritual direction. This fact is not altered if we accept Courcelle's hypothesis that the dialogue is based upon written sources. Nor is it even altered if we accept Mesnard's theory that the memorandum that Pascal submitted to Sacy essentially dealt with pedagogical issues. For from what we know about M. de Sacy, we cannot imagine him indulging in a purely academic discussion about anything. "Tout lui servait pour passer aussitôt à Dieu, et pour y faire passer les autres." Moreover, Fontaine specifies that Pascal has come to seek Sacy's counsel in ordering his spiritual life. "La fin de l'entretien," Henri Gouhier so correctly observes. "n'est nullement d'intéresser M. de Sacy à la philosophie de ces deux auteurs":

> On ne doit donc pas présenter l'entretien comme si Pascal venait défendre le droit de la philosophie à l'existence contre M. de Sacy qui le conteste. La question que pose Pascal est tout à fait différente. . . . Il y a deux philosophies dont la lecture, lui semble-t-il, peut être utile à la religion chrétienne à condition de savoir s'en servir. Le discours écrit qui fut soumis à M. de Sacy a donc une fin apologétique précise, et c'est bien ainsi que ce dernier l'a entendu.[88]

There is surely something curious about the way in which Pascal launches into his subject. Contrary to what we might expect in a classical dialogue, he gives not even the slightest clue as to the direction or thesis of his remarks. Here we encounter the first of the "points de suture" detected by Courcelle. It is at this point that Fontaine begins to make use of Pascal's collection of *excerpta* from the *Manuel* and *Propos* of Epictetus and the *Essais* of Montaigne. Though, as Courcelle observes, these "*excerpta* quasi textuels" are clear enough to permit their identification, Pascal takes liberties in their transcription and order. First he presents those ideas from each philosopher that he finds in essential agreement with Christian thought. Then he begins his critique of those ideas in Epictetus and Montaigne that run contrary to the Christian view of things.[89]

Pascal begins by telling Sacy that he can but admire Epictetus' conception of man's "devoirs." Though a pagan, Epictetus teaches that man must regard God as "son principal objet," submitting his will to divine Providence because he is persuaded that God cannot act otherwise than with justice:

> Vous ne devez pas, dit-il, désirer que ces choses qui se font se fassent comme

vous le voulez; mais vous devez vouloir qu'elles se fassent comme elles se font. Souvenez-vous, dit-il ailleurs, que vous êtes ici comme un acteur, et que vous jouez le personnage d'une comédie, tel qu'il plaît au maître de vous le donner. S'il vous le donne court, jouez-le court; s'il vous le donne long, jouez-le long. . . . C'est votre fait de jouer bien le personnage qui vous est donné; mais de le choisir, c'est le fait d'un autre. Ayez tous les jours devant les yeux la mort et les maux qui semblent les plus insupportables; et jamais vous ne penserez rien de bas, et ne désirerez rien avec excès.[90]

However, Pascal tells Sacy, Epictetus' view of things contains a serious flaw, an idea that runs completely contrary to Christian principles. "Il dit que Dieu a donné à l'homme les moyens de s'acquitter de toutes ses obligations; que ces moyens sont en notre puissance; qu'il faut chercher la félicité par les choses qui sont en notre pouvoir, puisque Dieu nous les a données à cette fin." In Pascal's view, such a doctrine of free will could be nothing less than tantamount to the Pelagian heresy. When he maintains that man can, through his own efforts, "connaître Dieu, l'aimer, lui obéir, lui plaire, se guérir de tous ses vices, acquérir toutes les vertus, se rendre saint ainsi et compagnon de Dieu," Epictetus loses himself "dans la présomption." These principles of Epictetus' "superbe diabolique" cause the philosopher to establish other erroneous principles: that death and pain are not really evils, that suicide is sometimes justified, and that the human soul "est une portion de la substance divine."[91]

In the margin of the translation of the *Propos* that Pascal consulted is the following note: "Erreur des stoïques qui croyoient que l'âme fust une particule de l'essence de Dieu."[92] In the mid-seventeenth century, the *Propos* and *Manuel* of Epictetus were the breviary, so to speak, of the neo-Stoics. Père Julien-Eymard d'Angers, the best authority on neo-Stoic thought, has observed that though Pascal detected this heterodox feature of Epictetus' theology, he nonetheless failed, along with almost the rest of the seventeenth century, to understand the pantheism inherent in Epictetus' thought. "Tout le XVIIe siècle, y compris le Pascal de l'*Entretien,* sauf, il est vrai, les deux extrêmes, c'est-à-dire Antoine Arnauld et La Mothe Le Vayer, ont cru au monothéisme d'Epictète ou de Sénèque; aucun n'a vu leur monisme foncier."[93]

Had Pascal suspected Epictetus' pantheism, we can hardly imagine him praising the philosopher to Sacy the way he does in the *Entretien.* "Voilà, monsieur, dit M. Pascal à M. de Saci, les lumières de ce grand esprit qui a si bien connu les devoirs de l'homme. J'ose dire qu'il mériterait d'être adoré, s'il avait connu son impuissance, puisqu'il fallait être Dieu pour apprendre l'un et l'autre aux hommes."[94] "Qu'il mériterait d'être adoré" strikes a very odd note. The notion must have scandalized M. de Sacy when he read or heard it. What Pascal means becomes clear only as the *Entretien* progresses.

In order to demonstrate that no philosophical system of human origin is capable of teaching both man's "devoir" and his "impuissance," Pascal now turns to the example of Montaigne. The fact that Montaigne professed himself to be a Catholic, he explains to Sacy, is of no consequence whatsoever with regard to the philosophical positions he adopts. "Comme il a voulu chercher quelle morale la raison devrait dicter sans la lumière de la foi, il a pris ses principes dans cette supposition; et ainsi en considérant l'homme destitué de toute révélation, il discourt en cette sorte:

> Il met toutes choses dans un doute universel et si général, que ce doute s'emporte soi-même, c'est-à-dire s'il doute, et doutant même de cette dernière supposition, son incertitude roule sur elle-même dans un cercle perpétuel et sans repos; s'opposant également à ceux qui assurent que tout est incertain et à ceux qui assurent que tout ne l'est pas, parce qu'il ne veut rien assurer. C'est dans ce doute qui doute de soi et dans cette ignorance qui s'ignore, et qu'il appelle sa maîtresse forme, qu'est l'essence de son opinion, qu'il n'a pu exprimer par aucun terme positif. Car, s'il dit qu'il doute, il se trahit, en assurant au moins qu'il doute; ce qui étant formellement contre son intention, il n'a pu s'expliquer que par interrogation; de sorte que, ne voulant pas dire "Je ne sais," il dit "Que sais-je" dont il fait sa devise, en la mettant sous des balances qui, pesant les contradictoires, se trouvent dans un parfait équilibre: c'est-à-dire qu'il est pur pyrrhonien. Sur ce principe roulent tous ses discours et tous ses *Essais*.[95]

Since the 1640s, the *Essais* of Montaigne, traditionally the handbook of the *honnête homme*, more and more had gained the reputation of what Lhermet calls "le livre cabalistique des sceptiques et des libertins."[96] As far as Port-Royal was concerned, Montaigne was definitely *personna non grata*. Sainte-Beuve even ventures the opinion that one of the great "originalités" of Port-Royal was "de n'offrir pas trace de Montaigne."[97] In the *Entretien*, Pascal is obviously aware of Sacy's prejudice against Montaigne. He takes particular care to point out to the theologian that Montaigne's "doute universel" afforded him a position from which to combat the atheists and Protestant heretics of his own day:

> C'est dans cette assiette, tout flottante et chancelante qu'elle est, qu'il combat avec une fermeté invincible les hérétiques de son temps, sur ce qu'ils s'assuraient de connaître seuls le véritable sens de l'Ecriture; et c'est de là encore qu'il foudroie plus vigoureusement l'impiété horrible de ceux qui osent assurer que Dieu n'est point. Il les entreprend particulièrement dans l'*Apologie de Raymond de Sebonde*; et les trouvant dépouillés volontairement de toute révélation et abandonnés à leurs lumières naturelles, toute foi mise à part, il les interroge de quelle autorité ils entreprennent de juger de cet être souverain qui est infini par sa propre définition, eux qui ne connaissent véritablement aucune des moindres choses de la nature![98]

Summarizing the *Apologie de Raymond Sebonde*, Pascal goes on to suggest that Montaigne's Skepticism might be a useful tool in the hands of a Christian apologist. Montaigne is not content simply to show the uncertainty of "axiomes ou notions communes parce qu'elles sont conformes dans tous les hommes" and the vanity of "opinions les plus reçues." He casts doubt even upon a science like geometry, "dont il montre l'incertitude dans les axiomes et dans les termes qu'elle ne définit point." Montaigne's critique of reason, Pascal argues, might be used to state the case for the authority of Revelation:

> C'est ainsi qu'il gourmande si fortement et si cruellement la raison dénuée de la foi, que lui faisant douter si elle est raisonnable . . . il la fait descendre de l'excellence qu'elle s'est attribuée, et la met par grâce en parallèle avec les bêtes, sans lui permettre de sortir de cet ordre jusqu'à ce qu'elle soit instruite par son Créateur même de son rang qu'elle ignore."[99]

Before Pascal can proceed to a critique of Montaigne's ideas, Sacy interrupts. "M. de Saci," Fontaine recounts, "se croyant vivre dans un nouveau pays et entendre une nouvelle langue, . . . se disait en lui-même les paroles de saint Augustin: 'O Dieu de vérité! ceux qui savent ces subtilités de raisonnement vous sont-ils pour cela plus agréables?' " Comparing Montaigne to Saint Augustine before his conversion, Sacy says he can feel but pity for "ce philosophe qui se piquait et se déchirait lui-même de toutes parts des épines qu'il se formait."[100]

We perhaps look ahead to the *Pensées* and perceive in Pascal's analysis of Epictetus and Montaigne the germ of the great themes "grandeur" and "misère." Sacy, however, finds the idea of using Skepticism to recommend the authority of Revelation extremely daring. His first speech in the *Entretien* is nothing less than a direct attack on profane reading. "On m'a peu conseillé," he tells Pascal, "de lire cet auteur [Montaigne], dont tous les ouvrages n'ont rien de ce que nous devons principalement rechercher dans nos lectures." Montaigne's ideas, he observes, "renversent les fondements de toute connaissance et par conséquent de la religion elle-même." Saint Augustine, Sacy recalls, had reproached the "académiciens" for having employed a system of universal doubt. Why, he asks his penitent, must Montaigne "s'égayer l'esprit en renouvelant une doctrine qui passe maintenant aux chrétiens pour une folie?" Why did Montaigne not put his great talents to better use: "en faire plutôt un sacrifice à Dieu qu'au démon"?[101]

Sacy then directly addresses the question of the relationship of profane philosophy to his penitent's own spiritual life. His comments lead us to believe that Pascal has already spoken to him about his conversion experience of the month before. "Vous êtes heureux, monsieur," he tells Pascal, "de vous être élevé au-dessus de ces personnes qu'on appelle des docteurs, plongés dans l'ivresse de la science, mais qui ont le coeur vide de la vérité. *Dieu a répandu dans votre coeur d'autres douceurs et d'autres attraits que ceux que vous trouviez dans Montaigne.*"[102]

After the Bible, no book was more frequently cited by confessors at Port-Royal than the *Confessions* of Saint Augustine. In urging Pascal to refrain from profane reading, Sacy cites the example of Saint Augustine:

> [Dieu] vous a rappelé de ce plaisir dangereux, *a jucunditate pestifera*, dit saint Augustin, qui rend grâces à Dieu de ce qu'il lui a pardonné les péchés qu'il avait commis en goûtant trop ces vanités. *Saint Augustin est d'autant plus croyable en cela, qu'il était autrefois dans ces sentiments; et comme vous dites de Montaigne que c'est par ce doute universel qu'il combat les hérétiques de son temps, ce fut aussi par ce même doute des académiciens que saint Augustin quitta l'hérésie des manichéens.* Depuis qu'il fut à Dieu, il renonça à cette vanité qu'il appelle sacrilège. . . . Il reconnaît avec quelle sagesse saint Paul nous avertit de ne nous laisser séduire par ces discours.[103] Car il avoue qu'il y a en cela un certain agrément qui enlève: on croit quelquefois les choses véritables, seulement parce qu'on les dit éloquemment. Ce sont des viandes dangereuses, dit-il, que l'on sert en de beaux plats; mais ces viandes, au lieu de nourrir le coeur, le vident. On ressemble alors à des gens qui dorment, et qui croient manger en dormant: ces viandes imaginaires les laissent aussi vides qu'ils étaient.[104]

At this point in their dialogue, Sacy and Pascal are totally at cross-purposes. Pascal's attempt to show how philosophy might serve the ends of Christian apology has been countered by Sacy's warning concerning the dangers of profane reading. Yet, for a moment, Sacy is drawn into Pascal's line of reasoning. Pascal's reference to the way in which Montaigne fought the heresies of his time has caused Sacy to recall that it was the Skepticism of the "académiciens" that led Augustine to acknowledge the errors of the Manichean heresy. Sacy has implicitly admitted that philosophy might serve some kind of *negative* role in apology.

Pascal appears to ignore totally Sacy's remarks concerning the dangers of philosophy.[105] "Encore tout plein de son auteur," he proceeds directly to a critique of Montaigne's position, distinguishing between what might be useful in the *Essais* and what is clearly unacceptable. "Je ne puis voir sans joie dans cet auteur," Pascal tells Sacy, "la superbe raison si invinciblement froissée par ses propres armes." Skepticism can serve to recommend Revelation by undercutting the authority of human reason. Yet Montaigne must be faulted for the practical moral standards he adopts:

> J'aurais aimé de tout mon coeur le ministre d'une si grande vengeance, si, étant disciple de l'Eglise par la foi, il eût suivi les règles de la morale. . . . Mais il agit au contraire de cette sorte en païen. De ce principe, dit-il, que hors de la foi tout est dans l'incertitude, et considérant combien il y a que l'on cherche le vrai et le bien sans aucun progrès vers la tranquillité, il conclut qu'on en doit laisser le soin aux autres. . . . C'est pourquoi il suit le rapport des sens et les notions communes, parce qu'il faudrait qu'il se fît violence pour les démentir.[106]

Montaigne and Epictetus, Pascal concludes, represent "les deux plus grands défenseurs des deux plus célèbres sectes du monde." Stoicism and Skepticism are the only two philosophical "sectes" "entre celles des hommes destitués de la lumière de la religion, dont les opinions soient en quelque sorte liées et conséquentes." They merit attention because they are "les seules conformes à la raison." Epictetus holds that man is capable of reaching God by using the wisdom that God has given him. Montaigne reaches the opposite conclusion. Man can never reach God by himself because his natural inclinations force him to seek happiness in "les biens visibles."[107]

Both Epictetus and Montaigne catch a glimpse of part of the truth concerning the human condition. "J'ai pris un plaisir extrême," Pascal tells Sacy, "à remarquer dans ces divers raisonnements en quoi les uns et les autres sont arrivés à quelque conformité avec la sagesse véritable qu'ils ont essayé de connaître:

> Car s'il est agréable d'observer dans la nature le désir qu'elle a de peindre Dieu dans tous ses ouvrages, où l'on en voit quelque caractère parce qu'ils en sont les images, combien est-il plus juste de considérer dans les productions des esprits les efforts qu'ils font pour imiter la vertu essentielle, même en la fuyant, et de remarquer en quoi ils y arrivent et en quoi ils s'en égarent, comme j'ai tâché de faire dans cette étude![208]

Pascal would appear to have effected a very clever synthesis of two rather different ideas. The first, that God's presence is manifest in his Creation, is a favorite theme of M. de Sacy. God created the world, Sacy tells Fontaine elsewhere in the *Mémoires*, "pour donner une grande idée de lui-même" and "pour peindre les choses invisibles dans les visibles."[109] The second, that philosophy sometimes manages to catch a glimpse of truths that are more fully disclosed in Revelation, is a notion to which the theologian is extremely hostile. Do not these two ideas, asks Pascal, really boil down to the same thing? If it is agreeable to take note of the designs of God in nature, is it not all the more so to find them "dans les productions des esprits"? Pascal admits that one must also observe the degree to which the philosophers, in their search for "la vertu essentielle," miss the mark completely ("s'en égarent"). "Même en la fuyant" is a theme that reoccurs with particular force in the *Pensées*.

At this point in the dialogue, we come upon another of the "points de suture" theorized by Courcelle. Of particular interest is Pascal's use of the term "cette étude" to describe the analysis of Epictetus and Montaigne that he has just completed. Is the word itself a relic from whatever source material Fontaine was using? Or does it simply reflect Fontaine's shift from using documentation to pure invention? In any event, what immediately follows appears to be solely the product of Fontaine's imagination. Before going on to explain why philosophy can never discover "la sagesse véritable," Pascal pauses to reassure Sacy that he is ready to accept the judgment of his *directeur* concerning the utility of profane philosophy:

> Il est vrai, monsieur, que vous venez de me faire voir admirablement le peu d'utilité que les chrétiens peuvent retirer de ces études philosophiques. Je ne laisserai pas néanmoins, avec votre permission, de vous en dire ma pensée, prêt néanmoins de renoncer à toutes les lumières qui ne viendront point de vous: en quoi j'aurai l'avantage, ou d'avoir rencontré la vérité par bonheur, ou de la recevoir de vous avec assurance.[110]

That the passage is of Fontaine's composition is clear enough. We easily recognize the narrator's habitual *formules de politesse*. But does this brief interlude contain a grain of truth? Is Fontaine perhaps relying on a tradition which recalled that Pascal took very seriously the role of penitent and the authority of his *directeur*? Or is he simply manufacturing a moment designed to throw a favorable light on his former master Sacy? After all, in writing the *Entretien* Fontaine had to contend with the fact that Pascal had already become, as Courcelle reminds us, "pour la postérité le grand homme du jansénisme."[111] On the other hand, it is interesting that Fontaine inserts this deference on the part of Pascal just before the dialogue's climax. Fontaine, at least, appears to think that Pascal is on the point of submitting an idea—perhaps even an apologetic scheme—to Sacy for his approval.

"La source des erreurs de ces deux sectes," Pascal goes on to explain to Sacy, "est de n'avoir pas su que *l'état de l'homme à présent diffère de celui de sa création*." Epictetus and the Stoics rightly perceive "quelques traces" of man's "première grandeur." Yet because they know nothing of the corruption of all mankind in Adam, they treat human nature as "saine et sans besoin de réparateur." Montaigne and the Skeptics, on the other hand, "éprouvant la misère présente et ignorant la première dignité" of the human condition, conclude that human nature is "nécessairement infirme et irréparable." "Ainsi ces deux états qu'il fallait connaître ensemble pour voir toute la vérité, étant connus séparément, conduisent nécessairement à l'un de ces deux vices, à l'orgueil ou à la paresse."[112]

It might seem, Pascal observes, that a synthesis of the philosophical systems of Epictetus and Montaigne might form, "en les alliant, une morale parfaite." Yet such is far from the case. "Au lieu de cette paix, il ne résulterait de leur assemblage qu'une guerre et qu'une destruction générale: car l'un établissant la certitude, l'autre le doute, l'un la grandeur de l'homme, l'autre sa faiblesse, ils ruinent la vérité aussi bien que la fausseté l'un de l'autre." The only solution is for these "lumières imparfaites" to give way to the truth of Revelation. Because they can neither coexist because of their "défauts" nor "s'unir à cause de leurs oppositions," the conflicting philosophies of Epictetus and Montaigne must therefore "se brisent et s'anéantissent pour faire place à la vérité de l'Evangile":

> C'est elle [l'Evangile] qui accorde les contrariétés par un art tout divin, et, unissant tout ce qui est de vrai et chassant tout ce qui de faux, elle en fait une sagesse véritablement céleste où s'accordent ces opposés, qui étaient incompatibles dans ces doctrines humaines.[113]

In arguing that only Revelation can resolve the "contrariétés" arrived at by human reason, Pascal invokes a doctrine dear to the theologians of Port-Royal. "Il n'appartient qu'à la grâce," Saint-Cyran had written, "d'allier les choses contraires, qui ne sont plus contraires lorsqu'elles sont alliées."[114] "Ces sages du monde," Pascal explains to Sacy, err in placing both the source of man's "grandeur" and the source of his "faiblesse" "dans un même sujet," i.e., human nature. Scripture, in its account of the Fall, teaches that man's "grandeur" and his "misère" have completely different origins: "tout ce qu'il y a d'infirme appartenant à la nature, tout ce qu'il y a de puissant appartenant à la grâce."[115]

"Il fallait être Dieu," Pascal had pointed out to Sacy earlier in their conversation, in order to be able to teach men both their "impuissance" and their "devoirs." When Pascal concludes that only Scripture is able to reconcile these principles that are incompatible in human doctrines, he invokes an idea central to Sacy's understanding of the Bible. The Bible, Sacy teaches throughout his scriptural commentaries, is a mirror of the Incarnation. The solution to the human enigma proposed by Scripture, Pascal takes care to observe, is but an image and an effect of that same incarnation:

> Voilà l'union étonnante et nouvelle que Dieu seul pouvait enseigner, et que lui seul pouvait faire, et *qui n'est qu'une image et qu'un effet de l'union ineffable de deux natures dans la seule personne d'un Homme-Dieu.*[116]

At this point in the course of their *entretien*, or so Fontaine reports, Sacy "ne put s'empêcher de témoigner à M. Pascal qu'il était surpris comment il savait tourner les choses." Pascal has just expressed Sacy's own understanding not only of the meaning of Christ's Incarnation in Scripture but of the relationship between nature and grace.[117] Conceding that his penitent's "lectures lui étaient utiles," Sacy compares Pascal to "ces médecins habiles qui, par la manière adroite de préparer les plus grands poisons, en savent tirer les plus grands remèdes." However, Fontaine makes it clear that Sacy has by no means changed his opinion concerning the dangers of profane reading. He cannot believe, he tells Pascal, that such "lectures" would benefit most people. Most of his penitents, he insists in his last speech in the dialogue, would lack sufficient "élévation pour lire ces auteurs et en juger, et savoir tirer les perles du milieu du fumier:

> *Aurum ex stercore Tertulliani,* disait un Père. Ce qu'on pouvait bien dire de ces philosophes, dont le fumier, par sa noire fumée, pouvait obscurcir la foi

> chancelante de ceux qui les lisent. C'est pourquoi il conseillerait toujours à ces personnes de ne pas s'exposer légèrement à ces lectures, de peur de se perdre avec ces philosophes, et de devenir l'objet des démons et la pâture des vers, selon le langage de l'Ecriture, comme ces philosophes l'ont été.[118]

In his final speech in the dialogue, Pascal, picking up Sacy's use of the word *utile*, recapitulates the way in which he thinks Epictetus and Montaigne might be put to use in Christian apologetics. In Epictetus, he finds "un art incomparable pour troubler le repos de ceux qui le cherchent dans les choses extérieures, et pour les forcer à reconnaître qu'ils sont de véritables esclaves et de misérables aveugles." Montaigne, on the other hand, "est incomparable . . . pour désabuser ceux qui s'attachent à leurs opinions et qui croient trouver dans les sciences des vérités inébranlables." Montaigne, he notes, might be a useful ally in convincing reason of its "peu de lumière" and of its "égarements." Hence, Skepticism might actually be used to debunk the notion that it is not reasonable to believe in such revealed mysteries as the Eucharist and the Incarnation. Pascal acknowledges that "ces lectures doivent être réglées avec beaucoup de soin." Epictetus might deceive some into thinking that man can work out his own salvation. "Montaigne est absolument pernicieux à ceux qui ont quelque pente à l'impiété et aux vices." Pascal ends what he has to say in the *Entretien* by insisting that neither the Stoics nor the Skeptics can lead a man to virtue. Rather, the complementary role of their opposing philosophies, taken together, is to "troubler dans les vices."[119]

We may perhaps think ahead to the *Pensées* and recognize the way in which Pascal will use ideas taken from Epictetus and Montaigne to trouble his *libertin* "dans ses vices." But what of the historical Sacy's reaction to Pascal's scheme? Given the distance that has separated the points of view of the two throughout the *Entretien*, Fontaine's conclusion seems far from satisfying:

> Ce fut ainsi que ces deux personnes d'un si bel esprit s'accordèrent enfin au sujet de la lecture de ces philosophes, et se rencontrèrent au même terme, où ils arrivèrent néanmoins d'une manière différente: M. de Saci y étant venu tout d'un coup par la claire vue du christianisme, et M. Pascal n'y étant arrivé qu'après beaucoup de tours, en s'attachant aux principes de ces philosophes.[120]

"S'accordèrent"? "Se rencontrèrent au même terme"? Fontaine hardly seems to have understood the real questions at issue in his dialogue. He writes as if Pascal has somehow come round to Sacy's point of view, albeit "d'une manière différente." We must not forget that, at least where Sacy is concerned, Fontaine's *Mémoires* often approach the genre of hagiography. As Courcelle observes, "Fontaine, malgré son désir de synthèse finale . . . dissimule mal qu'il partage la sévérité de Sacy à l'égard des 'détours' philosophiques de l'apologétique pascalienne."[121] But even if we take Fontaine's prejudice into account, the fact remains that no real synthesis or resolution has taken place by the end of the *Entretien*. Courcelle's perception on this point is particularly acute: "Il s'agit d'une rude prise de contact entre deux esprits de valeur, chacun d'une formation achievée, un peu sourds l'un à l'autre, nullement d'accord au départ, à peine plus à l'arrivée."[122]

If anything, Sacy has simply made an exception to his normal rule regarding profane philosophy. But can we believe Fontaine when he observes that Sacy conceded that his penitent's "lectures lui étaient utile"? Can this be taken as indicative of the fact that the real Sacy came round to giving a kind of guarded approval to Pascal's notion that profane philosophy might have limited use in Christian apologetics? Does Fontaine base his observation that "M. de Saci ne put s'empêcher de témoigner à M. Pascal qu'il était surpris comment il savait tourner les choses" on a cue that he found in his documentary materials? Or is this moment in the dialogue a pure and simple product of his imagination? The investigations of Courcelle and Mesnard have taught us to beware of the authenticity of the text of the *Entretien* almost every time that Fontaine slides into his transpositions to an indirect style. But, in the last analysis, we cannot give a definitive answer to these questions so long as Fontaine's original papers remain lost.[123]

Fontaine's interpretation of the materials upon which he based the *Entretien* may or may not give us a valid clue concerning the issue of the real dialogue between Pascal and Sacy. We can say with reasonable certainty that Pascal did submit to Sacy—orally or otherwise—some ideas concerning the utility of profane philosophy. Courcelle's research has established that much. And perhaps we are not wrong to imagine that Pascal was indeed interested in Sacy's reaction to his scheme. Yet surely M. Gounelle goes too far beyond the facts when he imagines that the *Entretien* recalls Pascal's having asked Sacy to approve the whole framework for his future *Apology*.[124]

Perhaps the most interesting question we might ask about the encounter recalled by the *Entretien* is not whether Pascal managed to modify Sacy's position concerning the utility of profane philosophy. Rather, since we are primarily interested in the evolution of Pascal's ideas prior to the writing of the *Pensées*, should we not wonder to what degree Sacy succeeded in altering *Pascal*'s point of view. If we discount those *formules de politesse* that are obviously attributable to Fontaine, the Pascal of the *Entretien* appears to ignore altogether what Sacy has to say about the dangers of profane reading. Yet surely this is more a function of Fontaine's lack of documentation on this point than it is indicative that Pascal found Sacy's position overscrupulous. Indeed, if Mesnard's hypothesis concerning the character of the *écrit* used by Fontaine is correct, this document, annotated by Sacy, never made its way back to Pascal.

If Sacy's admonitions in the *Entretien* do recall the spiritual direction given Pascal during his first retreat at Port-Royal-des-Champs, perhaps those words of caution later bore fruit in the realm of the penitent's personal piety. After "une seconde retraitte bien plus parfaite que la première, deux ans devant sa mort," Père Beurrier tells us, Pascal "vendit . . . sa bibliothèque, à la réserve de la Bible, de saint Augustin, et fort peu d'autres livres, et en donna tout l'argent aux pauvres."[125] Can we discern Sacy's direct influence in this act of *sacrificium intellectus*? Perhaps not. But we can note that Sacy alone at Port-Royal held such extreme opinions concerning the dangers of profane philosophy. Nicole and Arnauld were self-declared partisans of Descartes. Even Saint-Cyran had defended the study of pagan philosophy on the grounds that "au temps que l'Esprit de Dieu n'estoit pas encore répandu sur la terre, et que la raison humaine estoit en son règne . . . il n'estoit point nécessaire comme à présent, d'invoquer Dieu pour faire des livres."[126] Nor does Sacy follow a unanimous tradition when he cites those passages in the *Confessions* that are hostile to profane philosophy. Courcelle reminds us that Abelard and Petrarch had used other passages in the same work to argue in favor of the legitimacy of "lectures philosophiques, cicéroniennes ou platonisantes."[127]

In a table of contents added to manuscript M of the *Mémoires* by some member of the group responsible for copying out the document, we find a curious résumé of Fontaine's dialogue: "Sacy . . . ecoutte avec patience tout ce que M. Pascal luy raconte des différents sentiments des philosophes, et s'en sert pour l'engager à une étude plus solide."[128] In what "étude plus solide" did the author of this observation imagine that Sacy sought to engage Pascal? The circle of Jansenist sympathizers who copied out manuscript M were far closer to the living tradition of Port-Royal than we can ever hope to be. Could this comment, which does not quite seem to fit the *Entretien* recounted by Fontaine, possibly be a reference to Sacy's reputation as the chief biblicist at Port-Royal?

At what might be called the climax of the *Entretien*, Pascal astonishes Sacy by telling him that the conflicting philosophies of Epictetus and Montaigne must "s'anéantissent pour faire place à la vérité de l'Evangile." In chapters five and six, we shall see that this is precisely the apologetic strategy sketched by the *Pensées*. Pascal's ultimate proof of the truth of Christianity was to have been grounded in a demonstration of the credibility of the Bible. No source permits us to say with any certainty that Pascal ever consulted Sacy concerning such a demonstration. But if he did, the Sacy we know from the *Mémoires* could but have commended the project as "une étude plus solide."

SUBSEQUENT MEETINGS BETWEEN PASCAL AND SACY: THE "CONFERENCES" AT VAUMURIER

It is not possible to document another meeting between Pascal and Sacy until at least a year after Pascal's first retreat of January 1655. According to Jansenist historian Dom Clémencet, Pascal, "pendant les retraites qu'il fit en différents temps à Port-Royal-des-Champs," attended a series of meetings held at Vaumurier, the "petit chateau" built by the duc de Luynes so that he might live near the Solitaires. Dom Clémencet reports that Pascal was present at these meetings about the time of the composition of the *Provinciales*, i.e., between January 1656 and March 1657.[129]

The purpose of these gatherings at Vaumurier was to examine a translation of the New Testament just completed by M. de Sacy. According to Racine's *Abrégé de l'Histoire de Port-Royal*, Arnauld, Antoine Le Maître, Nicole, and the duc de Luynes were also present. Sacy had prepared the first draft of the translation, but it was Arnauld who was responsible for determining the "sens" of a passage when a point of doctrine was at issue. Nicole's role was constantly to consult the Protestant translation of the New Testament by Théodore de Bèze, "afin de l'éviter."[130]

Dom Clémencet's principal source of information about the meetings at Vaumurier was Marguerite Périer's *Additions au Nécrologe de Port-Royal*. "M. de Sacy," she writes, "a dit lui-même à MM. Périer, neveux de M. Pascal, qu'il avait traduit le Nouveau Testament trois fois." Sacy's first translation was in "un style très élevé." His colleagues objected that this high style "ne convenait point à l'Evangile," observing that "Notre-Seigneur n'a point parlé comme cela." At a subsequent meeting, the objections were of the reverse order: "Ils trouvèrent que le style était trop bas, et qu'il avilissait la parole de Dieu." According to Marguerite Périer, Pascal was present at these meetings and offered advice to Sacy concerning his translation:

> M. l'abbé Pascal m'a dit que M. Pascal mon oncle lui avait dit la même chose, dont il avait été lui-même témoin, et qu'il conseilla à M. de Sacy de garder cette dernière traduction bien du temps sans la voir, pour l'examiner ensuite, après que les premières idées dont on a l'esprit prévenu seraient effacées; c'est ce que fit M. de Sacy deux ou trois ans après.[131]

Sacy followed Pascal's advice and did not take up the translation again until 1666, four years after Pascal's death. At the meetings at Vaumurier in 1656 or 1657, Pascal and Sacy certainly had both opportunity and reason to discuss the subject of biblical exegesis. No source says that they did. Mlle Delassault advances the theory that Pascal had access to Sacy's yet unpublished translations of the Old Testament. She bases her hypothesis on a letter from Sacy to Barcos in which Sacy says that "qu'un seul" of his "amis" had seen those papers that were taken from him at the time of his arrest in 1666. Comparing Pascal's translation of Isaiah 59:9–11 (in fr. 735/489) to Sacy's version and finding that "Pascal suit exactement le texte de Sacy," she concludes: "Or, ces textes, que les amis de Sacy ne connaissaient pas, étaient communiqués à Pascal."[132]

The only other hint of a possible meeting between Pascal and Sacy is contained in the *Pensées*. Fragments 155/122 and 182/149 carry the designations "A.P.R." and "A.P.R. pour demain." These fragments have much in common with Etienne Périer's summary, in the preface to the Edition de Port-Royal of the *Pensées* (1670), of an outline of the projected *Apology* that Périer says Pascal presented to "plusieurs personnes très considérables de ses amis." Périer indicates that this "conférence"—at which Pascal presented "le plan de tout son ouvrage" as well as "l'ordre et la suite des choses qu'il y voulait traiter"—took place "il y a environ dix ou douze ans,"[133] i.e., between 1658 and 1660.

"Depuis Faugère, qui la formula le premier," Jean Mesnard tells us, "l'hypothèse a été constamment admise que 'A.P.R.' signifie 'A Port-Royal' et que le fragment qui porte ce titre est formé de notes prises en vue de la conférence où Pascal aurait exposé le plan de son *Apologie*."[134] If such is the case, Pascal would have surely seen Sacy again. Because he was confessor to the Solitaires, Sacy rarely left Port-Royal-des-Champs. However, we cannot be certain that Sacy was present at the "conférence" described by Etienne Périer. Philippe Sellier points out that nothing necessarily links Pascal's "discours" with fragments 155/122 and 182/149. In Sellier's opinion, "placer ce discours à Port-Royal demeure une pure hypothèse."[135]

It is interesting to note that Périer's summary of Pascal's "discours" reveals a significant parallel with an idea first traced in the *Entretien*. Only Genesis' account of the Fall, Pascal is reported to have told his audience, can resolve the paradox "misère"/"grandeur." The source of the errors of both Epictetus and Montaigne, Pascal tells Sacy in the *Entretien*, is that neither philosopher takes into account the fact "que l'état de l'homme à présent diffère de celui de sa création."[136]

In chapter four, we will take up the doctrine of the Fall as the hinge of Pascal's projected *Apology*. For the moment, let us recapitulate the evidence connecting Pascal and Sacy. If we put the *Entretien* aside, only two sources—Jacqueline Pascal and Marguerite Perier—permit us to document meetings between the theologian and the apologist. We search in vain for any reference to Sacy in the extant writings of Pascal. Sacy refers to Pascal but three times: once in the *Mémoires*,[137] once in his commentary on Genesis,[138] and once in a letter to Pascal's sister Mme Périer. The sketchiness of the evidence has meant that two eminent authorities on Pascal and Port-Royal have been able to reach very different conclusions concerning the degree to which Sacy and Pascal were allied.

Jean Mesnard, responding to l'Abbé L. Cognet's paper "Le Jugement de Port-Royal sur Pascal," expresses his doubt that Pascal "ait été aussi étroitement lié avec M. de Saci." "J'ai l'impression," Mesnard opines, "qu'ils se sont connus assez peu, et que l'admiration de M. de Saci est restée assez lointaine." Mesnard goes on to cite a letter of 1669 in which Pascal's nephews express their hesitancy about sending a copy of the first edition of the *Pensées* to M. de Sacy. L'Abbé Cognet replies that the letter cited by Mesnard by no means proves the absence of "une grande intimité entre Pascal et Saci." The Périer nephews, he argues, were "fort peu au courant de la vie privée de Pascal." Another letter, from Sacy himself to Mme Périer, convinces l'Abbé Cognet that Sacy was indeed "au courant de la vie intérieure de Pascal." Citing with admiration a fragment from the *Pensées*, Sacy adds: "Cette parole est d'autant plus considérable que celui qui l'a dite l'a pratiquée, et qu'elle est encore plus l'effusion de son coeur que de son esprit."[139]

The question of Sacy's influence on Pascal's thought has been more or less limited to a discussion of the *Entretien* and to an analysis of scattered and ambiguous references. I propose to launch out in a different direction. Using Sacy's biblical commentaries, we will follow a lead suggested by Philippe Sellier: "l'univers biblique de l'apologiste et celui de Sacy sont proches."[140] Chapter two begins with an examination of the circumstances surrounding Port-Royal's sponsorship of a complete new translation of the Bible. In undertaking the first Catholic commentary on the Bible in the vernacular, Sacy sought to defend a traditional view of Scripture against the beginnings of rationalist criticism. By examining his defense of the authority of the Bible, I hope to illuminate some little understood parts of the *Pensées*. By taking a look at the positions of Sacy's adversaries, I hope to clarify the mentality of the *libertin* for whom Pascal writes his *Apology*.

    1. Bibliothèque Nationale, MS. 4333, nouvelles acquisition françaises. Cited by Jean Mesnard in his response to Louis Cognet's paper "Le Jugement de Port-Royal sur Pascal," in *Blaise Pascal: l'homme et l'oeuvre*, p. 31 (italics mine).

    2. *Pascal et la Bible*, p. 184.

    3. *Le Maistre de Sacy et son temps*, p. 79.

    4. *L'Entretien de Pascal avec M. de Sacy: étude et commentaire*, p. 36.

    5. See below, pp. 7 and 36.

    6. See below, pp. 37–38, notes 137, 138, and 139.

    7. *Entretien avec M. de Saci*, Brunschvicg, 4:30–31.

    8. *Mémorial*, Lafuma, p. 618.

    9. "Lettre de Jacqueline Pascal à Madame Périer, 25 janvier, 1655," Brunschvicg, 4:61–62.

    10. Brunschvicg, 4:62–63.

    11. Brunschvicg, 4:64–66. Singlin's hesitancy concerning "des personnes de condition" is expressed in a letter of 16 November 1654 to Mère Marie des Anges (Brunschvicg 4:64 n. 1).

    12. *Memoires de Godefroy Hermant*, ed. A. Gazier, 2:528.

    13. Brunschvicg, 4:67.

14. "Extrait d'une lettre de Jacqueline à M. Pascal son frère, 19 janvier, 1655," Brunschvicg, 4:17.
15. "Lettre de l'abbé d'Etémare à Mlle Perier, 20 juin 1728," Brunschvicg 4:23–24.
16. Sainte-Beuve, *Port-Royal*, 1:813–14.
17. *Pensées*, 2d ed., 1:cxxi–cxxii.
18. *Oeuvres complètes*, 1:238.
19. *Pascal et son temps*, 2:322 ff.
20. P.-L. Couchoud, "L'Entretien de Pascal avec M. de Saci, a-t-il eu lieu?", pp. 216–17, 226–27.
21. *Le Maistre de Sacy et son temps*, pp. 68–72. The four "entretiens" which have been shown to have been pieced together from letters are the following: Fontaine's conversation with Sacy (*Mémoires*, 2:513), based upon a letter from Sacy to Barcos (Bibliotheque Municipale de Troyes, MS. 2222, f° 22); a conversation between Saint-Cyran and Singlin (*Mémoires*, 1:204–29), put together from letters written by Saint-Cyran to Singlin and M. de Rebours (see Couchoud's article, indicated in note 20); another purported conversation between Sacy and Fontaine (*Mémoires*, 1:391–92), fabricated from a letter of Sacy's (Bibliotheque Nationale, f. fr. MS. 1702, n.a., f° 270–74); an "entretien" between Saint-Cyran and A. Le Maître, which Couchoud (see note 20) shows to have been based on letters from Saint-Cyran to Le Maître and Singlin.
22. Sacy's epistolary direction of penitents is well documented by his *Lettres chrestiennes et spirituelles*. Mlle Delassault published much of the remainder of Sacy's extant correspondence in *Choix de lettres inédites de Louis-Isaac Le Maistre de Sacy*.
23. *Blaise Pascal: commentaires*, p. 78.
24. Brunschvicg, 4:23–24.
25. "Etablissement d'un texte critique de 'L'Entretien de Pascal avec M. de Saci'," p. 41.
26. Bibliothèque de la Société de Port-Royal, MS. 128 bis. The *Jugement* figures on pp. 285–302.
27. "Un nouveau manuscrit de l'Entretien de Pascal avec M. de Saci," p. 372.
28. Bibliothèque de la Société de Port-Royal, MS. 128 bis. Undated note inside front cover. Identified as handwriting of l'Abbé Cognet by M. André Gazier.
29. Bédier, pp. 30, 48.
30. *Port-Royal*, 1:698–99.
31. *Oeuvres complètes*, 1:954.
32. Bédier, pp. 37–38.
33. When citing the *Entretien* in his *Port-Royal*, Sainte-Beuve nearly always follows Tronchai's edition of 1736.
34. *Oeuvres complètes*, 1:954.
35. Bédier, p. 49.
36. Bibliothèque Mazarine, MS. 2465. The preface is dated 1730 and signed "f. E. M. R. A. Expr."
37. "Etablissement d'un texte critique," p. 43. Jean Mesnard has suggested to me the following modification of Bédier's manuscript tree:

```
          O
       x/ \v
      /   \
   M-/ D  \-G
     |y
     |
     B
     |z
     |
   F-/ \-J
    /   ⋮
   T⋯⋯⋯⋯
```

"Contrairement à ce que j'ai écrit dans mon Tome I," Mesnard tells me in a recent communication (1980), "Tronchai a suivi Faugère" (cf. *Oeuvres complètes*, 1:954).

38. Reproduced in Bédier, pp. 51–80.
39. Bédier, p. 26 (italics mine).
40. Bédier, p. 47.
41. Pierre Courcelle, *L'Entretien de Pascal et Sacy: ses sources et ses énigmes*, p. 145.
42. Courcelle, p. 165.
43. Courcelle, p. 145.
44. Courcelle, pp. 165–66.
45. Courcelle, p. 168.
46. Courcelle, p. 149.
47. See chapters 2 ("Pascal lecteur d'Epictète"), 3 (Pascal lecteur des *Essais*"), and 4 ("Sacy lecteur des *Confessions*").
48. *Oeuvres complètes*, 1:247–49.
49. Philippe Sellier, ed., *Pensées: nouvelle édition établie pour la première fois d'apres la copie de référence de Gilberte Pascal*, p. 17.
50. Brunschvicg, 4:67.
51. *Oeuvres complètes*, 1:249–50.
52. Brunschvicg, 4:17.
53. *Oeuvres complètes*, 1:237.
54. Courcelle, p. 170.
55. Lafuma, p. 272.
56. *Pascal et la Bible*, p. 130.
57. See Henri Gouhier's *Pascal et les humanistes chrétiens: l'affaire Saint-Ange*. Letters and documents are collected in Brunschvicg, 1:350 ff.
58. Gilberte Périer, *Vie de Monsieur Pascal*, Lafuma, p. 20.
59. Lafuma, p. 20.
60. "Lettre . . . 26 janvier, 1648," Lafuma, p. 272 (italics mine).
61. See *Pascal et la Bible*, pp. 39–67.
62. "Lettre de Pascal . . . au sujet du P. Noel, Jésuite," Lafuma, p. 210.
63. "Réponse de Pascal au très bon Révérend P. Noel, 29 octobre, 1647," Lafuma, p. 201 (italics mine).
64. Lafuma, p. 230 (italics mine). Cf. *Pensées*, fragment 217/185: "La foi dit bien ce que les sens ne disent pas, mais non le contraire de ce qu'ils voient. Elle est *au-dessus*, et non pas contre."
65. Lafuma, p. 230–31 (italics mine).
66. *Préface sur le Traité du Vide*, Lafuma, p. 231.
67. *Les Provinciales*, "dix-huitième lettre," Lafuma, p. 467.
68. *Pascal et la Bible*, p. 151.
69. Sainte-Beuve, 2:728.
70. Dom Clémencet, *Histoire générale de Port-Royal, depuis la réforme de l'abbaie jusqu'à son entière destruction*, 1:cix, xxvii.
71. Sainte-Beuve, 1:107.
72. N. Fontaine, *Mémoires pour servir à l'histoire de Port-Royal*, 1:388.
73. Fontaine, 1:386.
74. Fontaine, 1:388.
75. Fontaine, 1:337, 2:124.

76. Brunschvicg, 4:28–29. In the *Mémoires* of Fontaine, this episode immediately precedes the *Entretien*, providing an essential context for Sacy's dialogue with Pascal.

77. Fontaine, 1:339.

78. Fontaine, 2:53–54.

79. Fontaine, 2:54.

80. Fontaine, 2:52–53.

81. Cited by Jean Orcibal, *La Spiritualité de Saint-Cyran*, p. 109.

82. *Lettres chrestiennes*, 1:58–59.

83. Fontaine, 1:386.

84. Sainte-Beuve, 1:775.

85. Bédier, p. 53.

86. *Mémorial*, Lafuma, p. 618. "Dieu d'Abraham, Dieu d'Isaac, Dieu de Jacob, non des philosophes et des savants."

87. Bédier, p. 53.

88. *Blaise Pascal: commentaires*, p. 87.

89. Courcelle, p. 166.

90. Bédier, pp. 54–55.

91. Bédier, pp. 55–56.

92. *Les Propos d'Epictète, recueillis par Arrian, translatez du grec en françois par Fr. I. D. S. F.* [dom Jean de François Goulu] (Paris: 1609), I, I, 12, p. 5. Cited by Courcelle, p. 18.

93. Julien-Eymard d'Angers, O.F.M., "Le Stoïcisme d'après l'"Humanitas theologica' de Pierre Lescalopier, S.J." in *Bulletin de littérature écclésiastique* 56 (1955):35.

94. Bédier, p. 55.

95. Bédier, pp. 56–58. These excerpts are from Book 2. 12 of the *Essais*. Courcelle establishes that Pascal read the *Essais* in the edition of 1652.

96. *Pascal et la Bible*, p. 489.

97. Sainte-Beuve, 1:846.

98. Bédier, pp. 59–60. Cf. *Pensées*, fragment 220/188: *Essais*, 2. 12; 3. 13.

99. Bédier, pp. 63–65. Courcelle (p. 30) notes that "axiomes . . . communes" is an *excerpta*, not from the *Essais*, but from Descartes's *Méditation II*.

100. Bédier, pp. 65–66. Sacy cites the *Confessions*, 5. 4, where Saint Augustine asks, concerning the philosophy of the Manicheans: "*Numquid, Domine Deus veritatis, quisquis novit ista, jam placet tibi?*"

101. Bédier, pp. 66–67. In citing "renversent . . . religion elle-même," I follow text T, *Mémoires*, 2:65.

102. Bédier, pp. 67–68 (italics mine).

103. Cf. Colossians 2:8: "Make sure that no one traps you . . . by some empty, rational philosophy based upon the principles of this world" (Jerusalem Bible translation).

104. Bédier, p. 68 (italics mine). Sacy's speech is a composite of *excerpta* from the *Confessions*: 1. 14; 5. 14; 8. 7; 3. 4; 5. 6; 3. 6. In citing "ces vanités," I follow text B.

105. We may probably discount Fontaine's report that Pascal "lui témoigna être extrêmement édifié de la solidité de tout ce qu'il venait de lui représenter" (Bédier, p. 69). This has the ring of one of Fontaine's "formules de politesse."

106. Bédier, p. 69–70.

107. Bédier, p. 72. In citing "entre celles . . . conséquentes" and Pascal's recapitulation of the positions of the Stoics and the Skeptics, I follow text T, *Mémoires*, 2:68–69: "Car que peuvent-ils faire [i.e., "des hommes destituës de la lumière de la religion"] que de suivre l'un ou l'autre de ces deux systèmes? Le premier: il y a un Dieu; donc c'est lui qui a créé l'homme. Il l'a fait pour lui-même. Il l'a créé tel qu'il doit être pour être juste et pour devenir heureux.

L'homme peut donc connaître la vérité, et il est à portée de s'élever jusqu'à Dieu qui est son souverain bien. Second système: L'homme ne peut s'élever jusqu'à Dieu. Ses inclinations contredisent la loi. Il est porté à chercher son bonheur dans les biens visibles et même en ce qu'il y a de plus honteux. Tout paraît donc incertain, et le vrai bien l'est aussi; ce qui semble nous réduire à n'avoir ni règle fixe pour les moeurs, ni certitude dans les sciences." Bédier (p. 36) attributes this passage to Tronchai, "qui l'a composé, non pour son plaisir, mais pour réparer un texte inintelligible, et F et J sont ici inintelligibles." More research needs to be done on this passage. Is it indeed not derived from an *écrit* of Pascal's? If not, did Tronchai make use of passages from the *Pensées*? In any event, it certainly adds lucidity to Pascal's argument.

108. Bédier, pp. 72–73.

109. *Mémoires*, 2:53–54.

110. Bédier, p. 73.

111. Courcelle, p. 167.

112. Bédier, pp. 73–74 (italics mine). Cf. *Pensées*, fragment 182/149: "Mais vous n'êtes plus maintenant en l'état où je vous ai formés." In chapters 4 and 5, we take up the Fall as a doctrine central to Pascal's aplogetic strategy.

113. Bédier, pp. 74–75.

114. Saint-Cyran (Jean Duvergier de Hauranne, Abbé de), *Lettres chrestiennes et spirituelles*, p. 490. Cited by A. Gounelle, p. 104 n. 340.

115. Bédier, pp. 75–76.

116. Bédier, p. 76.

117. Like his master Saint-Cyran, Sacy always taught that only divine grace can reconcile principles which human reason perceives as contrary. The Gospel, he writes to one penitent, calls the Christian both to "joie" and to "un gémissement de ses fautes." Neither reason nor "notre amour propre," Sacy observes, can reconcile two such contrary emotions. But the Holy Spirit, drawn to an individual by faith, "les peut joindre ensemble parfaitement" (*Lettres chrestiennes*, 2:21).

118. Bédier, pp. 77–78.

119. Bédier, pp. 78–79.

120. Bédier, pp. 79–80. Manuscripts B, D, and J (and a later correction in manuscript M) give "qu'après beaucoup de détours."

121. Fontaine's hostility to profane philosophy is well documented elsewhere in the *Mémoires*. Consider, for instance, his judgment concerning Tertullian and Origen: "Tertullien et Origène s'étaient perdus par la raison et la philosophie, Origène par celle des Platoniciens, et Tertullien par celle des Stoïciens. Il était extrêmement adonné à la littérature profane, ce qui le rendait fort humain et l'accoutumait à se conduire par la raison . . . plus que par la foi" (*Mémoires*, MS. 2465, Bibliothèque Mazarine, pp. 285–86). This passage does not figure in Tronchai's edition of the *Mémoires*.

122. Courcelle, p. 167.

123. Jean Mesnard suggests that these materials may not be lost forever: "Si les papiers de Fontaine ne sont passés dans aucun des grands dépots jansénistes, ce n'est pas à dire qu'ils soient définitivement perdus. Leur découverte aurait une portée considérable" (*Oeuvres complètes*, 1:250). One might begin by checking the registers to see what convents existed in Melun at the beginning of the eighteenth century. Manuscript M tells us that Fontaine's "précieux manuscrit" passed into the hands of "une dame religieuse de la ville."

124. Gounelle, p. 36.

125. *Mémoires du P. Beurrier*, Bruschvicg, 10:391.

126. *Lettres chrestiennes* (1648), "seconde partie," p. 198. Cited by Gounelle, p. 77 n. 270.

127. Courcelle, pp. 168–69.

128. Bibliothèque Mazarine, MS. 2466.

129. *Histoire générale de Port-Royal*, 3:441.

130. In *Oeuvres complètes*, 4:624.

131. *Additions au Nécrologe* in Mesnard, *Oeuvres complètes*, 1:1139–40.

132. Delassault, pp. 74–78. Cf. Sacy's letter to Barcos of 8 January 1669, Bibliothèque Municipale de Troyes, MS. 2220, f° 20.

133. *Préface de l'Edition de Port-Royal*, Lafuma, p. 495.

134. *Les Pensées de Pascal*, p. 40.

135. *Pensées*, p. 18.

136. Bédier, p. 73.

137. Fontaine (1:385–86) reports that Sacy often counseled retreats to his penitents, "récitant souvent avec plaisir cette parole d'un homme d'esprit, qui lui semblait belle, *Que tout le mal du monde venait de ce qu'on ne pouvait demeurer tranquille dans sa chambre.*" Cf. *Pensées*, fr. 168/136.

138. See p. 122, n. 37.

139. In *Blaise Pascal: l'homme et l'oeuvre*, pp. 30–31. The letter from Louis and Blaise Périer cited by Mesnard is found in Brunschvicg 12:ccxlviii n. 1: " . . . Nous ne savons s'il en faut donner à P.-R. des Champs: si cela était, ce serait à MM. de Sacy, de Sainte-Marthe et de Tillemont." Sacy's letter to Mme. Périer is reproduced in Brunschvicg 6:83 n. 3: "Je ne doute pas, Mademoiselle, que vous n'ayiez eu dans l'esprit cette pensée de M. votre frère, qui me paroit admirable, et que je n'ai vu qu'en lui seul: *Il faut tacher*, dit-il, *de se consoler dans le plus grands maux, et de prendre tout ce qui arrive pour le meilleur, car l'essence du peché consistant à avoir une volonté opposée à celle que nous connaissons en Dieu, il est visible, ce me semble, que quand il nous decouvre sa volonté par les événements, ce serait un peché que de ne s'y pas conformer.* Cette parole . . . de son esprit." The passage, an extract from Pascal's letter to Mlle de Roannez (Lafuma, p. 266), was inserted into the 1669 edition of the *Pensées*. It bears an uncertain relationship to fragment 769/948.

140. *Pensées*, p. 21.

II

M. de Sacy and His Bible

SACY'S ROLE AT PORT-ROYAL

Sainte-Beuve describes the life of Monsieur de Sacy as "la ligne droite de Port-Royal."[1] Indeed, from beginning to end, the life of Isaac-Louis Le Maistre[2] (1613–84) is inseparable from the history of the Jansenist movement. His mother, Catherine Arnauld, was the eldest daughter of Antoine Arnauld, from among whose twenty children Port-Royal recruited the core of its cast of characters. The five sisters of Catherine Arnauld all became nuns at Port-Royal, among them the future Mère Angélique and Mère Agnès. Her oldest brother, Robert d'Andilly, and her youngest, "le grand Arnauld," were among the first of the Solitaires who retired to Port-Royal-des-Champs.

Sacy's childhood was austere and studious. After her separation from Isaac Le Maistre, Sacy's mother lived in close association with her sisters at Port-Royal and put Sacy under the spiritual direction of Saint-Cyran at a very early age. Though Sacy evidenced great talents in the *belles-lettres*, he decided early on against following his classmate and "petit oncle" Antoine ("le grand Arnauld") on to study at the Sorbonne. Saint-Cyran entirely approved of this act of humility. Fontaine's account of the episode underscores Sacy's early aversion to philosophy and his determination to avoid the contamination of the world:

> Quels combats n'eut-il point à soutenir pour ce sujet? Car presque tous Messieurs ses parents le souhaitaient. . . . De plus, l'exemple de M. Arnauld semblait l'y engager. . . . Mais ces raisons ne pouvaient lui faire vaincre ses répugnances. Un accident même qui arriva alors l'en détourna davantage. Un jeune bachelier nommé Chassi, s'étant préparé longtemps pour soutenir un acte . . . tomba malade et mourut au jour même qui était marqué pour l'acte. M. de Saci, qui savait profiter de tout, et à qui la ressemblance du nom rendait cet événement plus particulier, écrivit ce billet avec un dégoût encore plus grand de la Sorbonne: "J'avoue que l'équivoque de nos noms m'a fait peur. Je craindrais fort si, au lieu de m'attendre à répondre dans un acte devant les hommes dont on attend les louanges, je me voyais tout d'un coup surpris et obligé d'aller répondre de mes actions devant Dieu dont on doit attendre une rigoureuse justice. Cet homme m'effraie lorsque je vois qu'au lieu de prier ses amis à venir lui voir soutenir une thèse, il eût mieux fait de les prier à venir à son enterrement. Ces grands coups parlent; et si les jeunes gens n'en profitent, ils sont bien sourds à la voix de Dieu.[3]

In 1638, Sacy's two older brothers, Antoine Le Maistre and Simon de Séricourt, resolved to abandon successful careers in the law and in the military to retire to a life of penitence at Port-Royal-des-Champs. Sacy joined them for a temporary retreat and was living there later that year when the arrest of Saint-Cyran put an end to the experiment. After his return to Paris, Sacy's attempts to imitate the "austérités" practiced by his brothers led to a severe physical collapse.[4] After his recovery, he served as an assistant to Saint-Cyran's nephew, M. de Barcos, "dans la maison de M. de Saint-Cyran alors prisonnier." When Arnauld was forced into hiding by the furor surrounding his *Fréquente Communion*, Sacy accompanied him. "En M. de Saci," Sainte-Beuve observes, "se combinent l'esprit direct de Saint-Cyran par M. de Barcos . . . et en même temps l'esprit d'Arnauld par le sang et par cette collaboration intime."[5]

In 1640, Sacy's father died, permitting Mme Le Maistre to take the veil. Soon afterward, Sacy once again joined his brothers at Port-Royal-des-Champs, receiving the monastic tonsure and deeding all his worldly goods to the sisters at Port-Royal. After the death of Saint-Cyran, Sacy passed under the direction of Singlin, who began urging him to seek ordination to the priesthood. The prospect of orders and Singlin's offer of the position of spiritual director of the Solitaires were accepted by Sacy with great reluctance. Once ordained, he delayed celebrating his first Mass until after months of intense personal preparation. The date he chose for his first Mass, the feast of the Conversion of Saint Paul, serves to underline Sacy's own perception of the importance of the career on which he was about to embark. Sainte-Beuve records the date, 25 January 1650, as an event that all the Jansenist chronologies "mettent en première ligne pour l'importance." Sacy was thirty-seven years old. He would direct the course of Port-Royal for another thirty-four years. "Sa parole dirigera[it] jusqu'au bout."[6]

Though the Solitaires had no official status as a monastic order in the church, Sacy is best thought of as their father superior. "Port-Royal, le vrai Port-Royal complet," Sainte-Beuve insists, "n'a eu, en tout et pour tout, que trois directeurs *en chef*, M. de Saint-Cyran, M. Singlin, and M. de Saci."[7] It was Arnauld who governed the practical side of things at Port-Royal, defining doctrine and making decisions concerning polemical tactics. It was Sacy, however, around whom the spiritual life of the community centered. His influence was so great and his opinions remain so important for those seeking to understand the phenomenon of Port-Royal because he occupied the role of father confessor for so long and with such authority.

Even had he never come to meet Pascal, Sacy would have left his mark on French literature. Mlle Delassault presents detailed evidence that Corneille, Racine, Molière, and La Fontaine all used and sometimes imitated Sacy's translations.[8] By the time of his first meeting with Pascal in 1655,

Sacy had published translations of the *Fables* of Phaedrus and had adapted several of Terence's comedies for use in the "Petites Ecoles."[9] His subsequent literary effort was devoted to the translation of religious works into French, many of them for the first time. His translations of the *Imitation de Jésus-Christ* (1662), the *Sermons de saint Jean Chrysostome* (1666), and of a great number of Latin hymns and litanies achieved considerable popular success during his own lifetime.[10]

Sacy's greatest contribution to classical French prose was his translation of the entire Bible: "le grand et spécial monument de M. de Saci à titre d'écrivain et comme la mission singulière qu'il eut à remplir" (Sainte-Beuve).[11] A number of factors motivated Port-Royal's sponsorship of a complete new translation of the Bible. In the first place, no satisfactory French translation was available for use by Catholic laity. The various Protestant translations were both proscribed by the ecclesiastical authorities and suspect for nonorthodox interpretations. All the Catholic translations dating from the first half of the seventeenth century either remained incomplete (e.g., *la Bible dite de Richelieu*, 1642), had been censured for relying too heavily on Protestant translations (e.g., *la Bible de René Benoist*, 1566), or amounted to nothing more than revisions of the standard Louvain translation (e.g., the translations of Pierre de Besse, 1608, and of Pierre Frizon, 1621).

The Louvain Bible (1550 and 1578) served as the officially approved translation of Holy Scripture but had fallen into disuse, along with the subsequent translations based upon it, because of the great changes that had taken place in the French language. In Sainte-Beuve's estimation, "cette nouveauté d'élégance à laquelle l'époque de Louis XIV s'était aussitôt accoutumée" made these earlier translations seem, if not wholly inaccessible, at least somewhat barbaric when judged by the requirements of classical French prose.[12] Yet the French church was by no means anxious to sponsor a new translation to take the place of the Louvain Bible. As far as the ecclesiastical authorities were concerned, vernacular translations of the Bible had an extremely restricted use. Authorized neither for use in the liturgy nor for teaching and study, their unique approved function was that of private reading.

In seeking to do privately what the church had not yet seen fit to do officially—that is, publish a complete, explicated version of the Bible in French—Port-Royal was treading upon dangerous ground. The notion that the faithful have a right to read the Bible in the vernacular was considered radical, if not heretical. During the Counter Reformation, anything that might appear to countenance a position advanced by the Protestants was immediately suspect. Catholic translations of the Bible, without ever having been formally forbidden, were rigorously monitored, often censured, and never wholeheartedly endorsed by the Church of Rome. It was into what Sainte-Beuve calls "cette marge périlleuse à grand'peine laissée par Rome et par la Sorbonne" that M. de Sacy set forth when he undertook to publish the first complete Catholic translation of the Bible into French in more than a hundred years.[13]

THE *NOUVEAU TESTAMENT DE MONS* AND ARNAULD'S DEFENSE OF VERNACULAR TRANSLATIONS OF THE BIBLE

It was not until 1667 that the work of the "conférences" at Vaumurier (see chapter one) was brought to fruition with the publication of the *Nouveau Testament de Mons*. Following Pascal's advice, Sacy had set the translation aside for a number of years, taking it up again only just in time to complete the manuscript before his arrest in May 1666. The new translation was published in Amsterdam,[14] both the civil and the ecclesiastical authorities in Paris having refused their approbation. The *Nouveau Testament de Mons* is a translation based neither completely on the Greek text nor completely on the Vulgate. Rather, in the estimation of Mlle Delassault, it is "une version originale, conforme à l'esprit port-royaliste."[15]

The *Préface* (1667) of the *Nouveau Testament de Mons* serves to remind us that the neo-Augustinian movement had from almost its very beginnings envisaged the project of a complete new translation of the Bible. "Il y a près de trente ans que ceux qui y ont travaillé," Sacy points out to his readers, "ont eu ces vues dans l'esprit sans qu'elles les déterminassent à rien." "Ayant différé environ vint ans, il y en a près de dix qu'ils commencèrent à y travailler."[16] In other words, serious work on the new translation of the New Testament had begun in 1657, the year in which Dom Clémencet places Pascal at the "conférences" at Vaumurier.[17]

Sacy's *Préface* sets forth "les raisons qui ont fait souhaitter qu'on entreprist la traduction du Nouveau Testament." After acknowledging the work of the translators of the Louvain Bible, Sacy hastens to point out that the French language has undergone important changes in the century that has passed since the time of that translation. "Il faut reconnoistre que les changemens qui sont arrivez dans nostre langue depuis leur temps . . . ont tellement défiguré leur ouvrage . . . que si elle subsistoit encore ce n'estoit plus que par l'impuissance où l'on estoit de s'en passer, jusqu'à ce qu'on en eust donné une nouvelle." The authors of the present translation, Sacy explains, "ont cru que c'estoit un respect qu'on devoit à l'Evangile de ne le pas laisser dans un langage qui produit dans l'esprit de la plus part du monde des impressions contraires à la vénération que l'on doit avoir pour un livre si divin."[18]

The most essential "disposition" required of a reader of Scripture, Sacy emphasizes, is that of "un profond respect." "Il n'y a rien de plus contraire au bien des âmes que ce qui peut diminuer ce respect, ny rien qui soit plus capable de l'affoiblir *que de voir dans ces sortes de versions une si grande disproportion entre la Majesté de Dieu qui parle et la bassesse surprenant des paroles qu'on luy attribue.*" The style of the Gospels, because they reproduce the very words of Christ, must inspire respect and veneration. "L'Evangile est la bouche de Jésus-Christ. Il est assis dans le ciel, mais il parle continuellement sur la terre."[19]

According to Dom Clemencet's account (see chapter one), Sacy's first draft of his translation of the New Testament had made use of "un stile très élevé." Those present at the Vaumurier meetings had reacted negatively to such a style, arguing that "Jésus-Christ n'avoit point parlé comme cela."[20] Sacy must have succeeded in convincing his collaborators of the merits of "un stile très élevé," for in his *Préface* we find him presenting a theological rationale for the use of precisely this style. In striving to produce a translation worthy of conveying "la parole de Dieu," Sacy insists, the translators have only followed "l'esprit que l'Englise fait paroistre dans toutes les autres choses qui appartiennent au culte de Dieu":

> [L'Eglise] a soin que toutes les cérémonies qu'elle expose aux yeux des fidelles ayent quelque chose qui imprime du respect; qu'elle désire que les vases qui servent au sacrifice soient d'une matière précieuse; qu'elle croit que c'est honorer Dieu que d'employer ce qu'il y a de plus riche aux ciboires et aux calices qui enferment le corps et le sang du Sauveur. *Puisque donc qu'on a tant de soin que tout ce qui approche du corps de Jésus-Christ contribue à le faire respecter, il estoit juste de ne pas laisser sa parole dans un langage, qui n'estant guères propre à la faire révérer par la pluspart de ceux qui la lisent, pouvoit nuire à l'édification des fidelles.*[21]

Sacy's analogy between Christ's presence in the Eucharist and his presence in "la parole de Dieu" is fundamental to his understanding of the nature of Scripture. "Il y a un très-grand rapport entre la Parole du Fils de Dieu et son Corps dans le Sacrement de l'Eucharistie." Christians should venerate even that which is "obscur" in Scripture, Sacy explains, in the same way in which they adore Christ's hidden presence in the Holy Eucharist:

> Nous sommes très persuadez, qu'encore que nos yeux ne voient dans ce mystère que les espèces et les apparences extérieures du pain et du vin, Jésus-Christ néanmoins y est tout entier et qu'il se communique très-réellement à nous sous ces voiles dont il se couvre. Croyons de même que l'Evangile sous des paroles très-simples et sous les voiles mystérieux de ses paraboles, où il ne paroist rien de grand de d'extraordinaire, enferme néanmoins tous les thrésors de la sagesse et de la science de Dieu.[22]

In order to explain why Christ's presence in Scripture is so often hidden "sous des ombres et des figures," Sacy has recourse to an idea central to Augustinian theology. "Il estoit même nécessaire à l'homme dans l'estat où le péché l'a reduit, que Dieu luy proposast sa vérité de cette sorte pour humilier son orgueil par la peine qu'il auroit à en pénétrer les mystères et les secrets."²³ In the course of his translations, Sacy never hesitates to nuance the meaning of a given passage in order to emphasize a point of doctrine. For instance, he renders Luke 2:14, "Et in terra pax *hominibus bonae voluntatis*," as "Et paix sur la terre *aux hommes chéris de Dieu*" (italics mine). Such a translation obviously serves to throw into relief the Augustinian doctrine of predestination and election.

Such departures from the officially sanctioned text, the Vulgate, meant that Sacy's translations would immediately incur the wrath of the censors. As soon as it appeared, the *Nouveau Testament de Mons* was attacked by the Jesuits in a series of sermons preached by Père Meinbourg, who renewed the attack on Port-Royal mounted by Père Nouet in his condemnation of Arnauld's *La Fréquente Communion*. Arnauld responded with his *Défense de la traduction imprimée à Mons*, in which he set forth Port-Royal's position that the faithful should have the right to read the Bible in the vernacular.

Père Meinbourg condemned the translators of Port-Royal for having failed to leave the meanings of difficult passages of Scripture "indéterminez." Only Rome, he argued, has the right to decide questions of interpretation that reflect matters of doctrine. Arnauld answers that the translation was not intended for use by "gens sçavans qui entendent le Latin et le Grec" but rather for "des personnes qui ne sont pas sçavantes, mais pieuses . . . qui ne lisent le Nouveau Testament que pour nourrir leur foy." In any case, Arnauld argues, the ultimate tribunal in determining the meaning of difficult passages in the Bible is Scripture itself.²⁴

Père Meinbourg had accused the translators of the *Nouveau Testament de Mons* of having been "d'intelligence avec Genève." Arnauld cites thirty-two passages from Sacy's translation that Meinbourg had attacked, claiming to have discovered Protestant interpretations that, among other things, ruined the primacy of Peter, abolished the invocation of the saints, and called into doubt the Real Presence of Christ in the Eucharist. Meinbourg had not failed to take notice of Sacy's translation of Luke 2:14. He had demanded to know why "hominibus bonae voluntatis" had not been rendered "aux hommes de bonne volonté." "Bonne volonté," Arnauld replies, is simply not an accurate translation of the Greek text.²⁵

Meinbourg's anger had been particularly focused on Sacy's translation of John 12:8. Following the Greek text, Sacy had rendered the verse "Car vous avez toujours des pauvres parmy vous; mais pour moy vous ne m'aurez pas toujours." Meinbourg maintained that this translation undermined the doctrine of the Real Presence and betrayed the Calvinist sympathies of Port-Royal. Arnauld answers that the passage has nothing at all to do with Eucharistic doctrine, but rather refers to the approaching death of Jesus.

The Jesuits, when they use this verse to refute a Protestant interpretation of the Eucharist, Arnauld argues, invent an exegesis never once suggested by the Fathers of the Church.[26]

Arnauld's position on the question of the Real Presence is orthodox by any standard. Yet his interpretation of John 12:8, by virtue only of the fact that it happened to coincide with a Protestant interpretation of the same passage, was enough to condemn him in the eyes of contemporary theological opinion. In much the same way, Port-Royal's effort to produce a vernacular translation of the Bible, though intended as a direct offensive against the Protestants, ran aground on the reef of the Counter Reformation. The notion that the faithful have the right to read the Bible in the vernacular was simply too similar to the Protestant position to be accepted by an ecclesiastical mentality that all too often defined orthodoxy as any position contrary to that of the reformers. The *Nouveau Testament de Mons* would be proscribed by a whole series of episcopal mandates, culminating in its condemnation by Pope Clement IX.

In spite of the official reaction to the publication of the *Nouveau Testament de Mons*, Port-Royal continued to sponsor translations not only of the Bible but of the Mass, the offices, and the works of the Fathers. Opposition to their efforts continued to grow, the Faculty of Theology at the Sorbonne having declared in 1660: "Nous avons en horreur toutes les traductions de l'Ecriture, des Offices de l'Englise et des Pères."[27] From time to time, Port-Royal was able to gain the assistance of a sympathetic bishop. After the advent of the "Paix de l'Englise," Arnauld obtained Bossuet as censor, and a series of negotiations concerning the "Version de Mons" took place between Sacy and Bossuet at the Hôtel de Longueville. Bossuet probably would have sanctioned the translation had not the appointment of M. de Harlay as archbishop of Paris put an end to the discussions.[28]

In 1688, after the censure of a new translation of the breviary, Arnauld published a defense of translations of Scripture, the offices, and the Mass. If Latin were still the vernacular, he points out, would not the liturgy be understood by everyone? Such a state of affairs, he continues, would be very advantageous to the church, which could more easily "entretenir . . . les sentimens de piété dans le coeur des fidelles, par l'intelligence qu'ils auroient eue de tant de choses si édifiantes qui se disent dans le service divin." Yet, he takes care to point out, the church has acted wisely in retaining Latin as its liturgical language. The Mass and the offices have been spared the "infinité de changemens" to which they would have been exposed had they been translated into the vernacular. Arnauld takes the example of Marot's translation of the Psalms, "qui d'assez beaux qu'ils estoient en leur temps, sont devenus insupportables par le changement du François."[29] On the other hand, Arnauld insists, it would be wrong to suppose that the Council of Trent, though it confirmed the use of the Latin liturgy, had ever forbidden translations intended for "les personnes qui y assistent, et qui n'entendent pas le Latin."[30]

Arnauld laments the fact that the scholar who knows Greek and Hebrew is immediately suspected of being a heretic: "C'est un sophisme très-ordinaire quoique très-grossier: *Les hérétiques savent le grec et l'hébreu. Un tel fait le grec et l'hebreu. Donc il est hérétique, ou il faut craindre au moins qu'il ne le soit.*"[31] He contrasts the attitude of the Sorbonne with that of the theological faculty at Louvain, whose "Docteurs . . . s'appliquoient beaucoup à l'étude de l'Ecriture Sainte" and produced a translation of the Bible that lasted for a hundred years.[32] The French church, Arnauld protests, seems to have forgotten that Latin was a vernacular language ("la langue vulgaire de l'Occident") when Saint Jerome produced the Vulgate. If no Catholic translation is available, he argues, the faithful will be tempted to have recourse to Protestant ones.[33]

Those who oppose vernacular translations of the Bible, Arnauld observes, seem to base their opposition on two arguments. The first, that "le peuple n'est pas capable de . . . découvrir les sens allégoriques" of what is written in the Bible, seems absurd to Arnauld. Do those who advance this position, he asks, mean to argue that it is not the church's role to instruct the faithful concerning the meaning of Scripture? Moreover, are there not "mille choses dans la Bible, et surtout dans le Nouveau Testament très-propres à édifier la piété quoique prises dans le sens littéral?" A second argument advanced by those who oppose vernacular translations, "que la langue Françoise est une langue barbare qui ne peut estre assujettie à aucune règle de grammaire," strikes Arnauld as hardly worthy of consideration. "Comment M. l'Archeveque de Paris qui a fait l'honneur à l'Academie Françoise d'estre de son corps, pourra-t-il soutenir qu'on ait bien fait de donner au public . . . un si ridicule jugement d'une des plus belles langues de l'Europe."[34]

Arnauld's line of reasoning had not been contradicted by the public reaction to the *Nouveau Testament de Mons*. Its tremendous success, reflected in the fact that five editions appeared in the year following its publication, indicates that Sacy was responding to a genuine need for a new translation of the Bible.[35] Moreover, Sacy's translation satisfied the requirements of classical French prose. In Sacy's own words, he had tried to "rendre le langage de l'Ecriture clair, pur, et conforme aux règles de la grammaire."[36] Sacy's style, however, was not universally approved. Bossuet, who found in the translation "une affectation de politesse et d'agrément que le Saint-Esprit avait dédaignée dans l'original," thought that Sacy had gone too far in adopting the literary language of contemporary prose.[37] Literary tastes, however, undergo great changes. By the nineteenth century, Saint-Beuve would fault the critical perspective of both Bossuet and Sacy:

> Ce système d'élégance continue, que Bossuet trouvait souvent contraire à la simplicité de l'Esprit divin . . . cette sorte de monotonie tempérée, nous paraît à nous, aujourd'hui que le goût littéraire a changé et s'est enhardi, manquer précisément du cachet *littéraire* qui est propre à la Bible, et en fausser ce que nous en regarderions plus volontiers comme les ornements naturels. En un mot, la Bible traduite d'une façon qui eût semblé plus rude et tout inélégante à M. de Saci nous semblerait, pour les Psaumes, par exemple, ou pour Job, une traduction plus véritablement poétique et une oeuvre plus *littéraire*.[38]

SACY'S TRANSLATION OF THE OLD TESTAMENT: "LE LANGAGE OBSCUR DU SAINT ESPRIT"

Port-Royal's enemies had been steadily gaining in their influence at Versailles since Rome's condemnation of Jansenius' Five Propositions in 1653. The publication of the *Provinciales* had only further incited their wrath. M. de Sacy was forced to leave Port-Royal-des-Champs in 1661 and to go into hiding in Paris. On 13 May 1666, Sacy was arrested and imprisoned in the Bastille, where he remained until November 1668. During his imprisonment, the "Paix de l'Englise" was being worked out under the aegis of Mme de Longueville. But Sacy had no part in these negotiations. Though deprived of the sacraments and able to communicate with his penitents only through smuggled letters, Sacy viewed his stay in the Bastille as an event dictated by Providence itself. In Fontaine's judgment, "M. de Saci . . . semblait n'être entré à la Bastille que pour y achever la traduction de la Bible par celle de l'Ancien Testament."[39]

Sacy emerged from prison with several books of the Old Testament ready for publication. The censor, however, attempting to block their publication, required him to append to each completed chapter a series of "éclaircissements" that were then to be examined for evidence of doctrinal deviations. Sacy's commentaries were not in fact a part of his original plan. According to Fontaine, "il ne les avoit faites que par force, parce qu'autrement on n'auroit pu avoir de privilège."[40] Sacy was not displeased by the censor's decision. In his view, here was but another instance of the secret designs of Providence, a directive from on high to defend the Bible against the rising tide of rationalism and *libre pensée*.

Sacy devoted the last fifteen years of his life to completing his translations and commentaries. By 1679, the "Paix de l'Englise" had broken down and he was once again ordered to leave Port-Royal-des-Champs. The persecutions that would end in the complete destruction of Port-Royal had commenced. Sacy would spend the remaining five years of his life in exile at

Pomponne. His Bible had begun to appear in 1672 with the publication of *Proverbes*. Up until the end of his life, a new volume would appear at regular intervals: *L'Ecclésiaste, La Sagesse*, and *Isaïe* in 1673; the first two books of *Rois* in 1674; the *Douze petits prophètes* in 1679; *La Genèse* in 1682; and *L'Exode* and *Le Lévitique* in 1683.

Sacy's death, on 4 January 1684, preceded the first complete edition of his Bible. The remainder of the books of the Old Testament were found in manuscript form among his papers.[41] They were edited and published between 1685 and 1693 by Thomas Du Fossé, who completed Sacy's translations with his version of the *Cantique des Cantiques*.[42] Sacy's commentaries, completed only from *La Genèse* through the *Douze petits prophètes*, remained unfinished at his death. Du Fossé continued the explications through the four Gospels and was working on the *Actes des Apôtres* at the time of his own death. The rest of the New Testament was explicated by Charles Huré, in collaboration with Touret and Beaubrun.[43]

The first edition of the Sacy Bible appeared by books (32 volumes "in-8") between 1672 and 1696. It was reedited in a single edition (32 volumes "in-12") published in Lyon and in Amsterdam in 1696.[44] Subsequent editions, including eight in the following five years, serve to indicate the success of Sacy's translation.[45] He had given the French church its first complete translation of the Bible in more than a hundred years and Catholics their first explicated Bible in the vernacular. The importance of his translation in opening up the field of scriptural studies to a wider audience is indisputable. Yet shortly before his death, Sacy expressed to Fontaine serious reservations about the validity of his enterprise.

Fontaine, in his *Mémoires*, presents Sacy as having second thoughts concerning his attempt to remove the "obscurité" and the "rudesse" from Scripture. The public, Sacy fears, appreciates all too well his attempt to produce a translation that is "claire et . . . exacte par rapport à la pureté du langage." No longer finding those "difficultés qu'ils trouvoient auparavant dans l'Ecriture," readers have concluded that "leur curiosité y peut être satisfaite à peu de frais." His readers, Sacy continues, are for the most part content not to understand the great "vérités" and "mystères" revealed in the Bible. What they cannot bear is the "langage obscur et embarrassé dont le Saint-Esprit se sert pour les leur proposer." Such readers are pleased to find in Sacy's translations "une nouvelle clarté, qui les délivre des ténèbres qui étoient auparavant si fâcheuses . . . à leur orgueil et à leur curiosité."[46]

The success of his translation makes Sacy wonder if he has not, in trying to "rendre le langage de l'Ecriture clair, pur, et conforme aux règles de la grammaire," acted "contre les desseins de Dieu." "Qui peut m'assurer," he asks, "que ce ne soit pas là une méthode différente de celle qu'il a plu au

Saint-Esprit de chosir?" God himself has apparently "voulu que sa parole fût enveloppée d'obscurités."[47] The very obscurity of Scripture has played an important role in God's plan for the salvation of mankind:

> L'obscurité de l'Ecriture n'est pas moins utile et nécessaire au salut des hommes que la clarté. Dieu les a mêlées ensemble pour en former un tempérament divin . . . les âmes chrétiennes ont besoin, non seulement d'être nourries par des vérités manifestes, mais aussi d'être exercées et humiliées par ce qu'il y a de plus caché et de plus profond dans l'Ecriture. C'est ainsi que Dieu nous oblige à travailler . . . afin de gagner le pain de l'âme aussi bien que celui du corps. Il a choisi de plus la simplicité et la rudesse d'un langage négligé afin d'éprouver si nous cherchons la vérité pour elle-même.[48]

Sacy recalls the way in which Saint-Cyran had compared Scripture to the Incarnation. "Comme Dieu a réduit sa parole et son Verbe dans un état bas et méprisable par l'Incarnation, pour sauver les hommes par ce rabaissement, *il a voulu aussi honorer ce mystère dans son Ecriture, en proposant cette même parole sous des expressions foibles, informes et obscures,* afin de guérir ainsi les esprits superbes des hommes, et de les rendre capables de sa Grâce."[49] Therefore, Sacy concludes, it is not necessary for a translation of the Bible to be "claire" in order to edify the faithful. To the contrary, any translation that seeks to clarify Scripture too thoroughly "s'oppose peut-être . . . au Saint-Esprit qui est l'architecte et le principal ouvrier de l'édifice céleste."[50]

Sacy confides to Fontaine that he has taken note of the punishment that Scripture promises those "qui ajoutent quelque chose à la parole de Dieu." Yet how, he asks, can the translator otherwise proceed? "Combien y a-t-il d'endroits où l'on se voit presque nécessité de le faire pour éclaircir." How often the translator finds in the original text "des fautes contre la grammaire et contre les règles de langage des hommes." "Je tremble," Sacy continues, "quand je considère que le Saint-Esprit a voulu que l'Ecriture, telle qu'elle a été jusqu'ici dans les mains des fidèles, fût remplie de mauvais mots, de mauvaises phrases et quelquefois de discours qui paroissent confus et embarrassés." "Ai-je bien fait," he asks Fontaine, "lorsque j'ai eu dessein au contraire d'éviter toutes ses fautes apparentes, qui peuvent dégoûter bien des esprits, et de rendre ma traduction la plus nette et la plus intelligible que j'ai pu?"[51]

Sacy's reflections point up a fundamental conflict between Jansenism and the rationalist spirit of classicism, between the irrationality implicit in neo-Augustinian theology and the Cartesian rationalism of the age in which Port-Royal found itself. M. de Sacy was in many ways the product of the classical age in which he lived. His attempt to render the language of Scripture "clair, pur et conforme aux règles de la grammaire" is completely in accord with the aims of classical prose. In the last analysis, however,

Sacy is uncomfortable with the role he finds himself playing when he attempts to interpret the intentions of the Holy Spirit.

The fundamental assumption of the classical style is that rational discourse is possible. During the course of the seventeenth century, a whole range of subjects that formerly had been seen as beyond the scope of human reason were opened up to rational discourse. Astronomy and the natural sciences began to take their place alongside geometry and mathematics. This very spirit led to the beginnings of modern biblical criticism. The Bible began to lose its exemption from rational and textual analysis. It is no accident that Richard Simon, the father of modern biblical criticism, stands at the apogee of French classicism.

The idea that one may subject the Bible to scientific analysis is fundamentally repugnant to Monsieur de Sacy. He views Scripture as a part of the fabric of Revelation itself, as a mirror of the Incarnation. Since it is God's manifest will "que sa parole fût envelopée d'obscurités," all human means of illuminating a text, whether historical or linguistic, are of limited value. "Je vois dans l'Ecriture," Sacy tells Fontaine, "que le feu qui ne venoit point du sanctuaire étoit profane et étranger, quoiqu'il pût être plus clair et plus beau que celui du sanctuaire."[52]

"Il n'y a rien de si dangereux," Sacy tells Fontaine, "que de traduire ou d'expliquer publiquement l'Ecriture."[53] There is always the danger that those who wish to attack the authority of Scripture will make use of a new and easily comprehensible translation. "C'est pourquoy," Sacy states at the beginning of his *Préface à la Genèse*, "on a cru qu'on ne devoit pas produire un livre si saint en une langue qui le rend intelligible à tout le monde, *sans établir d'abord les fondemens inébranlables du profond respect qui luy est dû.*" In this preface to Genesis, designed to serve as an introduction to his entire translation of the Bible, Sacy addresses a proof of the infallibility of Scripture to those "qui estant Chrestiens de nom, et Payens de moeurs et de langage, entrent dans l'Eglise comme pour adorer Dieu et en mesme tems ne se souviennent de la religion que pour s'en railler, de Dieu que pour le deshonorer par leurs raisonnemens impies."[54]

THE BIBLE AND *LA LIBRE PENSEE*

To whom exactly does Sacy address his proof? What is the nature of their "raisonnemens impies"? *La libre pensée*, that movement of religious disbelief which since the beginning of the seventeenth century had begun to manifest itself among the *noblesse de cour* and in certain circles of the *bourgeoisie érudite*, was not a product of the scientific revolution. It had its origins in the Italian neo-Epicureanism of the Renaissance, more particularly in the neo-Averroism of the University of Padua. This reinterpretation of Aristotle furnished the *libres penseurs* of the seventeenth century with three principal themes: the refutation of miracles, the denial of the immortality of the soul, and the negation of the Creation. Prior to 1660, *la libre pensée* had for the most part not manifested itself in the form of outright atheism. The great majority of those who launched attacks on supernatural religion during the first half of the seventeenth century did so from the relatively safe position of fideism, or the notion that faith can accept what reason cannot.

It would be a mistake to take the position of Cyrano de Bergerac, for instance, as indicative of the general character of the attacks on the Bible by *la libre pensée* prior to 1660. The line of battle was drawn far short of the attacks on the divinity of Christ and the historicity of the Gospels that would begin to appear in the second half of the century. The controversy between those who sought to demolish supernatural religion and those who sought to defend it centered upon an issue that to twentieth-century eyes might seem relatively minor: Moses' authorship of the Pentateuch. The issue, however, was not a minor one for M. de Sacy. For him, to question Moses' authorship of Genesis was to rend irreparably the seamless garment of Scripture. Sacy particularly directs his argument in his *Préface à la Genèse* to those who "se servent . . . de la personne de Moyse et de ce qu'il dit dans les premiers Chapitres de ce livre touchant la création du monde, le paradis terrestre, la chute d'Adam, et le peché originel, pour en prendre des sujets de leurs discours plein d'insolence et de blasphème."[55]

The movement hostile to the authenticity of the Pentateuch had in the first half of the seventeenth century built a fairly coherent argument that these books were not the work of Moses. Early in the sixteenth century, Rabbi Aben Ezra had attributed the composition of the Pentateuch to Esdras.[56] This idea gained adherents during the course of the following century and was taken up again by Hobbes in chapter 33 of his *Leviathan* (1651). Just how popular the attribution of the Pentateuch to Esdras had become by the middle of the century is indicated by the care Pascal takes to refute the notion in fragments 415-18/970-72 of the *Pensées*.

Those attempting to discredit the historical accuracy of the Pentateuch based their arguments principally upon textual contradictions. In 1623, Séraphin Cumiranus published a whole series of such contradictions under the title *Conciliatio omnium fere locorum totius sacrae scripturae, quae inter se pugnare videntur.*[57] The apologists, however, followed quickly behind the detractors and attempted to reconcile the textual contradictions they had spelled out. Such is Père Garasse's aim in *La Doctrine curieuse* (1624), a work that provides us with a number of examples of the kinds of textual contradictions cited by the *libres penseurs*.

A few of the contradictions cited by Garasse pertain to New Testament texts. The *beaux esprits* pointed out that though Christ compared his coming death to the three days and nights Jonah spent in the belly of the whale (Matthew 12:40), "il ne demeura dans le ventre de la terre qu'un jour entier." More often, however, Garasse pictures them as objecting to contradictions they found in the Pentateuch. In Genesis 32:30, "Jacob se vante d'avoir veu Dieu face à face." In Exodus 33:20, however, God warns Moses: *Non videbit me homo et vivet*.[58] Garasse notes that his adversaries have particular trouble believing almost anything written in Genesis. Not only do they reject "ce qui est raconté au premier et second chapîtres de la *Genèse* touchant la création du premier homme" and the story of Adam's disobedience and fall as "choses si estranges et de si dure créance qu'il faudrait avoir perdu le sens pour les recevoir sans contradiction." They go on to speculate that perhaps the world always existed and that man himself "estoit né de pourriture comme les rats." Garasse reserves particularly harsh words for this second theory, which he identifies as one borrowed from "le maudit Lucilio Vanino."[59]

Other critics of scriptural infallibility scrutinized biblical chronologies and found irresolvable contradictions. Not only were the genealogies of the patriarchs found to vary according to whether one used the Hebrew, Greek, or Vulgate texts. Internal chronological contradictions in any given text were shown to cast doubt on the reliability of the Pentateuch as a historical document. For instance, according to the chronology of the Septuagint, Methuselah should have died fourteen years after the Flood. Yet this was clearly impossible, at least according to Genesis 5:27, which states that all mankind perished in the Flood except the eight in Noah's ark.[60] Isaac de la Peyrère made use of the same method to cast doubt on Moses' authorship of the whole of the Pentateuch. How, he asked in his *Systema theologicum*, could Moses have witnessed events that took place after his death: *Qui enim potuit Moses scribere post mortem suam?*[61]

In his *Préface à la Genèse*, Sacy refuses to accord those who raise such questions the status of scholars or exegetes. Sacy does not concede the point that the Bible is subject to the same kind of critical examination as any other human document. The fault of those who raise the problem of textual contradictions is a moral, not an intellectual, one:

> Ils s'imaginent s'attirer la réputation d'hommes d'esprit et de bon sens en déclarant qu'ils ne se laissent point aller à la prévention peu considerée d'un peuple crédule, qu'ils veulent des raisons qui les convainquent, et qu'ils ne sont point disposez à déférer aveuglement à l'autorité que l'on attribue à Jésus-Christ, ou à celle que l'on donne à Moyse et à toute l'Ecriture.[62]

For the most part, attacks by *la libre pensée* on the credibility of the Old Testament were not of a scholarly character. Nor, with the exception of Cyrano de Bergerac's *Etats et empires de la lune* (1658), did they take the form of direct antireligious propaganda. Cyrano's burlesque of the Fall, the Flood, and the entire supernatural element in the Bible stands very much by itself prior to 1660. By comparison, criticism of the Bible in the works of Naudé and La Mothe Le Vayer appears indirect, prudent, and intended for the already initiated. Both Naudé and La Mothe Le Vayer recognized religion as a necessary arm of absolute monarchy. Never intending to propagate antireligious ideas to any large public, they reserved their most radical ideas for their immediate circles.

Naudé, in his *Apologie pour tous les grands hommes soupçonnez de Magie* (1625), had outlined parallels between biblical events and ancient myths in order to draw the conclusion that Moses had borrowed from pagan sources.[63] La Mothe Le Vayer ridicules those who fear that parallels drawn between sacred and profane texts might cast doubt on Christianity's claim to represent a unique Revelation. Did not the Fathers themselves, he asks, suggest that certain biblical characters were "archetypes" of men who later appeared upon the stage of profane history? Had not even Saint Augustine seen in Cain, the founder of the world's first city, the "expresse figure" of Romulus, the founder of Rome? Moreover, he argues, why should Christianity, which has absorbed so many traditions, fear contamination from ideas coming from other cultures?:

> Les mots *Pleïades*, *Arcturus* et *Orion* se lisent sans scandale parmi les saintes moralités de Job. . . . Et si nous employons librement à l'embellissement des autels chrétiens quelques étoffes du Japon ou de la Chine que nous savons avoir été tissuës et travaillées par des mains idolâtres: Pourquoi ferions-nous difficulté de nous servir des dictions ou des pensées de ceux qu'une différente religion a séparés de nous et rendus même ennemis de nos vérités Evangeliques?[64]

In his *Parallèles historiques*, Le Vayer professes to suscribe to the traditional view that the pagan religions are but "singeries" by which the Devil has sought to mock Christianity. His examples, however, all point to the conclusion that very little indeed is peculiar to the rites and ceremonies of the Christian tradition. Circumcision, far from being unique to the Jews, is found "en usage dans beaucoup de provinces de l'Amérique." Nor is the monastic tradition found only in Christianity. "Les Chinois à l'autre bout de la terre ont des personnes de l'un et de l'autre sexe consacrées au culte de leurs Pagodes, et l'on y voit des monastères . . . peu différents, au rapport du Père Jarric, de ceux du Christianisme." Pilgrimages, confession, and baptism are practiced in India, and the cult of relics has numerous parallels in Buddhism and Islam. Even examples of prophecies and miracles are found in the pagan religions: "Une Rélation récente conte . . . qu'en en 1648 un Faquir . . . voyant une multitude infinie de pauvres pélerins accourus aux dévotions d'une Pagode, nourrit cent mille personnes."[65]

The example of La Mothe Le Vayer serves to remind us that *la libre pensée* amounted to something larger and more diffuse than a coherent literary or philosophical tradition. The fact that there existed even a few *esprits* for whom the vision of the Christian Revelation as unique and inviolable no longer made any sense, constituted a potential challenge of unprecedented proportions to the traditional authority of the Bible. Sacy's *Préface à la Genèse* represents the hardening of a whole conservative theological tradition in the face of the first stirrings of modern biblical criticism and the beginnings of a modern pluralistic view of man and the world. If we are to understand Sacy's whole enterprise in defending the authority of the Bible, we must look beyond the writings of the *beaux esprits* to their conversations within their own circles. Fortunately, we have access to this information. The apologists of the time, in order to refute their ideas, collected them and incorporated them into dialogues.

The *libres penseurs* described by Père Garasse can best be characterized as doubting anything they find of a supernatural character in Scripture. Moreover, they claim to be shocked by the style of the Old Testament, whose "incongruitez" and "barbarismes," they insist, could not possibly be the language "emané du Saint-Esprit."[66] Boucher, in *Les Triomphes de la religion chrestienne* (1638), presents a similar picture of the same group. His *libertins*, in addition to being suspicious of parallels they note between biblical events and pagan myths, claim to be horrified by the Old Testament's attribution of human features to God:

> Comment est-ce que cette Escripture peut estre inspirée de Dieu, puisqu'elle propose plusieurs choses injurieuses et indignes de sa Divine Majesté, luy attribuant des parties corporelles, des yeux, des oreilles, une bouche, des espaules, un ventre . . . et ce qui est plus injurieux, luy attribuant des passions d'esprit, disant qu'il travaille et se repose, qu'il sommeille . . . qu'il change ses oeuvres et se repent de quelques actions qu'il a faictes, choses toutes indignes de la grandeur de sa Majesté infinie?[67]

What links the diversity of the *libres penseurs* prior to 1660 is a spirit of rationality, the notion that every matter of inquiry is subject to rational explanation. Boucher's *libertins* find the Bible to be irrational and incoherent as a text. "Mais pourquoy," they want to know, "y a-[t]-il tant de confusions dans les livres de la Bible, où l'on voit plusieurs discours sans aucun ordre, si peu arangez et reiglez, que dans un mesme chapitre on trouvera une si grande diversité de sentences et si élloignées les unes des autres, qu'il est impossible d'y rien concevoir?"[68] It is this objection that Sacy attempts to rectify when he produces a translation of the Bible that is, in his own words, an effort to "rendre le langage de l'Ecriture clair, pur, et conforme aux règles de la grammaire."[69]

The *libertins* described by Boucher are unable to accept any biblical account that seems to conflict with science. They find the Bible as a whole to be fraught with "grands manquemens et défauts très-notables, touchant les propriétez naturelles des choses dont elle fait mention."[70] They can but dismiss as pure invention such episodes as Joshua's stopping of the sun[71] or the return of the spirit of Samuel.[72] The universal Flood, an event whose historicity Sacy takes great pains to defend, particularly provokes their doubts as to the credibility of the Bible. "Comment," they ask, "est-il possible que la nature ayt peu fournir d'une si grande quantité d'eaux pour noyer tout le monde?"[73]

Not all the *libres penseurs* espoused an outright disbelief in the supernatural events recorded in the Old Testament. Yet a book like Isaac de La Peyrère's *Systema theologicum ex Praeadamitarum hypothesi* (1655), in which he attempts to give a rational explanation of various Old Testament miracles, might have seemed to an apologist like Sacy even more dangerous than outright atheism. La Peyrère, unlike most of the *libertins*, does pretend to biblical exegesis. He interprets the two accounts of man's creation in Genesis to mean that there were two historical creations: that of Adam, from which the Jews descended; and another, several hundred years before, which produced the rest of the human race.[74]

La Peyrère attempts to remove the supernatural element from even the most miraculous episodes in the Old Testament. His notions anticipate both those of the eighteenth-century *philosophes* and those of the "rationalist" school of twentieth-century biblical criticism. For La Peyrère, the various miracles assisting the Israelites in the wilderness serve only to point out the true miracle that they were able to sustain themselves by a proper management of their herds.[75] The Flood was a historical event, but it was localized in the region of Palestine.[76] This is the very mentality that Desmarests de Saint-Sorlin, an apologist contemporary with Sacy, combats in his *Délices de l'Esprit*. His *libertin* argues that the passage of the Red Sea can be explained in a rational manner. Moses merely observed the tide and chose the favorable moment for his people to cross.[77]

SACY'S APOLOGETIC COUNTEROFFENSIVE: A DEFENSE OF THE LITERAL INSPIRATION OF SCRIPTURE

The Sacy Bible must be understood in the larger context of an apologetic countermovement that, during the course of the seventeenth century, sought to defend the Bible against the attacks of its rationalist detractors. Neo-Augustinianism, from its very beginnings, had significant contacts with this movement. Jansenius himself, in his commentary on the Pentateuch, had defended Moses' authorship of these books. Moses, he argues in response to those who had pointed out that the prophet's death takes place before the end of the narrative of the Pentateuch, was inspired by the Holy Spirit. In writing the final chapters of his narrative, Moses was making an inspired prediction of events that were to occur after his death.[78] Saint-Cyran always reacted violently against attempts to apply secular criteria to Scripture. The Bible, he argued in a long polemic against Père Sirmond, because it is a document of Revelation, is not subject to the standards by which literary works are judged.[79]

Pascal must be included among those who, under the influence of Port-Royal, came to the defense of the historicity of the Pentateuch. In outlining his projected *Apology* to the Solitaires, Etienne Périer reminds us in the *Préface de Port-Royal*, Pascal had made a point of arguing "par un très grand nombre de circonstances indubitables, qu'il était impossible que Moïse eût laissé par écrit des choses fausses."[80] A detailed analysis of Pascal's defense of Moses in the *Pensées* will appear in Chapter Six. For the moment, let us only note that Pascal's arguments inspired yet another defense of Moses, that of Filleau de la Chaise, who in 1672 published his *Discours sur les preuves du livre de Moïse*.

Port-Royal's role in organizing a defense of the historicity of the Old Testament lasted right up until the end. In 1678, the apostolic vicar to Belgium, pronouncing Spinoza's *Tractatus* "un des plus méchants livres du monde," called in Arnauld to write a refutation of its attacks on the Mosaic authorship of the Pentateuch. Arnauld, in turn, called upon Bossuet. The latter, who had just procured the condemnation of Richard Simon's *Histoire critique de l'Ancien Testament*, then proceeded to have Spinoza's works placed on the Roman Index.[81] At about the same time, Bossuet, again at the invitation of Arnauld, undertook to prove the authenticity of the biblical account of the Flood. Noting that "de nos jours on a bien osé publier en toute sorte de langues des livres contre l'Ecriture," Bossuet devoted an entire chapter of the second part of his *Discours sur l'histoire universelle* to a defense of the historicity of the Pentateuch.[82]

This movement in defense of Scripture reached its high-water mark about the time Sacy's Bible was being published. We are more interested, however, in those apologists who wrote prior to 1660. M. de Sacy, though he draws most of his defense of Scripture from Saint Augustine, nevertheless borrows several approaches from those defenders of the Bible who immediately preceded him. Of particular interest are two apologetic counteroffensives: the attempt to establish an accurate biblical chronology; and the effort to prove that the Bible was anterior to pagan myths.

The *libres penseurs* had often cited chronological errors in the Bible as proof of its fallibility. The apologists who followed behind them were especially anxious to fix the date of the Creation, from which other dates might then be computed. In 1632, J. d'Auzoles had published *La Sainte Chronologie*, in which he presented some 79 different opinions, arrived at by 122 different chronologists, concerning the date of the Creation. The dates var-

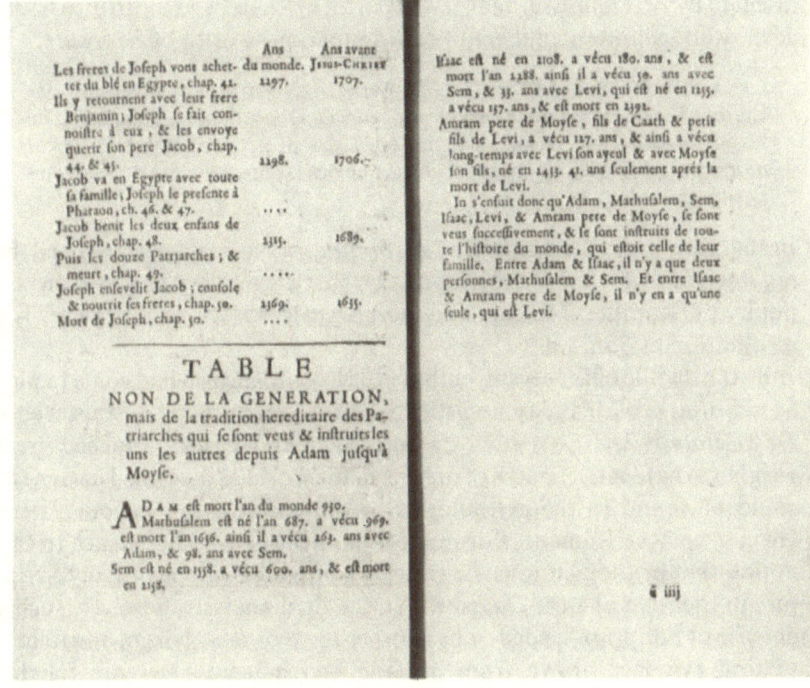

Figure 2. Chronological Table from Sacy's *Préface à la Genèse*, 1683 (Service photographique, Bibliothèque Nationale)

ied from the year 3083 B.C. to 6984 B.C.[83] By the time Sacy wrote his *Préface à la Genèse*, confusion still reigned in this particular field. Sacy attempts to put an end to the entire controversy by establishing two chronological tables based entirely on textual evidence from the Bible.

Sacy's first table is a chronology of biblical events from the Creation to the death of Joseph. A second, "Table non de la génération, mais de la tradition héréditaire des Patriarches qui se sont veus et instruits les uns les autres depuis Adam" (see figure 2), establishes the fact that only five persons separated Moses from Adam and the Creation. In the opinion of Mlle Delassault, "aucun historien avant Sacy n'avait tiré une conclusion aussi hardie."[84] Pascal, in fragment 327/296 of the *Pensées*, reaches precisely the same conclusion: "Sem, qui a vu Lamech, qui a vu Adam, a vu aussi Jacob, qui a vu ceux qui ont vu Moïse; donc le déluge et la création sont vrais."

A second argument taken up by Sacy attempts to turn the tables on the *libres penseurs* by putting comparatism—between the Bible and pagan myths—in the service of apology. The first generation of apologists, represented by Père Garasse, had viewed pagan myths only as an artifice of the devil, who had invented them to cast doubt on the truth of Scripture:

> Le Diable a prophané l'histoire du paradis terrestre par l'invention des champs Elyziens, le déluge de Noé par celuy de Deucalion, le changement de Nabuchodonosor par la métamorphose de Lycaon . . . en somme, les *Métamorphoses* d'Ovide ne sont autre chose que des larcins ridicules des Sainctes Ecritures.[85]

In 1641, however, Nierembergius' *De origine sacrae scripturae* reversed the argument and advanced the proposition that ancient myths prove the antiquity of Scripture: Mercury's caduceus recalls Moses' rod; Heracles is a recollection of Samson.[86]

By the middle of the seventeenth century, comparatism had come to play an important role in the apologists' defense of Scripture. H. Grotius, whose *De veritate religionis* is cited by both Sacy and Pascal, attached great weight to the fact that traces of origins of the world as described in Genesis could be found in the mythologies of the Indians, the Egyptians, the Greeks, and the Romans. Bogan (1658) attached such importance to this notion that he thought it useful to search for recollections of Holy Scripture in the *Iliad* and the *Odyssey*.[87] In the final analysis, however, such a defense of Scripture tended to be another form of rationalism, an attempt to find evidence drawn from profane and presumably more reliable sources.

Vossius, in his *De theologia Gentili* (1641), had come to view pagan myths as a kind of partial revelation, by which the Gentiles had been prepared to receive the truths set forth in Scripture.[88] An English apologist, E. Stillingfleet, sought "to make it appear what footsteps there are of the truth of Scripture history amid all the corruptions of Heathen Mythology."[89] Not all the apologists, however, trusted the method. Desmarests de Saint-Sorlin (1658) warns his *libertin* that pagan myths are distortions of the truth: "Le Démon ennemy du genre humain, ne pouvant entièrement destruire la vérité établie par des livres authentiques, a bien pu la contrefaire et la desguiser par des Fables et porter les hommes à adorer la fiction ornée de figures et de beau langage et à quitter pour elle la vérité simple et naïve."[90]

At Port-Royal, the theologians disagreed concerning the usefulness of comparatism. Arnauld feared that the method might lead some to conclude that paganism contained some elements of divine truth: "Ce sont d'horribles choses et capables d'inspirer à de jeunes libertins: qu'il faut avoir une religion, mais qu'elles sont toutes bonnes, et que le Paganisme même peut entrer en parallèle avec le Christianisme."[91] Sacy, surprisingly enough, found comparatism a useful tool in establishing the antiquity of biblical history. For instance, in a Greek myth, he finds traces of the biblical story of the tower of Babel: "Cette vérité de l'Ecriture a donné lieu à la fable des Géans, que les Poëtes disent avoir entasé des montagnes les unes sur les autres, pour attaquer et prendre le ciel."[92] Sacy accords particular importance to the myth of Saturn. He recalls that Tertullian, attempting in his *Apology* to prove that truth is more ancient than falsehood, had maintained that the Greek poets had forged this myth from the biblical story of Noah. Sacy insists on certain striking details. Saturn and Rhea were born of Ocean and Thetis, goddess of the sea: "Noé avait esté délivré du déluge dans lequel l'Océan avait inondé toute la terre." Saturn's symbol, the ship, for Sacy recalls Noah's Ark.[93]

Sacy rejects any notion that pagan myths contain traces of divine revelation. For him, as for Père Garasse and Desmarests de Saint-Sorlin, they are creations of Satan, parodies of biblical events forged in order to cast doubt on the authenticity of Scripture.[94] In his commentary on Leviticus 6:9[95] Sacy argues that the fire tended by the vestal virgins in Roman mythology is just such a parody. It is the Devil's attempt to reproduce in the cult of the pagans his own version of the perpetual fire that burned in the temple of the Jews. Always anxious to anchor his interpretation in Scripture itself, Sacy refers the reader to 1 Maccabees 3:48: "*Ils ouvrirent les livres de la Loy, où les Gentils cherchoient à trouver quelque chose qui eût du rapport avec leurs idoles*" (Sacy's translation). "Le démon," he explains, "a voulu imiter ce feu perpetuel de l'autel de Dieu par le feu des Vestales qui ne s'éteignoit jamais; selon ce qui est dit dans les Machabées, que les Payens cherchoient dans les livre saints quelque chose qu'ils pûssent imiter pour le culte de leurs idoles."[96]

A great distance separates Sacy's interpretation from that of modern biblical scholars. Compare, for instance, Sacy's translation with that of the Jerusalem Bible, which follows the Hebrew text: "Ils [les Juifs] déployèrent le livre de la Loi pour y découvrir ce que les païens demandaient aux représentations de leurs faux dieux."[97] Sacy unwittingly effects an ingenious exegesis on the basis of an incorrect text. Whereas he follows the Vulgate, nothing in the original Hebrew text substantiates his argument that the Gentiles modeled their own cult on what they found in the Scriptures of the Jews.

Richard Simon, a contemporary of Sacy's, set down the following critique of Sacy's translation of the Old Testament:

> M. Isaac Le Maistre avoit de certains talens, principalement pour écrire en François, qui ont pu lui donner quelque rang parmi les illustres auteurs du dix-septième siècle. Mais si on lui ôte cette qualité d'écrire avec politesse en sa langue, il lui reste peu de chose. Il a entrepris des ouvrages qui étaient beaucoup au-dessus de ses forces. . . . S'il avoit eu quelque connoissance de la langue hébraïque, et même du latin de la Vulgate, il aurait parlé autrement: il

y aurait reconnu un grand nombre de fautes considérables. Ses explications du sens spirituël sont pour l'ordinaire vagues et peu propres au texte qu'il veut expliquer, parce qu'elles ne coulent point du sens littéral.[98]

In the very decade Sacy was constructing his monumental defense of the historicity of the Old Testament, Richard Simon was laying the groundwork for modern textual criticism of the Bible. Simon's exposition of a multiple-source theory to explain the origins of the Pentateuch would mean that Sacy's ingenious defense of the Mosaic authorship of that document would never receive serious consideration by biblical scholars.[99] In the history of scriptural exegesis, Sacy's commentaries on the Old Testament represent a kind of last stand on the part of traditional exegesis. They are a final, comprehensive statement of a whole approach to the Bible that had endured since Saint Augustine and that came crashing down as a result of scholarship like Simon's.

In general, the Sacy Bible stands in the mainstream of both traditional exegesis and traditional apology. It does so because Sacy takes his inspiration from a source common to both of these, Saint Augustine. Sacy's biblical commentaries are also very much of their own time. When he puts comparatism in the service of defending the historicity of the Pentateuch, when he seeks to establish verifiable biblical chronologies, and when he reconciles apparent textual contradictions by explaining their "sens spirituel," Sacy makes himself heir to a definite seventeenth-century apologetic tradition, a tradition in which he is preceded by Garasse, Boucher, Grotius, and Desmarests de Saint-Sorlin.

On the other hand, because he seeks to counter the growing rationalism of an entire culture, Sacy often takes positions and reaches conclusions that appear extreme or exaggerated even by the standards of traditional apologetics. In defending the veracity of Genesis' account of the Creation, Sacy sets down a chronology of the patriarchs that is far more daring than that of any previous exegete. His amplifications of the traditional theory of the unity of the two Testaments likewise trespass the limits of classical exegesis. Sacy, following in the path traced by Saint-Cyran and Jansenius, develops the principle that the whole of Scripture must be viewed from the perspective of the Incarnation. In setting out to explicate the Old Testament, Sacy therefore assumes that every verse of this document somehow anticipates Christ himself.

Sacy offers his *Préface à la Genèse* as an introduction to his translation of the entire Bible. In addressing his *Préface* to those who question the authority of the Old Testament, Sacy has one principal purpose in mind. He will attempt to convince those who doubt the authority of Moses that they cannot do so without questioning the authority of Christ himself. Such an argument, the product of a Jansenist interpretation of classical

Augustinianism, represents the antirationalist character of Sacy's whole enterprise. His *Préface à la Genèse*, in which the argument is set forth, warrants our closer attention.

    1. Sainte-Beuve, 1:762.
    2. The name "Saci" has been taken to be an anagram of "Isaac"; presumably Sacy took this name when he became a Solitaire. Mlle Delassault, however, noting that the signature always appears as "Sacy," and not "Saci," suggests that "Sacy" was the name of a family property and that Sacy used the title "Sieur de Sacy" in the same way that his brothers used the titles "de Séricourt" and "de Vallemont" (p. 4).
    3. *Mémoires*, Bibliothèque Mazarine, MS. 2465, pp. 176–77.
    4. Fontaine (MS. 2465), p. 221.
    5. Sainte-Beuve, 1:765.
    6. Sainte-Beuve, 1:768.
    7. Sainte-Beuve, 1:777.
    8. See Delassault: pp. 55–58 for Corneille; pp. 58–60 for Racine; pp. 37–38 for Molière; pp. 28–29, 35, and 60 for La Fontaine.
    9. Gounelle, p. 30.
    10. See Delassault, "Deuxième Partie," chapters 2 and 7.
    11. Sainte-Beuve, 1:790.
    12. Sainte-Beuve, 1:790.
    13. Sainte-Beuve, 1:791.
    14. "Chez Gaspard Migeot, Mons" would appear to be a pseudonym for the press of Daniel Elzevier in Amsterdam. The *Historical Catalogue of the Printed Editions of Holy Scripture* (London: British and Foreign Bible Society, 1903) gives the following information concerning the *Nouveau Testament de Mons*: "This translation, begun by Antoine Le Maistre (1608–1658), was revised and completed by L.-I. Le Maistre [Sacy] (1613–1684), who used the original Greek. The whole was revised by Antoine Arnauld (1612–1694), Pierre Nicole (1625–1695) and others, with the help of the ancient versions and patristic commentaries" (p. 400). Nine editions of the *Nouveau Testament de Mons* appeared between 1667 and 1697, in spite of the fact that the translation was placed on the Index in 1668. This translation also served as the text for P. Quesnel's *Réflexions morales* on the New Testament, which were condemned as heretical in 1713 by Clement XI in the bull *Unigenitus*.
    15. Delassault, p. 155.
    16. *Le Nouveau Testament de Nostre Seigneur Jésus-Christ traduit en françois selon l'édition vulgate avec les différences du Grec*, "sixième édition," Préface, Première Partie.
    17. *Histoire générale de Port-Royal*, 3:441.
    18. *Nouveau Testament de Mons*, Préface, Première Partie.
    19. *Nouveau Testament de Mons*, Préface, Première Partie (italics mine).
    20. Clemencet, 3:441.
    21. *Nouveau Testament de Mons*, Préface, Première Partie (italics mine).
    22. *Nouveau Testament de Mons*, Préface, Première Partie.
    23. *Nouveau Testament de Mons*, Préface, Première Partie.
    24. Arnauld, *Défense de la traduction imprimée à Mons: contre les sermons de P. Meinbourg, Jésuite*, pp. 16–17, 22. This distinctively Augustinian doctrine is cited by Pascal from *De doctrina christiana* in fr. 283/251: "Qui veut donner le sens de l'Ecriture et ne le prend point de l'Ecriture est l'ennemi de l'Ecriture."

25. *Défense de la traduction*, p. 63.
26. *Défense de la traduction*, p. 94 ff.; p. 107.
27. Arnauld, *Défense des versions de l'Ecriture Sainte, des offices de l'Eglise, et des ouvrages des Pères et en particulier de la nouvelle traduction du Bréviaire*, p. 73.
28. Sainte-Beuve, 1:792.
29. *Défense des versions*, p. 5.
30. *Défense des versions*, p. 103.
31. *Défense des versions*, p. 62.
32. *Défense des versions*, p. 53.
33. *Défense des versions*, p. 58–59.
34. *Défense des versions*, pp. 161–62.
35. Delassault, p. 158.
36. Fontaine, 2:510.
37. Sainte-Beuve, 1:792.
38. Sainte-Beuve, 1:794.
39. Sainte-Beuve, 1:793.
40. Fontaine, 2:518.
41. Delassault, p. 161. *Ecclésiastique* appeared several months after Sacy's death. The remaining unpublished manuscripts—*Nombres, Deutéronome, Josué, Juges, Ruth, Livres III et IV des Rois, Paralipomènes, Estras, Tobie, Judith, Esther, Job, Jérémie, Ezechiel, Daniel, Machabées*—are identified in the bill of sale (Archives Nationales, Minutier Général, Etude LXXX, vente du 9 mars 1684) issued to Sacy's executor by the Libraire Desprez.
42. Sainte-Beuve, 1:793.
43. These distinctions are not noted by the catalogue of the Bibliothèque Nationale. The catalogue of the British Library (under the heading "Polyglot/Latin and French") attributes all commentaries to Sacy "except in the books of *Numbers, Deuteronomy, Joshua, Ruth, I and II Kings, I and II Chronicles, Ezra, Nehemiah, Esther, Job, Psalms, Song of Solomon, Jeremiah, Ezekiel, Daniel, Tobit, Judith, Baruch, I and II Maccabees*, the *Gospels* and *Acts* I–XIII, 18, where it is by Thomas du Fossé, *Acts* XIII, 19 to end and *Titus* to *Revelation*, where it is by Charles Huré, and *Romans* to *Timothy*, where the 'sens litteral' is by Touret . . . and the 'sens spirituel' by C. Huré."
44. Delassault, p. 162.
45. The catalogue of the Bibliothèque Nationale lists subsequent editions of the Sacy Bible as follows: Paris: 1696, 1700, 1696–1702; Anvers: 1700; Bruxelles: 1700; Liège: 1700; Paris: 1701; Bruxelles: 1701; Paris: 1728, 1730, 1742; Paris: 1834–36, 1837, 1841, 1843, 1846, 1851, 1858, 1867–68, 1875.
46. Fontaine, 2:509–10.
47. Fontaine, 2:510–11.
48. Fontaine, 2:515.
49. Fontaine, 2:516 (italics mine).
50. Fontaine, 2:515.
51. Fontaine, 2:511–12.
52. Fontaine, 2:510–11.
53. Fontaine, 2:511.
54. *La Genèse*, Préface, Première Partie, partie iii (italics mine). Pagination is missing in Sacy's *Préface*. Subsequent references will be to chapter subdivisions.
55. *La Genèse*, Préface, Première Partie, partie iii.
56. Delassault, p. 197, citing the *Biblia rabbinica* (Venitiis: 1524), p. 1.
57. Delassault, p. 205.

58. *La Doctrine curieuse des beaux esprits de ce tems ou pretendus tels*, pp. 592, 576.
59. Garasse, pp. 649–52.
60. Delassault, p. 210. Cf. Sacy's explication of Genesis 5:27.
61. *Systema theologicum ex Praeadamitarum hypothesi*, liber quartus, caput i, p. 152.
62. *La Genèse*, Préface, Première Partie, partie iii.
63. *Apologie pour tous les grands hommes . . . soupçonnez de Magie*, pp. 300–301.
64. "Rapports de l'Histoire Profane à la Sainte," in *Oeuvres de La Mothe Le Vayer*, vol. 6, "Lettre xciii," pp. 406–8.
65. *Oeuvres*, vol. 7, "Lettre cxvi," pp. 287–97.
66. Garasse, p. 638.
67. J. Boucher, *Les Triomphes de la religion chrestienne contenans les résolutions de trois cens soixante et six questions*, p. 182.
68. Boucher, p. 174.
69. Fontaine, 2:510.
70. Boucher, p. 177.
71. Boucher, p. 255. Cf. Joshua 10:12–14.
72. Boucher, p. 264. Cf. 1 Kings 28:8–21.
73. Boucher, p. 205.
74. Isaac de La Peyrère, *Systema theologicum ex Praeadamitarum hypothesi*, liber secundus, caput x, pp. 83 ff.
75. La Peyrère, liber quartus, caput vi, p. 175 ff.
76. La Peyrère, liber quartus, caput vii, p. 178.
77. *Les Délices de l'Esprit: dialogues dédiéz aux Beaux Esprits du monde*, partie ii (journée x), p. 23. Desmarests de Saint-Sorlin, though an apologist whose views were not dissimilar to those of Sacy, was a self-declared enemy of Port-Royal. Sainte-Beuve (1:779) credits him with masterminding Sacy's arrest and imprisonment.
78. C. Jansenius, *Pentateuchus sive Commentarius in V Libros Moysis*, praefatio, p. 1.
79. See Jean Orcibal's *Les Origines du Jansénisme*, 2:350, 372.
80. Lafuma, p. 496.
81. See Jean Orcibal's "Les Jansénistes face à Spinoza," pp. 449–52.
82. J.-B. Bossuet, *Discours sur l'histoire universelle*, deuxième partie, ch. XXVIII, pp. 323 ff.
83. Delassault, p. 211.
84. Delassault, p. 217.
85. Garasse, pp. 828–29.
86. Delassault, p. 218.
87. Z. Bogan, *Homerus sive comparatio Homeri cum scriptoribus sacris quoad norman loquendi*.
88. G.-J. Vossius, *De theologia Gentili et physiologia christiana sive de origine de progressu idolatriae*. For instance, Vossius argues that Noah is recalled by three pagan deities: Baccus, Janus, and Saturn. The Dionysian mysteries contain the memory of Noah's discovery of the effects of the fruit of the vine. Janus, represented in Roman mythology with two faces, recalls the fact that Noah had seen two worlds: before and after the Flood. Saturn, whose symbol is the ship, divided the world among his three sons: Jupiter, Neptune, and Pluto. Noah's three sons likewise fell heir to the post-deluvian world. (L.I., caput xix, pp. 75–77) Cf. Sacy's *Genèse*, ch. ix, 28–29, p. 350.
89. E. Stillingfleet, *Origines Sacrae or rational account of the grounds of Christian Faith as to the truth and divine authority of the Scriptures*, p. 599.
90. *Les Délices*, "Seconde Partie" ("journée x"), p. 25.

91. Arnauld, *Oeuvres de Messire Antoine Arnauld*, 3:400-401.

92. *La Genèse*, ch. XI, v. 9, p. 381.

93. *La Genèse*, ch. IX, v. 28-29, pp. 350-51.

94. Compare the position of Desmarests de Saint-Sorlin: "Si l'usage légitime est toujours premier que l'abus, il n'y a point lieu de douter que les superstitions suggérées par les Démons soient venues sur la terre depuis la Foy inspirée de Dieu . . . le Diable n'a composé le Paganisme que des larcins qu'il nous a faits; ses Fables sont controuvées sur nos Histoires" (*Les Délices* [ed. of 1652], pp. 43-44).

95. *Lévitique* 6:9: "Ordonnez ceci à Aaron et à ses fils: Voicy quelle est la loy de l'holocauste. Il brûlera sur l'autel toute la nuit jusqu'au matin. Le feu sera pris de l'autel même" (Sacy's translation). Cf. n. 52 above.

96. *L'Exode et Le Lévitique: traduits en françois avec l'explication du sens littéral et du sens spirituel*, p. 602.

97. *La Sainte Bible traduite en français sous la direction de l'école biblique de Jérusalem* (Paris: Editions du Cerf, 1956), p. 546. A straightforward note in the modern edition clarifies this passage: "Comme il n'y a plus de prophète, on ouvre au hasard le livre de la Loi pour y trouver une réponse divine. C'est ce que les païens demandaient à leurs faux dieux. Les Juifs consultent la Parole du vrai Dieu."

98. Richard Simon, *Critique de la bibliothèque des auteurs ecclésiastiques*, 2: pp. 327-28.

99. The Catholic church, however, required Catholic exegetes to maintain Mosaic authorship of the Pentateuch up into the twentieth century. Only in 1948 did the Pontifical Bible Commission authorize scholars' use of the Documentary Theory, the fundamentals of which had been established by Richard Simon in his *Histoire critique du Vieux Testament* (1678).

III

Sacy's *Préface à la Genèse*: Exegesis in the Service of Apology

THE SIGNIFICANCE OF THE *PREFACE*

A modern introduction to a translation of Genesis might very well not mention the New Testament at all. Sacy's *Préface à la Genèse*, however, is a document of a totally different order. Sacy proposes his *Préface* as an introduction to his translation of the entire Bible. His principal aim in this introduction is to exclude the possibility of a rationalist examination of the Old Testament by showing that the authority of Moses rests on that of Christ himself. That which the New Testament specifically designates as forming part of Revelation, Sacy will attempt to prove, cannot be subjected to ordinary standards of textual criticism.

Sacy's approach to this traditional idea of the unity of the two Testaments finds an important parallel in the *Pensées*. Pascal's "Preuve des deux Testaments à la fois," proposed in outline form in fragment 305/274, however, is never developed into a completely organized proof. In the *liasses* corresponding to the "table de 1658,"[1] Pascal organized part of the vast quantity of materials he had collected for this proof under such chapter headings as "Preuves de Moïse," "Preuves de Jésus-Christ," "Que la Loi était figurative," and "Prophéties." Even the most highly organized of these arguments, the proofs of Moses and Christ, however, are in far from finished form. The remainder of the material destined for the "Preuve des deux Testaments à la fois" is scattered throughout the other *liasses* and often consists only of extensive catalogues of biblical citations.

In the *Préface à la Genèse*, Sacy presents, in a highly organized form, many of the same arguments sketched by Pascal. Among these arguments are various proofs of Christ's divinity, a defense of the historicity of the Pentateuch, a critique of Islam, and a theory of "figuratifs." Sacy's *Préface*, a document long ignored by, or unknown to, commentators and editors of the *Pensées*, often suggests the finished form that Pascal's arguments might have taken in a proof designed to establish the authority and authenticity of the Bible. I will therefore present a summary and an analysis of the *Préface à la Genèse* in order to establish a comparative text of potential interpretive

LA GENESE

TRADUITE EN FRANCOIS.

Avec l'explication du fens litteral & du fens fpirituel.

Tirée des SS. Peres & des Auteurs Ecclefiaftiques.

A PARIS,
Chez LAMBERT ROULLAND, Imprimeur Libraire ordinaire de la Reyne, ruë S. Jacques, aux Ar nes de la Reyne.

M. DC. LXXXIII.
Avec Approbation & Privilege du Roy.

Figure 3. Title page, *La Genèse*, 1683 (Service photographique, Bibliothèque Nationale)

value. Specific comparisons with the *Pensées* will generally be reserved for subsequent chapters.

In analyzing Sacy's arguments, it seems necessary to treat them in more or less the order in which he presents them. Sacy's arrangement of his proofs has a definite apologetic purpose. He first shows how Christ himself established the authority of Moses as a prophet. He then presents a proof of Christ's divinity based upon the prophecies. Admitting that his argument might be taken to be a circular one, Sacy then produces additional proofs of Christ's divinity drawn (1) from the Fathers and (2) from outside Revelation. Only when he has firmly established the principle of the unity of the Old and New Testaments does Sacy then explain his approach to exegesis. Exegesis, in turn, is then put in the service of apology. Sacy's theory of "figuratifs" is the source of an argument designed to safeguard the Old Testament from rationalist analysis.

MOSES AND THE NEW TESTAMENT

"Le premier des livres de l'Ecriture est la *Genèse* et l'auteur qui l'a écrit est Moyse." At the very beginning of his *Préface à la Genèse*, Sacy undertakes a defense of the Mosaic authorship of the Pentateuch. He first invites his reader to consider Moses as a historical figure "sans comparaison plus ancien que tous ces auteurs si illustres dans le monde qui ont acquis à la Grece le nom de mère des sciences." Moses, Sacy points out to those who might be tempted to see traces of pagan myths in Scripture, preceded Homer by more than five hundred years.

Moses' miracles—the plagues called down upon Egypt and the parting of the Red Sea—merit respect in their own right according to Sacy. They are "certainement des oeuvres de Dieu." Yet Sacy does not ask his reader to accept such miracles on their own authority. The proof that authorizes them is of greater authority: "qui est que Moyse a esté Prophète et que c'est de Jésus-Christ mesme que nous apprenons la déférence et la vénération qui luy est deue."[2] The authority of Moses is established by the New Testament: "c'est le Fils de Dieu mesme qui rend témoignage à la loy que ce Saint a publiée." For instance, Sacy points out, the New Testament recounts that Jesus voluntarily submitted to the Law of Moses in his circumcision, in sending those he had cured to the priests of the Temple, and in a multitude of other matters.

Sacy goes on to argue that Jesus, by citing Moses as his own authority in his public teaching, establishes Moses' credibility as a prophet. Sacy lays particular emphasis on Luke 20:37–38. Jesus, seeking to prove the resurrection of the dead to the Sadducees, reminds them of the way in which Moses had addressed God:

Et quant à ce que les morts doivent ressusciter un jour, Moyse le déclare assez

> *lui-même, lors qu'étant auprès du buisson il appelle le Seigneur le Dieu d'Abraham, le Dieu d'Isaac et le Dieu de Jacob.*
> *Or Dieu n'est point le Dieu des morts, mais des vivans; parce que tous sont vivans devant luy* [Sacy's translation].

By citing Moses in connection with the Resurrection, Sacy concludes, Christ establishes a "grand principe": "que ce que Moyse enseigne dans ses livres estoit la figure de ce qui se devoit faire dans la loy nouvelle."[3]

Sacy's second proof of the authority of Moses proceeds from the first. Christ, not content simply to establish the "grand principe" that his life and miracles are prefigured in the writings of Moses, "explique luy-mesme quelques-unes de ces figures." As his primary example of such an explication performed by Christ, Sacy cites Jesus' words to Nicodemus in John 3:14–15:

> *Et comme Moïse éleva dans le désert le serpent d'airain, il faut de même que le Fils-de-l'homme soit élevé en haut afin que tout homme qui croit en lui ne périsse point, mais qu'il ait la vie éternelle* [Sacy's translation].

According to Sacy, this passage in the New Testament represents Christ's explication of a corresponding passage in the book of Numbers (21:8–9):

> *Et le Seigneur lui dit: Faites un serpent d'airain, et mettez-le pour servir de signe; quiconque étant blessé des serpens le regardera, sera guéri. Moïse fit donc un serpent d'airain, et il le mit pour servir de signe; et ceux qui ayant été blessés le regardoient, étoient guéris* [Sacy's translation].

The "serpent d'airain," Sacy explains, prefigures Christ on the Cross. The meaning of this "figure," however, remained incomplete until the event it anticipated came to pass. Moses' serpent was but an image of a serpent, "la figure et non le venin du serpent," because it prefigured the fact that Christ "porteroit une chair mortelle semblable à celle du péché et non le péché mesme." The healing of the bites of real serpents by the image set up by Moses prefigured the Redemption, in which "la veue et l'adoration de Jésus-Christ élevé sur la Croix guériroit les playes que nous a faites le démon, appelé dans l'Ecriture l'*ancien serpent*."[4] (See figure 4.)

Sacy's exegesis of this passage is by no means original. He adopts the interpretation of Saint Augustine, who had in turn expanded upon that of Saint Paul. While founding his interpretation upon Patristic and Pauline models, Sacy at the same time insists that it was Christ himself, not any subsequent exegete, who drew the parallel between himself and the serpent in Numbers 21:8–9. Christ himself authorizes a Christian interpretation of events in the Old Testament. Protestant exegetes, Sacy observes, imagine any explication of Scripture that is not purely literal to be "une chose inventée et arbitraire." They err not only in rejecting holy tradition but in ignoring the exegetical model proposed by Christ himself. "Le sens allégorique"

SACY'S *PREFACE A LA GENESE*

Figure 4. "Le Serpent d'airain"; illuminated chapter title, *Les Nombres*, Sacy Bible, 1702 (Service photographique, Bibliothèque Nationale)

bears the authority of Revelation itself. "Ce n'est pas un homme qui l'a inventé, mais c'est Jésus-Christ mesme qui nous assure, non seulement que Moyse a dit plusieurs choses qui ont rapport au Fils de Dieu, mais que *c'est de luy qu'il a écrit.*"[5]

Sacy cites additional examples of how Jesus' explication of passages from the Old Testament serves to establish the authority of Moses. Jesus had explained to the Jews that the manna that their fathers had eaten in the desert was but a "figure" of the Eucharist. (John 6:32). All subsequent Christian interpretations of this event, Sacy insists, are but elaborations of this essential and primary interpretation. Christ had warned the Jews that Moses himself would be the accuser of those who refused to accept his testimony (John 5:39). Moses appeared with Christ in the Transfiguration because Christ, "voulant donner aux Apostres une grande estime de Moyse," intended to make it clear that the Gospel would be "établi sur le témoignage de la loy donnée par Moyse."[6]

Sacy attaches particular importance to the words of the risen Christ on the road to Emmaus (Luke 24:27):

> *Et commençant par Moyse et continuant par les Prophètes, il leur expliquait ce qui avoit esté dit de luy dans toutes les Ecritures* [Sacy's translation].

Christ's specific reference to Moses after his Resurrection, Sacy explains, makes it clear that the Old Testament is an indispensable part of Revelation. In dictating the Pentateuch to Moses, the Holy Spirit "a eu Jésus-Christ en veue." In rendering himself "l'interprète" of what Moses had written, Christ unified the two Testaments and mandated the science of exegesis. From that point onward, the two Testaments had to be read as a single document with one meaning.[7] From the same perspective, Pascal concludes in the "Preuves de Jésus-Christ": "Moïse d'abord enseigne la Trinité, le péché originel, le Messie" (346/315).

"NECESSITE DE PROUVER AUX CHRESTIENS LA DIVINITE DE JESUS-CHRIST COMME LES SAINTS L'ONT PROUVEE AUTREFOIS AUX PAYENS"

Sacy's argument suddenly takes a new direction. He acknowledges that his adversaries may not accept the authority on which he has based his proof of Moses, i.e., the authority of the New Testament. He must therefore present a series of proofs of the divinity of Christ addressed not to the *libertins* but "aux Chrestiens." Sacy's chapter title reflects his anxiety over the state of contemporary Christianity. "Plust à Dieu," he laments, "que nostre siècle fust assez religieux pour n'avoir aucun besoin de cette preuve." A century earlier, Sacy recalls, the Council of Trent had attributed the success of the Lutheran and Calvinist heresies to a general "dérèglement de moeurs." In the course of the present century, Sacy observes, such a disregard for religion "s'est répandu avec un tel débordement, que l'excès des passions et l'amour du vice ont séché dans le coeur d'un grand nombre de personnes jusqu'aux moindres racines de la foy."

Sacy's proofs of Christ's divinity will be neither of his own devising nor drawn from contemporary apology. They will be assembled exclusively from the works of Saint Augustine. Augustine's proofs suit his purposes, Sacy explains, because they establish the divinity of Christ as a basis for proving the authenticity of the Old Testament. Sacy's account of Augustine's argument merits our attention. It is not lifted from Saint Augustine's writings as an entity, but rather pieced together "de divers endroits de ses ouvrages." We therefore have the opportunity to observe firsthand a neo-Augustinian synthesis of Augustinian texts. Sacy's exposition of Augustine's arguments, because it represents a process of selection, at the same time permits us to assess the extent to which Pascal's borrowings from the writings of Saint Augustine were guided by a neo-Augustinian perspective.

Sacy's first proof, for which he gives no specific reference in the writings of Saint Augustine, asserts that Christ proved his own divinity by predicting specific future events. Sacy puts special emphasis on the fulfillment of five prophecies:

1. John 12:32: Jesus' prediction of the "mort ignominieuse" that he was to suffer;
2. Acts 1:8: the prediction of the coming of the Holy Ghost at Pentecost;
3. Matthew 8:11: the conversion of the Gentiles;

4. Matthew 20:16: the reversal of the roles of the Jews and the Gentiles;
5. Luke 21:24: the destruction of Jerusalem.

Sacy emphasizes those events that are most easily confirmed by secular history. The accomplishment of the prediction of the Crucifixion and of the coming of the Holy Ghost, he observes, would not convince those who distrust the New Testament. The destruction of Jerusalem, however, predicted by Christ in Luke 21:24,

> *Ils passeront par le fil de l'épée: ils seront emmenés captifs dans toutes les nations; et Jérusalem sera foulée aux piés par les Gentils, jusqu'à ce que le temps des nations soit accompli* [Sacy's translation],

is confirmed by the most reliable secular sources. "Trente-sept ans après," Sacy insists, "nous voyons que cette ville malheureuse est prise et détruite en la même manière que Jésus-Christ l'avait dit." The principal witness to this event, Josephus, is a "témoin irréprochable." His testimony is all the more believable because of his great hostility to Christianity.[8]

Sacy asks his readers to consider two other of Christ's prophecies that were borne out by the course of history. At a time when idolatry still reigned throughout the earth, Jesus had predicted "*que toutes les nations . . . auroient un jour leur place dans le royaume du ciel avec Abraham, Isaac et Jacob*" (Matthew 8:11). The conversion of the Gentiles, Sacy contends, is the dominant theme in the history of the world since the death of Christ. The Jews, the "premiers" under the Old Covenant, in accordance with Jesus' prophecy in Matthew 20:16,

> *Ainsi les derniers seront les premiers, et les premiers seront les derniers* [Sacy's translation],

have fallen heir to the former fate of the Gentiles. "Ceux qui estoient alors les enfans du royaume estoient jettez dans les ténèbres extérieures."[9]

Sacy's second series of arguments, drawn from Augustine's *Third Epistle to Volusian*, are presented under the chapter heading "Ses Miracles et l'établissement miraculeux de son Eglise." According to Sacy, the most important of Jesus' miracles was his voluntary death on the Cross, "accompagnée de toutes les circonstances qu'il avait fait écrire tant de siècles auparavant par ses Prophètes." Sacy, however, is not yet ready to present his most important proof of Christ's divinity: the fulfillment of the Old Testament prophecies. First, he asks those who remain unconvinced of the authority of Scripture to consider the historical effects of Jesus' Resurrection, a proof that "toute la raison humaine et toute la puissance des hommes et des démons n'a pû résister."

The foundation of the Apostolic church, Sacy argues, would be inexplicable had not the Apostles really witnessed Jesus' Resurrection. In the

Gospels, these same Apostles are presented as "foibles" and "timides," as very much unlike the kind of men who could have founded a new religion on their own. After the Resurrection and Pentecost, the Apostles take on an entirely different character. They are "remplis tout d'un coup d'une force divine":

> Ceux qui sçavoient à peine leur propre langue, parlent tout d'un coup les langues de tous les peuples. Ceux qui estoient des hommes sans lettres et du commun du peuple . . . pénètrent en un moment les plus grands mystères de l'Ecriture, citent les paroles de Moyse et des Prophètes, et font voir qu'elles ont esté accomplies en la personne de Jésus-Christ.[10]

Sacy's emphasis on the historical effects of the Resurrection serves an important apologetic aim. It is meant to cause those who doubt the authenticity of Scripture to take another look at the evidence. Only at this point does Sacy then introduce his most telling proof: "Preuve des miracles par la Prophétie et de la Prophétie par les Juifs." The authenticity of the supernatural events in the life of Christ will be proved by the fact that they were predicted by the prophets. "La preuve invincible des miracles, qui confond les esprits les plus rebelles, c'est qu'ils ont esté prédits plusieurs siècles avant qu'ils ayent esté faits, et qu'ils ont esté l'accomplissement de la prophétie."

Before presenting an exposition of this proof, Sacy records two objections anticipated by Saint Augustine. In the time of the Fathers, the pagans had attributed Christ's miracles to magic. Prophecy, however, Sacy points out, does not fall within the domain of the magical arts:

> La prophétie n'appartient qu'à Dieu: Il est le seul Roy de tous les tems. Il n'y a point pour luy de passé ny d'avenir. . . . C'est pourquoy il a choisi luy-mesme la prédiction des choses futures comme le caractère de sa divinité, comme la marque essentielle qui distingue le Créateur de la créature.[11]

Following Saint Augustine, Sacy anticipates a second objection to the proof that he will present. Could not the Christians have falsified the Old Testament texts to make it look as though they predicted events in the life of Jesus? Sacy reminds the reader that Augustine had been presented with the same objection by the pagans:

> Saint Augustin nous assure que lorsque l'on faisoit voir aux Payens les écrits de Moyse, de David et des Prophètes, tout ce qui estoit arrivé à Jésus-Christ, et la ruine des idoles, laquelle ils voyoient de leurs propres yeux; ils avoüoient que ces prophéties estoient claires; mais ils ajoutoient que c'étoit pour cela même qu'ils les croyoient fausses, parce qu'ils estoient persuadez qu'elles avoient esté faites après la venue de Jésus-Christ, et que ceux qui les avoient écrites estoient plûtost des historiens que des Prophètes.[12]

Augustine, "pour répondre à cette objection," referred the pagans to the Jews, "qui leur déclaroient que Moyse avoit esté leur législateur et un homme envoyé de Dieu quinze cens ans avant Jésus-Christ." The pagans recognized the fact that the Jews, "tout ennemis qu'ils estoient de Jésus-

Christ, rendoient un témoignage que la vérité seule pouvoit tirer de leur bouche." Like Pascal, Sacy attaches great importance to the "perpétuité" of the Jews. Their fate since the destruction of the Temple represents "une des marques les plus claires de la vérité de nostre foy." Moses, "décrivant comme historien la mort d'Abel tué par Caïn et ce qui arriva à Caïn ensuite," Sacy explains, "a prophétisé la mort de Jésus-Christ tué par les Juifs et la punition qui l'a suivie."[13]

At every point in his argument, Sacy seeks to establish a further link between the Old and New Testaments. The story of Cain and Abel for him represents yet another instance of an event in the Old Testament whose meaning remained incomplete until the events it anticipated came to pass. Following Saint Augustine's interpretation in *De Consensu Evangelistarum*, Sacy presents an explication designed to demonstrate the prophetic character of the episode recorded in Genesis 15. Cain, marked with a sign, is condemned to "une vie errante et vagabonde." The Jews, carrying the "signe" of circumcision, are condemned to an existence in which they are "toujours agitez, sans établissement, sans considération, sans demeure fixe, bannis en tous lieux et méprisez en tous lieux."

According to Sacy's interpretation, the "état présent" of the Jews is one willed by God. In spite of extreme persecution, "ils subsistent." "Leur réprobation est devenue plus utile à l'Eglise que n'auroit esté leur conversion." Had they embraced Christianity, their witness to the Gentiles concerning the veracity of the Old Testament prophecies would have been suspect. God, therefore, "les a dispersez et les a fait subsistez depuis dix-sept siècles dans toute la terre comme des témoins irréprochables":

> Conservant avec un grand respect l'Ecriture sainte à la lettre de laquelle ils s'attachent inviolablement, ils présentent cette mesme Ecriture en tous lieux, afin que tous les hommes y lisent en des termes très-clairs et très convainquants la justification de nostre foy et la condamnation de leur perfidie.[14]

PROOFS OF CHRISTIANITY DRAWN FROM OUTSIDE REVELATION

In the next section of his *Préface*, Sacy broadens his arguments into a defense of the authority of Revelation. His arguments, he tells his readers, will first be drawn from outside Revelation itself. In a manner that recalls Pascal's argument in the *Entretien*, Sacy first demonstrates the inability of philosophy, and in particular of those "faux sages du siècle," to arrive at an explanation of the enigma of the human condition. Philosophy's remedies for the misery inherent in the human condition are easily judged to be but illusions. The philosophers promise "non seulement une santé, mais une béatitude parfaite à l'âme de l'homme accablée de langueur et de misère." How, Sacy asks, can philosophy make such promises? Philosophers have "ny assez de lumière pour discerner nos maux, ny assez de pouvoir pour nous en tirer."[15]

In a fragment of the *Pensées* marked "A.P.R. pour demain," Pascal outlines a critique of philosophy that bears a striking similarity to Sacy's expression of the same idea:

> C'est en vain, ô hommes, que vous cherchez dans vous-mêmes le remède à vos misères. Toutes vos lumières ne peuvent arriver qu'à connaître que ce n'est point dans vous-mêmes que vous trouverez ni la vérité ni le bien. Les philosophes vous l'ont promis, et ils n'ont pu le faire. Ils ne savent ni quel est votre véritable bien, ni quel est votre véritable état. . . . Comment auraient-ils donné des remèdes à vos maux qu'ils n'ont pas seulement connus. (182/149)

This fragment elaborates an idea that Pascal expresses to Sacy in the *Entretien*. Philosophy cannot resolve the enigma of the human condition because it knows nothing of the Fall, of the fact that "l'état de l'homme à présent diffère de celui de sa création."[16] Further along in fragment 182/149, Pascal restates the idea in almost its original form: "Vous n'êtes pas dans l'état de votre création."

How do we explain the similarity between Sacy's critique of philosophy in his *Préface à la Genèse* and Pascal's statement of the same idea in fragment 182/149? This fragment, carrying the title "A.P.R. pour demain," traditionally has been viewed as Pascal's outline of a presentation of the main points of his projected *Apology* that he delivered to the Solitaires at Port-Royal. Did Pascal's exposition of this idea make such a profound impression on Sacy that he later used it in his *Préface*? Or is Sacy borrowing Pascal's expression of this idea from the first edition of the *Pensées*?

The second of these two possibilities seems unlikely. Sacy presents the notion of philosophy's inability to arrive at an explanation of the human condition in order to then be able to explain how Scripture, in its account of the Fall, resolves this very enigma. Pascal, in his original draft of fragment 182/149, had incorporated this very idea into his argument:

> Ils ne savent ni quel est votre véritable bien, ni quel est votre véritable état. *Je suis la seule qui puis vous apprendre et quel est votre véritable bien et quel est votre véritable état. Je les enseigne à ceux qui m'écoutent, et les Livres que j'ai mis entre les mains des hommes les découvrent bien nettement.* . . . Comment auraient-ils donné des remèdes à vos maux qu'il n'ont pas seulement connus?[17]

Pascal struck through the lines that appear above in italics. This portion of fragment 182/149 was therefore not reproduced in the Edition de Port-Royal, the only version of the *Pensées* that Sacy could have consulted.

It seems impossible to say whether the idea of an opposition between Revelation and philosophy was Pascal's or Sacy's to begin with. Sacy's organization of the argument, however, helps illuminate Pascal's position. In the course of the *Pensées*, Pascal develops at length two themes that are never really synthesized: (1) the inability of philosophy to explain the origins of the human condition, and (2) a proof of the Old Testament's authority as Revelation. Sacy's argument, by which Scripture is shown to explain what philosophy cannot, suggests the missing link between these two great themes in the *Pensées*.

Sacy puts great emphasis on the corruption of man's reason in the Fall. Reason, "estant aussi malade et aussi obscure qu'elle estoit," would not be able to impart to the philosophers "ce qu'elle n'avoit pas elle-mesme." Sacy's next argument, however, involves an appeal to reason. Those who reject the proofs Sacy has just advanced concerning Christ's divinity and the authenticity of Scripture are guilty of faulty reasoning. "Rien n'est plus contraire à la raison, que de prétendre de détruire une autorité divine établie sur des preuves si convainquantes, en ne luy opposant que les vaines conjectures de l'esprit humain."[18]

In the second half of the seventeenth century, the word *raison* had two rather different meanings. According to the *Dictionnaire de l'Académie Française* (1694), it could mean either: (1) "la puissance le l'âme par laquelle l'homme discourt et est distingué des bestes" or (2) "le bon sens, le droit usage de la raison." This distinction between these two uses of the word reflects a corresponding dichotomy between "l'esprit" and "le jugement." The former is defined as a "faculté de pénétration," the latter as a "faculté pratique." It is to "raison" taken as "le jugement" and "le bon sens" that Sacy makes his appeal. In Sacy's view, "raison" in its first definition represents a "faculté de pénétration" that was irreparably corrupted in the Fall. Man's "puissance de l'âme par laquelle il discourt" is the very source of "les vaines conjectures de l'esprit humain."

Appealing to reason defined as "le bon sens," Sacy draws his next argument from the realm of *expérience*. Why, he asks, do those who refuse to accept Revelation reason in a manner totally at odds with their use of reason in everyday affairs? Sacy builds his argument on the notion of "la déférence que les hommes rendent à l'autorité." "Les hommes mesme du monde," Sacy points out, believe that it would be "déraisonnable que de ne se rendre pas à l'autorité quand elle est bien établie."

Sacy first appeals to the principles of hereditary nobility. The antiquity of certain families is established by "des titres non suspects" and confirmed by historical documents. If one said to a "personne de qualité" that his family was not "plus grande que celle des autres . . . cette personne s'offensera[it] avec raison de ces objections si frivoles." Sacy then draws another example of deference to authority from common law. All lands and revenues that men possess are founded on "certains papiers" that were written, signed, and authorized according to judicial forms and rules. "Si un homme prétendoit avoir trouvé des raisons par lesquelles il voudroit anéantir cette autorité sur laquelle les Juges forment leurs Arrests et décident souverainement de tous les biens des particuliers, il passeroit pour un insensé."

In a third example, Sacy comes close to suggesting that *libertinage* should be viewed as a crime against the state. The ancient law of France, he points out, inhibits women from succeeding to the throne, which it reserves to the princes of the blood. Anyone who might attempt to produce reasons calling into question such an established "loy du royaume" would be subjected to the most severe punishment. He would be taken to be not only an "extravagant," but an enemy of the state and of the sovereign.

Sacy then directly addresses the *libres penseurs*:

> Vous déférez à une autorité humaine. Vous croyez qu'un homme seroit insensé s'il raisonnoit contre des faits, et contre des titres et des lois autentiques, lorsqu'il s'agit de l'établissement ou d'une maison, ou d'un état. Et vous vous persuadez en mesme tems qu'il soit ou selon la raison ou selon la justice d'opposer des raisons imaginaires à cette foule de preuves que Dieu a établies dans tous les siècles, pour donner à la religion de Jésus-Christ une autorité qui fust digne, non seulement d'estre crue comme très-certaine, mais d'estre révérée comme le plus grande ouvrage que la sagesse et la puissance du Créateur ait pû faire sur la terre.

In their attempts to be "raisonnables," Sacy tells the *libertins*, they have erred against the fundamental principle of *bon sens*. For if human laws and ordinances have "une preuve" of their authority, "la Religion Chrestienne en a mille."[19]

The argument he has just advanced, Sacy advises his reader, is not one of his own devising. It carries the authority of Saint Augustine, who had formulated it in his polemic against the Manicheans. Sacy draws significant parallels between Augustine's adversaries and his own. The Manicheans, who promised to lead men to God "par la voye de la raison," thought it a "foiblesse que de se rendre à l'autorité." Like the *libres penseurs*, they refused to accept the "sainteté des livres de Moyse." Augustine had replied to the Manicheans that they had never doubted that Plato, Aristotle, and Cicero had really composed the works attributed to them. Why then did they doubt the authenticity of the books written by Moses?[20]

Having reviewed Augustine's argument, Sacy concludes that to doubt the authenticity of the Pentateuch is to adopt a position that is "la chose du monde la plus absurde." Suppose one applied to secular history the same standards that the *libres penseurs* apply to the Old Testament. One would have to conclude that one could be certain of nothing recorded in written records. One would find oneself in the absurd position of maintaining that "l'on pourra dire avec raison dans deux cens ans, que tous ceux qui vivent aujourd'huy ne vivent point, que tous ceux qui écrivent n'écrivent point, que tous les Rois qui règnent ne règnent point, et généralement que tout ce qui se passe aujourd'huy de plus grand et de plus remarquable dans le monde n'est qu'une fable." In two hundred years, Sacy reminds his adversaries, "on ne sçaura rien de ce qui se fait aujourd'huy, que ce qui s'en pourra lire dans les histoires."

Sacy contrasts the *libres penseurs* with those pagan philosophers who during the first centuries of Christianity were persuaded of the veracity of the new religion. During the time of Saint Augustine, almost all the Platonists, "sans comparaison les plus éclairez et les plus célèbres d'entre les Philosophes," renounced idolatry and converted to Christianity. Justin, Tertullian, Saint Cyprian, Saint Hilarius, and "tant d'autres" who were respected in society "par l'éminence de leur génie, de leur éloquence et de leurs écrits" put their talents in the service of the Faith.

By contrast, Sacy laments, the "grands esprits" of the seventeenth century "se flattent d'une certaine force de raisonnement en déclarant qu'ils ne croyent rien de tout ce qu'il y a de plus fort dans les preuves de nostre Religion." Those philosophers who are the most talented and the most eloquent use their gifts to attack and to undermine religion. Yet how, Sacy asks, can the *libres penseurs* think of themselves as reasonable when they "font profession de mépriser ce qui non seulement a persuadé, mais a ravi mesme en admiration, les plus grands esprits qui furent jamais."[21]

Sacy's purpose in formulating the notion that men ordinarily defer to the authority of historical records has been to point toward the credibility of Scripture. His next proof, which takes the form of a critique of Islam, likewise seeks to underline the historical character of the Bible and of Christianity in general. Like Pascal's analysis of the Moslem religion in "Fausseté des autres religions," Sacy's argument seems to be modeled on arguments drawn from Grotius' *De veritate religionis christianae*. Sacy's aim is to show those who maintain that Christianity is an imposture what a genuine invented religion looks like. By a process of comparison, he seeks to emphasize the authenticity of the historical records on which Christianity is founded.

Whereas Islam is founded on a single revelation purportedly received by Mohammed, Christianity represents a 1,500-year continuous revelation beginning with Moses and culminating in Christ. The Old Testament consists of legitimate historical documents that are the testimony of an entire people. The Koran, by contrast, is but the testimony of a single individual. Christ was predicted by Moses and a great number of prophets. "Mahomet n'est prédit de personne." (cf. *Pensées*, fragment 241/209) Christ predicted "de très-grandes choses qui se vérifient très-clairement." Mohammed personally convinced only his wife, "et par elle à beaucoup d'autres," that his attacks of epilepsy were "des communications . . . qu'il avoit avec l'Ange Gabriel."

The reader is invited to compare the teachings of Jesus and Mohammed. The Gospels represent "une morale divine et parfaitement sainte dans tous ses points." Those who adopted it spread the faith by martyrdom and "par une infinité de miracles." The Koran, by contrast, is both morally defective and unoriginal. Mohammed's teachings, "une religion brutale très-propre à gagner des hommes brutaux," were propagated "avec le fer et le feu" (cf. *Pensées* fr. 241/209). An analysis of the Koran reveals it to amount to no more than a plagiarism of "les véritez que les plus grands esprits avoient enseignées" prior to Mohammed and which Mohammed and his followers "ont . . . souillées dans leur bouche par le mélange de l'impiété et de l'erreur." Christ revealed a religion that had been prepared since the beginning of time. Mohammed, with the help of several renegade Jews and an apostate Christian monk, invented "une religion nouvelle."

An essential focus of Jansenism was man's inability to ensure his own salvation. Sacy can only regard with horror a religion which teaches that a man who dies fighting for the spread of Islam will go directly to paradise. There is nothing more important in a religion than its "fin," than the "récompense à laquelle doivent tendre toutes les actions de ceux qui la suivent." The beatitude that Mohammed promises those "qui seront assez fous pour le croire" shocks Sacy's fundamental conception of the incomprehensibility of the workings of divine justice. "Le Dieu de Mahomet qui promet aux siens une telle béatitude est digne, non de l'adoration, mais de l'exécration de tout le monde."

One can scarcely imagine the horror with which Sacy would have greeted Vatican II's proposal of a dialogue with Islam and other non-Christian religions. For him, the teachings of Mohammed are devoid of both revelation and historical credibility. Islam amounts to nothing more than a "superstition." Neither Judaism, from which it borrowed circumcision, nor Christianity, from which it plagiarized its moral teachings, it is "une secte monstrueuse composée de diverse erreurs qui s'entrecombattent."[22]

Sacy's analysis of Islam once again appeals to the notion of *bon sens*. Christianity, whose mysteries are beyond the scope of man's fallen *faculté de pénétration*, is a scandal to reason. Islam, however, unlike Christianity, violates the standards of *bon sens*. Christianity can be shown to be consistent in its teachings and verifiable in its historical foundations. Having used the example of Islam to make this point, Sacy then proceeds to the "Seconde Partie" of his *Préface à la Genèse*. In this section, he will put the science of exegesis in the service of apology. Scripture, when correctly interpreted according to the rules laid down by Christ and the Apostles, will be shown not to violate ordinary standards of *jugement* and *bon sens*.

SACY'S EXPOSITION OF HIS EXEGETICAL PRINCIPLES

Part two of Sacy's *Préface*, "De la manière dont on a traduit et éclairci la Genèse," seeks to provide the reader with an organized summary of Sacy's exegetical principles. His first concern is to establish the historicity of his text. Again taking up a defense of the Mosaic authorship of the Pentateuch, he produces a proof that, like those of the preceding section, is drawn from outside Revelation. Anyone who already accepts Moses' authority as a prophet will have no trouble believing that "l'Esprit de Dieu ait révélé à Moyse tout ce qui s'estoit passé avant luy." But for the benefit of those who believe nothing of Revelation, Sacy advances another proof, one that he establishes "sans avoir recours à la révélation."

Sacy asks his reader to imagine Moses speaking to those of his own generation concerning the books he has written:

> J'ai résolu d'écrire ce qui s'est passé depuis la création du monde jusqu'à ce tems. Et on ne peut pas en estre mieux informé que je le suis. Car Amram mon père m'a dit souvent: Mon fils, je vous diray toute l'histoire du monde jusqu'à nous, qui est celle de notre famille, selon que je l'ay apprise de Lévi mon ayeul, qui sçavoit tout ce qu'il m'en disoit d'Isaac son ayeul, avec lequel il avoit vécu trente-trois ans. Et pour ce qui est d'Isaac, il avoit appris tout ce qu'il en disoit à Lévi, de Sem, avec lequel il avoit vécu cinquante ans.

Sacy then asks his reader to imagine Sem speaking to Isaac and verifying the accounts that Isaac would then transmit to Moses through Levi and Amram:

> Vous pouvez bien me croire quand je vous parle du déluge: puisque je vous dis alors ce que j'ay vu de mes propres yeux. Et vous devez me croire quand je vous parle de la création du monde, et de tout ce qui est arrivé à Adam, puisque j'ay vécu près de cens ans avec Mathusalem mon bisayeul, qui avoit appris toutes ces choses d'Adam mesme, avec lequel il a vécu plus de deux cens soixante ans.

Such an argument has been calculated from what Sacy calls "la tradition héréditaire et domestique des Patriarches." In other words, by noting the length of the lifespan of each of the Patriarchs, he has established which of their lifespans overlapped. We must not confuse Sacy's argument with the modern notion of oral traditions. Because of the extremely long lives of the Patriarchs, Sacy argues, only five generations separated Moses from Adam. For Moses, the Flood and the Creation were historical events within living memory. "A parler mesme humainement," he concludes, "et sans avoir recours aux preuves surnaturelles, jamais histoire n'a mérité de trouver une si grande créance dans l'esprit des hommes que celle de la *Genèse*."[23]

Having established the authenticity of his text, Sacy next proceeds to explain his exegetical method. At the end of each chapter, he will append two explanatory sections: the first explaining "la lettre" and the second "l'esprit" of the chapter he has just translated. In clarifying the literal meaning, he will have recourse to the original Hebrew, following the counsel of "les plus sçavans Interprètes." In establishing the "sens spirituel," he will be guided by Saint Paul and Saint Augustine.

Sacy has already established the notion that the exegesis of the "sens spirituel" of the Old Testament is not a human invention but a part of Revelation itself. It is a science first established by Christ himself in the New Testament. Sacy now sets down the principle that the "sens spirituel" is not only a legitimate, but the *primary*, meaning of any given Old Testament text. As a point of departure, he cites Saint Paul's exegesis of a passage from Genesis in Galatians 4:21–31:

> *Dites-moi, je vous prie, vous qui voulez être sous la loi, n'entendez-vous point ce que dit la loi?*
> *Car il est écrit qu'Abraham a eu deux fils, l'un de la servante, et l'autre de la femme libre. Mais celui qui naquit de la servante, naquit selon la chair: et celui qui naquit de la femme libre, naquit en vertu de la promesse de Dieu. Tout ceci est une allégorie. Car ces deux femmes sont les deux alliances* [Sacy's translation].

Saint Paul, Sacy insists, does not simply say that one *may* found an allegory on this episode recounted by Genesis. "Il dit que toute cette histoire *est* une allégorie, pour nous montrer que cette histoire n'a esté écrite *que pour estre une image de la vérité*, et que l'intention du Saint Esprit a esté de représenter dans ces deux femmes un tableau vivant et animé de l'ancien Testament et du nouveau" (italics mine). In 1 Corinthians 10:6, Sacy goes on to point out, "Saint Paul . . . déclare en termes formels que *toutes les choses qui arrivoient autrefois* aux juifs *estoient des figures*, et qu'elles ont esté écrites pour servir d'instruction à toute l'Eglise."[24]

Sacy founds his whole theory of "figuratifs" on the example and authority of Saint Paul. One of the "maximes fondamentales" of the Christian religion, he observes, is that the Christian reader of the Old Testament "doit chercher l'esprit et la vérité qui est renfermée sous la lettre." However, Sacy by no means intends to abolish, or even to neglect, the literal meaning of the Old Testament. His exegesis, he assures his readers, will always be conducted with "une grande circonspection," endeavoring never to "s'éloigner du vray sens du texte." The "sens spirituel," though superseding the literal meaning of a given text, does not destroy it. "Encore que le Saint Esprit nous assure par la bouche de l'Apostre, qu'Agar et Sara ont esté les figures de l'ancienne alliance et de la nouvelle, *il ne s'ensuit pas néanmoins que ces deux femmes ne soient qu'une parabole, et qu'elles n'ayent pas esté effectivement.*"[25]

Sacy's emphasis on the literal and historical reality of events in the Old Testament can serve to prevent our misunderstanding of a fundamental exegetical principle set down by Pascal in the *Pensées*: "L'Ancien Testament . . . n'est que figuratif" (737/501). For instance, in fragment 489/590,

Pascal notes: "Les six jours que Moïse représente pour la formation d'Adam *ne sont que* la peinture des six âges pour former Jésus-Christ et l'Eglise" (italics mine). We might perhaps be tempted to interpret this fragment as anticipating a modern understanding of Genesis. In one of his first studies on Pascal, Jean Mesnard concluded that this fragment shows that the apologist "n'accorde aucune valeur historique au récit de la Création en six jours."[26] In chapter four, I shall show that Pascal, to the contrary, adheres to an extremely literal interpretation of the Creation and the Fall. Sacy constantly reminds his readers that the higher truth that an event in the Old Testament prefigures never excludes its historical reality. For example, Sacy identifies "la pierre dont Moyse fit sortir une source d'eau" (Exodus 17:6–7) as a "figure" of Christ's passion. Such an interpretation, Sacy insists, by no means suggests that the rock struck by Moses in the desert "n'ait pas esté réellement une pierre."[27]

In order to insure a proper balance between the spiritual and literal meanings of a given passage, Sacy explains, he will rely upon a rule first set down by Saint Augustine. This rule excludes two extreme approaches to the Old Testament. Those who maintain that the Old Testament never prefigures events in the New Testament "combattent formellement les paroles de Jésus-Christ et les Apostres." On the other hand, those who insist that "les plus petites circonstances" of the Old Testament are "prophétiques et mystérieuses" "semblent entreprendre une chose bien hardie et bien difficile." "*Illi mihi videntur multum errare; isti multum audere.*"[28]

Sacy interprets Saint Augustine's principle to mean that the exegete must always "fonder le sens spirituel sur la lettre mesme de l'Ecriture." From the perspective of medieval exegesis, Sacy's avowed intent to rehabilitate the "sens historique" of Scripture seems almost revolutionary. Medieval exegesis, in its passion for allegory, had tended to relegate the "sens littéral" of Scripture to a place of inferior importance. In the same way that the Jansenists sought to free theology from the trappings of scholasticism and ground it in Scripture and the Fathers, Sacy seeks to reorient biblical exegesis according to the instructions of Saint Paul and Saint Augustine.

It would be wrong, however, to view Sacy's emphasis on "la lettre de l'Ecriture" as pointing toward modern biblical criticism. Taken by itself, Sacy's principle of always basing the "sens spirituel" of a passage on "la lettre mesme" might seem to make common cause with Richard Simon's attempt to establish accurate biblical texts. Such is far from the case. Simon's very criticism of Sacy was that his explications of the "sens spirituel" were "peu propres au texte qu'il veut expliquer, parce qu'elles ne coulent point du sens littéral."[29] Sacy stands at the end of an exegetical tradition as old as Christianity itself, a tradition that had never ceased to amplify the wealth of *figures* it discovered in the Old Testament. With Simon began a movement in the direction of reducing the number of such *figures*. The effects of this trend are still being felt in contemporary biblical studies.

To turn to almost any page of Sacy's biblical commentaries is to enter a world alien to that of modern textual criticism. "Les plus petites circonstances" in fact very often do take on mysterious and prophetic meanings that are completely unlike those elucidated by the modern scholar. For instance, the description in Genesis 6:14 of the boards from which Noah's ark was to be constructed Sacy finds fraught with *figures*. These planks, "unies et applanies par-dessus, afin qu'estant jointes ensemble elles demeurassant tourjours fermes comme si ce n'eût esté qu'un même bois," prefigure the union that should exist between Christians. Their length is a symbol of the long wait of the soul to find God, their height an image of the elevation of the soul touched by grace.[30]

In his preface to *L'Exode*, Sacy further elaborates his theory of "figuratifs." His explanation of the way in which the ceremonies of the Law prefigure "les véritez de l'Eglise" parallels Pascal's treatment of the same subject. Once again, Sacy appeals to *expérience*:

> Si les hommes estiment tant et mettent presque hors de prix, la représentation des choses de la nature faitte par la main sçavante de ces sculpteurs anciens, ou de ces peintres célèbres dont ils considèrent les ouvrages comme des chef-d'ouevres de l'art; ne devrions-nous pas estimer et admirer infiniment davantage ces tableaux de l'Ecriture tracez par le doigt de Dieu qui est son Esprit, qui représentoient dès le tems de Moyse, non les ouvrages de la nature, mais les merveilles de la grâce, non les choses passées ou présentes comme font les peintres, mais celles qui devoient s'accomplir tant de siècles après?[31]

Sacy, always faithful to the thought of Saint-Cyran, derives such an approach to Scripture from a more general theological principle laid down by his master, the idea that nature is an image of grace. "Tout le monde," Saint-Cyran had written, "n'est qu'un tableau, et Dieu en créant les choses visibles n'a fait que peindre les invisibles, comme les peintres ne nous représentent que les visibles."[32] In other words, just as the visible world is but an image of the world to come, the Old Testament is an image of the New. All the ceremonies of the Law, all the "événemens visibles" of the Old Testament, represent "ce monde invisible que saint Paul appelle *un monde futur*, qui enferme tout ce qui devoit s'accomplir en la personne de Jésus-Christ et dans tout le corps de son Eglise."[33]

Sacy's explication of these "figures" that anticipate Christianity will not be limited to certain traditional motifs. To be sure, he gives extensive attention to the Passover as an image of the Eucharist, to the passage of the Red Sea as a figure of the Redemption, and to the Law as a figure of the Gospel. He goes on, however, to assign a figurative meaning to many passages that classical exegesis had tended to relegate to the status of historical detail.

"Les vestemens du grand Prêtre et les pierres prétieuses dont ils étoient enrichis," "[les] voiles qui couvroient le tabernacle," and "l'autel d'or" all are found to point toward "les véritez de l'Eglise"[34] (see figure 5). Perhaps most indicative of the way in which Sacy sees the finger of God tracing the outlines of the New Testament under the "voiles sacrez" of the Old is the interpretation he gives to the manner in which Moses defeated the tribe of Amalec. "En tenant les bras étendus," Moses prefigured the Cross on which Christ was to die.[35]

Sacy seeks to justify the multiplicity of "figures" he will find in the Old Testament by citing Augustine's description of the way in which the most seemingly insignificant details in the Bible serve the purposes of the Holy Spirit:

> Comme dans une harpe, tout sert pour faire résonner, et tout néanmoins ne résonne pas, n'y ayant que les cordes seules qui estant touchées avec art composent l'harmonie des sons: ainsi dans l'histoire sacrée, tout généralement n'est pas une figure et une prophétie; mais les moindres choses servent comme de jointure et de liaison pour les grandes qui sont prophétiques et mystérieuses.[36]

The comprehensiveness of Sacy's commentaries on the Old Testament reflect his assumption that every word in the Bible plays a role in unfolding the drama of man's salvation.

In his "instructions" to the reader of *L'Exode*, Sacy explains why some things in the Old Testament are not "figures." He draws the traditional distinction between "la loi morale" and "la loi cérémoniale." The former, exemplified in the Ten Commandments, must be observed by Christians just as "religieusement" as by the Israelites of old. Because "la loi morale" is a function of "la charité," its precepts are to be taken literally. On the other hand, "la loi cérémoniale" must be interpreted according to its "sens spirituel." Sacy directs his reader to regard

> tout ce qui est dit du tabernacle, qui étoit alors le temple de Dieu, de l'autel des holocaustes, des sacrifices sanglans, des différentes oblations, de l'autel des parfums, des festes solennelles, et de tout ce culte extérieur que Dieu avoit prescrit aux Israélites

as being subject to the kind of exegesis that discovers "la vérité et la lumière de Dieu cachées sous ces ombres et ces figures." The multitude of sacrifices that the Israelites were required to offer are but a single "*image* du grand et de l'unique sacrifice de la loy nouvelle."[37] Sacy's rule for distinguishing between "figure" and "réalité" in the Old Testament is the same principle proposed by Pascal in fragment 301/270: "Tout ce qui ne va point à la charité est figure."

Why, Sacy's reader may ask, is so much of the Old Testament hidden

Figure 5. *La Terre sainte*; engraving, Préface, Sacy Bible, 1702 (Service photographique, Bibliothèque Nationale)

beneath "figures"? Sacy's answer to this question ties his theory of "figuratifs" to his overall apology. Moses, Sacy explains, "a esté obligé d'y couvrir sous des ombres et sous des voiles sacrez les véritez les plus hautes" because he was writing for the Jews, "qui n'auroient pas esté capables de les comprendre s'il les eust expliquées plus clairemont."[38] From the beginning of time, God had chosen the Jews to be the witnesses of the fulfillment of his prophecies and the guardians of his Scriptures. Yet the central truth to which Scripture speaks, "une merveille si grande et si inouïe, que le Verbe Eternel, égal à Dieu son Père, daignât s'abaisser jusqu'à se faire homme pour sauver les hommes," would have been completely beyond their comprehension before the coming of Christ.[39]

The Jews' ignorance as to what was really written in the Law was a necessary part of the economy of Salvation. The Incarnation had to be announced by those who could later serve as non-suspect witnesses. Had the Jews recognized the "sens spirituel" of the Law, they would have received Christ as the Messiah. Had this happened, the Jews would not have been able to serve as hostile witnesses concerning the authenticity of the Old Testament prophecies.[40]

Sacy, attempting to explain God's choice of the Jews as his chosen people, advances a second reason for the figurative character of the Old Testament:

> Le démon qui voyait que le connoissance de Dieu étoit imprimée comme naturellement dans le fond de l'âme, avoit inventé une erreur très-dangereuse parmi les payens: . . . qui est que l'on ne pouvoit pas nier qu'il n'y eût un Dieu au-dessus de tous les autres, mais qu'il ne se mesloit que de régler le Ciel et le mouvement des astres. Et que ceux que l'on appeloit dieux, et que l'on révéroit par le culte des idoles (sous lesquelles cet Ange apostat se cachoit luy-même) étoient les maistres des biens de la terre.

In order to destroy this polytheism invented by the Devil, God "a voulu estre comme le Roy et le protecteur du peuple hébreu." By leading the Jews into the Promised Land and according them "des biens charnels et terrestres," God showed the pagans that he was master of earth as well as of heaven.[41]

Sacy proposes yet another explanation why God blessed the Israelites with "biens terrestres." Christ was to come in humility and poverty. It was therefore necessary "qu'il fist voir avant le tems de son Incarnation, qu'il estoit le maistre de ces mesmes biens qu'il devoit mépriser."[42] In the Old Testament, God therefore shows himself the master of "les biens terrestres." In the New Testament, by contrast, "Dieu détourne les hommes de ces biens terrestres pour leur faire goûter les biens du Ciel":

> Une des fins principales que Jésus-Christ a eues dans son Incarnation, a esté de nous apprendre que cette félicité temporelle que les Juifs et les Payens

recherchoient avec tant d'ardeur n'estoit qu'une illusion qui trompoit nos sens, et qui nous cachoit les biens vérietables où nous devons tendre; et que nôtre âme estant l'image de Dieu, ne devoit désirer, pour estre vraiment heureuse, que sa grâce sur la terre et sa gloire dans le ciel.[43]

The "biens spirituels" dispensed by Christ in the New Testament were reserved to the elect, just as the "biens terrestres" had been reserved for a chosen people in the Old Testament. However, by the special favor of God, the Patriarchs, the prophets, and several other Old Testament saints were permitted to penetrate the veil of "figures" in which the Law was hidden. Moses, for example, "a cru très-certainement que Jésus-Christ naîtroit et mourroit pour les hommes." Joshua, David, and Samuel were likewise "Chrétiens effectivement par une anticipation de grâce." Sacy warns, however, that one must not imagine that this grace was given to very many in the Old Covenant. Only a few recognized that the "grande variété" of sacrifices and legal observations were but the "figure des choses qui devoient s'accomplir en la personne de Jésus-Christ."[44]

Like Pascal, Sacy builds a whole exegetical principle on the opposition between the *juifs charnels* and the *juifs spirituels*. The former simply observed the external signs of the Law "sans y rien comprendre." The latter "pénétroient en mesme tems sous ses voiles la vérité qui y estoit cachée."[45] The *juifs spirituels* "ont été véritablement Chrestiens, quoy qu'ils n'en portassent pas le nom." The *réprouvés* among the Christians, on the other hand, fall into the very same category as the *juifs charnels*.[46]

Figures, Sacy theorizes, are the instrument used by God to blind those who were not meant to see (the *juifs charnels* and the *réprouvés*), and to enlighten the elect (including the *juifs spirituels*). Sacy's theory of "figuratifs" is a corollary of a larger theological principle, that of Predestination and Election. As in the *Pensées*, *figures* are the building blocks out of which is constructed a principle of central importance in Jansenist theology, *le Dieu caché*.

ON READING THE BIBLE

However much emphasis Sacy puts on the reasonableness of the arguments he presents in his *Préface*, he always reserves a place for those who have no need of such arguments. Many of the saints and martyrs, he notes, would have lacked the "lumière d'esprit" necessary for a complete understanding of many of the proofs he has advanced.[47] In his conclusion to the *Préface à la Genèse*, Sacy returns to the idea that proofs and arguments arrived at by human reason have only a limited value. In order to understand what is written in the books of the Bible, he insists, the reader must be guided "par le mesme Esprit qui les a dictez."[48]

In his letters to penitents, Sacy repeatedly stresses that the proper frame of mind for reading Scripture is not one of intellectual curiosity. Such a disposition leads one to discover in the Bible only "une lettre morte." Rather, one should approach Scripture in a spirit of prayer and meditation. However helpful any commentary, only the Holy Spirit can ultimately reveal to a reader the "sens spirituel" of a given passage in the Bible. This is because the organ of perception of the "sens spirituel" of Scripture is the heart, not reason.[49]

The Bible is not a document of human origin. "Il n'importe que ce soit Moyse . . . qui en ait esté le secrétaire. C'est Dieu certainement qui en est l'Auteur. *Ce sont ses pensées et ses paroles.*" If we commonly consult "un grand esprit humain" in order to understand what is written in "les livres des grands esprits," why then should be hesitate to ask the Holy Spirit to enlighten us as to the meaning of Scripture? No "sage du monde, ny vivant ny mort," has the power to "donner l'intelligence de ce livre à ceux qui ne seroient capables de l'entendre." Only God, "vivant dans le ciel, pendant que nous lisons sur la terre cette histoire sainte *qu'il a dictée à Moyse*," can reveal, through his Holy Spirit, "les grandes véritez qu'elle renferme."[50]

We have already accorded great importance to Sacy's conception of Scripture as an image of the Incarnation. In his conclusion to the *Préface à la Genèse*, Sacy presents this vision of the Bible in a striking analogy. In the most ancient of the Greek liturgies, he explains, "le prestre . . . prenoit sur l'autel le livre de l'Evangile, et se tournant vers le peuple l'élevoit en haut, et en formoit un signe de Croix . . . cependant tout le peuple, estant à genoux et prosterné, adoroit ce Livre sacré, *comme si c'eust esté Jésus-Christ mesme.*"[51]

Sacy's whole conception of the Bible is Christocentric. Christ is hidden in Scripture just as he was hidden in the Incarnation and is present under the veil of the Eucharist. This idea stands at the heart of Sacy's approach to exegesis. It is the cornerstone of his theory of the unity of the two Testaments. It is a principle to which we shall return as we endeavor to understand the place of the Bible in the thought of Pascal. Some critics who have treated the subject have distorted Pascal's fundamental conception of the nature of Scripture. Lhermet, for example, concluded that Pascal was "un initiateur du rationalisme scriptuaire" and called the apologist "le premier croyant qui se hasarda à considérer la Bible comme un livre ordinaire."[52] Such a view of Pascal's biblicism cannot be substantiated by a critical reading of the *Pensees*. Far from being an "initiateur du rationalisme scriptuaire," Pascal shares the attitude of Monsieur de Sacy concerning the inviolability of the Bible as a document of Revelation.

---

1. See Mesnard, *Les Pensées de Pascal*, p. 27.
2. *La Genèse*, Préface, Première Partie, partie i.

3. *La Genèse*, Préface, Première Partie, partie ii.
4. *La Genèse*, Préface, Première Partie, partie ii.
5. *La Genèse*, Préface, Seconde Partie, partie i. Cf. John 5:46.
6. *La Genèse*, Préface, Première Partie, partie ii. Cf. *Pensées*, fragments 285/253 and 660/818.
7. *La Genèse*, Préface, Première Partie, partie iii. Cf. *Pensées*, fragment 285/253.
8. *La Genèse*, Préface, Première Partie, partie iii.
9. *La Genèse*, Préface, Première Partie, partie iii. Cf., *Pensées* fragments 355/324; 357/324; 359/327; 370/338; 379/347. See pp. 200–202.
10. *La Genèse*, Préface, Première Partie, partie iv. Cf. *Pensées*, fragment 341/310: "L'hypothèse des apôtres fourbes est bien absurde."
11. *La Genèse*, Préface, Première Partie, partie v.
12. *La Genèse*, Préface, Première Partie, partie v.
13. *La Genèse*, Préface, Première Partie, partie v.
14. *La Genèse*, Préface, Première Partie, partie v.
15. *La Genèse*, Préface, Première Partie, partie vi.
16. Bedier, pp. 73–74.
17. The full text of this fragment, not given in most editions of the *Pensées*, has been restored in the recent edition of Philippe Sellier, who follows the text of the *Seconde Copie*. See *Pensées*, fragment 182, p. 108.
18. *La Genèse*, Préface, Première Partie, partie vi.
19. *La Genèse*, Préface, Première Partie, partie vi.
20. See Augustine, *Contra Faustum Manichaeum*, book 33, chapter 6.
21. *La Genèse*, Préface, Première Partie, partie vi.
22. *La Genèse*, Préface, Première Partie, partie vii. Cf. *Pensées*, fragments 241/209, 235/203, 239/207, 242/209, 37/1, 251/218, 276/243, 352/321, 694/454.
23. *La Genèse*, Préface, Seconde Partie, partie i. Cf. *Pensées*, fragment 741: "Cela vient de la longueur de la vie des premiers hommes. En sorte que Sem, qui a vu Lamech, etc. *Cette preuve suffit pour convaincre les personnes raisonnables de la vérité du Déluge et de la Création.*"
24. *La Genèse*, Préface, Second Partie, partie 1.
25. *La Genèse*, Préface, Second Partie, partie 1; *La Genèse*, p. 110.
26. "La Théorie des figuratifs dans les *Pensées* de Pascal," p. 240 n. 116.
27. *La Genèse*, p. 110.
28. *La Genèse*, Préface, Seconde Partie, partie i. Saint Augustine's principle was a particularly important one for those at Port-Royal. Jansenius, in the preface to his *Pentateuchus* (pp. 6–7) had restated the idea: "Duo extrema cavenda sunt: primum, ne relicto sensu litterali quem verba prae se ferunt, ad allegoricas expositiones declinetur. . . . Alterum est ne, in indagando sensu historico et litterali, nimium humanae philosophiae vel tribuamus, vel derogemus." Pascal, in fragment 284/252, renders the principle: "Deux erreurs: 1. prendre tout littéralement. 2. prendre tout spirituellement."
29. *Critique de la bibliothèque,* 2:328.
30. *La Genèse*, pp. 304–6.
31. *L'Exode et Le Lévitique*, Préface, pp. lvi–lvii.
32. Saint-Cyran, *Oeuvres chrestiennes et spirituelles*, t. 1. xxv, p. 178.
33. *L'Exode et Le Lévitique*, Préface, p. lvii.
34. *L'Exode et Le Lévitique*, Préface, pp. lx–lxii.
35. *L'Exode et Le Lévitique*, Préface, p. lxi. The reference is to Exodus 17:11–12: "And when Moses lifted up his hands, Israel overcame: but if he let them down a little, Amalec overcame."

36. *La Genèse*, Préface, Seconde Partie, partie i, citing *De civitate Dei*, book 16, chapter 2.
37. *L'Exode et Le Lévitique*, Préface, pp. lxv and lxiv.
38. *La Genèse*, Préface, Seconde Partie, partie ii.
39. *L'Exode et Le Lévitique*, Préface, p. xv.
40. *La Genèse*, Préface, Première Partie, partie v.
41. *L'Exode et Le Lévitique*, Préface, pp. xi–xii.
42. *L'Exode et Le Lévitique*, Préface, p. xvii.
43. *L'Exode et Le Lévitique*, Préface, pp. xxi, xix.
44. *L'Exode et Le Lévitique*, Préface, pp. xxxiv, xxxvi.
45. *L'Exode et Le Lévitique*, Préface, pp. xxxvi–xxxvii.
46. *La Genèse*, Préface, Seconde Partie, partie ii. Cf. *L'Exode et Le Lévitique*, Préface, p. xxxiv.
47. *La Genèse*, Préface, Première Partie, partie vi.
48. *La Genèse*, Préface, Seconde Partie, partie iii.
49. See *Lettres chrestiennes*, 1:25–26, 31, 57–59, 610–13; 2:270–71.
50. *La Genèse*, Préface, Seconde Partie, partie iii (italics mine).
51. *La Genèse*, Préface, Seconde Partie, partie iii (italics mine).
52. *Pascal et la Bible*, p. 432.

Part Two

The Bible

in the Argument of the *Pensées*

IV

Pascal's Biblicism:
The Apologetic Consequences of a
Literal View of the Fall

THE CENTRALITY OF THE FALL IN THE ARGUMENT OF THE *APOLOGY*

The role of the Bible in Pascal's projected *Apology* is above all one of documentation. Scripture serves as the ultimate authority in Pascal's attempt to establish the historicity of the two key elements in the history of the relationship between man and God: the Fall and the Incarnation. "Ordre," a dossier set down when Pascal organized his various arguments into twenty-seven provisional chapters, envisages these two events as constituting the two principal themes around which the *Apology* will be organized:

Première partie: Misère de l'homme sans Dieu.
Deuxième partie: Félicité de l'homme avec Dieu.

autrement

Première partie: Que la nature est corrompue, par la nature même.
Deuxième partie: Qu'il y a un Réparateur, par l'Écriture. (40/6)

This fragment, the best internal evidence of Pascal's plan for organizing his projected *Apology*, suggests a problem that goes to the heart of Pascal's apologetics. The Incarnation will be documented "par l'Ecriture." Man's fallen condition, however, will be proved "par la nature." Are we therefore to conclude that Pascal's proof of Christianity will have a dual source? Does Pascal intend to use the Bible only to document the historicity of the Incarnation? Will his proof of the Fall be drawn uniquely from outside Revelation?

Such a view of the overall scheme of the *Pensées* fails to take into account Pascal's understanding of the nature of Revelation. It serves only to sever Pascal's arguments from their theological roots. Pascal's dogmatic theology rarely fails to reflect the position of the neo-Augustinian theologians of Port-Royal. Though they admitted into their commentaries on Original Sin the notion that the effects of Adam's fault can be perceived in fallen nature, the theologians of Port-Royal always insisted that the only legitimate and acceptable proof of the Fall is to be found in Genesis.

It is no accident that fragment 40/6, which seems to draw a sharp distinction between the authority of *expérience* and that of Revelation, has attracted the attention of so many modern commentators on the *Pensées*. We are all heirs to an eighteenth-century conception of this work that continues to hold a powerful grasp on critics and ordinary readers alike. It is the notion that there exist "philosophical" sections of the *Pensées* that can be profitably read and understood totally apart from the theological and "dogmatic" character of the *Apology* as a whole.

As outlined in fragment 40/6, the "première partie" of Pascal's *Apology* might at first seem susceptible to such an interpretation. A dissection of the human condition through an analysis of "la nature même" (i.e., human nature) at first might appear to be a philosophical rather than a theological enterprise. Such an approach, however, will not stand the test of even the most elementary textual study. One is immediately presented with the implications of Pascal's use of the word *corrompue*. For Pascal, and for the reader of his time, this word invokes not simply some vague notion of the folly of the human condition but rather a concrete theological doctrine.

For reasons central to his apologetic strategy, Pascal will approach the doctrine of Original Sin through examples drawn from the realm of *expérience*. His ultimate demonstration, however, "Que la nature est corrompue," will find its final exposition in the specifically Christian doctrine of the Fall. His ultimate proof of the Fall will be founded upon Genesis' account of Adam's sin. "Sans l'Ecriture, sans le péché originel . . . on ne peut prouver absolument Dieu ni enseigner ni bonne doctrine ni bonne morale" (221/189).

Any attempt to assess the role of the Fall in Pascal's argument is infinitely complicated by the unfinished state in which the apologist left his papers at the time of his death. His notes, which represent an *Apology* interrupted in the course of its organization, give the misleading impression that Pascal envisaged two very different kinds of proofs of Christianity. Entire sections of the *Pensées*, including many of the most finished passages, seem to rule out a direct appeal to the authority of Revelation. Other large sections, by contrast, seek to document the historical credibility of that same Revelation. How Pascal would have effected a transition from this first order of arguments to the second has preoccupied almost every editor of the *Pensées* who has attempted to present the work as apology.[1]

Rather than viewing the *Pensées* as incorporating two separate blocks of arguments, such editors have shown us, it is much more in accord with Pascal's design to conceive of his projected *Apology* as a transition from the questions posed by *expérience* to the answers afforded by Revelation.

The doctrine of Original Sin, transmuted from a theoretical proposition suggested by *expérience* into an event whose historicity is confirmed by Scripture, is the model for Pascal's more fundamental transition from the insufficiency of reason to the certainty of Revelation.

From a purely thematic point of view, the doctrine of the Fall is one of the principal organizing forces of the *Pensées*. Over and over again, it enters into Pascal's very definition of Christianity, where it is always paired with the doctrine of the Incarnation. "La foi chrétienne ne va presque qu'à établir ces deux choses: la corruption de la nature et la Rédemption de Jésus-Christ" (681/427). "Cette religion . . . consiste à croire que l'homme est déchu d'un état de gloire . . . mais qu'après cette vie on serait rétabli par un Messie qui devait venir" (313/281). "Toute la foi consiste en Jésus-Christ et en Adam" (258/226).

These two doctrines, though fundamental to every orthodox school of Christian theology, take on a special significance in the *Pensées*. "En leur portant une attention presque exclusive, en renfermant en elles toutes les autres vérités," observes Jean Mesnard, "Pascal donne à son christianisme une couleur particulière, qui est celle de l'augustinisme."[2] By examining the place accorded the scriptural doctrine of the Fall in neo-Augustinian theology, I intend to clarify Pascal's adherence to a literal interpretation of Genesis. An understanding of Pascal's biblicism will in turn permit us to penetrate the internal logic of his argument when he puts the Fall in the service of apology.

To denote the idea that the Fall and the Incarnation together constitute the most fundamental mystery of the Christian faith, the doctrine of the Redemption, Pascal repeatedly makes use of the formula "Adam"/"Jésus-Christ." Even the most theologically minded modern reader will perhaps forget that Adam is for Pascal no less a historical figure than Jesus of Nazareth. The reader of today will perhaps automatically register the idea "mythological figure" when Pascal speaks of "Adam." Pascal's arguments, however, everywhere suppose Adam to be a historical personnage and the Fall to be a historical event. In order to enter into the internal logic of Pascal's arguments, the modern reader must find a way of temporarily suspending his view of the Fall as but metaphor.

The biblical commentaries of M. de Sacy afford us direct access to a closely reasoned exposition of the very literal understanding of Genesis that is implicit in the *Pensées*. Sacy's analysis permits us to recapture a vision of the origins of man that has long since been discredited both by science and by modern biblical scholarship. We evoke Sacy's interpretation in order to understand Pascal's view of sacred history. Yet we must constantly remind ourselves that reading Genesis as factual history is by no means an invention of Port-Royal, and that Sacy follows the precedent of the entire Christian tradition. Only in Sacy's own time did serious biblical scholars begin to doubt the historicity of Genesis' accounts of the Creation and the Fall.

"UN LIEU EFFECTIF": SACY'S PRESENTATION OF THE FALL AS A HISTORICAL EVENT

In his *Préface à la Genèse*, Sacy directs his reader's particular attention to his commentary on Genesis 3, Scripture's account of the Fall. This account, Sacy explains, is an episode whose "sens littéral" is of unparalleled importance in the whole of the Old Testament. It is the historical testimony on which the Church founds the doctrine of Original Sin. This doctrine, Sacy forewarns his reader, is one of those articles of faith "qui enferme toujours certaines obscuritez qui en sont inséparables."[3] Human reason, itself corrupted in Adam's fall, cannot hope to understand the source of its own limitations. Rather, reason must direct its full attention to the explanation afforded by Revelation:

> Lorsque nostre esprit envisage de plus près un mystère si profond, il s'éblouït d'abord, et il se trouve comme enveloppé d'un nuage de pensées qui le tiennent dans le doute, jusqu'à ce qu'il s'appuye sur la foy qu'il a receuë de Dieu, et *sur l'immobilité de sa Parole*.[4]

The obscure nature of the Fall and the necessity of relying upon the testimony of Scripture is a primary emphasis of Sacy's commentaries. It is likewise an idea echoed in his letters to penitents. "Il ne faut pas," Sacy counsels one gentleman under his direction, "trop raisonner sur le péché original." Instead, one must practice with regard to his "article" "ce que l'on pratique à l'égard de tous les autres mystères inconcevables à l'esprit humain."[5] The Holy Spirit, "parlant par la bouche de saint Paul," established the authority of this doctrine once and for all time in Romans 5:12.[6] To reject it means not only to "renoncer à tous les sentiments de la religion," but as well to "éteindre toutes les lumières de la raison."[7]

Having developed the idea that the doctrine of Original Sin is infinitely obscure to human reason, Sacy then introduces a paradox. Once this doctrine is enunciated by Revelation, it then illuminates that which is most mysterious in the human condition. "Cette vérité est comme un flambeau qui éclaircit ce qu'il y a plus inexpliqable dans l'état présent où la nature humaine est reduite."[8] Nothing is more evident than the corruption of man's reason. "Pour s'en convaincre," one has only to "faire attention à l'estat où naissent les enfans, aux ténèbres où leur âme est plongée, aux mauvaises inclinations qu'elle fait paroître si-tôt qu'elle commence d'agir." From such an observation, one can deduce at the very least the fact that man's present state "ne sçauroit estre celui de son origine." As Sacy sees it, then, the doctrine of the Fall, explaining so much about the human condition, is really "beaucoup moins obscure" than many of the other great mysteries of Christianity.⁹

Like Pascal, Sacy identifies the transmission of Adam's guilt to the rest of humanity as that aspect of the Fall which is the most contrary to human reason:

> Nous avons de la peine à comprendre comment la playe de la concupiscence dont Adam fut frappé au moment de sa révolte, et qui comme une maladie contagieuse se répandit dans toutes les parties de son âme et de son corps, est passée dans ses enfans, et ensuite dans la succession de tous les hommes . . . Il est sans doute que c'est là ce qui est le plus difficile à comprendre dans le péché originel.¹⁰

Yet, at the same time, Sacy does not hesitate to point out, everyday experience provides ample clarification of this mystery. In nature, one finds manifold examples of hereditary illnesses that follow the same pattern: "Nous voyons tous les jours qu'il y a des maladies héréditaires qui passent des pères aux enfans, qu'il y en a mesme, comme la lèpre et semblables, qui sont attachées à des familles entières, sans que la transfusion de cette maladie originelle soit interrompuë par le cours et le nombre des années."¹¹ Sacy's analogy supposes a literal reading of Genesis. He takes the whole of the human race to be a "famille entière" descended without exception from Adam, the father of mankind.

"L'expérience," Sacy goes on to point out, provides confirmation of the biological transmission not only of physical illnesses but of "vices tout de l'esprit." Such moral defects, "qui passent des pères aux enfans non seulement en des familles, mais en des Provinces entières," present an illustration that renders the Christian doctrine of the transmission of Original Sin all the more convincing:

> Que l'on considère les humeurs et les inclinations différentes de chaque païs, et l'on trouvera qu'il y en a où les hommes naissent naturellement fiers, vains, et glorieux, ce qui paroist dans les enfans mesmes. Il y en a d'autres où ils naissent artificieux dans leurs paroles et dans leur conduite. . . . Ces passions toutes spirituelles qui estoient dans les pères se reproduisent par la naissance dans l'esprit de leurs enfans.¹²

The effects of Adam's sin have penetrated nature in ways that are "si palpables et si sensibles," Sacy argues, that even the pagan philosophers "en ont esté frappez, quoi qu'ils n'en puissent pas découvrir la cause." These philosophers rightly realized that man, "ayant receu du ciel la lumière de la raison," should have been favored with "tous les avantages de la nature." Yet they only had to compare a newborn animal to a newborn child in order to realize that something had gone wrong at some point in man's earliest history. "*Celuy qui vient au monde comme le roy de tous les ani-*

maux," Pliny had observed in his *Historia naturalis*, "*naist comme un esclave et un criminel.*"[13]

In describing the pagan philosophers' perception of the effects of the Fall in nature, Sacy cites Saint Augustine: "*Rem viderunt, causam nescierunt.*"[14] Those "grands esprits" such as Aristotle and Cicero realized that God could not be other than "souverainement bon et juste." Yet when they took stock of the human condition, they found it to be "visiblement un état de condamnation et de supplice." As they had no knowledge of the Fall—"qui auroit autorisé cette misère de l'homme san faire injure à la justice de Dieu"—these philosophers were forced to invent "une cause vray-semblable et très-ingénieuse" to explain the contradiction between God's justice and man's misery.[15] "Ils ont inventé un péché originel, n'ayant pu découvrir le véritable."[16]

Sacy draws a critical distinction between the theoretical concept of man's having fallen from a more perfect state—which can be deduced from *expérience*—and the Christian doctrine of the Fall, "la véritable," which is grounded in Revelation. Only Genesis documents Original Sin as historical fact. To advance the notion that the story of man's Fall "n'est qu'une parabole" is to undermine the whole of Christian doctrine. Those who advance such an idea have fallen into one of the oldest of heresies. Philo, "expliquant l'Ecriture avec la perfidie d'un Juif et la présomption d'un Philosophe, a changé en une simple allégorie ce qu'a dit Moïse du Paradis."[17]

A nonhistorical interpretation of the Fall, Sacy warns, amounts to "une opinion fondée sur la témérité d'une conjecture phantastique de l'esprit humain." According to the universal opinion of the Fathers of the Church, Adam's sin was a historical event and the Garden of Eden "un lieu effectif."[18] Adam was the biological father of the entire human race:

> Il est certain qu'Adam . . . a eu un très grand nombre d'enfans, qui pendant sa vie, qui a esté de plus de neuf cens ans, ont composé des millions d'hommes et des peuples entiers.[19]

Therefore, all of humankind, including those who are yet unborn, themselves sinned in Adam's sin. To allegorize the Fall is to adopt the heretical position that a man born today is not corrupted just as fully as was Adam himself. It is to fall into the Pelagian heresy, to "détruire la vérité de l'Histoire Sainte" and to "renverser les fondemens les plus inébranlables de la foy et de la religion."[20]

In placing the Fall at the center of his framework for Christian doctrine, in making it the "fondement" of all the other revealed mysteries, Sacy presents us with the essence of neo-Augustinian theology. Without the Fall, not even the Incarnation has any real meaning, "puisque le Fils de Dieu . . . n'est descendu du ciel et ne s'est revestu de notre nature *qu'afin que le second homme réparast les ruines du premier.*"[21] To treat Adam as but a symbol of human weakness is to disrupt the divinely authorized analogy between Christ and Adam. To question the historicity of Adam is to doubt the historicity of the Incarnation. Those who call themselves Christians while "faisant profession" of denying the reality of the Fall find themselves "condamnez en ce point de stupidité et d'un manquement d'esprit et de raison par les plus sages d'entre les Payens."[22]

The Fall never stands alone in Sacy's dogmatic theology. It is always paired with the Incarnation:

> Depuis que le Verbe s'est fait chair et a demeuré au milieu de nous, si nous avions oublié en quelque sorte la première dignité de nostre création, sçachons au moins l'estimer par le prix inestimable de nostre redemption.[23]

The *Bible de Royaumont*, a synopsis of Scripture pieced together from Sacy's commentaries by Fontaine, emphasizes the unity of the Fall and the Incarnation by recalling the idea of *felix culpa* from the liturgy of Holy Saturday. Adam's sin, viewed from the totality of sacred history, was both a necessary and happy event:

> Tous les hommes sont infiniment obligez au Sauveur qui a réparé ce mal d'une manière si avantageuse que l'Eglise puisse maintenant appeler le péché d'Adam *un péché nécessaire*, et sa faute *une faute bienheureuse.*[24]

God permitted Adam's sin in the first place, Sacy writes to one penitent, "pour en tirer un plus grand bien que celui de la justice originelle, par le mérite de la grâce de Jésus-Christ. Cette pensée est si solide et si véritable que toute l'Eglise s'écrie dans ses prières de la feste de Pâque: *O péché vraiment nécessaire . . . O heureuse faute qui a esté réparée par un remède et par un Sauveur si grand et si divin.*"[25]

In his commentary on Genesis, Sacy explains how God produced from the Fall an even greater good than man's original state of innocence:

> Dieu a tiré du péché d'Adam, non seulement l'élévation singulière de la nature humaine au plus haut degré qu'elle pouvoit monter, mais encore un prodigieux rehaussement de sa propre gloire . . . quoy qu'il soit vray que Dieu estant l'Estre souverain, ne peut rien ajoûter á sa grandeur qui est infinie, on peut dire néanmoins, que lors qu'il s'est abaissé si profondément pour sauver les hommes, *il s'est relevé en quelque sorte au-dessus de luy-mesme: parce que sa puissance estant demeurée la mesme, sa bonté a paru ensuite sans comparaison plus grande.*[26]

In the whole story of man's fall from grace, Sacy observes, there is nothing "qui ne conspire à la gloire du Créateur et à la confusion de la créature."[27]

This vision of the purpose of the Fall profoundly influences Sacy's exegesis of the traditional analogy between Christ and Adam first set down by Saint Paul.[28] Because the Fall and the Incarnation are but different sides of the same mystery, one must constantly look for parallels between the life of Christ and "toutes les circonstances du péché du premier homme." Christ, the second Adam, became Incarnate "pour guérir les blessures profondes que la nature humaine a receuës dans la chute du premier." The life of Christ recapitulates specific details of the Fall in order to reverse their effects. Because Adam was tempted, "Jésus-Christ aussi a voulu l'estre."[29]

Sacy's juxtaposition of Adam's temptation and Christ's is the perfect illustration of his conception of the unity of the Old and New Testaments, of the Fall and the Incarnation. The three "flèches mortelles" with which Satan "a percé le coeur de nos premiers parents" prefigure the three ways in which the Devil would tempt Christ. Or rather, the three temptations of Christ recapitulate the three means by which human nature was corrupted and reverse their consequences in order to regenerate man's fallen nature.[30]

When he partook of the forbidden fruit, Adam subjected human nature to "la sensualité," or "la concupiscence de la chair." Satan, tempting Christ in the midst of his forty-day fast in the desert, challenged him to turn stones into bread, "ce qui auroit esté une faute d'intempérance." Adam and Even succumbed to the sin of "la curiosité," or "la concupiscence des yeux," in believing Satan's promise that their eyes would be opened to discern good and evil. Christ was tempted in like manner when Satan, taking him to the pinnacle of the Temple, asked him to demonstrate his divinity by throwing himself to the ground: "ce qui auroit esté tenter Dieu par une *curiosité criminelle*." Satan caught Adam and Eve in a third snare, "la présomption," "lorsqu'il leur a persuadé qu'ils deviendroient semblables à Dieu." Christ was tempted by the same "piège de l'orgueil" when Satan offered him all the kingdoms of the world in exchange for falling down and worshiping him.[31]

Christ's manner of refuting Satan's temptations, Sacy observes, is "bien différente" from the actions of "nos premiers pères." Unlike Eve, "il ne *raisonne* point avec le démon . . . il ne luy parle point avec doute de la certitude des ordonnances de Dieu." Instead, Christ counters Satan "par l'épée de la parole de Dieu." All three of Christ's responses, Sacy observes, are citations drawn from Holy Scripture. "*L'homme ne vit pas seulement de pain, mais de toute parole qui sort de la bouche de Dieu.*" "*Vous ne tenterez point le Seigneur vostre Dieu.*" "*Vous adorerez le Seigneur vostre Dieu et vous ne servirez que luy seul.*"[32] By opposing Eve's attempt to "raisonner" with Satan to Christ's reliance on the Word of God, Sacy establishes a fundamental dichotomy between reason and Revelation. If man fell through attempting to rely on his reason, his salvation lies in accepting Revelation as recorded in Scripture.

In Sacy's view, it is not only the New Testament that is mysteriously part of the Incarnation. The Old Testament, even before the historical Incarnation, had begun to restore man's communication with God. The editors of the first edition of the Sacy Bible to be published separately from Sacy's commentaries (1702) set this idea at the beginning of their *Préface*. They present a synthesis of Sacy's conception of sacred history that particularly clarifies Pascal's understanding of the origins of the Old Testament.

The *Préface* of 1702 opens by describing the whole universe as a "grand volume, dans lequel Dieu a imprimé tous les caractères de sa Divinité." Likewise, the human heart is a book in which God has traced "les règles de sa conduite, par la lumière naturelle." "La lumière naturelle," however, no longer can serve as a means of knowing God. In fact, the contemplation of the universe "dissipe beaucoup plus notre esprit qu'elle ne l'éclaire." "Si nous étendons nos vues sur tout ce monde visible, c'est bien moins pour nous élever jusqu'à son Auteur, que pour chercher dans quelques-unes des parties de cet Univers l'objet de nos désirs corrompus, de nos attaches criminelles, de nos passions déréglées." Man's inability to perceive God in nature is a direct result of the corruption of his natural reason in Adam's sin:

> Le péché [originel] a tellement brouillé ces divins caractères; il a repandu de si profondes ténèbres sur nos esprits; il a corrompu nos coeurs jusqu'à un tel point, que l'ignorance et la foiblesse sont devenues notre partage.[33]

In order to "remédier" the "funestes effets" of Original Sin and to "dissiper nos ténèbres les plus épaisses," God did not choose to rehabilitate human reason directly. Instead, He made use of a process that the church has come to call Revelation:

> Il nous a dévelopé ses mistères les plus cachez. Il nous a expliquez ses volontez dans toute leur étendue. En un mot, il nous a fait présent d'un nouveau Livre, dans lequel nous pouvons, sans crainte d'être trompez, lire sans cesse les règles de notre conduite, tant par rapport à cet Auteur de notre être, que par rapport à nous-mêmes. . . . Le livre n'est rien autre chose que LA SAINTE BIBLE.[34]

According to the *Préface* of 1702, the Fall resulted in the complete rupture of communications between God and man. "Dieu s'est éloigné de lui, et ne l'a plus honoré de sa conversation." Yet man did not remain in complete ignorance of God right up until the time of the Incarnation. "Sa miséricorde ne l'a pas entièrement abandonné. S'il ne lui a plus parlé lui-même, il lui a fait parler par des hommes qu'il a inspirez, et dont il a conduit la langue et la plume." In fact, God never stopped intervening in human history. Only with Moses' writing of the Pentateuch, however, were these interventions—including the most important, God's alliance with the Jews "en la personne d'Abraham"—set down for the instruction and illumination of subsequent generations.[35]

This view of sacred history finds a significant parallel in Pascal's description of the origins of the Old Testament in fragment 711/474. To prevent the story of the Fall from being forgotten by subsequent generations of mankind, God spoke through his servant Moses:

> La création du monde commençant à s'éloigner, Dieu a pourvu d'un historien unique contemporain, et a commis tout un peuple pour la garde de ce livre, afin que cette histoire fût la plus authentique du monde et que tous les hommes pussent apprendre par là une chose si nécessaire à savoir, et qu'on ne pût la savoir que par là.

In this fragment, the "chose si nécessaire à savoir" to which Pascal refers is the Fall. Only the Bible, in Moses' account of this event, provides an accurate and historically reliable exposition of its circumstances.

Both Pascal and Sacy view the whole of sacred history from the perspective of two central events. "Tout le sistème des Ecritures saintes," concludes the *Préface* of 1702, "roule sur la chute d'Adam qui a rendu l'homme criminel et malheureux, et sur la venue du Messie qui l'a rétabli dans l'innocence."[36] "Toute la foi," Pascal's *Apology* seeks to demonstrate, "consiste en Jésus-Christ et en Adam" (258/226).

Pascal's argument will demonstrate the need for a revealed religion by showing that nature, "dans l'homme et hors de l'homme," "marque partout un Dieu perdu" (708/471). In his commentary on Genesis, Sacy did not fail to note the usefulness of such an argument. "Un des plus grands esprits de nostre siècle," he points out to his readers, used the Fall as the cornerstone of an *Apology* for Christianity. According to Sacy, Pascal's argument is as follows:

> Que de quelque obscurité que soit couvert le péché originel, ses effets néanmoins qui éclatent de toutes parts, luy rendent un témoignage si évident, que s'il est difficile de croire ce point de nostre Religion, il paroist encore plus difficile de ne le pas croire . . . *L'homme est plus incompréhensible sans ce mystère, que ce mystère n'est incompréhensible à l'homme.*[37]

When he identifies this doctrine as central to Pascal's apologetic purposes, Sacy provides us with an important critical perspective. Sometimes, almost to the exclusion of all other Christian doctrines, the Fall seems to have preoccupied the theologians of Port-Royal. Pascal's organization of his defense of the Christian religion did not fail to reflect this preoccupation.

PARALLELS IN THE *PENSEES*: THE SPECIFICITY OF REVELATION AND THE PARADOX OF THE DOCTRINE OF ORIGINAL SIN

In Sacy's analysis, the doctrine of the Fall is a paradox. From the perspective of human philosophy, the doctrine is "obscure" and completely beyond the grasp of reason. Yet, once enunciated by Revelation, the same doctrine clarifies what is most mysterious in the human condition. This same paradox is the touchstone of Pascal's *Apology*:

> Pour moi, j'avoue qu'aussitôt que la religion chrétienne découvre ce principe: que la nature des hommes est corrompue et déchue de Dieu, cela ouvre les yeux à voir partout le caractère de cette vérité. Car la nature est telle, qu'elle marque partout un Dieu perdu, et dans l'homme, et hors de l'homme.
> Et une nature corrompue. (708/471)

Every time Pascal presents the Fall as a transcendent doctrine beyond human understanding, he then proceeds to introduce the paradoxical idea that this same doctrine is the key to the human enigma. This paradox, in turn, takes its place within a larger system of paradoxes, a system that constitutes the core of what modern critics call Pascal's "dialectic":

> Incompréhensible que Dieu soit, et incompréhensible qu'il ne soit pas; que l'âme soit avec le corps, que nous n'ayons point d'âme; que le monde soit créé, qu'il ne le soit pas; etc.; que le péché originel soit, et qu'il ne soit pas. (656/809)

The paradox of the Fall, in effect, serves as the model from which the three principal dialectical oppositions of the *Pensées*—"misère"/"grandeur," "l'homme sans Dieu"/"l'homme avec Dieu," and "figure"/"vérité"—take their inspiration and derive their force.

Pascal's exposition of the obscurity of the doctrine of the Fall takes the form of a series of variations on the same theme. One development stresses the doctrine's inherent irrationality. "Le péché originel est folie devant les hommes, mais on le donne pour tel. Vous ne me devez donc pas reprocher le défaut de raison en cette doctrine, puisque je la donne pour être sans raison" (574/695). One cannot expect man to be able to grasp this doctrine, "puisque c'est une chose contre se raison et que sa raison, bien loin de l'inventer par ses voies, s'en éloigne quand on le lui présente" (574/695). As does Sacy, Pascal insists that human reason, unaided by Revelation, would never be able to deduce—or, for that matter, to invent—the doctrine of Original Sin.

To explain reason's incapacity to perceive the Fall by relying upon its own forces, Pascal has recourse to an idea borrowed from Jansenius: the notion of man's "deux états."[38] Because he is not in the state of his creation, man cannot perceive an event that took place prior to (and resulted in) the corruption of his reason. Man's ability to deduce the Fall would presuppose his ability to conceive of his original state of innocence. That too, however, escapes the powers of man's present rational faculties:

> Nous ne concevons ni l'état glorieux d'Adam, ni la nature de son péché, ni la transmission qui s'en est faite en nous. Ce sont choses qui se sont passées dans l'état d'une nature toute différente de la nôtre et qui passent l'état de notre capacité présente. (683/431)

Elsewhere, Pascal insists upon the obscurity of the Fall from a somewhat different perspective. His emphasis is on God's design in hiding this truth from human reason:

> Dieu, pour se réserver à soi seul le droit de nous instruire de nous-même, voulant nous rendre la difficulté de notre être inintelligible à nous-même, en a caché le noeud si haut ou pour mieux dire si bas, que nous étions bien incapables d'y arriver. De sorte que ce n'est pas par les superbes agitations de notre raison, mais par la simple soumission de la raison, que nous pouvons véritablement nous connaître. (164/131)

Reason, even in its most "superbes agitations," is incapable of deducing the cause of "la difficulté de notre être." Only "par la simple soumission de la raison" to Genesis' account of the origins of the human condition can man hope to understand those truths that God has hidden from reason.

Like Sacy, Pascal points out that the most unintelligible and difficult aspect of the doctrine of Original Sin is the notion that all men fell in Adam. "Le mystère le plus éloigné de notre connaissance . . . est celui de la transmission du péché":

> Car il est sans doute qu'il n'y a rien qui choque plus notre raison que de dire que le péché du premier homme ait rendu coupables ceux qui, étant si éloignés de cette source, semblent incapables d'y participer. Cet écoulement ne nous paraît pas seulement impossible. Il nous semble même très injuste. Car qu'y a-t-il de plus contraire aux règles de notre misérable justice que de damner éternellement un enfant incapable de volonté pour un péché où il paraît avoir si peu de part, qu'il est commis six mille ans avant qu'il fût en être. Certainement rien ne nous heurte plus rudement que cette doctrine. (164/131)

It may seem odd that Pascal, in an apology whose stated aim is to "rendre la religion aimable,"[39] chooses to put such emphasis on the most difficult, and indeed most frightening, aspect of the doctrine of the Fall. Pascal is not, however, merely echoing the position of Port-Royal on the question of the culpability of unbaptized infants for the sake of doctrinal orthodoxy. He invokes the idea of the transmission of Original Sin with a particular apologetic objective in view. In chapter five I shall examine in detail the way in which Pascal puts the doctrine of the Fall in the service of apology. For the moment, it seems important not to neglect the extent to which the apologist is caught up in the defense of a neo-Augustinian interpretation of the doctrine of Original Sin, a defense that spills over from the *Ecrits sur la Grâce* and the *Provinciales* into the argument of the *Pensées*.

In order to appreciate the rigor with which Pascal adheres to a neo-Augustinian interpretation of the Fall in the fragment we have just examined (164/131), we may do well to recall the position of Pascal's adversaries. The theologians of Port-Royal accused the Jesuits of having revived the

Pelagian heresy by teaching that men are born with sufficient grace to work out their own salvation. Pascal's response, in the *Ecrits sur la Grâce*, clearly sets forth the position taken by Port-Royal:

> Ce péché ayant passé d'Adam à toute sa postérité, qui fut corrompue en lui comme un fruit sortant d'une mauvaise semence, tous les hommes sortis d'Adam naissent dans l'ignorance, dans la concupiscence, coupables du péché d'Adam et dignes de la mort éternelle.[40]

Pascal draws a sharp distinction between an orthodox view of the Fall and that of the Calvinists, who teach that "le péché d'Adam s'est communiqué à toute sa postérité, *non pas naturellement*, comme le vice d'une semence au fruit qu'elle produit, mais par un décret de Dieu."[41] In order to affirm what Philippe Sellier calls "la solidarité organique d'Adam et ses descendants,"[42] Pascal borrows from Saint Augustine not only the image of "un fruit sortant d'une mauvaise semence" but as well, like Sacy, the image of "la contagion."[43] Pascal's emphasis on the hereditary nature of the transmission of Original Sin underscores his defense of the Fall as a historical event. All men are guilty of Adam's sin beause all are his biological descendents.

Pascal's view of the practical consequences of the Fall places him on the side of what Sellier describes as "l'anti-humanisme augustinien."[44] Shortly before Pascal began writing his *Apology*, the Pelagian theses on the salvation of the "anciens justes" had begun to reappear. La Mothe Le Vayer, in his *De la vertu des païens* (1641), had made use of the theology of the Jesuits to argue that Socrates and Aristotle had worked out their own salvation. Pascal's position stands in direct contradiction to the humanism of his time. Outside the church, he writes in a letter to Charlotte de Roannez, "il n'y a que malédiction."[45] Prior to Christ's Incarnation, he concludes in fragment 332/301, "tous les peuples étaient dans l'infidélité et dans la concupiscence." The virtue of the pagans, when analysed from the standpoint of Christian theology, can be shown to be but a deception:

> Un bâtiment également beau par dehors, mais sur un mauvais fondement, les païens sages le bâtissaient. Et le diable trompe les hommes par cette ressemblance apparente, fondée sur le fondement le plus différent." (796/960)

Pascal's analysis of the "anciens justes" throws into relief the literalistic character of neo-Augustinian theology. His emphasis is on the specificity of the Christian Revelation. The "païens sages," though they achieved a kind of virtue, were incapable of achieving that specific virtue which alone leads to salvation. The former is of human origin, the latter can be obtained only through the merits of Christ's death. Pascal's analysis recalls Sacy's judgment on the pagan philosophers' perception of the Fall: "Ils ont inventé un péché originel, n'ayant pas pu découvrir le véritable."[46] Though they were able to deduce from *expérience* the fact of man's fall from a better state, their conclusion was of no use whatsoever in advancing their salvation. The Fall deduced by the pagan philosophers was not "le véritable," the one revealed in Genesis and bound up with the mystery of the Redemption. Like the virtue of the "païens sages," it is built on a "mauvais fondement" and falls totally outside Revelation.[47]

Pascal's rigorous adherence to a neo-Augustinian view of the Fall has profound consequences with regard to the kind of apology he writes. The corruption of human reason is permanent and irreparable. In the words of the *Bible de Royaumont*, the Fall "aura *jusqu'à la fin du monde* [ses] si effroyables suites."[48] The Incarnation, though it reversed the Fall by taking human flesh into the Godhead, did not rehabilitate human reason. Therefore, since human reason is irreparably impaired, apology cannot make use of metaphysical proofs:

> Les preuves de Dieu métaphysiques sont si éloignées du raisonnement des hommes et si impliquées, qu'elles frappent peu. Et quand cela servirait à quelques-uns, cela ne servirait que pendant l'instant qu'ils voient cette démonstration. Mais une heure après, ils craignent de s'être trompés. (222/190)

Pascal notes that he has considered the usefulness of those apologies that seek to prove "la divinité par les ouvrages de la nature." Such proofs, when addressed to "personnes destituées de foi et de grâce," are supposed to rekindle in their minds the idea of a Supreme Being. Yet, Pascal observes, such apologies rarely have their intended effect. Those unbelievers who are asked to ponder the course of the moon and of the planets in the hope of finding God, "ne trouvent qu'obscurité et ténèbres." Metaphysical proofs of God's existence, Pascal concludes, have the worst possible effect on those to whom they are addressed. "Rien n'est plus propre à leur en faire naître le mépris" (644/781).

Why are proofs drawn from nature of so little use? Had not Saint-Cyran taught that nature is the very *image* of Grace? The great majority of Christian apologists in the seventeenth century made use of metaphysical proofs drawn from scholastic philosophy. To understand why Pascal rules out the use of such proofs, it is useful to recall the opening of the *Préface* to the 1702 edition of the Sacy Bible. Though the universe is indeed "un grand volume dans lequel Dieu a imprimé tous les caractères de sa Divinité," the Fall has "tellement brouillé ces divins caractères" and "répandu de si profondes ténèbres sur nos esprits," that "la lumière naturelle" is no longer an avenue to knowledge of God.[49] Such is exactly the position of Pascal. In fact, he goes so far as to argue that it is Christianity's very rejection of "la raison naturelle" in favor of a radical reliance on Revelation that distinguishes it from all other religions:

> Toutes les religions et les sectes du monde ont eu la raison naturelle pour guide. Les seuls chrétiens ont été astreints à prendre leurs règles hors d'eux-mêmes, et à s'informer de celles que Jésus-Christ a laissées aux anciens pour être transmises aux fidèles. (634/769)

Pascal warns that proofs drawn from scholastic reasoning might lead the unbeliever to "le déisme." Those who do not really understand Christianity might imagine that deism—"l'adoration d'un Dieu considéré comme grand, puissant et éternel"—is a step in the direction of Christianity. But such is not the case. "Le déisme . . . [est] presque aussi éloigné de la religion chrétienne que l'athéisme." "[Ce] sont deux choses que la religion chrétienne abhorre presque également" (690/449).

Once again, we encounter the literalism of Pascal's neo-Augustinian theology. Revelation, like the Incarnation, limits itself to specific and concrete manifestations. Analogies arrived at by purely human reason are ultimately devoid of meaning. The virtue of the "païens sages" and their deduction of man's fall from a better state must not be taken to bear any real relationship to that unique virtue merited by Christ's sacrifice or to the Fall as recounted by Genesis. Likewise, there exists an unbridgeable gulf between the god of the deists and the God revealed in Christ.

Those who confound deism and Christianity think that they have discredited the Christian God when they have but proved the impossibility of the god of the deists. "Ils concluent que cette religion n'est pas véritable, parce qu'ils ne voient pas que toutes choses concourent à l'établissement de ce point, que Dieu ne se manifeste pas aux hommes avec tout l'évidence qu'il pourrait faire" (690/449). The god of the deists must necessarily manifest himself in the universe. The God of the Christians, by contrast, has chosen to hide Himself in the Incarnation, in Scripture, and in Revelation. The opponents of Christianity, when they discredit the god of the deists by documenting his apparent absence in the universe, only confirm what Christianity already teaches.

The doctrine of the Fall accounts for God's apparent absence in the universe. Man's corrupted reason, it tells us, prevents him from perceiving God in nature. The hidden character of the Christian Revelation invalidates the anti-deist argument as an argument against Christianity:

> Qu'ils en concluent ce qu'ils voudront contre le déisme, ils n'en concluront rien contre la religion chrétienne, qui consiste proprement au mystère du Rédempteur, qui unissant en lui les deux natures, humaine et divine, a retiré les hommes de la corruption et du péché pour les réconcilier à Dieu en sa personne divine." (690/449)

Pascal's limitation of man's knowledge of God to what is contained in Revelation profoundly affects the scope of his projected *Apology*. Mysteries like the Fall and the Incarnation are beyond the grasp of man's fallen reason. Therefore, he explains, it has been necessary to rule out metaphysical proofs either of God's existence or of particular Christian doctrines:

> C'est pourquoi je n'entreprendrai pas ici de prouver par les raisons naturelles, ou l'existence de Dieu, ou la Trinité, ou l'immortalité de l'âme, ni aucune des choses de cette nature; non seulement parce qu je ne me sentirais pas assez fort pour trouver dans la nature de quoi convaincre des athées endurcis, mais encore parce que cette connaissance sans Jésus-Christ est inutile et stérile. Quand un homme serait persuadé que les proportions des nombres sont des vérités immatérielles, éternelles et dépendantes d'une première vérité en qui elles subsistent et qu'on appelle Dieu, je ne le trouverais pas beaucoup avancé pour son salut. (690/449)

In discarding the use of metaphysical proofs, Pascal observes that the Bible, the very source of Revelation, never once makes use of ontological or metaphysical arguments. "C'est une chose admirable que jamais auteur canonique ne s'est servi de la nature pour prouver Dieu" (702/463). A document addressed to fallen humanity, Scripture takes into account the corruption of man's reason. It presents something more accessible to man's intellect than metaphysical proofs: the intervention of God in history. "Le Dieu des chrétiens ne consiste pas en un Dieu simplement auteur des vérités géométriques et de l'ordre des éléments." Rather, He is the God who has visibly intervened in human history: "le Dieu d'Abraham, le Dieu d'Isaac, le Dieu de Jacob" (690/449).

"L'ORDRE DU MONDE": THE FALL TRANSLATED INTO THE LANGUAGE OF *EXPERIENCE*

Before proceeding to a historical proof of Christianity, Pascal's apologetic itinerary calls for what amounts to a radical departure from traditional Christian apologetics. Revelation, though beyond the grasp of reason, will be shown to bear a direct and demonstrable relationship to the whole of human experience. The doctrine of the Fall will be shown to afford the unique answer to an enigma upon which reason and philosophy, and indeed the net experience of the human race, have been unable to cast any light.

Pascal's demonstration derives its force from the idea that the Fall is a paradox. While totally escaping rational analysis, this doctrine at the same time illuminates what is most enigmatic in the human condition. Though "folie devant les hommes" and "une chose contre [la] raison," the doctrine of Original Sin nevertheless surpasses "toute la sagesse des hommes."[50] Without it, it is impossible even to define man. "Sans cela que dira-t-on qu'est l'homme? Tout son état dépend de ce point imperceptible" (574/695). "Sans ce mystère le plus incompréhensible de tous nous sommes incompréhensibles à nous-mêmes. Le noeud de notre condition prend ses replis et ses tours dans cet abîme" (164/131).

In fragment 690/449, having just established the Fall and the Incarnation as the core of Christian theology, Pascal suggests "qu'on examine *l'ordre du monde* sur cela, et qu'on voie si toutes choses ne tendent pas à l'établissement des deux chefs de notre religion" (italics mine). What does Pascal have in mind when he suggests that "l'ordre du monde" will provide confirmation of the doctrine of the Fall? Does he plan to use an argument like the one we have already seen Sacy use? Does he intend to explain that the hereditary transmission of physical illnesses renders the transmission of Original Sin more credible?[51]

Evidence exterior to the *Pensées* suggests that Pascal did consider such a tactic. Filleau de la Chaise, in his *Discours sur les Pensées*, presents Pascal as attaching particular importance to the way in which the Bible "faisait voir clair dans *l'ordre du monde*" (italics mine). According to Filleau, Pascal proposed to a group of friends that he intended to demonstrate that Genesis' account of the Fall "démêl[ait] ces questions impénétrables qui ont tant tourmenté les plus grands esprits du paganisme":

> Pourquoi, par exemple, cette étrange diversité entre les hommes, qui sont tous de même nature? Comment la chose du monde la plus simple, qui est l'âme, ou la pensée, peut-elle se trouver si diversifiée? . . . Si l'âme passe des pères aux enfants, comme les philosophes le croyaient, d'où peut encore venir cette diversité? Pourquoi un habile homme en produit-il un sans esprit? Comment un scélérat peut-il venir d'un honnête homme? Comment les enfants d'un même père peuvent-ils naître avec des inclinations différentes?

"Toutes ces difficultés," Pascal would have pointed out to his adversary, "ne cessent-elles pas par cette chute de la nature de l'homme, que ce livre [*la Genèse*] dit être tombé de son premier état?"[52]

The irregularities in human heredity, Filleau presents Pascal as arguing, are "des suites nécessaires de l'assujettissement de l'âme au corps . . . qui la fait dépendre de la naissance, du pays, du tempérament, de l'éducation, de la coutume et d'une infinité de choses de cette nature, qui n'y devraient faire aucune impression."[53] In other words, the Fall subjected man to "cette étrange diversité" that has been the great stumbling block in philosophy's attempt to explain the origins of human nature. From the same historical event results "cette confusion qu'on voit dans le monde, qui a fait douter à tant de philosophes qu'il y eût une providence":

> Pourquoi les méchants réussissent-ils presque toujours, et pourquoi ceux qui semblent justes sont-ils misérables et accablés? Pourquoi ce mélange monstreux de pauvres et de riches, de sains et de malades, de tyrans et d'opprimés? Qu'ont fait ceux-là pour naître heureux, et avoir tout à souhait; ou par où

ceux-ci ont-ils mérité de ne venir au monde que pour souffrir? Pourquoi Dieu a-t-il permis qu'il y eût tant d'erreurs, tant d'opinions, de moeurs, de coutumes, de religions différentes?[54]

Filleau reports that Pascal went on to show that Scripture explains the origins of an enigma that human philosophy has been unable to resolve. "Tout cela est encore éclairci par un petit nombre de principes qui se trouvent dans ce livre: . . . que ce n'est pas ici le lieu où Dieu veut que se fasse le discernement des bons et des méchants . . . que ce n'est pas ici non plus le lieu de récompense; que ce jour viendra; que cependant Dieu veut que les choses demeurent dans l'obscurité; qu'il a laissé marcher les hommes dans leurs voies; qu'il les laisse courir après les désirs de leur coeur."[55]

Filleau's *Discours* provides us with a valuable perspective on the apologetic method of the *Pensées*. Those particular arguments concerning the Fall's clarification of the mystery of human diversity do not appear in the *Pensées* at all. Pascal would seem to have laid them aside as too specific for use in illustrating how "l'ordre du monde" reflects the consequences of the Fall. Instead, Pascal adopts a more global approach.

In fragment 181/148, Pascal attempts to embrace the whole of human experience. His emphasis is not on the inexplicable diversity of human experience, but rather on the one goal that all men hold in common:

> Tous les hommes recherchent d'être heureux. Cela est sans exception, quelques différents moyens qu'ils y emploient. Ils tendent tous à ce but. Ce qui fait que les uns vont à la guerre et que les autres n'y vont pas est ce même désir qui est dans tous les deux, accompagné de différentes vues. La volonté [ne] fait jamais la moindre démarche que vers cet objet. C'est le motif de toutes les actions de tous les hommes. Jusqu'à ceux qui vont se pendre.
> Et cependant depuis un si grand nombre d'années jamais personne, sans la foi, n'est arrivé à ce point où tous visent continuellement. Tous se plaignent, princes, sujets, nobles, roturiers, vieux, jeunes, forts, faibles, savants, ignorants, sains, malades, de tous pays, de tous les temps, de tous âges et de toutes conditions.

The collective experience of the whole of human history, Pascal observes, "une épreuve si longue, si continuelle et si uniforme," should have served to convince us of "notre impuissance d'arriver au bien par nos efforts." "Mais l'exemple nous instruit peu":

> Il n'est jamais si parfaitment semblable qu'il n'y ait quelque délicate différence, et c'est de là que nous attendons que notre attente ne sera pas déçue en cette occasion comme en l'autre. Et ainsi, le présent ne nous satisfaisant jamais, l'expérience nous pipe, et de malheur en malheur nous conduit jusqu'à la mort qui en est un comble éternel. (181/148)

This paradigm of the human condition serves to demonstrate that man's present state could not possibly be the state in which he has always been.

Man's search for the "souverain bien" is the clue to the enigma of the human situation, the most telling symptom of his fallen state:

> Qu'est-ce donc que nous crie cette avidité et cette impuissance, *sinon qu'il y a eu autrefois dans l'homme un véritable bonheur, dont il ne lui reste maintenant que la marque et la trace toute vide*, et qu'il essaie inutilement de remplir de tout ce qui l'environne, recherchant des choses absentes le secours qu'il n'obtient pas des présentes, mais qui en sont toute incapables, parce que ce gouffre infini ne peut être rempli que par un objet infini et immuable, c'est-à-dire que par Dieu même. Lui seul est son véritable bien. *Et depuis qu'il l'a quitté*, c'est une chose étrange qu'il n'y a rien dans la nature qui n'ait été capable de lui en tenir la place: astres, ciel, terre, éléments, plantes, choux, poireaux, animaux, insectes, veaux, serpents, fièvre, peste, guerre, famine, vices, adultère, inceste. *Et depuis qu'il a perdu le vrai bien*, tout également peut lui paraître tel, jusqu'à sa destruction propre, quoique si contraire à Dieu, à la raison et à la nature tout ensemble. (181/148; italics mine)

Pascal's argument is not entirely of his own invention. Presenting the same analysis of man's present state in the "Lettre sur la mort de son père," (1651), Pascal says he draws upon the observations of "deux très grands et très saints personnages."[56] Philippe Sellier identifies Pascal's sources, perhaps not to our surprise, as Jansenius and Saint Augustine, indicating in particular the opening of the *Confessions*.[57] On the other hand, it would be a mistake to exaggerate the role of Pascal's sources and fail to recognize his originality in this passage. The apologist has taken a traditional motif of Christian polemics—that the impulse to find a lost God is at the root of all human activity—and turned it to his own purposes by giving it a more global expression.

In order to illustrate the way in which "l'ordre du monde" reflects man's fallen condition, Pascal seeks to avoid citing any example that might be objected to as in any way less than universally valid. He therefore borrows from the *philosophes* their conclusion that the absolute common denominator of the human condition is man's search for "le souverain bien." His emphasis is on the universal validity of this principle. All men search for the "souverain bien," "*sans exception*." "La volonté ne fait jamais *la moindre* démarche *que* vers cet objet." "*Personne*, sans la foi, n'est arrivé à ce point où *tous* visent *continuellement*" (181/148).

Pascal's example seeks to embrace—vertically and horizontally—the whole of human experience. From the perspective of history, mankind's whole collective experience—"une épreuve *si longue, si continuelle, et si uniforme*"—testifies to man's failure in his quest for happiness. To reinforce the idea that this failure is common to all sorts and conditions of men, Pascal makes use of a sociological *dénombrement*: "princes, sujets . . . de toutes conditions." His use of enumeration to render his illustration global in its application recurs with particular effect in an exposition of the fact that "rien dans la nature" has been able to fill the void of God's absence in man's heart:

> Et depuis qu'il l'a quitté, c'est une chose étrange qu'il n'y a rien dans la nature qui n'ait été capable de lui en tenir la place: astres, ciel, terre, éléments, plantes, choux, poireaux, animaux, insectes, veaux, serpents, fièvre, peste, guerre, famine, vices, adultère, inceste. (181/148)

This second *dénombrement* is, in part, a survey of all the traditional categories of created things: "astres," "ciel," "terre," "plantes," "animaux." "Eléments" falls under the category of "terre," "choux" and "poireaux" under "plantes," and "insectes, veaux, serpents" under "animaux." To these categories of naturally created things, Pascal then adds those phenomena that have invaded nature since the Fall ("peste, guerre, famine") and concludes his *dénombrement* of "rien dans la nature" by picturing man as seeking "le souverain bien" even in his own "vices," of which "adultère" and "inceste" serve as specific examples. His argument is reinforced with an example that represents the furthermost extreme of man's search for happiness, "sa destruction propre" (181/148)

Such a straightforward analysis of this passage, however, does not take into account what Jean Mesnard calls "une ironie très apparente."[58] Not all Pascal's examples strike with the same effect. "Guerre" reiterates an idea proposed earlier in the passage: "Ce qui fait que les uns vont à la guerre et que les autres n'y vont pas est ce même désir [d'être heureux] qui est dans tous les deux, accompagné de différentes vues" (181/148). Likewise, the idea that man seeks a lost God not only in all of created nature but even in "vices" such as adultery finds its place immediately within the rational framework of Pascal's argument. On the other hand, is there not something unusual in the notion that man seeks his lost Creator in "insectes, veaux, serpents," in "choux" and in "poireaux"?

"Veaux" is probably an allusion to the Golden Calf of Exodus 32. "Serpents" perhaps recalls the *ancien serpent* who tempted Eve, or perhaps the "fiery serpents" of Numbers 21. And one might take "poireaux" and "choux" to be emblems of ordinary human activity, as representing man's search for God in the cultivation of his everyday garden.[59] It seems important, however, not to overlook the function of these examples on a purely rhetorical level. Pascal cites "choux," "poireaux," "serpents," and "insectes" to achieve a particular effect. Because they are slightly nonsensical, these examples serve to make the point that in the whole of the created universe there exists not even the most minor exception to the principle of man's search for the "souverain bien" or to the conclusion that man has not been able to find what he lost at the Fall in even the most particular of created things.

Pascal's choice of examples such as "choux" and "serpents" has a definite ironic function. To search for God in any created thing, he implies, is as foolish as to search for happiness in a cabbage or a snake. Fragment 181/148 is of obvious scriptural inspiration and reflects Pascal's constant meditation on the early apostolic preaching recorded in the Pauline Epistles. The folly of searching for God in created things was a favorite theme of Saint Paul,[60] as it would be for Saint Augustine, Jansenius, and the theologians of Port-Royal.

While bearing in mind the close parallel between Pascal's exposition of how "l'ordre du monde" reflects man's search for paradise lost and Sacy's observation that the doctrine of the Fall "éclaircit ce qu'il y a de plus inexplicable" in the human condition,[61] we should attempt to place fragment 181/148 in the larger context of Pascal's apologetic strategy. By showing that the doctrine of the Fall bears a direct and demonstrable relationship to the most fundamental common denominator of human experience, Pascal seeks to persuade his interlocutor to consider the whole of Revelation. The Fall is a doctrine anchored in historical fact. So too, Pascal will attempt to demonstrate, is the rest of Revelation.

THE ABSENCE OF A SCRIPTURAL EXPOSITION OF THE FALL IN PASCAL'S ARGUMENT

In chapter five, I shall trace Pascal's use of the Fall to effect a transition from experience to Revelation. In chapter six, I shall examine his proofs of the historicity of Revelation. First, however, a problem remains to be considered. Given the centrality of the Fall not only to Pascal's argument but to his very definition of Christianity (681/427; 313/281; 258/226; 690/449), it seems striking that nowhere in the text of the *Pensées* is to be found an exegesis of chapter three of Genesis. In the extensive catalogue of biblical citations that figure in the *Pensées*, there is not to be found a single citation that seems to anticipate an exposition of the Fall in explicitly biblical terms.[62] Considering the importance of the doctrine that such missing citations would have served to document, this lacuna warrants our consideration.

In this chapter, an attempt has been made to show that Pascal's interpretation of the Fall cannot be viewed as other than literal and historical. Making use of the *Ecrits sur la Grâce*, I have pointed out the obvious implications of Pascal's insistence on Adam's fatherhood of the entire human race. Sacy's understanding of the specificity of Revelation has thrown into relief an equally stringent view on the part of Pascal with regard to the concrete and historical forms that, he argues, Revelation always takes. In effect, I have argued that Pascal's arguments everywhere and always presuppose a historical Fall.

The whole force of Pascal's proof of the authenticity of the *Pentateuch* points to the importance he attaches to the Fall as a historical event. Moreover, evidence external to the *Pensées* indicates that Pascal intended to make use of the very scriptural exposition of the Fall that does not figure in his notes for the *Apology*. Etienne Périer, in his *Préface* to the Edition de Port-Royal (1670), and Filleau de la Chaise, in his *Discours*, present Pascal as directing his *libertin* to Genesis in order to find the solution to the enigma of the human condition.[63]

Why does Pascal never present an exegesis of Genesis 3 in the course of an argument built around the doctrine of the Fall? Might we conjecture that Pascal simply assumed his reader's acquaintance with Genesis 3 and never thought it necessary to present the Fall in explicitly scriptural terms? If so, Pascal's failure to document a doctrine of capital importance in his argument would seem totally at odds with his usual practice of documenting every other facet of Christian doctrine with citations drawn from the Bible. Once the Bible had been shown to be historically credible, an exegesis of Genesis 3 could have served as Pascal's ultimate proof of the doctrine of the Fall.

This consideration brings us to a second possibility. Is not the logical place for a scriptural exposition of the Fall *after* a historical proof of the credibility of Revelation? This part of Pascal's projected *Apology* is after all the most unfinished, at times consisting only of lists of biblical citations. Perhaps Pascal, interrupted in his work by devastating illness, simply never had time to develop what in fact amounted to an essential aspect of his argument. This idea has merit. Critics rarely accord enough importance to the fact that the *Pensées* represents an *Apology* interrupted not only in the course of its organization but in the course of its writing.

The only problem with this second hypothesis is that from what we can judge from the text itself (i.e., from the arrangement and contents of the 28 *liasses*), Pascal did not anticipate any extensive treatment of the Fall subsequent to his historical proofs. To the contrary, the Fall is assigned a major thematic role in those sections that *precede* the historical proofs. It figures, in fact, in the most finished sections of the *Pensées*. Its very purpose is to provide a means of convincing the *libertin* to take a closer, and perhaps more sympathetic, look at the whole of Revelation.

The absence of a scriptural exposition of the Fall in those sections of the *Apology* that precede the historical proofs is undoubtedly bound up with Pascal's apologetic method. In chapter five, I shall argue that Pascal refrains from citing the authority of Revelation until he has proved its historical credibility. I shall make a critical distinction between the perspective of the *libertin* and that of Pascal himself. From the point of view of the apologist, the Fall is a doctrine grounded in indisputable historical fact. As far as the *libertin* is concerned, however, it remains no more than a plausible theory. For the *libertin*, the potential credibility of the Fall resides not in its status as a scriptural doctrine but rather in its apparent empirical confirmation by "l'ordre du monde."

In developing the idea that the Fall is a paradox, Pascal clarifies the direction of his apologetic method. Analyzing man's "deux états," he draws a conclusion concerning the Fall's ability to illuminate human nature that is quite different from that of fragment 181/148. Man, because of the corruption of his natural reason, is able to conceive "ni l'état glorieux d'Adam, ni la nature de son péché." Yet even if human reason could comprehend these mysteries, the course of man's salvation would not be significantly advanced. "Tout cela nous serait inutile à savoir pour en sortir." (683/431)

Though only the doctrine of the Fall can make sense of human nature, Pascal insists, such a demonstration is not the ultimate end of his *Apology*. "Ce qu'il nous importe de connaître est que nous sommes misérables, corrompus, séparés de Dieu, mais rachetés par Jésus-Christ." Explaining the doctrine of the Fall in either scriptural or theological terms would have little chance of leading the nonbeliever to such a recognition. Therefore, the doctrine of the Fall is to be presented in terms of human experience, in terms with which Pascal's interlocutor can personally identify. "Et c'est de quoi nous avons des preuves admirables sur la terre" (683/431).

The entire first half of Pascal's *Apology* grows out of the idea that the Fall has left a visible imprint on nature, on man, on man's perception of the universe, and on man's perception of himself. "Misère"/"grandeur," the principal dialectical thread running through the first twelve/eleven dossiers of the *Pensées*, represents Pascal's attempt to translate the doctrine of the Fall into the language of human experience.

"Misère"/"grandeur" is a commonplace in neo-Augustinian theology. The *Bible de Royaumont* makes Adam and Eve the first model of this emblem of man's fallen condition:

> Ils voyoient partout des traces sanglantes de leur péché. Ils se souvenoient des biens ineffables qu'ils avoient goûtez . . . et ressentant les maux qu'ils s'étoient attirez eux-mêmes, cette triste comparaison qu'ils pourvoient faire infiniment mieux que nous par l'expérience et la lumière qui ne peut tomber dans aucun des hommes, les abîma dans une profonde douleur.[64]

Pascal has taken this theological commonplace and transformed it into the cornerstone of his *Apology*. By universalizing Adam's predicament ["Félicité de l'homme avec Dieu"/"Misère de l'homme sans Dieu" (40/6)], he turns the doctrine of the Fall to the uses of apology.

---

1. See Marie-Louise Hubert, *Pascal's Unfinished Apology*, chapter 1, for an overview of these various editions.

2. *Les Pensées de Pascal*, p. 140.
3. *La Genèse*, Préface, Seconde Partie, partie ii.
4. *La Genèse*, p. 234 (italics mine).
5. *Lettres chrestiennes*, 2:326–27.
6. "Car comme le péché est entré dans le monde par un seul homme, et la mort par le péché; ainsi la mort est passée dans tous les hommes par ce seul homme en qui tous ont péché" (Sacy's translation).
7. *La Genèse*, pp. 233–34.
8. *La Genèse*, p. 253.
9. *Lettres chrestiennes*, 2:326–28.
10. *La Genèse*, p. 247.
11. *La Genèse*, p. 247.
12. *La Genèse*, pp. 247–48.
13. *La Genèse*, pp. 248–49.
14. Cf. *Pensées*, fragment 238/206: "*Rem viderunt, causam non viderunt.*"
15. *La Genèse*, pp. 250–52.
16. *La Genèse*, Préface, Seconde Partie, partie ii.
17. *La Genèse*, pp. 108–9. Philo (54 B.C.), attempting to render the Old Testament acceptable to the Greek mentality of Alexandrian Jews, had formulated what would be known in the middle ages as "anagogical" exegesis. Long before him, the Greek philosophers, shocked by the morality of the Homeric epics, had allegorized the *Iliad* and the *Odyssey* in order to make the gods symbolize forces of nature or aspects of the soul. Philo, borrowing their method, turned all the characters of Genesis into symbols of vices or virtues.
18. *La Genèse*, p. 89.
19. *La Genèse*, p. 210.
20. *La Genèse*, p. 109.
21. *La Genèse*, p. 160 (italics mine).
22. *La Genèse*, p. 252.
23. *Les Pseaumes de David*, 1:547. Commentary on Psalm 48, v. 12.
24. *L'Histoire du Vieux et du Nouveau Testament, avec des explications édifiantes, tirées des Saint Pères . . . par le Sieur de Royaumont*, "figure" 4, p. 8. Long attributed to Sacy himself, the *Bible de Royaumont* is probably the work of Nicolas Fontaine.
25. *Lettres chrestiennes*, 2:331.
26. *La Genèse*, p. 196 (italics mine).
27. *La Genèse*, p. 168.
28. Cf. Romans 5:12–21.
29. *La Genèse*, p. 173.
30. *La Genèse*, p. 173–74.
31. *La Genèse*, p. 174. See Matthew 4:1–10.
32. *La Genèse*, pp. 174–75. Cf. Deuteronomy 8:3, 6:16, 6:13.
33. *La Sainte Bible . . . traduite en françois . . . avec de courtes notes tirées des Saints Pères*, Préface, p. i.
34. *La Sainte Bible*, Préface, p. i.
35. *La Sainte Bible*, Préface, p. xxviii.
36. *La Sainte Bible*, Préface, p. xxviii.
37. *La Genèse*, pp. 252–53. Cf. *Pensées*, fr. 164/131: "L'homme est plus inconcevable sans ce mystère, que ce mystère n'est inconcevable à l'homme." Sacy cites as his reference "*Pensées sur la Religion*, article 3." The Edition de Port-Royal, "article 3" of which includes the passage cited by Sacy, gives "inconcevable" instead of "incompréhensible."

38. See Philippe Sellier, *Pascal et Saint Augustin*, pp. 236–37.
39. Cf. the title of *liasse* XVIII/XVII, "Rendre la religion aimable."
40. Lafuma, p. 317.
41. Lafuma, p. 319 (italics mine).
42. *Pascal et Saint Augustin*, p. 254.
43. In the *Comparaison des chrétiens des premiers temps avec ceux d'aujourd'hui* (Lafuma, p. 361), Pascal explains that the modern church practices infant baptism in order to deliver unbaptized enfants from "la contagion du monde." Cf., Sacy, *La Genèse*, p. 248, for a discussion of "la contagion."
44. *Pascal et Saint Augustin*, p. 262.
45. Lafuma, p. 267.
46. *La Genèse*, Préface, Seconde Partie, partie ii.
47. Pascal devotes an entire *liasse*, "Fondements" (XIX/XVIII), to developing the idea of the specificity of Revelation.
48. *L'Histoire du Vieux et du Nouveau Testament*, figure 3, p. 6 (italics mine).
49. *La Sainte Bible*, Préface, p. i.
50. Cf. 1 Corinthians, 1:25: " . . . Ce qui paraît en Dieu une folie, est plus sage que la sagesse de tous les hommes" (Sacy's translation).
51. Sacy's argument in *La Genèse*, (pp. 247–50).
52. Brunschvicg, 12:ccxii. *Discours sur les pensées de M. Pascal où l'on essaie de faire voir quel était son dessein.*
53. Brunschvicg, 12:ccxii. Cf. fragment 159/126: "La coutume est une seconde nature qui détruit la première. Mais qu'est-ce que nature? Pourquoi la coutume n'est-elle pas naturelle? J'ai grand peur que cette nature ne soit elle-même qu'une première coutume, comme la coutume est une seconde nature."
54. Brunschvicg, 12:ccxiii.
55. Brunschvicg, 12:ccxiii.
56. Lafuma, p. 277.
57. *Pensées*, p. 104 n. 4. "Fecisti nos ad Te, et inquietum est cor nostrum donec requiescat in Te" (*Confessions* 1. i). Sellier observes that "Et depuis qu'il a perdu . . . à la nature tout ensemble" is a "lieu commun de la polémique chrétienne," a traditional theme that runs from Tertullian right up through the seventeenth century (p. 104 n. 5).
58. *Les Pensées de Pascal*, p. 298.
59. The use of "choux" to represent ordinary human activity has at least one literary precedent in Rabelais's account of the world discovered in Pantagruel's mouth (bk. 2, chap. 32).
60. One calls to mind particularly St. Paul's speech to the men of Athens in Acts 17:24–28.
61. *La Genèse*, p. 253.
62. See Sellier's "Index des Citations Bibliques de l'Oeuvre Pascalienne" in his *Pascal et la Liturgie*, p. 118. Two minor fragments, neither found in the two *Copies* nor destined for the *Apology*, cite Genesis 2 and 3. Fr. 795/959, written for the *Ecrits sur la Grâce*, records "*In quacumque die*" (Genesis 2:17): "*for in what day soever* thou shalt eat of it [the tree of knowledge of good and evil] thou shalt die" (Douay). Fr. 751/919, part of the *Mystère de Jésus*, cites Genesis 3:5: "*Eritis sicut dii scientes bonum et malum*," the serpent's promise to Eve. Neither of these citations can be taken as envisaging any major exposition of the Fall as a scriptural doctrine.
63. Lafuma, pp. 495–96; Brunschvicg, 12:ccviii–ccix.
64. *L'Histoire du Vieux et du Nouveau Testament*, figure 4, p. 8.

V

From *Expérience* to Revelation: The Role of the Fall in Pascal's Apologetic Strategy

ORDERING PASCAL'S ARGUMENT: THE *COPIES* AND THE "LIASSE TABLE DE 1658"

Fragment 660/820, set down subsequent to Pascal's ordering of his overall argument in the dossiers of 1658, contains a reflection that is particularly relevant to the way in which Pascal puts the doctrine of the Fall in the service of apology. Pascal distinguishes between two kinds of proofs, those carrying the force of reason, and those whose source is Revelation itself:

> Il y a deux manières de persuader les vérités de notre religion: l'une par la force de la raison, l'autre par l'autorité de celui qui parle.
> On ne se sert point de la dernière, mais de la première. On ne dit point: Il faut croire cela, car l'Ecriture, qui le dit, est divine. Mais on dit qu'il le faut croire par telle et telle raison, qui sont de faibles arguments, la raison étant flexible à tout. (660/820)

Why, I asked in chapter four, does Pascal never present an explicitly biblical exposition of the Fall? How, considering Sacy's insistence on a historical presentation of the doctrine, can the apologist sometimes present the Fall as if it were only a metaphor? Fragment 660/820 suggests that the answer to these questions lies in an examination of Pascal's apologetic strategy. The ultimate proofs of Christianity lie in Revelation. Yet one cannot begin by citing the authority of a document whose authenticity, in the mind of the interlocutor, remains far from certain. Arguments drawn from *expérience* and based upon "la force de la raison" are, of course, in the final analysis, "faibles, la raison étant flexible à tout." Yet such arguments, documented "par telle et telle raison," may be sufficiently plausible to convince the *libertin* that the proofs of Revelation at least warrant his consideration.

Sacy's proof of the Fall as outlined in the preceding chapter helps to bring Pascal's ultimate apologetic aim into sharper focus. In elucidating the doctrine of Original Sin in scriptural terms, Sacy is primarily interested in defending the historical integrity of the doctrine itself. Pascal, however, seeks to put that same doctrine in the service of a defense of the credibility of the whole of the Christian Revelation. He therefore avoids saying, with regard to the Fall, "Il faut croire cela, car l'Ecriture, qui le dit, est divine." Rather, making use of "la force de la raison," he attempts to demonstrate that the doctrine, taken in abstract terms, squares with a purely empirical analysis of the human condition. His aim is to effect a transition from an abstract idea illustrated by human experience to the specifically Christian doctrine of the Fall as revealed in Scripture.

The notion of transition presupposes that of order. To follow Pascal's transmutation of the idea of the Fall from *expérience* to Revelation, it will be necessary to follow a text of the *Pensées* that reflects the arrangement of Pascal's papers when he organized his overall argument. Editions of the *Pensées* that follow the example of the Edition de Port-Royal and class the fragments according to theme (including the edition of Brunschvicg), necessarily distort the original disposition of Pascal's argument.[1] Likewise, the editions of Chevalier, Dedieu, and Stewart—which attempt to reconstruct Pascal's plan for organizing his *Apology*—fail to reflect the order in which Pascal left his unfinished manuscript at the time of his death. Nor does the original autograph of the *Pensées* faithfully represent such an order. Pascal's papers had circulated in the form of an unbound manuscript for almost fifty years prior to Louis Périer's constitution of the *Recueil original* at the beginning of the eighteenth century. As Louis Lafuma observes, "le *Recueil original* ne donne pas . . . l'état des papiers de Pascal en 1662, mais leur état en 1710."[2]

Fortunately, there exist two manuscripts in the Bibliothèque National ("manuscrits français" 9203 and 12449) that do reflect the state in which Pascal left his papers at the time of his death: the *Première Copie* (C1), the basis of the Lafuma edition of the *Pensées*, and the *Seconde Copie* (C2), which has been presented for the first time in the recent edition (1976) of Philippe Sellier. These two *Copies*, transcriptions of Pascal's papers made under the direction of the Périer family shortly after the apologist's death, present an *Apology* sufficiently organized to merit preserving its original disposition. "La première chose que l'on fit," recounts Etienne Périer, "fut de . . . faire copier [les écrits] tels qu'ils étaient, et dans la même confusion qu'on les avait trouvés."[3]

When compared with corresponding pages in the *Recueil original*, the *Copies* have been found to reproduce scrupulously the original order of Pascal's paragraphs. Jean Mesnard observes: "On se trouve souvent en présence de véritables copies figurées; les fragments portés dans les marges de l'*Original* demeurent dans les marges."[4] Yet, whereas the *Recueil original* classes Pascal's arguments in no discernible order, the *Copies* reveal that Pascal had ordered the overall scheme of his *Apology* in twenty-seven provisional chapters. This classification, Mesnard points out, must be attributed to Pascal himself:

> Emettra-t-on l'hypothèse que ces unités auraient été constituées avec les originaux par les éditeurs? Pascal lui-même nous met en garde contre cette erreur. Dans plusieurs fragments écrits de sa main, il se réfère lui-même aux divisions que les *Copies* nous restituent, faisant allusion, rappelons-le, plus qu'à un *plan*, à un *classement*. Ainsi: "Il faut mettre au chapitre des Fondements ce qui est en celui des Figuratifs . . . " (Laf. 223), "Voyez Perpétuité" (Laf. 222).[5]

In order to be able to speak of Pascal's development of the idea of the Fall, it is not enough simply to know that it was Pascal himself who constituted the contents of each individual dossier in the classification of 1658. We must be sure that the *order* of the chapters as presented by the two *Copies* represents Pascal's intended sequence. A table that figures at the head of each of the *Copies* (see figure 6) was obviously used by the copyists to order the first twenty-seven *liasses*. Can this table, however, be attributed to Pascal himself? It does not figure in the *Recueil original*. Nor is an original version of this table in the hand of Pascal anywhere to be found.

Lafuma and Tourneur, the first editors to make use of the *Copies*, did not consider the "liasse-table" to reflect an arrangement of the titled dossiers that could be attributed to Pascal himself. No edition of the *Pensées* until that of Sellier ever included it as part of Pascal's text. Jean Mesnard's analysis of the table itself, however, has changed the direction of contemporary critical thought on the matter of Pascal's ordering of the first twenty-seven *liasses*. According to Mesnard, the table appearing in the two *Copies* is a "copie figurée." In other words, it is the copyist's reproduction of the exact disposition on the page of yet another table, presumably one in Pascal's own hand that at some point became lost from the *Recueil original*.

Mesnard first notes that the table is divided into two columns, "que le copiste a voulu égales," despite the fact that the second column contains more chapter headings than the first. The editor, he concludes, evidently sought to respect "non seulement le texte, mais la disposition d'un original précieux . . . ce qui ne se serait guère justifié si Pascal n'en était pas l'auteur." Second, Mesnard goes on to point out, the copyist reproduced and then struck out the chapter heading "Opinions du peuple saines," replacing it with the title "Raisons des effets," which appears at the head of the liasse itself. The copyist, as elsewhere in the two *Copies*, "a tenu à reproduire même les lignes rayées par Pascal, en les rayant à son tour: hésitation dont il n'y aurait eu aucun intérêt à garder le souvenir si elle avait été le fait des éditeurs."[6]

Mesnard's third argument is perhaps his most convincing. Whereas the

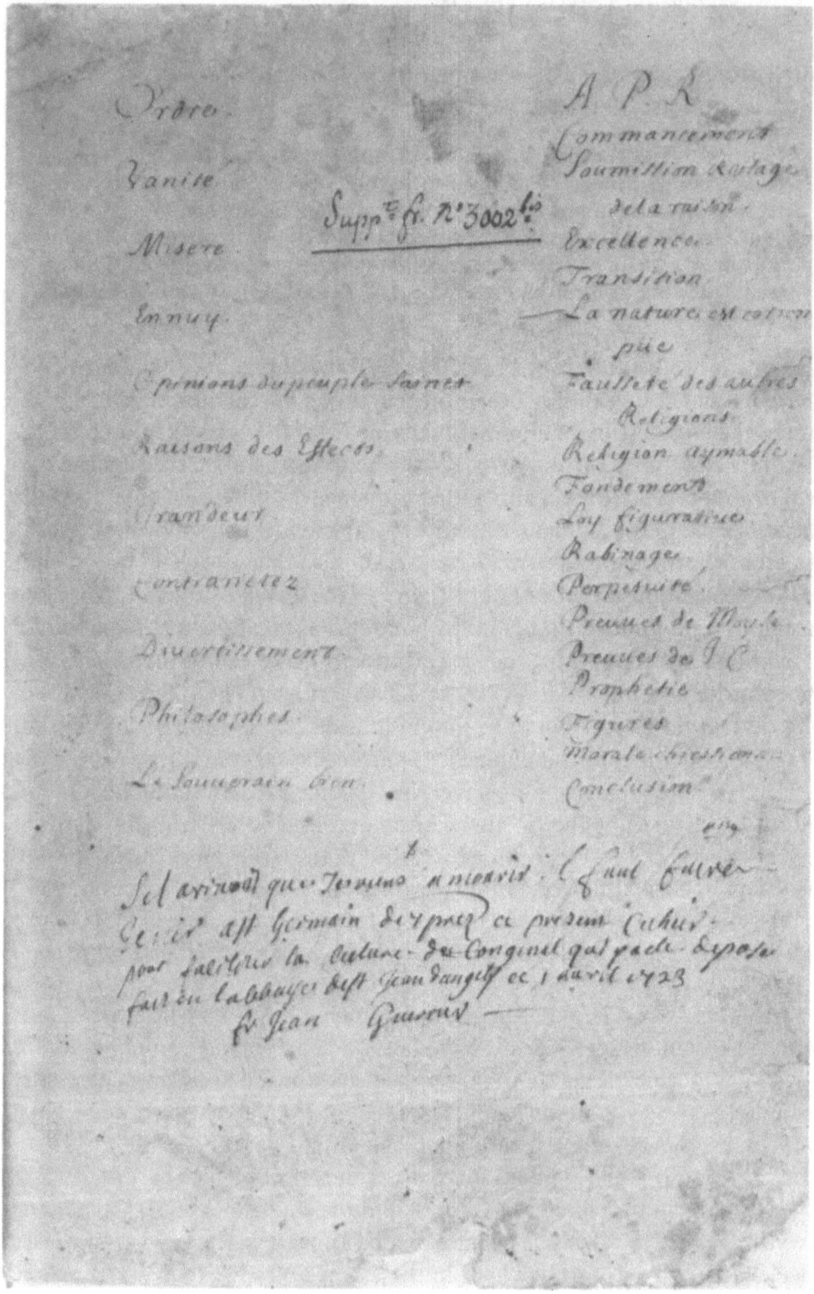

Ordre	A P R
	Commancement
Vanité	Soumission & usage
	de la raison
Misere	Excellence
	Transition
Ennuy	La nature est corrompue
Opinions du peuple saines	Faussete des autres Religions
Raisons des Effects	Religion aymable
	Fondement
Grandeur	Loy figurative
	Rabinage
Contrarietez	Perpetuité
	Preuves de Moyse
Divertissement	Preuves de J C
	Prophetie
Philosophes	Figures
	Morale chrestienne
Le Souverain bien	Conclusion

Supp.te fr. N° 3002 bis

S'il arrivoit que je meurs avant... [illegible annotation dated 1723, signed Jean...]

Figure 6. The "Liasse-Table" of 1658, as reproduced in the *Première Copie* (Bibliotheque Nationale, MS français 9203, 1° folio) (Service photographique, Bibliothèque Nationale)

Copies present twenty-seven titled *liasses*, the table records twenty-eight chapter headings. The additional heading, "La nature est corrompue," refers to a chapter that does not exist. Why, asks Mesnard, would the editors—supposing they had made up the table and arranged the *liasses*—have added such a title? On the basis of these three observations, Mesnard reaches a rather startling conclusion: "La table des matières est donc elle-même une *pensée*, la plus précise et la plus complète de toutes celles qui suggèrent un plan de l'*Apologie*."[7] In turn, Mesnard's judgment on the authenticity of the "liasse-table" serves to reinforce the credibility of his conclusions concerning the two *Copies*: "Lire les *Pensées* selon les enseignements tirés des *Copies*, c'est se rapprocher de Pascal autant qu'il est possible."[8]

Our present endeavor, tracing the *development* of Pascal's treatment of the Fall, would hardly be feasible were it not for Mesnard's resolution of the problem of the "table de matières." In following the order of the first twenty-seven *liasses* of Pascal's manuscript as recorded by the two *Copies*, we can be sure that we are following an order proposed by the apologist himself. This demonstration of Pascal's proposed transition from *expérience* to Revelation is constructed upon the assumption that the general order of Pascal's argument is no longer a matter of serious dispute.

Reading through the dossiers of 1658 in the order proposed by the "liasse-table," it soon becomes apparent that Pascal's arguments fall into two very distinct categories. Significantly enough, these two categories reflect the two columns of chapter titles of the "liasse-table." The ten titles in the left-hand column of the table constitute what M. Mesnard calls the "étape préparatoire" of Pascal's *Apology*: "Montrer que la religion chrétienne est 'vénérable' et 'aimable.' " The eighteen titles of the right-hand column, on the other hand, propose an "étape démonstrative": " 'montrer qu'elle est vraie.' "[9]

Pascal's two classes of arguments can be envisaged from another perspective, that of their documentation. Whereas the first ten chapters refrain from ever appealing to the authority of Revelation, the "étape démonstrative" is documented with an extensive series of citations drawn from Scripture. The dichotomy between proofs drawn from *expérience* and those drawn from Revelation suggested by the "liasse-table," however, may be highly misleading. It would be a mistake to see Pascal as taking refuge in Revelation for the simple reason that *expérience* can furnish no certain knowledge. Fideism, however appropriate a description of Montaigne's *Essais*, is far removed from the ultimate aim of Pascal's *Apology*.

The *liasses* of 1658 do not envisage two separate blocks of proofs, one drawn from human experience and another founded in Revelation. To the contrary, they chart an apologetic course that effects a transition from the uncertainty of *expérience* to the historical demonstrability of Revelation. The first five chapters of the "étape démonstrative" ("A.P.R."—"Transition") particularly serve to effect such a transition. The complete title of chapter XVI/XV, which stands at the head of the dossier itself, is of primary significance: "Transition de la connaissance de l'homme à Dieu." In effect, it describes the overall movement of the whole *Apology*.

No theme in the whole of the *Pensées* better reflects the idea of a transition from *expérience* to Revelation than Pascal's treatment of the Fall. In following its exposition throughout the course of the twenty-seven dossiers of 1658, we go directly to the heart of Pascal's apologetic method.

"MISERE"/"GRANDEUR": THE FALL PRESENTED AS PHILOSOPHICAL HYPOTHESIS

Chapters III/II-XI/X ("Vanité"-"Le Souverain Bien") approach the doctrine of the Fall in terms that deliberately avoid citing the authority of Scripture. The paradox "misère"/"grandeur," derived from an empirical analysis of the human condition, is made to stand in provisionally for the specifically Christian doctrine of Original Sin. Those chapters that document man's "Vanité," "Misère," and "Ennui" draw their illustrations principally from the *Essais* of Montaigne. In those rare instances in which Scripture is cited, it is cited not as something apart from human experience but as simply another piece of empirical documentation. "Salomon et Job ont le mieux connu et le mieux parlé de la misère de l'homme . . . l'un connaissant la vanité des plaisirs par *expérience*, l'autre la réalité des maux" (22/403;[10] italics mine).

Only in the dossier "Grandeur" (VII/VI) does Pascal first begin to suggest a paradox central to his apologetic strategy. Man's "misère," taken by itself, might suggest nothing contradictory about the human condition or mysterious about man's origins. Once man's "grandeur" is documented, however, a paradox emerges. Man's "grandeur" proceeds from his capacity for reason. "Je puis bien concevoir un homme sans mains, pieds, tête. . . . Mais je ne puis concevoir l'homme sans pensée. Ce serait une pierre ou une brute" (143/111). Yet it is this very reasoning capacity that enables man to recognize his own "misère." "Un arbre ne se connaît pais misérable" (146/114). "Ce qui est nature aux animaux, nous l'appelons misère en l'homme" (149/117). "La grandeur de l'homme est grande en ce qu'il se connaît misérable" (146/114).

Out of this paradox proceeds Pascal's first step in a demonstration of the relationship of the Fall to the human condition. Man's recognition of his "misère" implies his knowledge of some alternative to the present human condition. "Nous reconnaissons que, sa nature étant aujourd'hui pareille à celle des animaux, *il est déchu d'une meilleure nature qui lui était propre autrefois*" (149/117; italics mine). In other words, had man not fallen from some better state, he would have no reason to find fault with his present lot. Had he not some memory, however dim, of some happier existence, he would be unable to conceive of his present "misère."

Pascal does not attempt to draw any further conclusions from the argument he has just proposed. For the moment, he remains content simply to reinforce the credibility of his idea through two analogies. The first, drawn from the political sphere, is that of the "roi dépossédé." Making use of an episode recounted by Montaigne,[11] he contrasts the official who has been deprived of his post with the king who has lost his throne:

> Trouvait-on Paul Emile malheureux de n'être pas consul? Au contraire, tout le monde trouvait qu'il était heureux de l'avoir été, parce que sa condition n'était pas de l'être toujours. Mais on trouvait Persée si malheureux de n'être plus roi, parce que sa condition était de l'être toujours, qu'on trouvait étrange de ce qu'il supportait la vie. (149/117)

Pascal's example, aimed at illustrating the point that men only yearn for what was once rightfully theirs, derives its force from the notion of inherent kingship: "Qui se trouve malheureux de n'être pas roi, sinon un roi dépossédé?" (149/117).

Pascal's second illustration seeks to appeal to his interlocutor's basic common sense: "Qui se trouve malheureux de n'avoir qu'une bouche? Et qui ne se trouverait malheureux de n'avoir qu'un oeil? On ne s'est peut-être jamais avisé de s'affliger de n'avoir pas trois yeux, mais on est inconsolable de n'en point avoir" (149/117). Both Pascal's examples are drawn from concrete human experience. Both seek to reinforce the idea that man would not be aware of his present "misère" had he not fallen from a better state.

Pascal's interlocutor could have pointed out, of course, that men do in fact yearn for stations and possessions that they have never experienced themselves. Pascal does not record such an objection, but one suspects he intended it to be planted in the mind of his interlocutor. It is an objection that he answers in the chapter "Le Souverain Bien," where he explains that men seek a lost God in all their yearnings for created things (181/148).

In the chapter "Grandeur," the Fall remains on the level of metaphor, though a metaphor whose fitness in describing the human situation is attested to by the most fundamental of analogies drawn from common experience. Pascal's aim is to get his interlocutor to agree that man's present state cannot possibly be that of "autrefois." The apologist has not yet used the definition "péché originel," nor has he suggested that man himself is responsible for his present "misère." In the following dossier, Pascal takes his argument one step further. Introducing the term "péché originel," he begins to situate the Fall in a more specifically Christian context.

"Contrariétés" (VIII/VII) exploits the implications of the paradox "misère"/"grandeur" in order to reach the conclusion that the doctrine of the

Fall provides a plausible explanation of the total contradiction inherent in the human condition. Pascal begins by recapitulating an argument that he uses in the *Entretien*. The two principal schools of philosophy—the "dogmatistes" and the "pyrrhoniens"—while each having discerned one side of the proposition "misère"/"grandeur," have never been able to reconcile these two conflicting descriptions of the human condition. Pascal states the enigma of the human situation in terms of a "guerre ouverte" between these two philosophical positions. The "dogmatistes" argue that one cannot doubt "des principes naturels."[12] To which the Skeptics "opposent, en un mot, *l'incertitude de notre origine*, qui enferme celle de notre nature" (164/131; italics mine).

From the perspective of ordinary human reason, the impasse presented by these two conflicting philosophical positions is irresolvable. "Il faut que chacun prenne parti, et se range nécessairement ou au dogmatisme ou au pyrrhonisme, car qui pensera demeurer neutre sera pyrrhonien par excellence." Yet each of these positions obviously falls short of embracing the whole of the human condition. Neither is absolutely tenable:

> Que fera donc l'homme en cet état? Doutera-t-il de tout? Doutera-t-il s'il veille, si on le pince, si on le brûle? Doutera-t-il s'il doute? Doutera-t-il s'il est? On n'en peut venir là, et je mets en fait qu'il n'y a jamais eu de pyrrhonien effectif parfait. La nature soutient la raison impuissante et l'empêche d'extravaguer jusqu'à ce point.
>
> Dira-t-il donc au contraire qu'il possède certainement la vérité, lui qui, si peu qu'on le pousse, ne peut en montrer aucun titre et est forcé de lâcher prise? (164/131)

"La nature confond les pyrrhoniens et la raison confond les dogmatiques" (164/131).

Pascal extrapolates from this philosophical impasse what is perhaps his most memorable description of the enigma called man:

> Quelle chimère est-ce donc que l'homme, quelle nouveauté, quel monstre, quel chaos, quel sujet de contradiction, quel prodige, juge de toutes choses, imbécile ver de terre, dépositaire du vrai, cloaque d'incertitude et d'erreur, gloire et rebut de l'univers. (164/131)

He then immediately states the central question of the chapter "Contrariétés": "Qui démêlera cet embrouillement?" (164/131). The two most enlightened schools of human philosophy have failed to give satisfactory answers. What authority, what source of knowledge, therefore, can be called upon to help resolve the enigma of the paradox "misére"/ "grandeur"?

The *Entretien avec M. de Saci*, which poses this question in almost precisely the same terms, envisages a direct appeal to the authority of Scripture. A synthesis of Montaigne's skepticism and Epictetus' positivism, Pascal points out to Sacy, is out of the question. "Il ne résulterait de leur assemblage qu'une *guerre* et qu'une destruction générale":

> Car l'un établissant la certitude et l'autre le doute, l'un la grandeur de l'homme, et l'autre sa faiblesse, ils ruinent la vérité aussi bien que la fausseté l'un de l'autre. De sorte qu'ils ne peuvent subsister seuls à cause de leurs défauts, ni s'unir à cause de leurs oppositions, et qu'ainsi *[il faut qu']* ils se brisent et s'anéantissent pour faire place à la vérité de l'Evangile. C'est elle qui accorde les contrariétés par un art tout divin, et unissant tout ce qui est de vrai, et chassant tout ce qui est de faux, *elle en fait une sagesse véritablement céleste où s'accordent ces opposés, qui étaient incompatibles dans ces doctrines humaines.*[13]

At this point in the dossier "Contrariétés," Pascal indeed seems to have considered introducing the idea that Scripture alone can reconcile the conflicting truths of purely human philosophy. Immediately following the question "Qui démêlera cet embrouillement?" he originally set down—and then struck out—the following paragraph (see figure 7):

> *Certainement cela passe le dogmatisme et le pyrrhonisme et toute la philosophie humaine. L'homme passe l'homme. Qu'on accorde donc aux pyrrhoniens ce qu'ils ont tant crié, que la vérité n'est pas de notre portée ni de notre gibier, qu'elle ne demeure pas en terre, qu'elle est domestique du ciel, qu'elle loge dans le sein de Dieu et que l'on ne la peut connaître qu'à mesure qu'il lui plaît de la révéler. Apprenons donc de la vérité incréée et incarnée notre véritable nature.* (164/131)[14]

This similarity of this passage to the one just cited from the *Entretien* is striking. Though Scripture is not named, it is, of course, the source of what God has chosen to "révéler." "La vérité incréée et incarnée," the classical theological definition of the Second Person of the Trinity, embraces the written record of Christ's life on earth, i.e., the Gospel. Yet, in striking this passage, Pascal momentarily sets aside such a clear-cut dichotomy between *expérience* and Revelation. His apologetic strategy has undergone considerable refinement since the time of his conversation with Sacy. He is not yet ready to insist that only Revelation can clarify "notre véritable nature."

Pascal ultimately intends to present an explanation of man's present state that is grounded in the authority of Scripture. To do so at this point might mean losing the confidence of his interlocutor. Not yet having laid the groundwork for a historical proof of the credibility of the Bible, he cannot yet present the Fall in strictly historical terms. Nowhere in the section "Contrariétés" is there any mention of Genesis, the garden of Eden, or even of Adam.

Pascal's revised answer to the question "Qui démêlera cet embrouillement?" stops short of the appeal to Revelation traced in his first response. It aims at getting the *libertin* to look beyond the purely human and ordinarily rational sphere of things:

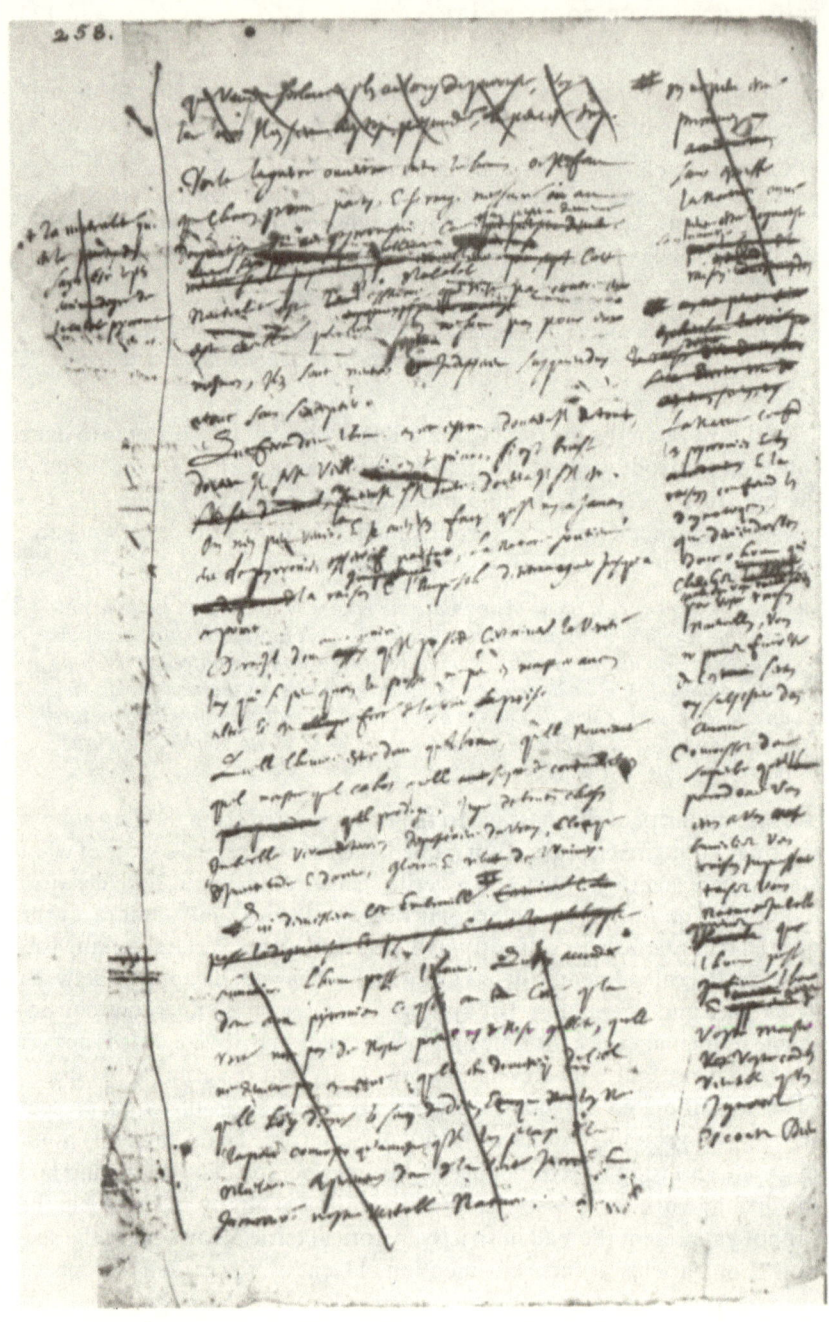

Figure 7. Passage suppressed in the dossier "Contrariétés" in the *Recueil original* (Bibliothèque Nationale, MS français 9202, folio 258) (Service photographique, Bibliothèque Nationale)

> La nature confond les pyrrhoniens et la raison confond les dogmatiques. Que deviendrez-vous donc, ô homme qui cherchez quelle est votre véritable condition *par votre raison naturelle?* Vous ne pouvez fuir une de ces sectes ni subsister dans aucune.
> Connaissez donc, superbe, quel paradoxe vous êtes à vous-même! Humiliez-vous raison impuissante! Taisez-vous, nature imbécile! Apprenez que l'homme passe infiniment l'homme et entendez de votre Maître votre condition véritable que vous ignorez.
> Ecoutez Dieu. (164/131; italics mine)

At this point, Pascal's text once again reminds us that we are dealing with a series of not totally finished arguments. "Ecoutez Dieu" seems to imply that some answer based upon divine inspiration is about to follow. Instead, Pascal picks up the Fall at the point at which he left off dealing with it in the *liasse* "Grandeur." He does not again take up the testimony of "la sagesse de Dieu" until the great "Prosopopée" of the chapter "A.P.R."

Pascal's shift in emphasis at this point reflects a change in his apologetic strategy. Following the admonition "Ecoutez Dieu," Pascal had originally written: "*N'est-il pas clair comme le jour que la condition de l'homme est double? Certainement*" (164/131). The section that follows this struck line reflects Pascal's hesitancy in assuming that, for his interlocutor, the implications of the paradox "misère"/"grandeur" are in fact "clair comme le jour." In the very next sentence, the apologist begins to recapitulate an argument already set forth in the dossier "Grandeur." His presentation of the Fall, far from being divorced from the evidence of *expérience*, is at this point deduced from the case already built for the paradox "misère"/"grandeur." Pascal, in effect, presents a closely argued explication of the idea that he has heretofore presented under the guise of the metaphor of the "roi dépossédé":

> Car enfin, si l'homme n'avait jamais été corrompu, il jouirait dans son innocence et de la vérité et de la félicité avec assurance. Et si l'homme n'avait jamais été que corrompu, il n'aurait aucune idée ni de la vérité, ni de la béatitude. Mais, malheureux que nous sommes, et plus que s'il n'y avait point de grandeur dans notre condition, nous avons une idée du bonheur et ne pouvons y arriver, nous sentons une image de la vérité et ne possédons que le mensonge, incapables d'ignorer absolument et de savoir certainement, tant il est manifeste que nous avons été dans un degré de perfection dont nous sommes malheureusement déchus. (164/131)

Every time Pascal takes up the theme of the Fall again in the course of the 27 *liasses* of 1658, he pushes the concept a bit further in the direction of an explicitly Christian doctrine. In "Contrariétés," he introduces the notion that the Fall is a paradox. The transmission of Original Sin to Adam's descendents, though an idea completely contrary to reason, clarifies what is most mysterious in the human condition. "Le noeud de notre condition prend ses replis et ses tours dans cet abîme" (164/131). Pascal's introduction of this paradox at this point has a twofold purpose. In the first place, the idea that the Fall illuminates the enigma "misère"/"grandeur" places the doctrine in the realm of that which is empirically confirmable. At the same time, Pascal's emphasis on the inherent obscurity of the Fall serves to remove the doctrine from the sphere of rational examination.

In his first draft of fragment 164/131, Pascal had gone on to describe the Fall as a doctrine accessible only through Revelation, as a principle that God has hidden from human intelligence:

> *D'où il paraît que Dieu, pour se réserver à soi seul le droit de nous instruire de nous-même, voulant nous rendre la difficulté de notre être inintelligible à nous-même, en a caché le noeud si haut ou pour mieux dire si bas, que nous étions bien incapables d'y arriver. De sorte que ce n'est pas par les superbes agitations de notre raison, mais par la simple soumission de la raison, que nous pouvons véritablement nous connaître.* (164/131)

Pascal's suppression of this passage hardly means that he has abandoned the position that the mystery of the Fall is fundamentally inaccessible to human reason. Sacy's commentaries on Genesis serve to remind us that this notion stands at the heart of neo-Augustinian theology. The experience of working with the *Copies* teaches us that when Pascal strikes a passage it is usually less because he is abandoning the idea than because he intends to use that idea elsewhere. This would seem the case in fragment 164/131. Pascal recognizes that in removing the Fall too far beyond the limits of human understanding, he risks alienating his interlocutor. Pascal has not yet introduced the idea that God has hidden himself in Revelation. Nor does he intend to until he has laid the groundwork for this principle in his exposition of how Scripture must be interpreted. "Le Dieu caché" will be presented as a biblical doctrine.

Pascal strikes two other ideas at the end of "Contrariétés" in the interest of his larger apologetic strategy. At this point, his plan originally called for a demonstration of how the theoretical implications of the paradox "misère"/"grandeur" square with the "fondements" of the Christian doctrine of Original Sin. From the formula "misère"/"grandeur," Pascal has deduced two propositions: (1) that man once enjoyed an existence superior to his present lot; and (2) that man somehow fell from this former state of "félicité." These propositions, Pascal intended to argue, square precisely with the "deux vérités" taught by the Christian doctrine of the Fall:

> *L'autorité inviolable de la religion nous* [fait] *connaître qu'il y a deux vérités de foi également constantes: l'une que l'homme dans l'état de la création . . . est élevé au-dessus de toute la nature, rendu comme semblable à Dieu et participant de la divinité. L'autre, qu'en l'état de la corruption et du péché il est déchu de cet état et rendu semblable aux bêtes. Ces deux propositions sont également fermes et certaines.* (164/131)

In striking this passage (see figure 8), Pascal anticipates the reaction of

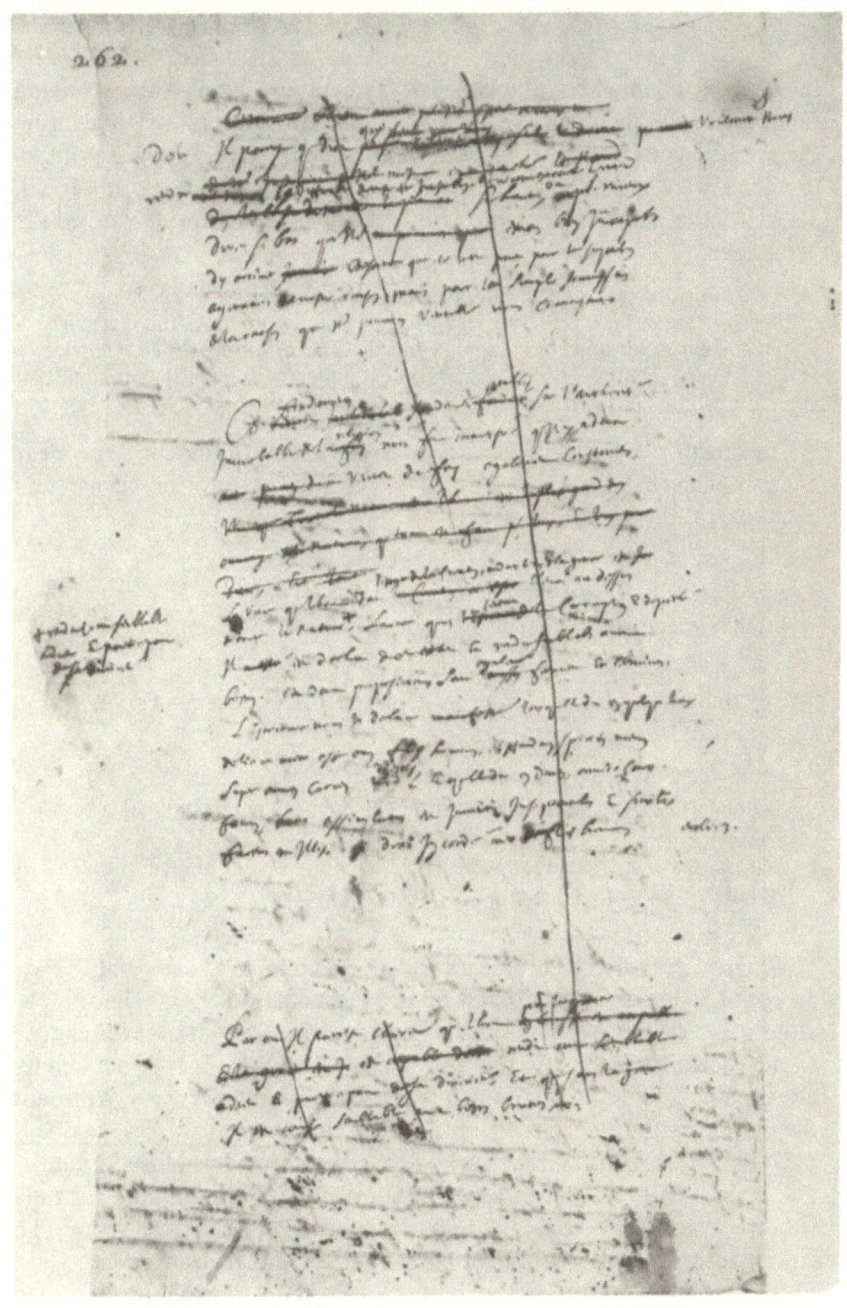

Figure 8. Scriptural citations crossed out in the dossier "Contrariétés" in the *Recueil original* (Bibliothèque Nationale, MS français 9202, folio 262) (Service photographique, Bibliothèque Nationale)

the *libertin*. To invoke "l'autorité inviolable de la religion" without having first established the credibility of such an authority would risk alienating the nonbeliever altogether. For the same reason, Pascal suppresses a second idea (see figure 8). Various passages in Scripture, he had observed, attest to the same two propositions as does the formula "misère"/"grandeur":

> *L'Ecriture nous les* [ces deux propositions] *déclare manifestement lorsqu'elle dit en quelques lieux*: Deliciae meae esse cum filiis hominum. Effundam spiritum meum super omnem carnem. Dii estis. Etc. *Et qu'elle dit en d'autres*: Omnis caro foenum. Homo assimilatus est jumentis insipientibus et similis factus est illis. Dixi in corde meo de filiis hominum.—*Eccl., 3*. (164/131)

The function of these six biblical verses in Pascal's argument seems clear enough. The first three attest to man's original state of innocence and communication with God:

> Proverbs 8:31: ". . . My delights were to be with the children of men";
> Joel 2:28: ". . . I will pour out my spirit upon all flesh";
> Psalm 81:6: "I have said: You are gods and all of you the sons of the most High."

The second three citations, on the other hand, underscore man's corruption since his fall from divine favor:

> Isaiah 40:6: "All flesh is grass";
> Psalm 48:12: "Man [when he was in honor did not understand; he] is compared to senseless beasts, and is become like to them";
> Ecclesiastes 3:18: "I said in my heart concerning the sons of men, that God would prove them, and show them to be like beasts."
> (Douay translation)

When he documents Scripture's recognition of man's "deux états," Pascal seems to be following no particular exegetical tradition.[15] His aim obviously is to establish the Fall as a biblical doctrine. Yet why does he choose to cite such diverse texts as Joel and Ecclesiastes? Why does he not simply cite Genesis 3? We can only conclude that Pascal is not yet ready to present the Fall in historical terms. The six biblical citations hardly serve to document the Fall as a historical event. Rather, they provide additional confirmation of man's dual condition as already expressed in the formula "misère"/"grandeur." Pascal, however, strikes what he has just written. To cite Scripture, he realizes, might necessitate an immediate demonstration of the credibility of the Bible. The apologist wants to avoid being drawn into such an argument prematurely.

Pascal's suppression of the three passages that we have just considered reveals a great deal about his apologetic method. Pascal shows calculated restraint when he refrains from invoking either "l'autorité inviolable de la religion" or the testimony of the Bible. He tailors his argument in order to anticipate the objections of the *libertin*. His strategy recalls fragment 660/820: "On ne dit point: Il faut croire cela, car l'Ecriture, qui le dit, est divine. Mais on dit qu'il le faut croire par telle et telle raison." By exploiting the implications of the formula "misère"/"grandeur," Pascal seeks to persuade the *libertin* that the Fall is a potentially credible hypothesis. A direct exposition of Genesis 3 could never achieve this end. At this point in the dialogue, the *libertin* still views Genesis as but a collection of myths.

"A.P.R.": THE TRANSITION TO REVELATION

The foregoing hypothesis concerning Pascal's suppression of a historical presentation of the Fall finds a confirmation in the disposition of the chapter "A.P.R." The *Copies* reveal that Pascal once again strikes arguments that might cause him to be drawn into a discussion of the historical credibility of Genesis. "A.P.R." (XII/XI) picks up Pascal's argument at precisely the point where "Contrariétés" leaves off. *Liasse* VIII/VII concludes with the idea of "incompréhensibilité": "Sans ce mystère le plus incompréhensible de tous nous sommes incompréhensibles à nous-mêmes" (164/131). "A.P.R." commences with the following notation: "Après avoir expliqué l'incompréhensibilité."

"A.P.R." is a chapter of transition. Philippe Sellier describes the *liasse* as "une plaque tournante dans le projet d'*Apologie*: concluant la réflexion anthropologique des liasses III-XI [II-X], elle annonce une recherche plus proprement religieuse."[16] After restating the major conclusion of "Contrariétés"—that the paradox "misère"/"grandeur" implies man's fall from "un degré de perfection"—"A.P.R." places this idea in a new perspective, that of "la véritable religion." Jean Mesnard gives a particularly useful description of the interrelationship between these two chapters:

> De l'analyse de l'homme se déduisent donc certains caractères de la véritable religion: elle devra obligatoirement expliquer les "effets" observés. C'est à quoi satisfait le christianisme, selon l'esquisse de raisonnement proposée dans le chapitre *Contrariétés* et développée dans le fragment *A.P.R.* La "Sagesse de Dieu" ouvre le principe qui fait "reconnaître la cause de tant de contrariétés qui ont étonné tous les hommes et qui les ont partagés en de si divers sentiments." Ce principe se résume dans le fait de la chute: "Vous n'êtes plus maintenant dans l'état où je vous ai formés."[17]

Pascal has laid the groundwork for the idea of "la véritable religion" in the three *liasses* that intervene between "Contrariétés" and "A.P.R." "Divertissement" (IX/VIII) has served as a forceful illustration of fallen man's attempt to regain what he lost in the Fall through terrestrial pursuits. "Philosophes" (X/IX) has recapitulated Pascal's arguments concerning the inability of reason and philosophy to explain or to resolve the enigma "misère"/"grandeur." "Le Souverain Bien" (XI/X) has postulated the hypothesis that the search for a lost Creator is at the root of all human activity.

All three of these chapters orient the nonbeliever in the direction of Revelation. They seek to demonstrate that man is inherently incapable of working out his own salvation. "Divertissement" documents the ultimate folly of terrestrial pursuits. The philosophers, though recognizing this folly, have counseled an equally useless course:

> Notre instinct nous fait sentir qu'il faut chercher notre bonheur hors de nous. Nos passions nous poussent au-dehors, quand même les objets ne s'offriraient pas pour les exciter. Les objets du dehors nous tentent d'eux-mêmes et nous appellent, quand même nous n'y pensons pas. Et *ainsi les philosophes ont beau dire: "Rentrez-vous en vous mêmes, y trouverez votre bien." On ne les croit pas. Et ceux qui les croient sont les plus vides et les plus sots.* (176/143; italics mine)

Man's search for "le souverain bien" is the key to the enigma posed by the paradox "misère"/"grandeur." It is the most telling symptom of man's fallen state:

> Qu'est-ce donc que nous crie cette avidité et cette impuissance, sinon qu'il y a eu autrefois dans l'homme un véritable bonheur, dont il ne lui reste maintenant que la marque et la trace toute vide, et qu'il essaie inutilement de remplir de tout ce qui l'environne? (181/148)

At the beginning of "A.P.R." (see figure 9), Pascal restates "misère"/"grandeur" as the very enigma that "la véritable religion" would have to resolve:

> Les grandeurs et les misères de l'homme sont tellement visibles qu'il faut nécessairement que la véritable religion nous enseigne et qu'il y a quelque grand principe de grandeur en l'homme et qu'il y a un grand principe de misère. Il faut encore qu'elle nous rende raison de ces étonnantes contrariétés. (182/149)

Taking up the Fall once again, Pascal presents this very doctrine as meeting the requirements that he has just set down. In "Contrariétés," the proposition "man is not in the state of his creation" was deduced from the testimony of human experience. In "A.P.R.," however, it is "la Sagesse de Dieu" that reveals a mystery that neither reason nor philosophy has been able to penetrate. "N'attendez point, dit-elle, ô hommes, ni vérité ni consolation des hommes. Je suis celle qui vous ai formés et qui peux seule vous apprendre qui vous êtes" (182/149).

"La Sagesse de Dieu" is Pascal's personification of Revelation. The "'Prosopopée," in which Divine Wisdom addresses men directly, is a literary form borrowed from the first and eighth chapters of Proverbs. Pascal makes use of this convention, which allows him momentarily to set aside the whole question of the historicity of Revelation, to demonstrate that the Christian doctrine of the Fall squares exactly with the criteria that "la véritable religion" would have to satisfy.

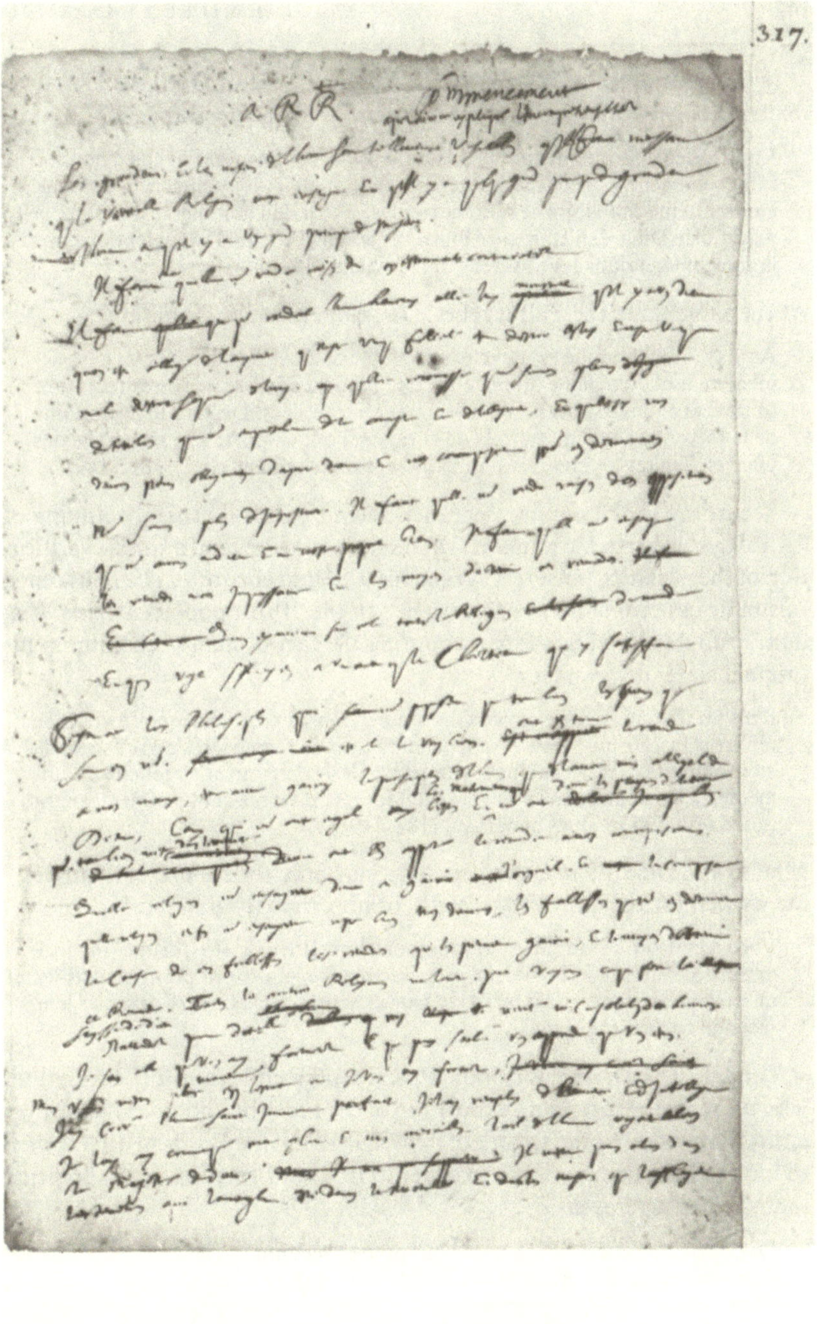

Figure 9. First page of "A.P.R." in the *Recueil original* (Bibliothèque Nationale, MS français 9202, folio 317) (Service photographique, Bibliothèque Nationale)

In its description of man as created in the image of God, the Christian doctrine of the Fall incorporates a "grand principe de grandeur":

> Vous n'êtes plus maintenant en l'état où je vous ai formés. J'ai créé l'homme saint, innocent, parfait. Je l'ai rempli de lumière et d'intelligence. Je lui ai communiqué ma gloire et mes merveilles. L'oeil de l'homme voyait alors la majesté de Dieu. Il n'était pas alors dans les ténèbres qui l'aveuglent, ni dans la mortalité et dans les misères qui l'affligent. (182/149)

At the same time, the Fall teaches "un grand principe de misère":

> Aujourd'hui l'homme est devenu semblable aux bêtes et dans un tel éloignement de moi qu'à peine lui reste-t-il une lumière confuse de son auteur, tant toutes ces connaissances ont été éteintes ou troublées. Les sens indépendants de la raison et souvent maîtres de la raison l'ont emporté à la recherche des plaisirs. Toutes les créatures ou l'affligent ou le tentent. . . . (182/149)

According to the requirements set down by Pascal at the beginning of "A.P.R.," "la véritable religion" would have to go beyond a simple verification of the paradox "misère"/"grandeur." "Il faut encore qu'elle nous rende raison de ces étonnantes contrariétés." In the "Prosopopée," Divine Wisdom resolves this enigma by recounting the fact of man's rebellion in his original state of "grandeur":

> Il n'a pu soutenir tant de gloire sans tomber dans la présomption, il a voulu se rendre centre de lui-même et indépendant de mon secours. Il s'est soustrait de ma domination et, s'égalant à moi par le désir de trouver sa félicité en lui-même, je l'ai abandonné à lui, et révoltant les créatures qui lui étaient soumises je les lui ai rendues ennemies. (182/149)

Man's fall from divine favor accounts, not only for his present "misère," but as well for the "trace toute vide" of his original "grandeur":

> Voilà l'état où les hommes sont aujourd'hui. Il leur reste quelque instinct impuissant du bonheur de leur première nature, et ils sont plongés dans les misères de leur aveuglement et de leur concupiscence qui est devenue leur seconde nature. (182/149)

Though it is Divine Wisdom, Pascal's personification of Revelation, who presents the foregoing exposition of the Fall, the apologist has not yet entirely abandoned the sphere of *expérience*. Divine Wisdom directs men to look to human experience in order to find confirmation of the doctrine that she has just revealed:

> De ce principe que je vous ouvre vous pouvez reconnaître la cause de tant de contrariétés qui ont étonné tous les hommes et qui les ont partagés en de si divers sentiments. *Observez maintenant tous les mouvements de grandeur et de gloire que l'épreuve de tant de misères ne peut étouffer, et voyez s'il ne faut pas que la cause en soit en une autre nature.* (182/149; italics mine)

Pascal is not yet ready to anchor the doctrine of the Fall in sacred history. "La Sagesse de Dieu" makes no specific reference to any of the historical details of Genesis' account of the Fall.[18] On close examination, we find that the first "prosopopée" is closely modeled after those very biblical citations suppressed at the end of "Contrariétés." "Je l'ai rempli de lumière" recalls Joel 2:28. "Je lui ai communiqué ma gloire" represents the same idea as "Dii estis" (Psalm 81:6). "L'oeil de l'homme voyait alors la majesté de Dieu" recalls Proverbs 8:31. Likewise, those citations that were to document man's corruption reappear in Divine Wisdom's narrative. "Dans la mortalité" reflects Isaiah 40:6. "L'homme est devenue semblable aux bêtes" recalls Psalm 48:12 and Ecclesiastes 3:18.[19] These ideas, however, in their present development in "A.P.R.," avoid a specifically scriptural exposition.

The *Copies* reveal that in "A.P.R." Pascal once again considered invoking the authority of Scripture. A second version of the "prosopopée," labeled "A.P.R. pour demain," contains a struck passage of great significance. This second version begins by elaborating the idea that God alone has knowledge of man's origins:

> C'est en vain, ô hommes, que vous cherchez dans vous-mêmes le remède à vos misères. Toutes vos lumières ne peuvent arriver qu'à connaître que ce n'est point dans vous-mêmes que vous trouverez ni la vérité ni le bien. Les philosophes vous l'ont promis et ils n'ont pu le faire.
> Ils ne savent ni quel est votre véritable bien, ni quel est votre véritable état. (182/149)

The lines that follow, struck in the manuscript (see figure 10) and the *Copies*, represent a very different apologetic strategy than that traced by the first "prosopopée":

> *Je suis la seul qui puis vous apprendre et quel est votre véritable bien [et quel est votre véritable état]. Je les enseigne à ceux qui m'écoutent, et les Livres que j'ai mis entre les mains des hommes les découvrent bien nettement. Mais je n'ai pas voulu que cette connaissance fût si ouverte. J'apprends aux hommes ce qui les peut rendre heureux: pourquoi refusez-vous de m'ouïr?* (182/149)

Nowhere in the *Pensées* do we find a better statement of Pascal's vision of the nature of Revelation. Yet why does the apologist stop short of identifying the source of the Christian doctrine of the Fall as "les Livres que j'ai mis entre les mains des hommes"? We must posit the same explanation that we proposed to explain Pascal's suppression of similar passages at the end of "Contrariétés." Since the authority of the Bible has yet to be demonstrated, Pascal refrains from presenting the Fall as a scriptural doctrine. To invoke the testimony of Scripture is to encounter "le Dieu caché": "Je n'ai pas voulu que cette connaissance fût si ouverte" (182/149).

In "A.P.R.," Pascal is still primarily concerned with prompting the *liber-*

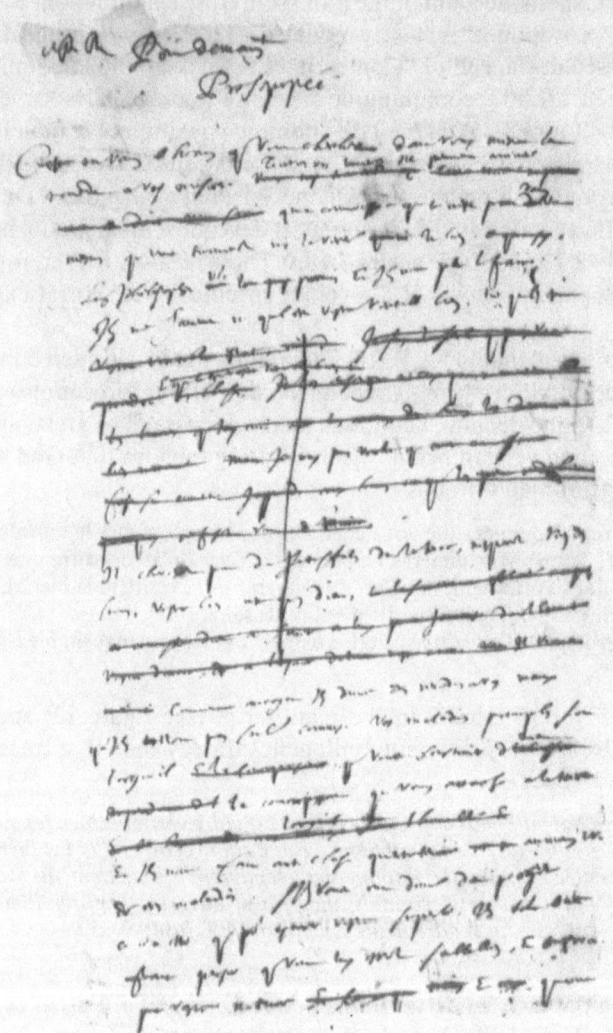

Figure 10. "Prosopopée" from "A.P.R." (Bibliothèque Nationale, MS français 9202, folio 321); page from the *Recueil original* showing lines suppressed by Pascal (Service photographique, Bibliothèque Nationale)

tin to consider the arguments of Revelation. He has not yet abandoned the sphere of *expérience*. "La Sagesse de Dieu," the personification under which Revelation is first introduced in the *Apology*, invites men to verify the doctrine of the Fall by examining themselves: "Ces deux états étant ouverts, il est impossible que vous ne les reconnaissiez pas. *Suivez vos mouvements, observez-vous yous-même, et voyez si vous n'y trouverez pas les caractères vivants de ces deux natures.*"[20]

Divine Wisdom's exposition of the Fall represents a critical juncture in Pascal's projected *Apology*. "A.P.R." indeed brings to an end the anthropological reflections of *liasses* III-XI [II-X] and announces the beginning of an "étape démonstrative." Pascal's transition from experience to Revelation, however, is by no means yet completed. Significantly enough, the chapter that follows "A.P.R." bears the title "Commencement." From the perspective of Pascal's apologetic strategy, we are indeed presented with a new beginning. In the next four chapters ("Commencement"—"Transition"), the apologist will lay the groundwork for a historical proof of Revelation.

THE "CONFERENCE" OF 1658: THE TESTIMONY OF ETIENNE PERIER AND FILLEAU DE LA CHAISE

The passages crossed out by Pascal in the *liasse* "A.P.R." appear all the more significant when considered in the light of two contemporary accounts of the apologist's own description of his projected *Apology*. The title "A.P.R." has long been taken to stand for "à Port-Royal" and the *liasse* itself to be Pascal's notes for a summary of his project delivered to the "Solitaires" in 1658. This "conférence," critics have always assumed, is the same one described by Etienne Périer in his *Préface* to the Edition de Port-Royal and by Filleau de la Chaise in his *Discours sur les Pensées de M. Pascal*. Yet, when one compares these two accounts with "A.P.R.," striking differences emerge. The very appeal to the testimony of Scripture suppressed in "A.P.R." occupies a place of central importance in the accounts of Périer and Filleau.

In his *Préface* (1670), Etienne Périer recounts that Pascal, "il y a environ dix ou douze ans," had presented an "abrégé," "de vive voix," of his projected *Apology*:

> Il le fit donc en présence et à la prière de plusieurs personnes très considérables de ses amis. Il leur développa en peu de mots le plan de tout son ouvrage; il leur représenta ce qui en devait faire le sujet et la matière; il leur en rapporta en abrégé les raisons et les principes, et leur expliqua l'ordre et la suite des choses qu'il y voulait traiter.[21]

Périer's account of Pascal's "plan de tout son ouvrage" closely mirrors the arrangement of the dossiers of 1658. The apologist "entreprit de montrer que la religion chrétienne avait autant de marques de certitude et d'évidence que les choses qui sont reçues dans le monde pour les plus indubitables." "Pour entrer dans ce dessein," Pascal began with "une peinture de l'homme" that in fact corresponds to his exposition of the paradox "misère"/"grandeur" in *liasses* III–XII [II–XI]. The purpose of this "peinture" was to convince the *libertin* that he must look beyond the limits of his own experience: "Après avoir ainsi connu ce qu'il est, [il doit souhaiter] de connaître d'où il vient et ce qu'il doit devenir."[22]

Périer gives far greater attention to the "étape démonstrative" of the *Apology* than to the arguments designed to trouble the *libertin*. To "misère"/"grandeur" and the other arguments that make up *liasses* III–XII [II–XI], he devotes only a cogent summary. His essential emphasis focuses on the historical proofs of *liasses* XVIII–XXV [XVI–XXIV]. Périer gives the impression that Pascal, in the "conférence" that "A.P.R." supposedly envisages, was primarily concerned with outlining a series of historical proofs of Christianity.

"L'ayant mis dans cette disposition de chercher à s'instruire sur un doute si important," Périer continues, Pascal next proposed presenting his interlocutor with the conclusions of the "philosophes." When these failed to shed any light on man's origins and destiny, the apologist then suggested that the *libertin* consider the explanations of various religions. "Il lui fait ensuite parcourir tout l'univers et tous les âges, pour lui fair remarquer une infinité de religions." When all these religions as well were shown to contain nothing but "vanités," "folies," "erreurs," "égarements," and "extravagances," Pascal then introduced his primary historical argument. He called the *libertin*'s attention to the singular circumstances surrounding the religion and history of the Jews.[23]

Up until this point, Périer has not gone into detail concerning Pascal's precise arguments. When he recalls that Pascal drew his hearers' attention to the "circonstances si extraordinaires" surrounding "le peuple juif," Périer, as if to reflect Pascal's own emphasis, suddenly enters into the particulars of Pascal's arguments. "Après lui avoir représenté tout ce que ce peuple a de singulier, il s'arrête particulièrement à lui faire remarquer un livre unique par lequel il se gouverne, et qui comprend tout ensemble son histoire, sa loi et sa religion."[24]

In Périer's account of Pascal's apologetic strategy, the *libertin* finds the explanation of the paradox "misère"/"grandeur" in the "livre unique" of the Jews. "*A peine a-t-il ouvert ce livre*, qu'il y apprend que le monde est l'ouvrage d'un Dieu et que c'est ce même Dieu qui a créé l'homme à son image." When the *libertin* compares this description of man with the "peinture" that the apologist has already drawn, he realizes that man today "est bien éloigné de posséder tous ces avantages qu'il a du avoir lorsqu'il est sorti des mains de son auteur." This contradiction, however, is at once resolved "*dès qu'il poursuit la lecture de ce même livre*":

Il y trouve qu'après que l'homme eût été crée de Dieu dans l'état d'innocence . . . la première action qu'il fit fut de se révolter contre son créateur, et d'employer tous les avantages qu'il en avait reçus pour l'offenser.[25]

According to Périer, Pascal's exegesis of what his interlocutor has just read in Genesis 3 was to provide a simple and direct explanation of the enigma "misère"/"grandeur":

> M. Pascal lui fait alors comprendre que ce crime ayant été le plus grand de tous les crimes en toutes ses circonstances, il [l'homme] avait été puni non seulement dans ce premier homme, qui, étant déchu par là de son état, tomba tout d'un coup *dans la misère*, dans la faiblesse, dans l'erreur et dans l'aveuglement; mais encore dans tous ses descendants, à qui ce même homme a communiqué et communiquera encore sa corruption dans toute la suite des temps.[26]

Pascal would have gone on to point out to his interlocutor that "cette vérité" (i.e., the Fall) is attested to by "divers endroits de ce livre." After Genesis' account of Adam's fall, the Bible no longer speaks of man's "grandeur." "Il n'y est plus parlé de l'homme que par rapport à cet état de faiblesse et de désordre." Rather, Scripture insists "souvent" that "toute chair est corrompue," that "les hommes sont abandonnés à leurs sens" and that all men are afflicted with "une pente au mal dès leur naissance."[27]

Périer's account of Pascal's "conférence" reflects the central argument of both "Contrariétés" and "A.P.R." According to Périer, Pascal intended to point out to the *libertin* "que cette première chute est la source, non seulement de tout ce qu'il y a de plus incompréhensible dans la nature de l'homme, mais aussi d'une infinité d'effets qui sont hors de lui, et dont la cause est inconnue."[28] At the same time, however, Pascal's "discours" makes use of a demonstration that is consciously suppressed in the text of the *Pensées*.

Périer presents Pascal as grounding his explanation of the enigma "misère"/"grandeur" in an exegesis of the first three chapters of Genesis. "A.P.R." suppresses all references to Scripture, striking Divine Wisdom's appeal to the authority of "les Livres que j'ai mis entre les mains des hommes." Those "divers endroits de ce livre" that Pascal cites in Périer's account correspond to the very biblical citations struck by Pascal at the end of "Contrariétés." Etienne Périer presents Pascal as making use of the very scriptural exposition of the Fall whose absence we have documented in the *liasses* of 1658.

The same differences that make one wonder if Etienne Périer is really describing the "conférence" supposedly envisaged by "A.P.R." tend to confirm the credibility of his account. Much of what Périer recounts might have been fabricated from the text of the Edition de Port-Royal of the *Pensées*. On the other hand, the tactic of presenting the *libertin* with Genesis' account of the Fall nowhere figures in Périer's text of the *Pensées*. The two principal passages in which Pascal reveals that he was considering such a strategy—"les Livres que j'ai mis entre les mains des hommes" and the list of scriptural citations that corresponds to Périer's "divers endroits"—did not appear at all in the Edition de Port-Royal. Struck in the original manuscript, these passages were apparently considered by the editors of the first edition of the *Pensées* to be ideas rejected by Pascal. The scriptural exposition of the Fall recounted by Périer either is a complete fabrication or else represents an argument outlined by Pascal himself "de vive voix."

Lafuma advances the theory that Etienne Périer made use of Filleau de la Chaise's *Discours sur les Pensées de M. Pascal* in composing his account of Pascal's "conférence" of 1658.[29] If this is the case, and Filleau can be taken to be the more reliable witness of the two, there emerges an even greater contrast between "A.P.R." and the "conférence" it supposedly envisages. From start to finish, Filleau's emphasis is on Pascal's exposition of a historical demonstration of Christianity. Filleau relegates the arguments of the "étape préparatoire" to a place of secondary importance. The theme "misère"/"grandeur"—which occupies ten chapters in the dossiers of 1658—appears only in truncated form in Filleau's account.

According to Filleau, Pascal was primarily concerned with impressing upon his audience the demonstrable character of his projected defense of Christianity. The apologist first of all rejected those metaphysical proofs customarily employed by theologians as "peu proportionnées à l'état naturel du coeur humain." Arguing that the vast majority of men "ont la tête peu propre aux raisonnements métaphysiques," Pascal "montra clairement qu'il n'y a que les preuves morales et historiques, et de certains sentiments qui viennent de la nature et de l'expérience qui soient de leur portée."[30]

Metaphysical proofs, Pascal had gone on to show, are not those that are commonly accepted as leading to certainty and on which are founded "les choses qui sont reconnues dans le monde pour les plus certaines." Using such proofs, for example, one would have great difficulty ever proving that the city of Rome actually exists, that Mohammed ever lived, or that the Great Fire of London ever took place.[31] "Cependant ce serait être fou d'en douter, et de ne pas exposer sa vie là-dessus pour peu qu'il y eût à gagner":

> Les voies par où nous acquérons ces sortes de certitudes, pour n'être pas géométriques, n'en sont pas moins infaillibles, et ne nous doivent pas moins porter à agir: et ce n'est même que là-dessus que nous agissons presque en toutes choses.[32]

According to Filleau, Pascal's proof of the credibility of Christianity was to be of the same order as those proofs commonly accepted by men in everyday life.

Filleau tells us that Pascal began by painting the human condition in terms of the paradox "misère"/"grandeur":

Jamais ceux qui ont le plus méprisé l'homme n'ont poussé si loin son imbécillité, sa corruption, ses ténèbres; et jamais sa grandeur et ses avantages n'ont été portés si haut par ceux qui l'ont le plus relevé.[33]

Pascal then sketched the inability of philosophy to resolve this paradox. If certain philosophers had reached the conclusion "que les hommes naissent méchants, aucun ne s'était avisé d'en dire la raison, ni même de la chercher."[34]

At this point, Pascal would have suggested that perhaps an "auteur" of mankind exists who might be able to afford men "des marques de leur origine" and to explain what "dessein il aurait eu en leur donnant l'être." This possiblity means the *libertin*'s examining an "infinité de religions" claiming knowledge of God the Creator. None is found to provide any answer. Some of these religions are found to worship gods "plus ridicules que les hommes." Others could be demonstrated to contain "rien de surnaturel" or to be "sans preuves." Only when the *libertin* was "près de tomber dans le désespoir" would Pascal have revealed the existence of "un certain peuple" meriting his attention "par quantité de circonstances merveilleuses et uniques."[35]

Like Etienne Périer, Filleau assigns singular importance to an argument that does not at all figure in "A.P.R.": the unique historical character of the Pentateuch. Pascal would have pointed out to his *libertin* that only the Jews, among all the peoples of the earth, have conserved their history and genealogy intact from the beginning of the world:

> Ce sont des gens sortis d'un même homme, et qui ayant toujours eu un soin extraordinaire de ne point s'allier avec les autres nations et de conserver leur généalogies, peuvent donner au monde, plutôt qu'aucun autre peuple, une histoire digne de créance, puisque enfin ce n'est proprement que l'histoire d'une seule famille, qui ne peut être sujette à confusion; mais pourtant d'une famille si nombreuse, que s'il s'était mêlé de l'imposture, il serait impossible, comme les hommes sont faits, que quelqu'un d'eux ne l'eût découverte et publiée; outre que cette histoire étant la plus ancienne de toutes, elle n'a pu rien emprunter des autres, et que par cela seul elle mérite une vénération particulière.[36]

Filleau de la Chaise recounts a scheme whereby Pascal would have established the historical credibility of Genesis before proceeding to an exposition of how the Fall resolves the enigma "misère"/"grandeur." The *libertin*, "ravi de cette découverte, et résolu de la pousser comme sa dernière ressource," would have discovered that in the same "livre unique" that recounts the history of the Jews, "il y trouve aussi celle de la naissance du monde." Continuing his reading, the *libertin* would have learned that God had created Adam in his own image, "libre dans ses jugements et dans ses actions," but that Adam had made use of "ce présent si précieux de la liberté" "à violer le premier commandement qu'il en avait reçu."[37]

As in Etienne Périer's account of Pascal's "conférence," a straightforward exegesis of Genesis 3 serves to explain man's present dual condition. If man's aspirations to "grandeur" can be seen to be the product of his clouded memory of his former state, his "misère" can be shown to be the direct result of Adam's rebellion:

> Il n'est pas besoin d'exagération pour persuader, ni beaucoup de lumière pour comprendre que ç'a été le plus grand de tous les crimes, en toutes ses circonstances. Aussi fut-il puni comme il méritait . . . il perdit en ce moment tous les avantages dont il n'avait pas voulu bien user; son esprit se remplit de nuages; Dieu se cacha pour lui dans une nuit impénétrable; il devint le jouet de la concupiscence et l'esclave du péché; de tout ce qu'il avait de lumière et de connaissance, il n'en conserva qu'un désir impuissant de connaître, qui ne servit plus qu'à le tourmenter . . . il devint ce monstre incompréhensible qu'on appelle l'homme; et communiquant de plus sa corruption à tout ce qui sortit de lui, il peupla l'univers de misérables, d'aveugles et de criminels comme lui.[38]

Filleau attributes to Pascal an additional proof of the authenticity of Genesis' account of the Fall. This argument, which does not figure in the original text of the *Pensées*, concerns the supernatural character of the Bible's account:

> Ces grandes idées sont d'un caractère tout différent de ce que l'esprit humain est capable de produire. Mais parce que les hommes sont faits de telle sorte, que dès qu'ils sont accoutumés aux choses, ils ne peuvent presque plus juger s'ils étaient capables ou non de les imaginer. . . . Qu'ils croient, s'ils le peuvent, qu'il n'y a nulle impossibilité que Moïse et ceux qui l'ont suivi . . . aient pu avancer de leur tête une chose aussi incompréhensible que le péché originel, et qui paraît si contraire à la justice de Dieu.[39]

Curiously enough, a quite similar exposition of this same idea appears in the Edition de Port-Royal of the *Pensées* under the chapter heading "Moïse":

> Moïse était habile homme. Cela est clair. Donc, s'il eût eu dessein de tromper, il eût fait en sorte qu'on ne l'eût pu convaincre de tromperie. Il a fait tout le contraire; car s'il eût débité des fables, il n'y eût point eu de Juif qui n'en eût pu reconnaître l'imposture.

But the passage is nowhere to be found in the original text. Fragment 268/236 contains the phrase "Moïse était habile homme." However, the context is quite different: "Si donc il se gouvernait par son esprit, il ne devait rien mettre qui fût directement contre l'esprit." Unless we imagine that they had access to a lost "pensée," it would appear that the editors of the Edition de Port-Royal made use of Filleau's account in constructing the passage.

Jean Mesnard points out that Filleau de la Chaise often glosses over Pascal's central arguments and emphasizes "des points secondaires."[40]

However, Filleau's treatment of the Fall does shed a great deal of light on the connection between Divine Wisdom's exposition of man's "deux états" in "A.P.R." and Pascal's later development of a proof of the authenticity of the Pentateuch. Mesnard has suggested that Filleau made use of the *Copies* in reconstructing Pascal's arguments.[41] Indeed, Filleau's outline, like that of Etienne Périer, does reflect the arrangement of the twenty-seven *liasses* of 1658. That is, with one important exception. Both Filleau and Périer present Pascal as showing the *libertin* that the resolution of the paradox "misère"/"grandeur" is to be found in Genesis 3. The *liasses* of 1658 systematically exclude any such approach. Moreover, in the "conférence," Pascal's presentation of the Fall presupposes a historical proof of the Pentateuch. In the dossiers of 1658, Pascal's proofs of the Pentateuch come *after* his exposition of the Fall in "A.P.R."

The heading "A.P.R. Pour demain," which figures in the middle of fragment 182/149, certainly seems to suggest that Pascal is setting down something that he intends to use "à Port-Royal." However, we can by no means be sure that the entire dossier bears a direct relationship to the "conférence" described by Etienne Périer and Filleau de la Chaise. As Philippe Sellier points out, "placer ce discours à Port-Royal demeure une pure hypothèse." Sellier reminds us that Périer notes that Pascal's presentation took place "sur-le-champ sans avoir été prémédité ni travaillé."[42] Yet almost in the same breath, we should remember, Périer pictures Pascal explaining to his friends "l'ordre et la suite des choses qu'il y voulait traiter."[43] Though it is impossible to square the apologetic strategy proposed in "A.P.R." with the "conférence" described by Périer and Filleau, the fact remains that "A.P.R." is the only title in the *liasse-table* that does not bear a thematic relationship to the *liasse* to which it corresponds. Perhaps the fragment was set down not prior to, but subsequent to, Pascal's presentation. Perhaps it represents, not his notes for the "conférence," but rather his reworking of one particular idea: how to present the Fall without having to take up the question of the credibility of the Old Testament.

Given the overall movement of the *Apology*, some exposition of the Fall must take place at this point in Pascal's argument. Throughout the first ten *liasses*, the whole theme "misère"/"grandeur" has been moving toward this exposition. The Fall is Pascal's primary example of the plausibility of Revelation. Yet Pascal's exposition cannot evoke historical arguments that have yet to be presented. "A.P.R." resolves this problem by borrowing the "prosopopée" from Proverbs and personifying Revelation as Divine Wisdom.

"A.P.R." represents a significant shift in Pascal's apologetic strategy. Filleau and Périer present the apologist as proposing to confront the *libertin* directly with the testimony of Genesis. "A.P.R." repeatedly excludes this tactic. Might we speculate that such a change in strategy grew out of the hypothetical "conférence" at Port-Royal? Perhaps one of the Solitaires pointed out the inherent weakness in Pascal's original argument: the *libertin* would not accept the testimony of Genesis. Perhaps the apologist, during the remainder of his stay "à Port-Royal," set down "A.P.R." in order to respond to this objection, tailoring his arguments to avoid citing the direct testimony of Genesis. Pascal's hesitations, signaled by the struck passages in the dossier, lead us to consider what has been a thorny issue for commentators on the *Pensées*: the degree to which Pascal was acquainted with *le libertinage érudit*.

PASCAL'S *LIBERTIN*

In her *Vie de Monsieur Pascal*, Gilberte Pascal recounts that her brother "se sentit tellement animé contre les athées que, voyant dans les lumières que Dieu lui avait données, de quoi les convaincre et les confondre sans ressources, il s'appliqua à cet ouvrage, dont les parties qu'on a ramassées nous font avoir tant de regret qu'il n'ait pas pu les rassembler lui-même et avec tout ce qu'il aurait pu ajouter encore en faire un composé d'une beauté achevée."[44] Père Beurrier, to whom Pascal made his last confession, records in his *Mémoires* that after "une retraite spirituelle" Pascal had resolved "de combattre fortement les impies et les athées, qui étaient en grand nombre dans Paris."[45] Who precisely were these "athées" and "impies" whom Pascal had in mind when he formulated the arguments recorded in the *Pensées*? To what extent were they familiar with that tradition of *libertinage érudit* whose attacks on the credibility of the Bible we examined in chapter two?

Unlike Sacy's biblical commentaries, the *Pensées* hardly ever undertake a point-by-point refutation of the philosophical theories advanced by the most famous of the *libertins* of the seventeenth century. In a sense, this is surprising, for Pascal had ample opportunity to meet and observe at first-hand some of the chief exponents of these ideas. At the "Académie mathématique" of Père Mersenne, the young Pascal and his father moved in the same scientific circles as La Mothe le Vayer, Gassendi, and Isaac La Peyrère. At the "Académie parisienne" of Le Pailleur, he would have had the opportunity to meet the English philosopher Hobbes. René Pintard points out that Pascal's friendship with Père Mersenne afforded the future apologist direct access to the world of *la libre pensée*:

> Mersenne avait commencé sa carrière d'écrivain en attaquant les "Déistes, athées et libertins de ce temps," puis les "Sceptiques ou Pyrrhoniens," dans des livres massifs, bourrés d'arguments mais aussi d'analyses des doctrines et d'allusions aux textes, véritable encyclopédie des philosophies libertines. . . . Chercheur infatigable, et devenu plus indulgent, il avait contracté alliance avec les esprits les plus divers, vu naître les dialogues les plus audacieux de La Mothe le Vayer, accueilli cordialement Campanella, patronné en France le *De Cive* de Hobbes. . . . Fréquenter Mersenne, c'était avoir accès

aux doctrines irréligieuses de l'antiquité, à celles des naturalistes italiens et des déistes français; c'était tenir entre ses mains, si l'on daignait la prendre, la clé . . . des systèmes les plus hardis des "novateurs"; c'était rejoindre, à leur source, tous les courants d'idées qui troublaient ou préoccupaient, sur les questions religieuses, le monde savant.[46]

Considering all the circumstances that might have permitted Pascal to penetrate the thought of the *libertins érudits* and discern the degree to which their attacks on the biblical vision of the universe threatened to undermine the coherence of the Christian position, Pintard observes, it is disconcerting that the *Pensées* accord so little importance to this challenge:

A ceux qui se demandent si, dans un univers aux dimensions indéfiniment agrandies, les cadres de l'histoire traditionnelle des hommes ne sont pas remis en question, il parle tranquillement de la Création et du Déluge. De même, au moment où quelques curieux . . . redonnent vie au problème de la pluralité des mondes . . . le poète des Deux Infinis tient le savant strictement assujetti aux préoccupations du peintre de la nature humaine. Qu'il s'agisse du temps ou de l'espace, Pascal laisse la pensée profane ou libertine tâtonner seule devant les horizons nouveaux.[47]

Pintard finds it difficult to discover in the *Pensées* "ou cette adaptation constante aux curiosités des philosophes libertins que beaucoup de critiques y reconnaissent, ou cette ampleur et cette minutie d'information que laissaient supposer le témoignage de Mme Périer et celui, plus sujet à caution, du Père Beurrier." According to Pintard, Pascal hardly even seems to recognize the existence of those objections to Christianity that were peculiar to "l'érudition libertine" in mid-seventeenth-century France. "Pas une allusion claire aux paradoxes nouveaux des libertins." "Aucun discussion méthodique des questions sur lesquelles ils s'en prenaient aux dogmes." "Pas un seul nom de ces rationalistes italiens qui apparaissaient comme les adversaires les plus redoutables de la foi."[48]

In Pintard's estimation, Pascal envisages a very traditional kind of atheism. The deism that he condemns so severely (690/449) "convient beaucoup mieux au stoïcisme antique qu'à ce que les 'curieux' du siècle découvraient . . . dans les *Quatrains du Déiste*." The skepticism he portrays bears none of the distinguishing characteristics of the philosophy of La Mothe le Vayer:

Tout près de Pascal, de même, le scepticisme se renouvelle. La Mothe le Vayer, dépouillant avec acharnement géographes et voyageurs, prolonge, aggrave les analyses de Montaigne; il promène au coeur même du sanctuaire la lampe tremblotante du doute; bien plus, il puise dans son érudition des rapprochements entre les croyances chrétiennes et celles des Gentils qui acheminent, de façon assez insidieuse, vers une histoire comparée des religions. Point d'autre scepticisme, pour le Pascal de l'Apologie, que celui des académiciens et des pyrrhoniens de l'antiquité ou que celui de leur disciple Montaigne.[49]

It is in the famous argument known as the "pari" (680/418) that critics and readers alike have thought they have been able to catch the clearest glimpse of Pascal's interlocutor in the *Pensées*. But any attempt to fix either the character or the identity of this interlocutor has always resulted in a lively disagreement among those critics who take up the question. Responding to Lucien Goldmann's paper "Le pari est-il écrit 'pour le libertin'?" (1954), Henri Gouhier points to a key text in the *Pensées*:

> Il n'y [a que] trois sortes de personnes: les uns qui servent Dieu l'ayant trouvé, les autres qui s'emploient à le chercher ne l'ayant pas trouvé, les autres qui vivent sans le chercher ni l'avoir trouvé. Les premiers sont raisonnables et heureux, les derniers sont fous et malheureux, ceux du milieu sont malheureux et raisonnables. (192/160)

In Gouhier's estimation, "il s'agit d'un dialogue, non pas avec le libertin, mais avec celui qui commence à chercher Dieu, ou du moins qui est malheurex."[50] Paul Bénichou, taking part in the same discussion, disagrees: "Je ne vois pas ici un libertin malheureux, quelqu'un qui cherche en gémissant. Je vois un sceptique, purement et simplement."[51]

Jean Mesnard, also responding to Goldmann's paper, notes that Pascal does not use the word *libertin* all that often. When he does, Mesnard insists, it is in "un sens relativement technique." Mesnard places great emphasis on the evolution of the point of view of Pascal's interlocutor during the course of the *Apology*: "A la fin de l'*Apologie*, lorsqu'on arrive au chapitre 'Morale Chrétienne,' par exemple, on peut dire que le libertin est considéré comme pratiquement converti. . . . Il y a, je crois, dans le mouvement même de l'*Apologie*, une progression, théorique, conventionnelle sans doute, mais qu'il importe de souligner pour savoir dans quelle situation Pascal imagine le libertin au moment où il compose ce fragment du *Pari*." While writing the *Apology*, Mesnard suggests, Pascal certainly had in mind "quelques individualités déterminées": "Cette perspective nous est absolument imposée par l'apostrophe à Miton, qui apparaît plusieurs fois."[52]

In his study of "Pascal et les libertins," Pintard very much agrees that Damien Miton, along with the Chevalier de Méré, was Pascal's chief model for the *libertin* who is his interlocutor in the *Pensées*. Pascal sought to draw the attention of these two "théoriciens de l'"honnêté' " to Christianity, not by refuting the arguments of the *érudits*, but by appealing to their "appétit de bonheur":

> Il les imagine, il les voit, et l'affection se mêle au zèle religieux pour . . . les débusquer de leur tranquillité. . . . Rude ou charitable, l'incitation est pressante; et elle se fait directe, personnelle même: "Une lettre d'exhortation à un ami pour le porter à chercher" [39/5]. . . . Plus qu'en des philosophes de profession présentant des objections bien classées, Pascal a trouvé ses interlocuteurs en ces esprits brillants et désinvoltes, en ces hommes avides de vi-

vre, êtres de chair et de sang qui ont des convoitises, des joies, des déceptions, des vanités, des faiblesses et qui s'offrent par elles à ses prises. Il ne les lâchera plus; et c'est ainsi que leur image s'imprimera fortement dans ce texte même des *Pensées* qui garde si peu de traces des doctrines des savants libertins.[53]

Pintard's portrait of Miton and Méré certainly corresponds more closely to the *libertin* pictured in the *Pensées* than does that of the *beaux esprits* whose attacks on the Bible we examined in chapter two. And it is equally clear that Pascal's whole apologetic strategy is addressed to a *libertin* of a hedonistic and agnostic temperament far more directly than it is to the *érudits*, whom he hardly ever even mentions. Yet it would be a mistake to think that Pascal ever supposed Miton and Méré, for instance, to be free from a whole series of prejudices inherited from their close association with the tradition of *libertinage érudit*.

In his *Mémoires*, Père Beurrier presents three portraits of *libertins* whose confidence he was able to gain during his years as curé of Saint-Etienne-de-Mont. M. Pintard has criticized these portraits as representing "types conventionnels."[54] Herein, however, lies their value. Père Beurrier gives a picture, however distorted by his apologetic purposes, not of professional *érudits* or philosophers, but of three conventional atheists in mid-seventeenth-century Paris: a lawyer, a doctor, and a priest. His description of their objections to Christianity permits us to see the extent to which the principal conclusions of the whole tradition of *libertinage érudit* had been absorbed into the point of view of the conventional atheist.

The atheist lawyer, who tells Beurrier that he is only one among twenty thousand of his persuasion in Paris, explains that religion is but a tool of the state, "inventée pour maintenir les peuples dans la soumission . . . aux souverains par la crainte des enfers imaginaires." "Nous n'en croyons point," he tells Beurrier, "non plus que de paradis. Nous croyons que quand nous mourons tout est mort pour nous."[55] The doctor explains that his position is based upon "trois articles": "le premier, que la plus grande de toutes les fables, c'est la religion chrestienne; le second, que le plus ancien de tous les romans, c'est la Bible; le troisième, que le plus grand de tous les fourbes et de tous les imposteurs, c'est Jésus-Christ."[56]

Père Beurrier's doctor's exposition of the second article of his creed particulièrement merits our attention: "Je vous réitère que votre Bible est un vray roman, dans lequel il y a mille contes à dormir debout, il y a plusieurs niaiseries et contradictions, plusieurs choses impossibles, plusieurs imaginations mal pensées, mal digérées et encore plus mal écrites."[57] Nor should we fail to note the atheist priest's total rejection of the doctrine of the Fall: "Toutes les actions que nous croions péché ne l'estoient point, mais des inclinations purement naturelles, venant de nos inclinations et passions . . . il n'y avoit non plus de péché originel, et par conséquent . . . toutes les inclinations et passions que nous avions estoient aussy innocentes que la nature mesme."[58]

Without going so far as to argue that the *libertins* depicted by Père Beurrier represent an exact picture of those individuals Pascal had in mind when writing the *Pensées*, we can nonetheless note that their opinions represent prejudices that the apologist had to take into account when framing the outline of his apologetic strategy. Pascal's suppression of a historical exposition of the Fall in the dossiers "Contrariétés" and "A.P.R." would appear to reflect the fact that he has taken the measure of his interlocutor's potential hostility to the testimony of the Bible. To encounter the suspicion with which the *beaux esprits* regarded Genesis, we are by no means obliged to look to the "paradoxes nouveaux" of a La Mothe le Vayer. The whole spectrum of *libre pensée* in seventeenth-century France in large measure took its inspiration from Italian neo-Epicureanism of the previous century. One of the mainstays of this school was the affirmation of the eternity of the universe and the complete negation of the doctrine of the Creation. Whether cited by Père Garasse in the 1620s, by Boucher in the 1630s, or by Desmarests de Saint-Sorlin in the 1650s, the *libertins* all share a profound distrust of Genesis' account of the origins of the world.[59]

Only once in the *Pensées* does Pascal refer directly to an argument concerning Genesis formulated by one of the *érudits*. In fragment 478/575, in connection with those who would seek to found "des opinions extravagantes sur l'Ecriture," he mentions the "préadamites." This seems a fairly certain reference to a theory that Isaac de la Peyrère had sought to propagate since the 1640s. La Peyrère was hardly what modern students of the Bible would call a *libertin*. In fact, he advanced the curiously modern notion that "la Bible n'enseigne que ce qui regarde notre salut."[60] One of the first exegetes to attempt to subject the Bible to rational examination, La Peyrère sought to make sense of Genesis' two accounts of the Creation. He hypothesized two Creations: Adam's, from which the Jews descended; and a much earlier one, from which would have sprung the "préadamites" and the rest of humanity. An attempt to reconcile the Bible with increasing evidence that the human race was far older than the dates suggested by Genesis, La Peyrère's theory could but have been for Pascal a very dangerous kind of innovation. The author of the *Pensées* understands the doctrine of Original Sin to presuppose Adam's fatherhood of the entire human race.[61]

The third article of faith in the *credo* cited by Père Beurrier's atheist doctor provides us with another important perspective on the extent to which Pascal might have imagined his *libertin* to be acquainted with the chief tenets of *le libertinage érudit*:

Enfin, le troisième article que je vous réitère, c'est qu'il y a eu trois grands imposteurs au monde, à sçavoir Moyse, Jésus-Christ et Mahomet, mais Jésus-Christ est le plus grand, il a été le plus adroit et le plus subtil de tous. Aussi y a-t-il mieux réussy dans son entreprise, ayant tellement leurré le simple peuple et surtout ses disciples, qui estoient sans esprit, sans lettres et sans jugement, par les menaces de l'enfer imaginaire et les promesses d'une vie heureuse éternellement, et par ses faux miracles, qu'ils ont répandu partout sa doctrine et sa religion.[62]

According to Antoine Adam, Père Beurrier makes a conscious reference to the famous libertine doctrine *De Tribus Impostoribus*.[63] In a recent article, Georges Couton presents a convincing case that Pascal supposed his *libertin* to be familiar with this doctrine. Not only was the *thesis* of the *Trois Imposteurs* part of the public domain. Pascal's friend Père Mersenne believed in the existence of a book "très impie, très digne des flammes éternelles par lequel les Déistes et Athées essaient de persuader que Moïse et le Christ, à l'imitation de Mahomet, sont des imposteurs."[64] Since no such book has ever come to light, Couton hypothesizes the existence "d'un manuscrit recopié sans qu'aucune copie soit venue jusqu'à nous, ou d'une édition très confidentielle, totalement disparue." Besides, Couton argues, it really makes no difference whether such a book ever existed: "la thèse, à défaut du livre, était largement répandue."[65]

As we shall see in chapter six, the three key historical chapters in the dossiers de 1658—"Fausseté des autres religions" (XVII/XVI), "Preuves de Moïse" (XXIII/XXII), and "Preuves de Jésus-Christ" (XXIV/XXIII)—can very much be viewed as serving to neutralize the thesis of the *Trois Imposteurs*. Couton gives particular attention to the first of these chapters, noting that the editors of the Edition de Port-Royal assigned it the title "Contre Mahomet." In chapter three, I argued that Sacy's aim in his analysis of Islam was to show those who maintain that Christianity is an imposture what a genuine invented religion looks like.[66] Couton finds the arguments of Sacy and Pascal so similar that he wonders if Sacy's section on Islam in the *Préface à la Genèse* was not put together "en rassemblant les thèmes des *Pensées*."[67]

Returning to the question of why the *Pensées* contain so few traces of the doctrines of *le libertinage érudit*, we might wonder why Pascal never more clearly states the position of his adversaries with regard to the testimony of Genesis or the thesis of the *Trois Imposteurs*. With regard to the second of these, Couton offers a plausible explanation: "c'eût été lui donner trop d'importance."[68] Indeed, Pascal's whole apologetic strategy turns upon never showing his hand. The apologist anticipates potential objections on the part of his interlocutor, steering clear of sore points that might cause his argument to become sidetracked. At the same time, he rigorously avoids making mention of anything that might constellate a set of opposing and perhaps prefabricated theories in the mind of an opponent who is not unacquainted with the traditional arguments of *la libre pensée*. When Pascal "avait à conférer avec quelques athées," Mme Périer recalls for us, he never began by establishing "les principes qu'il avait à dire."[69]

Pascal ultimately hopes to be able to persuade the *libertin* to reconsider the testimony of the Bible. For the moment (i.e., in "Contrariétés" and "A.P.R."), he does not want to risk inviting his adversary to take a cursory look at Genesis, only to have him reject it out of hand. In the dossier entitled "Lettre pour porter à rechercher Dieu" (XLVI/série III), Pascal notes the example of those who think they have given the Christian religion a fair hearing when they have done no more than devote "quelques heures à la lecture de quelque livre de l'Ecriture" (681/427).

In "A.P.R.," Divine Wisdom presents the proposition that the Fall may be deduced from the paradox "misère"/"grandeur" as a formulation the logic of which the *libertin* cannot fail to see: "Ces deux états étant ouverts, il est impossible que vous ne les reconnaissiez pas" (182/149). In another fragment, however, he notes that his friend Miton has not been able to follow the argument to its logical conclusion: "Miton voit bien que la nature est corrompue et que les hommes sont contraires à l'honnêté. Mais il ne sait pas pourquoi ils ne peuvent voler plus haut" (529/642).

Pascal's strategy, we should remember, was to prove that "la nature est corrompue, *par la nature même*." (40/6; italics mine) Miton is willing to acknowledge that human nature "est corrompue." But because he understands the word *corrompue* only in a static and passive sense, he has failed to understand the whole point of Pascal's line of reasoning. Human nature is not simply inherently corrupt. It *has been corrupted*. All the arguments of "Contrariétés" and "A.P.R." have been designed to permit the *libertin* to go a step further and recognize why humanity cannot "voler plus haut." The apologist, however, deliberately refrains from calling his attention to the account of the Fall in Genesis. The *libertin*'s prejudice against that document could well cloud his judgment. Instead, he is invited to observe the effects of the Fall in himself: "Suivez vos mouvements, observez-vous vous-même, et voyez si vous n'y trouverez pas les caractères vivants de ces deux natures" (182/149).

Philippe Sellier draws an important parallel between Pascal's analysis of Miton and Saint Augustine's description of Cicero:

> Miton ressemble . . . à Cicéron: Augustin souligne que dans le livre III du *De Républica* ce dernier présente l'homme comme un être produit par une nature-marâtre, nu, fragile, sans force . . . et pourtant habité d'une parcelle du feu divin. Le grand orateur accuse la nature. C'est donc qu'il a bien vu la réalité, mais en a ignoré la cause. . . . Parce qu'il n'était pas instruit de l'Ecriture, il ignorait les causes exactes de l'état présent.[70]

Sellier goes on to present a view of Pascal's apologetic strategy that is quite different from the one that I proposed in my analysis of "A.P.R." "Les esprits ordinaires," he argues, "ne voient plus très bien par eux-mêmes, mais ils reconnaissent la vérité si on la leur montre. C'est pourquoi l'apologiste, tout en s'appuyant sur l'expérience, *n'hésite pas à ouvrir la Bible devant ses interlocutors*: ('Il y a deux vérités de foi également constantes . . . aux bêtes brutes.')"[71]

The passage that Sellier cites as proof that Pascal "n'hésite pas à ouvrir la Bible" is none other than the lines struck by the apologist in "Contrariétés" (164/131). I have argued that Pascal's striking of these lines, in which he sets down various biblical verses attesting to man's condition before and after the Fall,[72] indicates that he indeed had second thoughts about presenting scriptural evidence of humanity's fallen condition.

In our attempt to assess Pascal's apologetic strategy, we should constantly keep in mind fragment 660/820:

> Il y a deux manières de persuader les vérités de notre religion: l'une par la force de la raison, l'autre par l'autorité de celui qui parle.
> On ne se sert point de la dernière, mais de la première. On ne dit point: Il faut croire cela, car l'Ecriture, qui le dit, est divine. Mais on dit qu'il le faut croire par telle et telle raison, qui sont de faibles arguments, la raison étant flexible à tout.

We should remember as well that our apologist does not consider himself to be engaged in an ordinary kind of dialogue when he attempts to lead his interlocutor to Christianity. The *libertin*'s heart must be predisposed by Grace to recognize the truth of Revelation, else the fruits of any arguments will be useless:

> C'est pourquoi ceux à qui Dieu a donné la religion par sentiment du coeur sont bien heureux et bien légitimement persuadés. *Mais [à] ceux qui ne l'ont pas nous ne pouvons la donner que par raisonnement, en attendant que Dieu la leur donne par sentiment du coeur.* Sans quoi la foi n'est qu'humaine et inutile pour le salut. (142/110; italics mine)

The "raisonnement" by which Pascal says Christianity must be imparted to the unbeliever—"en attendant" God's Grace—represents the first of the two "manières de persuader" envisaged by fragment 660/820. Because reason, however, is "flexible à tout," "par raisonnement" represents only a provisional stage in Pascal's apologetic itinerary. "A.P.R.," which brings to a close the "étape préparatoire" of the *Apology*, refrains from citing Scripture to an interlocutor who has no appreciation of the Bible's status as Revelation. At the same time, the "prosopopée" of Divine Wisdom looks forward to the moment when Pascal will be able to say with regard to the Fall: "Il faut croire cela, car l'Ecriture, qui le dit, est divine."

"PREUVES CONVAINCANTES": TOWARD A HISTORICAL PROOF OF REVELATION

Taking up the "prosopopée" of Divine Wisdom for the third time at the end of "A.P.R.," Pascal introduces an idea that announces the governing theme of the second part of the *Apology*: Revelation itself contains "preuves convaincantes" of its credibility. Divine Wisdom reassures Pascal's interlocutor as to the character of the arguments that are to follow:

> Je n'entends pas que vous soumettiez votre créance à moi sans raison, et ne prétends point vous assujettir avec tyrannie. Je ne prétends point aussi vous rendre raison de toutes choses. Et pour accorder ces contrariétés, j'entends vous faire voir clairement par des preuves convaincantes des marques divines en moi qui vous convainquent de ce que je suis, et m'attirer autorité par des merveilles et des preuves que vous ne puissiez refuser, et qu'ensuite vous croyiez les choses que je vous enseigne. . . . (182/149)

The first line of Pascal's resumption of the "prosopopée" recapitulates a line crossed out when Divine Wisdom's discourse was broken off earlier in the fragment: "*Je ne demande pas de vous une créance aveugle.*"[73] What intervenes between Pascal's striking of this idea and its restatement is significant. The apologist, in a reflection addressed more to himself than to his interlocutor, formulates an argument designed to predispose the *libertin* to listen to what "la sagesse de Dieu" is about to say:

> Je voudrais savoir d'où cet animal qui se reconnait si faible a le droit de mesurer la miséricorde de Dieu. . . . Tout troublé de la vue de son propre état, il ose dire que Dieu ne le peut pas rendre capable de sa communication. Mais je voudrais lui demander si Dieu demande autre chose de lui sinon qu'il l'aime et le connaisse, et pourquoi il croit que Dieu ne peut se rendre connaissable et aimable à lui. . . . Si Dieu lui découvre quelque rayons de son essence, ne sera-t-il pas capable de le connaître et de l'aimer en la manière qu'il lui plaira se communiquer à nous? (182/149)

The position of the agnostic, who simply claims that he has no knowledge of anything beyond the scope of his own reason, amounts to a "présomption insupportable." Though apparently founded on "humilité," it is neither "sincère" nor "raisonnable." When he concludes that God is incapable of rendering himself "connaissable," the *libertin* exceeds the limitations of his own powers of reason. Revelation, Pascal will point out to him, has not been deduced by man. It is a manifestation of God's desire to "se rendre parfaitement connaissable." "Nous ne pouvons l'apprendre que de Dieu" (182/149).

In taking up again the "prosopopée," Pascal introduces an idea that serves as a transition to the entire second part of his *Apology*. There exist "preuves convaincantes" that are of an entirely different order than those drawn from *expérience*. As Jean Mesnard, commenting on the passage just cited, observes: "Les véritables preuves du christianisme sont donc données par Dieu et non trouvées par l'homme. Elles n'appartiennent pas à la nature, mais à l'histoire, sur laquelle Dieu a imprimé son sceau. L'histoire est en effet le lieu de la révélation."[74]

Pascal's historical proof of Revelation will not attempt, as do Sacy's biblical commentaries, to answer every objection to the historicity of Christianity. "Je ne prétends point," warns "la sagesse de Dieu," "vous rendre raison de toutes choses." The whole of Revelation is beyond the scope of human reason. At the same time, however, Revelation is accompanied by "marques divines" and "merveilles" that will attest to its authenticity and authority (182/149).

"La sagesse de Dieu," we must remember, is Pascal's personification of Revelation. Those "marques divines" and "'merveilles" that Divine Wisdom says will lend her authority are the very signs and events that signify Scripture's divine origin. Jean Mesnard gives a particularly helpful description of the character of these "marques divines" and of their place in Pascal's overall argument:

> Ces signes obligent la raison à se soumettre parce qu'elle ne saurait les poser elle-même; mais ils l'invitent aussi à s'exercer puisque, comme les expériences en physique, ils constituent les "principes" à partir desquels le raisonnement doit conclure à l'intervention de Dieu et à la divinité de la doctrine qu'ils accompagnent.[75]

It seems doubtful that Pascal intended for the last four (three in Lafuma's edition) paragraphs of "A.P.R." to figure in his continuation of the "prosopopée."[76] These paragraphs develop an idea that contrasts sharply with the idea of "preuves convaincantes," the notion that God has hidden himself from "quelques-uns":

> Dieu a voulu racheter les hommes et ouvrir le salut à ceux qui le chercheraient. Mais les hommes s'en rendent si indignes qu'il est juste que Dieu refuse à quelques-uns à cause de leur endurcissement ce qu'il accorde aux autres par une miséricorde qui ne leur est pas due. (182/149)

Pascal goes on to develop the theme of "le Dieu caché." This development, from a theological perspective, is a necessary corollary to what Divine Wisdom has revealed about Revelation. It accounts for the fact that not all men have in fact acted upon the evidence of the "marques divines" of Revelation. "Il y a assez de lumière pour ceux qui ne désirent que de voir et assez d'obsurité pour ceux qui ont une disposition contraire" (182/149). Yet, toward the end of the page on which he sets down this argument, Pascal decides that it really belongs in the section "Fondements de la religion" (XIX/XVIII). The *Copies* show us that the following page, on which the passage was completed, was filed in chapter XIX/XVIII.[77] Once again, we find Pascal delaying the introduction of a theme that might confuse the issue at hand: persuading the interlocutor that Revelation is worthy of his attention.

In the following chapter, I shall attempt to reconstruct Pascal's plan for a historical proof of Revelation. His exposition of the Fall will have important consequences with regard to the organization of this proof. Because the analogy "Adam/Jésus-Christ" takes its authority from Revelation itself, a historical proof of Christianity must envisage both Testaments. Proving the historicity of the Fall will mean first establishing the authenticity of the Pentateuch. It is with this aim in mind that Pascal opens the dossiers "Perpétuité" (XXII/XXI), "Preuves de Moïse" (XXIII/XXII) and "Contre la fable d'Esdras" (XXIX).[78]

In those chapters, Pascal will take up the very issue—the authority of Scripture—that we have portrayed him as repeatedly avoiding in the first part of the *Apology*. Yet we must not forget that all along Scripture has been, so to speak, waiting in the wings to be brought forward. Even that most "psychological" paradigm of the "étape préparatoire," the argument of the "pari," looks forward to the moment when the Bible can be opened. The *libertin*, dumbfounded by the proposition the apologist has advanced, protests: "N'y a-t-il point moyen de voir le dessous du jeu?" Pascal does not fail to reply: "Oui, l'Ecriture et le reste." (680/418)

---

1. As Sister Marie-Louise Hubert observes, "dismissing altogether Pascal's plan of the *Apology* and reverting to the system of the Port-Royal editors, Brunschvicg classified the *Pensées* according to content, unintentionally creating a cleavage between the so-called 'psychological' and 'dogmatic' parts of the *Apology*" (*Pascal's Unfinished Apology*, p. 9).

2. Lafuma, p. 494. See also, Mesnard, *Les Pensées de Pascal*, p. 15.

3. "Préface de l'Edition de Port-Royal," Lafuma, p. 498. Mesnard remarks: "Confusion, nous l'avons vu, qui n'était pas sans ordre, sinon pourquoi la respecter?" (*Les Pensées de Pascal*, p. 21).

4. "Aux origines de l'édition des *Pensées*: les deux Copies," in *Les "Pensées" de Pascal ont trois cents ans*, p. 23.

5. "Aux origines de l'édition des *Pensées*," p. 24.

6. *Les Pensées de Pascal*, p. 28.

7. *Les Pensées de Pascal*, p. 28.

8. "Aux origines de l'édition des *Pensées*," p. 29.

9. "Aux origines de l'édition des *Pensées*," p. 27.

10. Fr. 22/403 occurs in *liasse* i/*série* i. Fragment 103/69, "Job et Salomon," indicates that it was to be placed in the *liasse* "Misère" (IV/III). Pascal took Solomon to be the author of Ecclesiastes. Cf. Sacy's *L'Ecclésiaste de Salomon* (Bruxelles: Chez Fricx, 1699), Preface, p. iii: "Le Saint-Esprit parle aux hommes par la bouche de Salomon."

11. *Essais*, I, 20, "Que Philosopher, c'est apprendre à mourir."

12. A more elaborate statement of the "fort des dogmatistes" is developed in fr. 142/110. The arguments are those Pascal uses himself in establishing man's "grandeur": " . . . La connaissance des premiers principes comme qu'il y a espace, temps, mouvement, nombres, [est] aussi ferme qu'aucune de celles que nos raisonnements nous donnent. Et c'est sur ces connaissances du coeur et de l'instinct qu'il faut que la raison s'appuie et qu'elle y fonde tout son discours."

13. Bédier, p. 75 (italics mine). For ["il faut qu' "] I follow text T.

14. Lafuma, following C1, and Sellier, following C2, reproduce all struck-out passages in

italics. Brunschvicg, however, following the example of the Edition of Port-Royal, leaves out entirely all passages struck in the *Recueil original*.

15. Sacy finds a reference to the Fall in only one of Pascal's six citations. Commenting upon Psalm 48:12 ("Et l'homme tandis qu'il estoit élevé en honneur, ne l'a pas compris. Il a esté comparé aux bêtes qui n'ont aucune raison, et il leur est devenu semblable."), Sacy presents the very explication that Pascal must have had in mind: "La grande dignité de l'homme . . . c'est d'avoir esté créé à l'image de Dieu même et d'avoir reçu de son créateur le pouvoir de le connoître et de l'aimer. Cependant, il n'a point connu ni sçu estimer le prix de sa propre dignité" (*Les Pseaumes de David*, 1:546–47).

16. *Pensées*, p. 111 n. 1.

17. *Les Pensées de Pascal*, p. 206.

18. The notation "Adam. Jésus Christ" falling at the end of the second "prosopopée" cannot be taken to be part of Divine Wisdom's speech. The "prosopopée" is closed with a quotation mark at the end of the sentence "Je puis seule vous faire entendre qui vous êtes." Rather, the notation represents Pascal's note to himself concerning the direction of his argument from this point onward.

19. See above, p. 138.

20. This fragment, though recorded in the section immediately following the "prosopopée," is obviously destined to be placed in Divine Wisdom's speech.

21. Lafuma, p. 495.

22. Lafuma, p. 495.

23. Lafuma, p. 495.

24. Lafuma, p. 495.

25. Lafuma, pp. 495–96 (italics mine).

26. Lafuma, p. 496 (italics mine).

27. Lafuma, p. 496. These "divers endroits" in fact correspond to the second three Scriptural citations suppressed by Pascal at the end of "Contrariétés" (164/131). "Que toute chair est corrompue" recalls Isaiah 40:6 and "les hommes sont abandonnés à leurs sens" Psalm 48:12 and Ecclesiastes 3:18. "Qu'ils ont une pente . . . leur naissance," however, corresponds to a citation perhaps déjà cataloguée by Pascal in the dossier "Rabbinage": fragment 309/278, titled "du péché originel," records: "Sur le mot de la *Genèse* 8, *la composition du coeur de l'homme est mauvaise dès son enfance*."

28. Lafuma, p. 496.

29. Lafuma, p. 494.

30. Brunschvicg, 12:cciii–cciv.

31. Filleau's reference to "l'embrasement de Londres" reveals the extent to which he has added his own illustrations to his report of Pascal's "conférence." Pascal's death (19 August 1662) occurred some two years before the Great Fire of London (1664).

32. Brunschvicg, 12:cciv.

33. Brunschvicg, 12:cciv.

34. Brunschvicg, 12:ccvi.

35. Brunschvicg, 12:ccvi–ccvii.

36. Brunschvicg, 12:ccvii. Cf. *liasses* XXII/XXI ("Perpétuité") and XXIII/XXII ("Preuves de Moïse").

37. Brunschvicg, 12:ccvii–ccix.

38. Brunschvicg, 12:ccx.

39. Brunschvicg, 12:ccxv.

40. *Pascal*, p. 149.

41. *Pascal*, p. 147.

42. *Pensées*, pp. 17–18.

43. Lafuma, p. 495.
44. Lafuma, p. 24.
45. Mesnard (ed.), *Oeuvres complètes*, 1:868.
46. "Pascal et les libertins," in *Pascal Présent*, p. 111.
47. "Pascal et les libertins," p. 116.
48. "Pascal et les libertins," pp. 116, 112–13.
49. "Pascal et les libertins," pp. 113–14. Cf. *Pensées*, fragments 38/4 and 164/131.
50. In *Blaise Pascal: l'homme et l'oeuvre*, pp. 139–40.
51. In *Blaise Pascal: l'homme et l'oeuvre*, p. 150.
52. In *Blaise Pascal: l'homme et l'oeuvre*, pp. 155–56. Cf. fragments 433/853; 494/597; 529/642.
53. "Pascal et les libertins," pp. 126, 124.
54. Antoine Adam, *Les Libertins au XVIIe siècle*, p. 110. The extracts from the *Mémoires* of Père Beurrier are reproduced on pp. 111–19.
55. Adam, pp. 112–13.
56. Adam, pp. 115–16.
57. Adam, pp. 116–17.
58. Adam, p. 119 (italics mine).
59. See pp. 56–61, above.
60. *Systema theologicum*, pp. 183–84. French translation cited from Jean Steinman's *Richard Simon et les origines de l'exégèse biblique*, p. 56.
61. *Systema theologicum*, liber secundus, caput x, pp. 83 ff. See pp. 60 and 110–11, above.
62. Adam, p. 117.
63. Adam, p. 120 n. 6.
64. Mersenne, *Quaestiones . . . in Genesim* (1623), col. 672; cited by Georges Couton, "Libertinage et Apologétique: les *Pensées* de Pascal contre la thèse des Trois Imposteurs," p. 187.
65. Couton, p. 188.
66. See pp. 83–84, above.
67. Couton, p. 190.
68. Couton, p. 188.
69. Lafuma, p. 25.
70. *Pascal et Saint Augustin*, pp. 239–40.
71. *Pascal et Saint Augustin*, p. 240 (italics mine).
72. See pp. 138–39, above.
73. The quotation marks are Pascal's. It is not the apologist but rather "la sagesse de Dieu" who refrains from demanding "une créance aveugle."
74. *Les Pensées de Pascal*, p. 162.
75. *Les Pensées de Pascal*, p. 162.
76. The "prosopopée" would appear to end with "si elles sont ou non."
77. The *Seconde Copie*, while transcribing the remainder of the passage in order to complete "A.P.R.," notes in the margin: "Cette suite s'est trouvée dans le chapitre 'Fondements de la religion.'" Sellier places this "suite" in chapter XIX as fr. 274. Lafuma, however, leaves it in "A.P.R.," obscuring Pascal's reminder to himself of where the argument was to be placed and our perception of Pascal's constant preoccupation with apologetic strategy.
78. This *liasse* does not figure in the *Première Copie*. Lafuma presents the relevant fragments in his section "Fragments non enregistrés," frs. 970–72.

VI

L'Ecriture et le Reste: Pascal's Historical Demonstration of the Credibility of Christianity

"LA PLUS GRANDE DES PREUVES"

That large body of material in the *Pensées* relating to Pascal's treatment of the Old Testament prophecies has long been neglected by critics and readers alike. Such neglect is largely a function of the fact that the dossiers in which this material is contained rarely transcend the stage of documentation. More than any other single part of the *Pensées*, these dossiers represent an *Apology* interrupted in the course of its organization.

The dossiers of 1658, however, make it clear that Pascal intended to rest his entire case in favor of the credibility of Christianity on a proof built upon this very material. The transitional chapters, which prepare the way for Pascal's historical demonstration, contain a number of significant references to this definitive argument. "Excellence" (XV/XIV) rules out metaphysical proofs in favor of those "preuves solides et palpables" represented by the prophecies (221/189). "Soumission" (XIV/XIII) rejects an argument based upon miracles in order to make way for the same ultimate proof: "les prophéties accomplies sont un miracle subsistant" (211/180). Chapters XVI/XV and XVII/XVI advance the idea that the prophecies set Christianity apart from all the other religions the world has ever known.

Those chapters in which Pascal develops his historical demonstrations likewise anticipate a definitive argument founded upon a juxtaposition of Old and New Testament texts. In order to establish the historical credibility of these two sets of texts, the apologist opens the dossiers "Preuves de Moïse" and "Preuves de Jésus-Christ." Laying the groundwork for examining the prophecies will require a special system of interpretation. "Pour examiner les prophéties il faut les entendre" (305/274). "Que la Loi était figurative" (XX/XIX), in which this system is worked out, seeks to prove the existence of a figurative level of meaning in the Old Testament. "Car si on croit qu[e les prophéties] n'ont qu'un sens, il est sûr que le Messie ne sera point venu" (305/274). "Fondements" (XIX/XVIII), in turn, provides a theological rationale for the existence of "les deux sens de l'Ecriture." The theory of "le Dieu qui se cache," forged to explain why the Bible requires a special system of interpretation, sets into motion a chain of investigations that lead Pascal's interlocutor to consider the origins of sacred history and in particular the "témoignage" of the Jews.

An examination of the "étape démonstrative" from the perspective of "la plus grande des preuves" greatly clarifies the overall movement of Pascal's proposed *Apology*. By pointing up the central role of the Bible in Pascal's apologetic strategy, such an approach permits us to grasp the empirical nature of the proof of Christianity envisaged by the *Pensées*. Reason, "froissée par ses propres armes"[1] in the "étape préparatoire," is to a certain extent rehabilitated in the course of Pascal's historical demonstration. The evidence of the prophecies is the final stage in a strategy designed to convince reason that empirical evidence warrants its abdication in the face of the case built for the credibility of Revelation.

"SOUMISSION ET USAGE DE LA RAISON"

Strictly speaking, Pascal's historical demonstrations begin with the chapter "Fondements" (XIX/XVIII). In order to place the historical dossiers in their larger apologetic context, however, we begin with an overview of those transitional chapters that seek to orient the *libertin* toward an examination of sacred history. While recapitulating the major themes of the "étape préparatoire," these chapters anticipate, in a number of key fragments, that definitive proof based on the prophecies that Pascal reserves for his ultimate argument.

"Commencement" (XIII/XII) undertakes a critique of the *libertin*'s position that religion is irrelevant. Pascal begins by pointing out that one necessarily organizes one's life according to one of two propositions. "Il faut vivre autrement dans le monde selon ces diverses suppositions: Si on pouvait y être toujours. S'il est sûr qu'on n'y sera pas longtemps et incertain si on y sera une heure" (187/154). The first of these propositions is obviously false. All of mankind stands under the ultimate sentence of death: "Le dernier acte est sanglant, quelque belle que soit la comédie en tout le reste. On jette enfin de la terre sur la tête, et en voilà pour jamais" (197/165).

The majority of men choose to deceive themselves and lead their lives as if they were going to remain in the world forever. "Nous sommes plaisants de nous reposer dans la société de nos semblables, misérables comme nous, impuissants comme nous" (184/151). Yet their behavior is contrary to the most elementary standards of reason. To make his point, Pascal produces an illustration drawn from *expérience*:

> Un homme dans un cachot, ne sachant pas si son arrêt est donné, n'ayant qu'une heure pour l'apprendre, cette heure suffisant, s'il sait qu'il est donné,

pour le faire révoquer, il est contre nature qu'il emploie cette heure-là non à s'informer si l'arrêt est donné, mais à jouer au piquet.
Ainsi il est surnaturel que l'homme, etc. (195/163)

Pascal's parable is meant to be applied directly to the situation of the *libertin*. Instead of seeking to avoid the finality of death through "divertissement," reason dictates that he spend his time searching for a way to avoid this final judgment. At the very least, he should be concerned to find out whether death is the end of all things. "Il importe à toute la vie de savoir si l'âme est mortelle ou immortelle" (196/164). The answer to this question will dictate how he will organize his life in this world. If the soul is mortal, one would obviously want to live very differently than if the Christian vision of things is true and there is a hell to avoid and a heaven to prepare for.

To avoid posing the question in the first place is, by ordinary standards of human reason, "contre nature." The *libertin*, who considers man's final destiny irrelevant, is the most unreasonable of all men:

> L'immortalité de l'âme est une chose qui nous importe si fort, qui nous touche si profondément, qu'il faut avoir perdu tout sentiment pour être dans l'indifférence de savoir ce qui en est. Toutes nos actions et nos pensées doivent prendre des routes si différentes, selon qu'il y aura des biens éternels à espérer ou non, qu'il est impossible de faire une démarche avec sens et jugement, qu'en réglant par la vue de ce point, qui doit être notre dernier objet.[2] (681/427)

"Les impies qui font profession de suivre la raison doivent être étrangement forts en raison" (183/150). "Les athées doivent dire des choses parfaitement claires" (193/161). Yet the position of the *libertin*, who refuses to consider Revelation, is far from reasonable. The supposition that "l'âme soit matérielle" is far from "parfaitement claire" (193/161).

"Vous devez vous mettre en peine de rechercher la vérité," Pascal counsels the *libertin*, "car si vous mourez sans adorer le vrai principe vous êtes perdu." The *libertin*'s response, "mais . . . s'il avait voulu que je l'adorasse il m'aurait laissé des signes de sa volonté," is precisely the opening Pascal has been waiting for. "Aussi a-t-il fait," Pascal answers, "mais vous les négligez. Cherchez-les donc, cela le vaut bien" (190/158). In affirming the proposition that God has left "des signes de sa volonté" in the world, Pascal leads his interlocutor to anticipate an argument in favor of Revelation based upon empirical evidence.

The following dossier, "Soumission et usage de la raison" (XIV/XIII), aims at convincing the *libertin* that he will not be asked to abandon reason when examining the arguments in favor of accepting Revelation. The chapter elaborates an idea first expressed by Divine Wisdom in "A.P.R.": "Je n'entends pas que vous soumettiez votre créance à moi sans raison" (182/149). "La conduite de Dieu," Pascal reassures his interlocutor, "est de mettre la religion dans l'esprit *par les raisons* et dans le coeur par la grâce" (203/172; italics mine).

According to Philippe Sellier, Pascal's arguments in this chapter should be taken as a "critique de la raison pure."[3] In Pascal's view, reason's authority extends only to the physical world, to those phenomena that can be assessed empirically. Revelation, however, is of another order: "La foi dit bien ce que les sens ne disent pas, mais non pas le contraire de ce qu'ils voient. Elle est *au-dessus*, et non pas contre" (217/185; italics mine). Built into the correct use of reason is the idea that reason must yield in those domains in which it has no authority. "La raison ne se soumettrait jamais si elle ne jugeait qu'il y a des occasions où elle se doit soumettre" (205/174).

In making the judgment of whether or not to submit to that which appears to transcend its proper domain, however, reason continues to exercise its rightful authority:

> Il faut . . . savoir douter où il faut, assurer où il faut, en se soumettant où il faut. Qui ne fait ainsi n'entend pas la force de la raison. Il y en a qui faillent contre ces trois principes, ou en assurant tout comme démonstratif, manque de se connaître en démonstration, ou en doutant de tout, manque de savoir où il faut se soumettre, ou en se soumettant en tout, manque de savoir où il faut juger. (201/170)

Whereas reason has no authority to judge Revelation itself, it is capable of analyzing those signs of an empirical nature, like the prophecies, that accompany Revelation. That Pascal is thinking ahead to the prophecies when he formulates a theory of the limited uses of reason in chapter XIV/XIII is clearly indicated by Fragment 202/171. This fragment, containing a single citation from the Acts of the Apostles (17:11) might seem at first to have been misfiled in a dossier on the uses of reason. "*Susceperunt verbum cum omni aviditate, scrutantes Scripturas si ita se haberent.*"[4] In fact, Pascal is recording an instance of the correct use of reason: those Jews in the Acts of the Apostles who diligently studied the Old Testament prophecies in an attempt to evaluate the apostles' claim that Jesus was the Messiah.

Pascal intends to make use of the very same prophecies to convince the unbeliever that the case for Revelation warrants his "soumission." Reason will have a key role to play in this process. It will be acting in its proper sphere as it examines the Old Testament prophecies and their fulfillment in the New Testament. It will exercise an act of *jugement* in deciding whether or not such evidence warrants its abdication. "Il n'y a rien de si conforme à la raison que ce désaveu de la raison" (213/182).

Fragment 211/180 reflects a critical juncture in Pascal's formulation of the overall character of his *Apology*. Originally, Pascal seems to have intended to found his defense of Christianity upon a proof of the authenticity of miracles. Three extensive dossiers (XXX–XXXII/*séries* XXXII–XXXIV), dating from 1656–57, attest to this project.[5] The classed dossiers of 1658, however, make no reference to such a proof. Fragment 211/180 even seems to indicate that these dossiers would not have figured at all in the *Apology*:

> Jésus-Christ a fait des miracles . . . parce que les prophéties n'étant pas encore accomplies . . . rien ne témoignait que les miracles. Il était prédit que le Messie convertirait les nations: comment cette prophétie se fût-elle accomplie, sans la conversion des nations? Et comment les nations se fussent-elles converties au Messie, ne voyant pas ce dernier effet des prophéties qui le prouvent? Avant donc qu'il ait été mort, ressuscité et converti les nations, tout n'etait pas accompli, et ainsi il a fallu des miracles pendant tout ce temps. *Maintenant il n'en faut plus . . . car les prophéties accomplies sont un miracle subsistant.* (211/180; italics mine)

In Sellier's estimation, "Pascal s'est rendu compte que la rareté, la limitation dans l'espace, des phénomènes jugés miraculeux ne permettaient pas de fonder une argumentation."[6] It is significant that Pascal classes this reflection in the chapter in which he formulates a theory of reason. Miracles, like Revelation, do not fall within the scope of reason's comprehension. The "prophéties accomplies," however, provide empirical evidence on which reason may act without exceeding its own limitations.

In the following chapter, "Excellence de cette manière de prouver Dieu" (XV/XIV), Pascal rules out metaphysical proofs of God's existence, a logical consequence of the theory of reason's limitations in the preceding chapter. "Les preuves de Dieu métaphysiques sont si éloignées du raisonnement des hommes et si impliquées, qu'elles frappent peu" (222/190). Reason must be presented with arguments that are "palpables" and "solides":

> Tous ceux qui ont prétendu connaître Dieu et le prouver sans Jésus-Christ n'avaient que des preuves impuissantes. Mais pour prouver Jésus-Christ nous avons les prophéties, qui sont des preuves solides et palpables. Et ces prophéties étant accomplies et prouvées véritables par l'événement marquent la certitude de ces vérités et partant la preuve de la divinité de Jésus-Christ. (221/189)

In "Transition" (XVI/XV), Pascal presents a picture of the state of uncertainty to which the *libertin* has ideally been reduced by the arguments of the "étape préparatoire":

> En voyant l'aveuglement et la misère de l'homme, en regardant tout l'univers muet et l'homme sans lumière abandonné à lui-même et comme égaré dans ce recoin de l'univers sans savoir qui l'y a mis, ce qu'il y est venu faire, ce qu'il deviendra en mourant, incapable de toute connaissance, j'entre en effroi comme un homme qu'on aurait porté endormi dans une île déserte. . . . Je vois d'autres personnes auprès de moi d'une semblable nature, je leur demande s'ils sont mieux instruits que moi. Ils me disent que non. Et sur cela ces

misérables égarés, ayant regardé autour d'eux et ayant vu quelques objets plaisants, s'y sont donnés et s'y sont attachés. (229/198)

Pascal's interlocutor, at least as pictured in this fragment, has made definite progress. The arguments of "Vanité" and "Divertissement" have led him to see the folly of seeking solace in temporal things. "Pour moi je n'ai pu y prendre d'attache [aux objets plaisants] (229/198). He has agreed at least to consider Revelation, to attempt to find out "si ce Dieu n'aurait point laissé quelque marque de soi" (229/198). At this point Pascal looks forward to what he hopes will be the unbeliever's reaction when confronted with the historical proofs of Christianity. The *libertin* will see that God has indeed left "quelque marque de soi" in the fallen world:

> Je vois plusieurs religions contraires, et partant toutes fausses excepté une. Chacune veut être crue par sa propre autorité et menace les incrédules. Je ne les crois donc pas là-dessus. Chacun peut dire cela. Chacun peut se dire prophète. *Mais je vois la chrétienne où je trouve des prophéties, et c'est ce que chacun ne peut pas faire.* (229/198; italics mine)

The prophecies are the "marque" that distinguish Christianity from all other religions. "La fausseté des autres religions" (XVII/XVI) takes the example of Islam: "Mahomet non prédit. Jésus-Christ prédit" (241/209). The same chapter joins to this new theme the central argument of the "étape préparatoire"—that "la vraie religion" must embrace and explain the paradox "misère"/"grandeur." "Après avoir entendu toute la nature de l'homme, il faut, pour faire qu'une religion soit vraie, qu'elle ait connu notre nature. Elle doit avoir connu la grandeur et la petitesse, et la raison de l'une et de l'autre. Qui l'a connue, que la chrétienne?" (248/215).

"LE DIEU QUI SE CACHE": THE HIDDEN CHARACTER OF REVELATION

Pascal's ultimate proof of Christianity will be founded on the prophecies. In order to interpret the prophecies, one must be aware of their figurative nature. The theory of "le Dieu caché," elaborated in "Fondements de la religion" (XIX/XVIII), provides a theological rationale for the existence of "figures." "Il faut mettre au chapitre des 'Fondements,' " Pascal notes in fragment 256/223, "ce qui est en celui des 'Figuratifs' touchant *la cause des figures*" (italics mine).

Throughout the course of the *Apology* so far, the *libertin* has repeatedly protested that he can find no evidence of God's presence in the world. He has concluded that if God exists, he must have hidden himself from human knowledge. The teachings of Christianity, Pascal replies in "Fondements," square precisely with this conclusion. The Christian religion, far from teaching that God's presence is manifest in the world, insists that He is knowable only through Revelation. "Nous ne connaissons Dieu que par Jésus-Christ. Sans ce médiateur est ôtée toute communication avec Dieu" (221/189). Any religion that did not proclaim God's hidden nature would contradict the whole of practical human experience. "Dieu étant ainsi caché, toute religion qui ne dit pas que Dieu est caché n'est pas véritable" (275/242).

Even in Revelation, Pascal goes on to point out, God remains "un Dieu véritablement caché." Christ, in whom was revealed all that can ever be known about God, was far from "évidemment Dieu" in the Incarnation (260/228). Just as Christ remained "inconnu parmi les hommes," so "sa vérité demeure parmi les opinions communes, sans différence à l'extérieur." Christ is likewise hidden in the Holy Eucharist. Reason is completely unable to distinguish "l'Eucharistie parmi le pain commun" (258/225).

God's hidden nature extends to the historical evidence that accompanies Revelation. Though the prophecies said that the Messiah would be born in Bethlehem, Christ did not deny that he was from Nazareth. And though the prophets predicted the Messiah would be born of a virgin, Christ never made a point of denying that he was the "fils de Joseph" (265/233). Nor do the genealogies of Jesus recorded in the New Testament make it perfectly clear that he is a linear descendant of David (268/236). The prophets, however, had not predicted that the Messiah would be manifestly the Son of God:

> Que disent les prophètes de Jésus-Christ? Qu'il sera évidemment Dieu? Non. Mais qu'il est *un Dieu véritablement caché*, qu'il sera méconnu, qu'on ne pensera point que ce soit lui, qu'il sera une pierre d'achoppement, à laquelle plusieurs heurteront, etc.[7] (260/228)

The figurative nature of the prophecies is a function of the fact that "Dieu s'est voulu cacher" (275/242). Pascal's explanation of the reason why God has hidden himself in Scripture is founded upon Saint Augustine's doctrine of predestination and election. If God had permitted but a single religion, "elle eût été trop reconnaissable" (268/236). Even the unjust, even those predestined to damnation, would have been able to perceive the truth of Christianity. "Si Jésus-Christ n'était venu que pour sanctifier, toute l'Ecriture et toutes choses y tendraient, et il serait bien aisé de convaincre les infidèles." God's plan, however, was not to save all men. Christ came not only "*in sanctificationem*," but as well "*in scandalum*" (269/237).

Had the prophecies not been figurative in nature and veiled in "obscurités," "on ne serait pas aheurté à Jésus-Christ" (260/228). Yet such was not God's plan. "On n'entend rien aux ouvrages de Dieu si on ne prend pour principe qu'il a voulu aveugler les uns et éclaircir les autres" (264/232). To blind those who were not predestined to recognize Christ as the Messiah was "un des desseins formels des prophètes" (260/228). Christ came not only to save those whom he was meant to redeem but to condemn those doomed from the beginning of time:

> Jésus-Christ est venu aveugler ceux qui voient clair et donner la vue aux aveugles, guérir les malades, et laisser mourir les sains, appeler à pénitence et justifier les pécheurs, et laisser les justes dans leurs péchés, remplir les indigents et *laisser les riches vides*. (267/235)

Pascal's use of the word *laisser* to describe the fate of the *réprouvés* recalls a central principle of Augustinian theology. In condemning some men and in saving others, God is not acting arbitrarily or contrary to mercy and justice. All men, who fell in Adam, merit eternal damnation. God simply *abandons* the unjust to a fate that by right all men deserve. His mercy in saving the elect infinitely transcends any human standard of justice. God has hidden himself in Revelation so as to separate the *élus* from the *réprouvés*. In those signs that, like the prophecies, accompany Revelation, "il y a assez de clarté pour éclairer les élus et assez d'obscurité pour les humilier." In the same signs, "il y a assez d'obscurité pour aveugler les réprouvés et assez de clarté pour les condamner et les rendre inexcusables" (268/236).

Just as all men are by right damned as a result of the Fall, so too is God unknowable as a result of man's fallen reason. Yet just as God transcends human standards of justice in saving the elect, so too he transcends his own hidden nature in the Incarnation. God has "tempéré sa connaissance," modified his unknowable nature, in order to save those who search for him. In a passage transposed from "A.P.R.," Pascal envisages the prophecies as a kind of extraordinary dispensation of grace given to those "qui le cherchent de tout leur coeur":

> Voulant paraître à découvert à ceux qui le cherchent de tout leur coeur, et caché à ceux qui le fuient de tout leur coeur, Dieu a tempéré sa connaissance en sorte qu'il a donné *des marques de soi* visibles à ceux qui le cherchent et non à ceux qui ne le cherchent pas.
> Il y a assez de lumière pour ceux qui ne désirent que de voir, et assez d'obscurité pour ceux qui ont une disposition contraire. (274/149; italics mine)

The prophecies are "marques . . . visibles" only to those whose hearts are oriented toward a figurative understanding of them. Those whose hearts are fixed on earthly and temporal things will be blinded by the veiled nature of "figures." In Pascal's scheme of things, however, those searching for God "de tout leur coeur" must already have been touched by his grace. Their hearts must already have been turned away from temporal things. Otherwise they would not be searching. "Tu ne me chercherais pas," says Christ in a fragment destined for the *Mystère de Jésus*, "si tu ne me possédais" (756/929).

"LES DEUX SENS DE L'ECRITURE"

The system of scriptural interpretation set down in "Que la Loi était figurative" (XX/XIX) spells out the exegetical implications of God's having hidden himself in Scripture. Pascal will rest his whole case for the credibility of Revelation on the notion of the unity of the Old and New Testaments. "Pour prouver tout d'un coup les deux [Testaments] il ne faut que voir si les prophéties de l'un sont accomplies en l'autre" (305/274). Given the principle of God's hidden nature, however, one must assume that the "marques visibles" through which He manifests himself in Revelation are subject to the paradox "aveugler"/"éclaircir."

"Pour examiner les prophéties il faut les entendre" (305/274). If taken literally, the Old Testament prophecies do not in fact square with the phenomenon of Christianity as described in the Gospels. On the surface, they predict the coming of a "grand prince temporel" (319/287) who will restore Israel to its former glory. "Si on croit qu[e les prophéties] n'ont qu'un sens, il est sûr que le Messie ne sera point venu." If, however, the prophecies can be shown to have "deux sens," "il est sûr qu'il sera venu en Jésus-Christ. *Toute la question est donc de savoir si elles ont deux sens*" (305/274; italics mine).

Pascal envisages a fivefold proof that the Old Testament contains a figurative level of meaning:

Que l'Ecriture a deux sens,
que Jésus-Christ et les apôtres ont donnés
dont voici les preuves.
1. Preuve par l'Ecriture même.
2. Preuves par les rabbins. Moïse Maïmon dit qu'elle a deux faces, prou[vées]. Et que les prophètes n'ont prophétisé que de Jésus-Christ.
3. Preuves par la Kabbale.
4. Preuves par l'interprétation mystique que les rabbins mêmes donnent à l'Ecriture.
5. Preuves par les principes des rabbins qu'il y a deux sens. (305/274)

The arguments Pascal proposes in proofs 2–5 are in fact never fully developed in the course of his notes for the *Apology*. Only the dossier "Rabbinage" (XXI/XX) even gives us a general idea of his intentions for making use of the rabbinical tradition to prove the "deux sens" of Scripture. A note in the dossier indicates that all Pascal's documentation regarding the exegetical tradition of the rabbis is taken from the *Pugio fidei adversus Mauros et Judaeos*, a thirteenth-century polemic written by the Spanish Dominican Raymond Martini. This work, an attempt to prove to the Jews that Jesus was the Messiah predicted by the Old Testament prophets, had remained unpublished until the seventeenth century. In 1651, the Hebraic scholar Joseph de Voisin, a friend of Arnauld and of Port-Royal, brought out the first edition of the *Pugio fidei*, to which he added a commentary in which he sought to clarify the history and the principles of the rabbinic tradition.

"Rabbinage" consists of Pascal's notes taken from the *Pugio fidei* and from Voisin's commentaries. Fragment 308/277 outlines a brief "chronologie du rabbinisme," in which the apologist notes the origins and principal authors of the Talmud. Fragment 309/278, titled "Du péché originel," seeks to document a "tradition ample du péché originel selon les Juifs." By showing that the rabbis, departing from the text of Genesis' account of Adam's fall, went on to deduce a theory of universal human corruption, Pascal seeks to provide an instance of the way in which the Jewish tradition itself penetrated the literal meaning of a biblical text and arrived at its figurative significance.

Pascal's aim is to demonstrate that the Talmudic tradition assumes two distinct levels of meaning in the Bible. His notes, however, seem to anticipate going beyond such documentation to argue that the specifically Christian doctrine of Original Sin is already implicit in the Jewish exegetical tradition:

> Sur le mot de la *Genèse* 8, *la composition du coeur de l'homme est mauvaise dès son enfance*. R. Moïse Haddarschan: ce mauvais levain est mis dans l'homme dès l'heure où il est formé. *Massechet Succa*: ce mauvais levain a sept noms dans l'Écriture. Il est appelé mal, prépuce, immonde, ennemi, scandale, coeur de pierre, aquilon: tout cela signifie la malignité qui est cachée et empreinte dans le coeur de l'homme. *Midrasch Tillim* dit la même chose, et que Dieu délivrera la bonne nature de l'homme de la mauvaise. . . . Tout cela se trouve dans le *Talmud*. . . . (309/278)

Pascal goes on to note that the rabbis assign figurative meanings to other texts of Scripture that when taken literally appear to bear no relationship to the theme of "le mauvais levain":

> *Bereschit Rabba* sur le *Psaume* 35: *Seigneur, tous mes os te béniront, parce que tu délivres le pauvre du tyran*. Et y a-t-il un plus grand tyran que le mauvais levain? Et sur les *Proverbes*, 25[21]: *Si ton ennemi a faim, donne-lui à manger*. C'est-à-dire, si le mauvais levain a faim, donnez-lui du pain de la sagesse dont il est parlé *Proverbes*, 9[5]. . . .
> *Midrasch Tillim* dit la même chose, et que l'Ecriture en cet endroit, en parlant de notre ennemi, entend le mauvais levain. . . .
> *Midrasch Kohelet* sur l'*Ecclésiaste*, 9 [13-18]: *Un grand roi a assiégé une petite ville*. Ce grand roi est le mauvais levain, les grandes machines dont il l'environne sont les tentations. (309/278)

Pascal obviously intends to argue that the rabbis' allegorizing of such texts means that the Jewish tradition recognizes the existence of a figurative level of meaning in Scripture. "Rabbinage," however, never spells out this argument. It remains a dossier of transcribed notes. Nor does Pascal elsewhere in the *Pensées* ever develop this line of argument. Jean Mesnard suggests that "Rabbinage" might not have figured at all in Pascal's ultimate argument: "le programme tracé risquait de conduire à un étalage d'érudition peu adapté au lecteur 'honnête homme' que visent les *Pensées*."[8]

As set forth by "Que la Loi était figurative," Pascal's proof of the "deux sens" of Scripture rests entirely on the first of the five "preuves" envisaged by fragment 305/274: "Preuve par l'Ecriture même." Yet perhaps we should not be too quick to banish the arguments suggested by "Rabbinage" from Pascal's definitive version of his *Apology*. One of the distinctive features of Pascal's defense of Christianity is the importance he assigns to the Jewish roots of Christianity. His central argument is that "la véritable religion" was not fabricated in one piece, like Islam, but predicted and prepared for by the 4,000-year-old tradition of the Jews. "Rabbinage" takes its place in the *Apology* as yet another indicator of the historical character of the Christian religion.

The Sacy Bible provides a number of important clarifications of Pascal's "Preuve par l'Ecriture même" of the dual nature of Scripture. That the Old Testament prefigures the New is of course the cardinal assumption of the whole Christian exegetical tradition. Biblical scholarship as practiced at Port-Royal was particularly concerned with working out a theoretical rationale for this assumption. As Henri Gouhier explains, this concern must have had an important formative influence on Pascal:

> L'herméneutique de la future "Apologie" a été élaborée dans un milieu où l'on tient pour évident que la Bible a deux sens. . . . A cet égard, on ne saurait trop insister sur la présence de Pascal aux séances qui, à partir de 1657, se tiennent au château de Vaumuriers, chez le duc de Luynes, pour préparer, avec M. de Sacy, la traduction du Nouveau Testament . . . qui devait paraître dix ans plus tard.[9]

The most concise account of the rationale that the theologians of Port-Royal had worked out for the existence of a figurative level of meaning in the Bible is found in the preface to the 1702 edition of the Sacy Bible. In Sacy's view, the Bible is incarnate in human language in a way that parallels Christ's Incarnation in human flesh: "Dieu y parle aux hommes un langage humain." Because metaphor is an essential attribute of human language, the Bible makes particular use of figurative language:

> Le langage de l'Ecriture . . . s'accommode aux idées et à la manière de concevoir des hommes. D'où vient qu'elle parle de Dieu comme s'il avoit un corps et qu'il nous ressemblât. Non seulement elle luy donne des yeux, une bouche et des mains; elle luy attribue de la colère, de la compassion, de la fureur, et quelques autres de nos passions. Par là, elle représente Dieu, non tel qu'il est, ni comme la raison le fait connoître, *mais comme l'imagination a accoutumé de se le figurer*, malgré les lumières de la raison et de la Foi.[10]

In Augustinian theology, the imagination is the lowliest and weakest of human faculties. Pascal calls it "cette maîtresse d'erreur et de fausseté . . . cette superbe puissance ennemie de la raison" (78/44). Yet it is to this very faculty, and not to reason, that Scripture addresses its use of metaphor and figurative language. Just as Christ became Incarnate in the lowliest of human states, so the Bible takes into account the corrupt state of man's reason.

What distinguishes the Bible's use of metaphor from that of "tous les autres livres" is the fact that its "figures" are organized into a completely coherent system, into an organized level of meaning known as the "sens spirituel." This level of meaning may in human terms best be compared to the "sens de l'auteur" of any other book. "Rien n'est plus utile pour pénétrer le sens d'un auteur, que de savoir le but qu'il s'est proposé.[11] The Old Testament's use of "figures" is likewise a function of the "but" that its "Auteur" "s'est proposé":

> Le but de l'Ancien Testament est de représenter Jésus-Christ, mais Jésus-Christ caché sous le voile des Figures et sous l'obscurité des Prophéties. Le but du Nouveau Testament est de montrer Jésus-Christ à découvert, et de faire voir qu'il est la vérité des Figures, et l'accomplissement des Prophéties. Ainsi les deux Testaments se regardent et s'expliquent l'un l'autre. Le Nouveau Testament . . . est caché dans l'Ancien, et l'Ancien est manifesté dans le Nouveau.[12]

The "figures" found in the Old Testament may be divided into three categories: "légales," "historiques," and "naturelles":

> (1) Les figures légales sont tout ce qui regardent le Temple . . . et les cérémonies de la Loi de Moïse.
>
> (2) Les historiques comprennent les évenements et les traits divers qui composent l'Histoire du Peuple Juif: comme, par exemple, le mariage d'Abraham avec deux femmes, l'une libre et l'autre esclave . . . l'histoire de Jacob et d'Esaü, celle du Serpent d'airain . . . C'étoient des Images de ce que le Messie devoit faire un jour. Les Juifs en conviennent, et Jésus-Christ lui-même dans son Evangile.
>
> (3) Les figures naturelles comprennent tout ce que Moïse a écrit de l'Univers, de la création, de la chute du premier homme. . . . L'homme formé d'abord de la terre, animé ensuite du souffle de Dieu est l'image de l'homme revêtu d'un corps corruptible qui ressuscitera un jour immortel.
>
> Toutes ces choses étoient encore des peintures mistérieuses, des Emblèmes, qui représentoient à l'esprit autre chose que ce que les yeux du corps y voyoient. S. Paul compare le second Adam avec le premier . . . S. Pierre regarde le Déluge et ce qui arriva à la famille de Noé comme une figure de ce qui arrive aux Chrétiens dans leur baptême.[13]

In the course of his commentary on the Bible, Sacy provides a number of different proofs of the existence of a figurative level of meaning in the Old Testament. Three in particular recall arguments formulated by Pascal in "Que la Loi était figurative." On a purely literal level, Sacy admits, Scripture indeed appears to contradict itself. Two propositions that are "contradictoires dans les mots" can, however, "s'accorder très-bien dans le sens." Christ's admonition to his disciples to become like little children (Matthew 18:3) contradicts Saint Paul's admonition "Gardez-vous de devenir des enfans" (1 Corinthians 14:20) only on the most literal level. If the authors of Holy Scripture "ont parlé d'une manière sensée et raisonnable," there must exist a level of meaning in the Bible on which all contradictions are resolved.[14] Pascal states the same argument: "Tout auteur a un sens auquel tous les passages contraires s'accordent ou il n'a point de sens du tout" (289/257).

In his preface to the book of Psalms, Sacy points out that the Bible often declares itself to be speaking in enigmas. He takes the example of Psalm 77 [2]: "J'ouvrirai ma bouche pour vous parler en paraboles; je vous parlerai en énigmes de ce qui s'est fait dès le commencement" (Sacy's translation). After such a declaration, one expects the text that follows to be "rempli d'obscuritez et de paroles énigmatiques." Yet in fact, Sacy observes, Psalm 77 contains only references to "des événemens très connus et dont l'intelligence étoit très-facile à toutes sortes de personnes." Therefore, one must conclude that the apparently clear "sens historique" contains "d'autres véritez plus importantes sous l'écorce de la lettre."[15] Pascal uses the same argument to demonstrate that the prophecies cannot be taken literally. The prophets, like the psalmist, declare themselves to be speaking in enigmas: "Ils ont dit que l'on n'entendrait point leur sens et qu'il était voilé" (291/260).

For Sacy, the ultimate proof of the figurative nature of the Old Testament is to be found in the New Testament. Such a position is completely consistent with the overall orientation of biblical scholarship at Port-Royal. Seeking to bypass scholasticism and return to the principles of the Primitive Church, the Jansenists sought to follow the example of Saint Augustine and found scriptural exegesis upon models authorized by the New Testament itself. The whole of Christian tradition, Sacy observes, has always accepted a figurative reading of the Old Testament:

> Si quelques personnes se trouvent encore choquées de ce qu'on adjoint ces sens spirituels [à la lettre de l'Ancien Testament], on les supplie de se souvenir que l'on n'a fait en cela que suivre l'exemple de tous les saints Pères . . . de saint Paul . . . et de Jésus-Christ, qui s'est servi avantageusement de ces sortes d'explications. . . . Ainsi on ne peut blâmer avec justice ceux qui imitent en ce point Jésus-Christ, saint Paul, les Evangélistes et tous les saints Interprètes de l'Ecriture.[16]

The definitive proof of the figurative character of the Old Testament is the testimony of the risen Christ in Luke 24:44–45: "*Jésus-Christ leur ouvrit l'esprit, afin qu'ils entendissent les Ecritures et leur fit comprendre qu'il falloit que tout ce qui avoit été écrit de luy dans la loy de Moïse, dans les*

Prophètes et dans les Pseaumes fût accompli."[17] Those who reject an allegorical interpretation of the Old Testament reject the authority of Christ himself. "Ils ressemblent en quelque façon aux Juifs."[18]

For Pascal as well, the definitive proof of the "deux sens" of the Old Testament resides in the exegetical model provided by Christ himself in the New Testament. Fragment 285/253 recalls the appearance of the risen Christ to his disciples on the road to Emmaus (Luke 24:13–32): "Jésus-Christ leur ouvrit l'esprit pour entendre les Ecritures." In the *Pensées*, however, we must distinguish between Pascal's own position and those proofs that he intends to make use of in convincing the unbeliever that the Old Testament contains a figurative level of meaning. He cannot appeal to the authority of the New Testament without falling into a circular argument. The aim of the whole *Apology* is to demonstrate the credibility of the New Testament through the fulfillment of the prophecies.

Pascal's proof of the "deux sens" of the prophecies closely parallels Sacy's arguments. Like the 1702 preface to the Sacy Bible, Pascal calls his interlocutor's attention to the fact that Scripture often speaks in metaphors. Such metaphors, when "faux littéralement," can nevertheless be shown to be "vrai spirituellement." Pascal takes the example of Psalm 109:1: "*Sede a dextris meis.*"[19] In such a passage, "il est parlé de Dieu à la manière des hommes":

> Cela ne signifie autre chose sinon que l'intention que les hommes ont en faisant asseoir à leur droite, Dieu l'aura aussi. C'est donc une marque de l'intention de Dieu, non de sa manière de l'exécuter.
> Ainsi quand il est dit: *Dieu a reçu l'odeur de vos parfums et vous donnera en récompense une terre grasse* [Genesis 8:21, 27–28], c'est-à-dire . . . Dieu aura la même intention pour vous parce que vous avez eu pour [lui] la même intention qu'un homme a pour celui à qui il donne des parfums.
> Ainsi *iratus est, Dieu jaloux*, etc.[20] (303/272)

Such metaphors would be ridiculous if taken literally. Indeed, as Pascal had read in Boucher's *Les Triomphes de la religion chrestienne*,[21] detractors of the Bible had argued that Scripture's attribution of human features to God called into question its divinely inspired status:

> Comment est-ce que cette Escriture peut estre inspirée de Dieu puisqu'elle propose plusieurs choses injurieuses et indignes de sa Divine Majesté, luy attribuant des parties corporelles, des yeux, des oreilles, une bouche . . . et ce qui est plus injurieux, luy attribuant des passions d'esprit.[22]

To such detractors, Pascal replies that Scripture necessarily speaks "à la manière des hommes": "Les choses de Dieu étant inexprimables, elles ne peuvent être dites autrement" (303/272). The Bible's attribution of human characteristics to God must be interpreted "spirituellement."

Like Sacy, Pascal appeals to the fact that Scripture often declares itself to be speaking in enigmas. He casts his argument in terms of a practical illustration:

> Quand on surprend une lettre importante où l'on trouve un sens clair, et où il est dit néanmoins que le sens en est voilé et obscurci, qu'il est caché en sorte qu'on verra cette lettre sans la voir et qu'on l'entendra sans l'entendre, que doit-on penser sinon que c'est un chiffre à double sens? Et d'autant plus qu'on y trouve des contrariétés dans le sens littéral. (291/260)

Like Psalm 77 in Sacy's illustration, the prophecies appear to be clear enough in their literal interpretation. "Les prophètes ont dit clairement qu'Israël serait toujours aimé de Dieu et que la Loi serait éternelle." Yet the prophets, like the psalmist, declare themselves to be speaking in enigmas. "Ils ont dit que l'on n'entendrait point leur sens et qu'il était voilé." Therefore, one must conclude, the prophecies take the form of a "chiffre à double sens" (291/260).

Pascal's next argument grows out of the same illustration. Just as one would have to conclude that a letter had a "double sens" if there were manifest contradictions in its "sens littéral," so one can conclude that "le *Vieux Testament* est un chiffre" (307/276) on the basis of its textual contradictions. Fragment 294/263 envisages a brief list of such "contrariétés." In Genesis, Jacob predicts that "the sceptre shall not be taken away from Juda."[23] Hosea, on the other hand, contains the prophecy that Israel will find herself "sans roi ni prince."[24] Leviticus speaks of the Law as "éternelle."[25] A whole series of other texts, however, announce that the Law handed to Moses will be changed.[26] In Genesis, God contracts an "alliance éternelle" with Abraham.[27] Yet Jeremiah announces an "alliance nouvelle."[28] All of Deuteronomy celebrates the excellence of the Law. In Ezechiel, however, God declares that he has given his people "préceptes mauvais."[29]

Such contradictions in the Old Testament cannot be resolved unless one has recourse to a figurative level of meaning. The Jews, practitioners of literal exegesis, "ne sauraient accorder la cessation de la royauté et principauté prédite par Osée avec la prophétie de Jacob." Nor can one "accorder tous les passages" if one takes the Law, the sacrifices described in the Old Testament, and the "royaume" referred to by Jacob and Hosea as "réalités." "Il faut donc par nécessité qu'ils ne soient que figures" (289/257).

Pascal's argument everywhere assumes that the whole of the Old Testament has in reality but a single author. The modern notion that each of the books of the Bible must be studied in its historical context is far removed from his conception of the nature of Scripture. So far removed, that his argument does not even envisage an objection based upon such an assumption. The whole of the Old Testament may be compared to a given work of a single author. "Pour entendre le sens d'un auteur, il faut accorder tout les passages contraires" (289/257). This model may be applied directly to Scripture:

> Ainsi pour entendre l'Ecriture, il faut avoir un sens dans lequel tous les passages contraires s'accordent. Il ne suffit pas d'en avoir un qui convienne à plusieurs passages accordants, mais d'en avoir un qui accorde les passages même contraires.
> Tout auteur a un sens auquel tous les passages contraires s'accordent ou il n'a point de sens du tout. On ne peut pas dire cela de l'Ecriture et des prophètes, ils avaient assurément trop bon sens. (289/257)

Pascal never seems to envisage the objection that perhaps the Bible as a whole has no overall "sens auquel tous les passages contraires s'accordent." It never occurs to him that the *libertin* might argue that each of the books of the Old Testament belongs to a different historical period and was written by a different author. As far as he is concerned, every word in the Bible—from the first of Genesis to the last of Revelation—finds it ultimate significance in Christ himself. "En Jésus-Christ toutes les contradictions sont accordées" (289/257). Another factor must also be taken into account: Pascal's supposition that the *libertin* also views the Bible as a single literary document is by and large a correct one.

Nowhere in the writings of the *libertins* does one find an attempt to discredit the Bible based upon a historical awareness of the cultural and chronological differences that separate the various authors of the books of the two Testaments. Such an objection would have to be based on a historical view of Scripture that Spinoza and Richard Simon were only beginning to formulate in the very period in which Pascal lived. Though Pascal's unbeliever by no means admits the Bible's divinely inspired status, he nonetheless approaches it as a single book.

Pascal dismisses the possibility that the whole Bible "n'a point de sens du tout" with the notion that the human authors of Scripture "avaient assurément trop bon sens" (289/257). In a comparison of the Bible with the Koran, Pascal admits that Scripture contains "obscurités . . . aussi bizarres que celles de Mahomet." Yet the Bible, unlike the Koran, contains "des clartés admirables et des prophéties manifestes et accomplies." These "clartés" merit "qu'on révère les obscurités" (251/218). "Tous ces sacrifices et cérémonies étaient donc figures ou sottises. Or il y a des choses claires trop hautes pour les estimer des sottises" (298/267).

Having deduced the proposition "le *Vieux Testament* est un chiffre" (307/276) from evidence internal to the Old Testament, Pascal then turns to the New Testament. He points out that the New Testament constantly applies the qualification "vrai" or "véritable" to Old Testament events or personages: "*Vere Israelita, Vere liberi, Vrai pain du ciel*"[30] (285/253). In assigning this qualification to such terms, the New Testament indicates that their models in the Old Testament were but "figures" of the "réalités" that were to come. This principle, confirmed in Saint Paul's observation "*toutes choses leur arrivaient en figures*" (1 Corinthians 10:11) (285/253), is the "clé du chiffre." "Dès qu'une fois on a ouvert ce secret, il est impossible de ne le pas voir" (298/267). The New Testament itself is the "clé" to the figurative meaning of the Old Testament:

> Combien doit-on donc estimer ceux qui nous découvrent le chiffre et nous apprennent à connaître le sens caché, et principalement quand les principes qu'ils en prennent sont tout à fait naturels et clairs. C'est ce qu'a fait Jésus-Christ et les apôtres. Ils ont levé le sceau. Il a rompu le voile et a découvert l'esprit. (291/260)

In the course of his proof of the figurative nature of the Old Testament, Pascal works out a rationale for the existence of such a level of meaning. His argument is a corollary of the principle "le Dieu caché." "L'unique objet de l'Ecriture est la charité." "Tout ce qui ne va point à la charité est figure" (301/270). Those blind to "charité" will likewise fail to see that which is hidden by "figures." "Figures" serve to separate the pure of heart from those who have their hearts fixed upon temporal things. This is particularly true of the way "figures" operate in the prophecies:

> Dieu, pour rendre le Messie connaissable aux bons et méconnaissable aux méchants, l'a fait prédire en cette sorte. Si la manière du Messie eût été prédite clairement, il n'y eût point eu d'obscurité, même pour les méchants. Si le temps eût été prédit obscurément, il y eût eu obscurité même pour les bons. . . . Mais le temps a été prédit clairement et la manière en figures.
> *Par ce moyen les méchants, prenant les biens promis pour matériels, s'é-garent malgré le temps prédit clairement, et les bons ne s'égarent pas.*
> *Car l'intelligence des biens promis dépend du coeur, qui appelle bien ce qu'il aime*, mais l'intelligence du temps promis ne dépend point du coeur. Et ainsi la prédiction claire du temps et obscure des biens ne déçoit que les seuls méchants.[31] (287/255; italics mine)

Pascal gives another reason for the existence of "figures." "Dieu diversifie ainsi cet unique précepte de charité pour satisfaire notre curiosité, qui recherche la diversité." His argument recalls Sacy's notion that the language of Scripture "s'accommode aux idées et à la manière de concevoir des hommes."[32] "Curiosité," like "l'imagination," is a manifestation of man's fallen reason. Scripture, incarnate in human language, uses *figures* to appeal to fallen reason's fascination with "diversité." "*Une seule chose est nécessaire* [cf. Luke 10:42], et nous aimons la diversité. Et Dieu satisfait à l'un et à l'autre par ces diversités qui mènent à ce seul nécessaire" (301/270).

In dossier LXI (*série* XIX), we find Pascal reorganizing the chapter "Que la Loi était figurative" and adding additional "raisons pourquoi figures." The figurative character of the Old Testament, he observes, is a function of the fact that a "peuple charnel" was made the "dépositaire" of a "testament spirituel." The prophecies of the Messiah had to be put in the hands of a people who would "porte[r] à la vue de tout le monde ces livres qui prédisent leur Messie, assurant toutes les nations qu'il devait venir, et en la manière prédite dans les livres qu'ils tenaient ouverts à tout le monde." In order to ensure that this people conserved these books "jusqu'au Messie," it was necessary to appeal to their self-interest. "Pour faire réussir tout cela, Dieu a choisi ce peuple charnel, auquel il a mis en dépôt les prophéties qui prédisent le Messie comme libérateur et dispensateur des biens charnels que ce peuple aimait" (738/502).

Pascal argues, in effect, that the "charnel" nature of the Jews was a necessary part of God's plan. "Dieu s'est servi de la concupiscence des Juifs pour les faire servir à Jésus-Christ" (507/614). It ensured that the Jews, seeing temporal prosperity promised to them, showed a "diligence," "fidélité," and "zèle extraordinaire" for what was written in their sacred texts. At the same time, however, it was necessary that the Jews remain ignorant of the "sens caché" of the Law and the Prophets:

> "Si le sens spirituel eût été découvert, ils n'étaient pas capables de l'aimer; et, ne pouvant pas le porter, ils n'eussent point eu le zèle pour la conservation de leurs livres et de leurs cérémonies. Et, s'ils avaient aimé ces promesses spirituelles et qu'ils les eussent conservées incorrompues jusqu'au Messie, leur témoignage n'eût point eu de force, puisqu'ils en eussent été amis.
> Voilà pourquoi il était bon que le sens spirituel fût couvert. (738/502)

Pascal's explanation of why the Jews had to remain ignorant of what was really written in the Law and the Prophets closely parallels Sacy's treatment of the same subject. In the *Préface à la Genèse*, Sacy advanced the idea that it was Moses himself who first began the process of veiling "les véritez les plus hautes" under the form of "figures." The Jews "n'auroient pas esté capables de les comprendre s'il les eust expliquées plus clairement."[33] The central truth to which these "figures" point—"une merveille si grande et si inouïe que le Verbe Éternel, égal à Dieu son Père, daignât s'abaisser jusqu'à se faire homme pour sauver les hommes"—would have been completely beyond their comprehension.[34] Moreover, had the Jews recognized the "sens spirituel" of the Law, they would have accepted Christ as the Messiah. Had this happened, they would not have been able to serve later as hostile witnesses concerning the authenticity of the Old Testament prophecies. "Leur réprobation est devenue plus utile à l'Église que n'auroit esté leur conversion."[35]

PASCAL'S VISION OF SACRED HISTORY: THE "TEMOIGNAGE" OF THE JEWS

According to Filleau de la Chaise, Pascal intended to assign a major place in the *Apology* to an argument founded upon the "circonstances merveilleuses et uniques" surrounding the history of the Jews.[36] The dossiers of 1658, however, fail to envisage such a development. In order to get a more complete idea of Pascal's historical proofs than that afforded by the project of 1658, it is necessary to consider dossiers XLVIII–LII (*séries* VI–X). The argument formulated in these dossiers, which concerns the unique historical character of the Jewish nation, fits perfectly into the *Apology* envisaged by the dossiers of 1658 when inserted between "Perpétuité" and the "Preuves de Moïse." These later dossiers lay the groundwork for Pascal's proof of the Pentateuch in the "Preuves de Moïse" and at the same time document a theory that the apologist advances in "Perpétuité," that Christianity "a toujours été sur la terre" (313/281).

In "Perpétuité," Pascal applies the theory of "figures" to Judaism and concludes that the religion of the Old Testament is *already* Christianity. The core of Christian theology—"qui consiste à croire que l'homme est déchu d'un état de gloire et de communication avec Dieu . . . mais qu'après cette vie on serait rétabli par un Messie qui devait venir"—is already fully present in the Law and the Prophets, though veiled under "figures." If the majority of the Jews had to remain "charnels" and blind to the "sens spirituel" of their religion in order to insure its transmission down through the ages, "il y avait cependant des saints . . . qui attendaient en patience le Christ promis dès le commencement du monde" (313/281). The Old Testament "saints" were, to recall Sacy's definition of them, "Chrètiens effectivement par une anticipation de grâce, quoy qu'ils n'en portassent pas le nom"[37]:

> Noé . . . a mérité de sauver le monde en sa personne par l'espérance du Messie, dont il a été la figure. Abraham était environné d'idolâtres quand Dieu lui a fait connaître le mystère du Messie qu'il a salué de loin. Au temps d'Isaac et de Jacob, l'abomination était répandue sur toute la terre, mais ces saints vivaient en leur foi, et Jacob mourant et bénissant ses enfants s'écrie . . . . *J'attends, ô mon Dieu, le sauveur que vous avez promis.* . . .
> Les Egyptiens étaient infectés et d'idolâtrie et de magie, le peuple de Dieu même était entraîné par leur exemple, mais cependant Moïse et d'autres voyaient celui qu'ils ne voyaient pas et l'adoraient. . . .
> Les Grecs et les Latins ensuite ont fait régner les fausses déités, les poètes ont fait cent diverses théologies, les philosophes se sont séparés en mille sectes différentes. *Et cependant, il y avait toujours au coeur de la Judée des hommes choisis qui prédisaient la venue de ce Messie qui n'était connu que d'eux.* (313/281; italics mine)[38]

Preoccupied with establishing a vision of sacred history based upon his theory of "figures," Pascal does not emphasize the unique character of Judaism in "Perpétuité." In dossier LII (*série* X), however, perhaps after having reread the fragment cited above, he recasts the same argument so as to throw into relief the notion of the Jews' unique character as a nation. "Ceci est effectif," he notes, as if he has just seen the larger implications of what he had written in fragment 313/281:

> Pendant que tous les philosophes se séparent en différentes sectes, il se trouve en un coin du monde des gens qui sont les plus anciens du monde, déclarant que tout le monde est dans l'erreur, que Dieu leur a révélé la vérité, qu'elle sera toujours sur la terre. *En effet, toutes les autres sectes cessent, celle-là dure toujours.* Et depuis quatre mille ans ils déclarent qu'ils tiennent de leurs ancêtres que l'homme est déchu de la communication avec Dieu, dans un entier éloignement de Dieu, mais qu'il a promis de les racheter. (696/456; italics mine)

Whereas "Perpétuité" envisages only the Old Testament "saints" ("des hommes choisis"), the later dossiers embrace the house of Israel as "un peuple tout entier." "La rencontre de ce peuple m'étonne et me semble digne de l'attention" (694/454). What strikes Pascal as most unique about the Jews is the fact that they exist "toujours," still observing the same laws and observing the same traditions that he reads about in the Old Testament. "Cela," he will point out to his interlocutor, "n'a point d'exemple dans le monde ni sa racine dans la nature" (736/492). Pascal takes the present "état des Juifs" to be living proof of the historicity of Christianity.

If "miracles," i.e., the whole supernatural side of Christianity, "ne paraissent pas d'abord convaincants," the Judaic "fondements de cette religion . . . ne peuvent être mis en doute par quelque personne que ce soit." Even while rejecting everything else, the *libertin* must assent to the observable phenomenon of the "état des Juifs." "Il est certain que *nous voyons* en plusieurs endroits du monde un peuple particulier, séparé de tous les autres peuples du monde, qui s'appelle le peuple juif" (694/454; italics mine).

Dossiers XLVIII (*série* VI) and LI (*série* IX) present two versions of Pascal's argument. In the first, titled "Avantages du peuple juif," the apologist draws his interlocutor's attention to a whole series of "choses admirables et singulières" that characterize the Jewish people. Whereas all other races in the world were formed as a result of the intermarriage "d'une infinité de familles," the Jews have conserved their status as "une seule famille." Though "étrangement abondant," this nation "est tout sorti d'un seul homme [Abraham], et étant ainsi tous une même chair et membres les uns des autres, composent un puissant État d'une seule famille. Cela est unique." Moreover, this people "est le plus ancien qui soit en la connaissance des hommes." Dans la recherche que nous faisons," Pascal observes, the antiquity of the Jews merits "une vénération particulière." For if God has manifested himself in history from the beginning of the world, "c'est à ceux-ci qu'il faut recourir pour en savoir la tradition" (691/451).

The Jewish nation is set apart from all other peoples that have ever existed not only by its antiquity but by its "durée." This singular people "a toujours continué depuis son origine jusqu'à maintenant":

> Car au lieu que les peuples de Grèce et d'Italie, de Lacédémone, d'Athènes, et de Rome, et les autres qui sont venus si longtemps après, soient péris il y a si

longtemps, ceux-ci subsistent toujours, et, malgré les enterprises de tant de puissants rois qui ont cent fois essayé de les faire périr . . . ils ont toujours été conservés néanmoins (et cette conservation a été prédite); et, s'étendant depuis les premiers temps jusques aux derniers, leur histoire enferme dans sa durée celle de toutes nos histoires. (691/451)

The singular character of the Jews becomes even more evident when one examines the Law by which they govern themselves. "La plus ancienne loi du monde" which is contained in "le plus ancien livre du monde," the Law of the Jews is the "seule qui ait toujours été gardée sans interruption dans un État." The Jews' singular attachment to their Law seems inexplicable when compared with the transmutation of the laws of other nations:

Cette loi est en même temps la plus sévère et la plus rigoureuse de toutes, en ce qui regarde le culte de leur religion, obligeant ce peuple . . . à mille observations particulières et pénibles,.sur peine de la vie, de sorte que c'est une chose bien étonnante qu'elle se soit toujours conservée constamment durant tant de siècles par un peuple rebelle et impatient comme celui-ci, pendant que tous les autres États ont changé de temps en temps leurs lois, quoique tout autrement faciles. (691/451)

In dossier LI (*série* IX), Pascal contrasts Judaism with other world religions. Islam, the religion of the Romans, and that of the Egyptians are easily shown to be products of "des faiseurs de religions." That "religion précédente" on which Christianity is founded, however, bears the marks of *la véritable religion*. It is the only rèligion aside from Christianity itself which teaches that man has fallen into a state of corruption from a state of communication with God. It is the only religion which teaches "qu'il viendra un Libérateur pour tous." The Jews declare that they have been "formés exprès" by God "pour être les avant-coureurs et les hérauts de ce grand avènement, et pour appeler tous les peuples à s'unir à eux dans l'attente de ce Libérateur" (694/454).

Before he can begin to deal with the prophecies, Pascal must demonstrate the historicity of the Old Testament. The singular circumstances surrounding the Jewish nation serve to draw the *libertin*'s attention to the fact that the "histoires" of the Jews "précèdent de plusieurs siècles les plus anciennes que nous ayons" (694/454). The same book that chronicles the history of the Jews and contains their Law also records their prophecies of the Messiah. To prove the historicity of the Pentateuch is to establish the authenticity of the prophecies.

Pascal's whole proof of the authenticity of the Pentateuch is built around the figure of Moses. "La création du monde commençant à s'éloigner, Dieu a pourvu d'un historien unique contemporain, et a commis tout un peuple pour la garde de ce livre, afin que cette histoire fût la plus authentique du monde" (711/474). What distinguishes the Pentateuch from all other ancient works is the fact that it was written by an author who

Figure 11. Moses parting the Red Sea; illuminated chapter title, *L'Exode*, Sacy Bible, 1702 (Service photographique, Bibliothèque Nationale)

had direct access to the events that he chronicles. "Toute histoire qui n'est pas contemporaine est suspecte" (688/436).

In order to show that Moses was indeed a "contemporain" of those events that he reports in the Pentateuch, Pascal has recourse to a theory that we have already encountered in Sacy's *Préface à la Genèse*. "Ce n'est pas la longueur des années, mais la multitude des générations qui rendent les choses obscures. Car la vérité ne s'altère que par le changement des hommes" (324/292). The longevity of the Patriarchs ensured the accurate transmission of historical data from Adam to Moses:

> La longueur de la vie des patriarches, au lieu de faire que les histoires des choses passées se perdissent, servait au contrairie à les conserver. . . . Lorsque les hommes vivaient si longtemps, les enfants vivaient longtemps avec leurs pères. Ils les entretenaient longtemps. Or de quoi les eussent-ils entretenus sinon de l'histoire de leurs ancêtres, puisque toute l'histoire était réduite à celle-là, qu'ils n'avaient point d'études, ni de sciences, ni d'arts, qui occupent une grande partie des discours de la vie? Aussi l'on voit qu'en ce temps les peuples avaient un soin particulier de conserver leurs généalogies. (322/290)

The 2,000 years that separate Moses from Adam in fact only amount to five generations. "Sem qui a vu Lamech, qui a vu Adam, a vu aussi Jacob, qui a vu ceux qui ont vu Moïse" (327/296). The origins of the world were to Moses what events are to us that took place 300 years ago. "Cette preuve suffit pour convaincre les personnes raisonnables de la vérité du Déluge et de la Création. Et cela fait voir la Providence de Dieu, lequel, voyant que la Création commençait à s'éloigner, a pourvu d'un historien qu'on peut appeller contemporain" (741).[39]

Pascal's entire defense of the historicity of the Pentateuch rests on two assumptions: its Mosaic authorship and the accuracy of biblical chronologies. Evidence elsewhere in the *Pensées* indicates that the apologist gathered material to sustain his position on both these points. Dossier XXIX, "Contre la fable d'Esdras," anticipates the need to refute one longstanding objection to the Mosaic authorship of the Pentateuch. Various fragments relative to "l'*Histoire de la Chine*" envisage a defense of biblical chronologies.

The noncanonical Fourth Book of Esdras recounts that the original texts of the Pentateuch were burned during the Babylonian Exile and reconstituted by Esdras. Pascal, in a dossier written prior to the classification of 1658, assembles arguments aimed at proving that the account is but a "fable." The fact that Pascal did not include this dossier, or even a single allusion to it, in the classification of 1658 perhaps indicates that it would not have figured in the *Apology* at all. The dossier's chief interest lies in showing that Pascal, in the earliest stages of his work, anticipated a proof of the Old Testament founded upon the authority of Moses. His arguments seek to counter any potential use of the "fable d'Esdras" by those "qui voudraient ruiner la vérité de notre religion, fondée sur Moïse" (416/972).

After noting several references in the early Fathers that seem to indicate their acceptance of Esdras' reconstitution of the Pentateuch, Pascal assembles a set of evidence meant to refute the story's historicity. It is significant that he first of all has recourse to the testimony of canonical Scripture: "2 *Macchabées*, 2" recounts that Jeremiah hid the ark containing the Law at the time of the going into Exile (415/971). Pascal notes that "Josèphe en toute l'histoire d'Esdras ne dit pas un mot de ce rétablissement" (415/971) and cites Philo the Jew to the effect that the Law reached the translators of the Septuagint in the characters in which it was anciently written. He goes on to argue that if the sacred texts survived the persecution of Antiochus and Vespasian, "où l'on a voulu abolir les Livres," it makes no sense to suppose that they perished under the Babylonians, "où nulle persécution n'a été faite" (417/970).

If Pascal's attempt to refute "la fable d'Esdras" remains marginal to the major proofs envisaged by the dossiers of 1658, such is not the case with his defense of traditional biblical chronologies. Shortly after having set down his "Preuves de Moïse," the apologist came across evidence that directly challenged the chronological basis of his arguments. In 1658, the Jesuit Martin Martini published his *Sinicae Historiae*, in which the chronologies of the Chinese were shown to cast doubt upon traditional assumptions concerning the antiquity of human history. Christian chronologists, calculating backward through the genealogies of the Old Testament, had fixed the date of the Creation at the year 4404 B.C. The chronologies of the Chinese showed human history to be much more ancient,

Pascal's first reaction to the *Sinicae Historiae* is vividly recorded in fragment 663/822, "*Histoire de la Chine*":

> Je ne crois que les histoires dont les témoins se feraient égorger.
> (*Lequel est le plus croyable des deux: Moïse ou la Chine?*)
> Il n'est pas question de voir cela en gros: je vous dis qu'il y a de quoi aveugler et de quoi éclairer.
> Par ce mot seul je ruine tous vos raisonnements. —"Mais la Chine obscurcit, dites-vous." Et je réponds: "La Chine obscurcit, mais il y a clarté à trouver. Cherchez-la.
> Ainsi tout ce que vous dites fait à un des desseins, et rien contre l'autre. Ainsi cela sert et ne nuit pas.
> Il faut donc voir cela en détail, il faut mettre papiers sur table." (663/822)

"Personally," Pascal imagines himself telling the *libertin*, "I would prefer to place my trust in the Christian tradition, whose credibility is sealed by the blood of the martyrs." It is not simply a matter of posing an empirical question—a question in fact struck by Pascal in his draft of this imaginary exchange—*lequel est le plus croyable: Moïse ou la Chine*? The apparent evidence of the Chinese chronologies is but a further demonstration of the way in which God has hidden Revelation from the wise. "La Chine obscurcit."

Pascal's response to the *Sinicae Historiae* is not so clear cut as fragment 663/822 might lead us to believe. While drafting one fragment in which the *libertin* is told that the whole issue really has little bearing on the state of his spiritual progress, the apologist at the same time begins searching for arguments that might refute the evidence of the Chinese chronologies. Fragment 716/481, "Contre l'*Histoire de la Chine*," cites evidence in favor of biblical chronologies from the *Essais* of Montaigne: "Les histoires de Mexico, des cinq soleils, dont le dernier est il n'y a que huit cents ans." According to Montaigne (*Essais* III, 6), the Aztecs divided the history of the world into five ages, the first of which ended in a universal flood and the last of which began only 800 years ago with the appearance of a fifth sun. Pascal, familiar with Saint Augustine's theory of the six ages of the world,[40] sees a parallel in the "histoires de Mexico." As Sellier so correctly observes, "Pascal . . . pensait que les Aztèques confirmaient la chronologie biblique, contre les prétentions de la Chine à une extrême antiquité."[41]

Fragment 688/430, "Antiquité des juifs," was likewise composed in response to the *Sinicae Historiae*. Pascal classes the "histoires" of the Chinese, along with those of the Greeks and the Egyptians, in the category of noncontemporary writings:

> Qu'il y a de différence d'un livre à un autre! Je ne m'étonne pas de ce que les Grecs ont fait l'*Iliade*, ni les Egyptiens et les Chinois leurs histoires.
> Il ne faut que voir comment cela est né. Ces historiens fabuleux ne sont pas contemporains des choses dont ils écrivent. Homère fait un roman, qu'il donne pour tel et qui est reçu pour tel: car personne ne doutait que Troie et Agamemnon n'avaient non plus été que la pomme d'or. . . . Quatre cents ans après, les témoins des choses ne sont plus vivants; personne ne sait plus par sa connaissance si c'est une fable ou une histoire. (688/436)

The Pentateuch, by contrast, was written by an "historien contemporain" (711/474). It bears an additional mark of its authenticity: it has formed an entire people. "Il y a bien de la différence entre un livre que fait un particulier, et qu'il jette dans le peuple, et un livre qui fait lui-même un peuple. On ne peut douter que le livre ne soit aussi ancien que le peuple" (688/436).[42] Whereas the chronologies of the Chinese were written subsequently to the events that they report and are in reality but "fables," the Pentateuch is as old as the Jews themselves.

The foregoing fragments reveal that Pascal was indeed aware of a challenge to the biblical chronologies on which he bases his defense of the authenticity of the Old Testament. In the *Pensées*, however, the issue remains a largely unresolved problem. Once again we are presented with an *Apology* interrupted in the course of its revision by Pascal's premature death. What we should note is that Pascal's faith in the accuracy of the biblical chronologies does not seem to have been shaken in the least by the evidence presented in the *Sinicae Historiae*. The arguments that we find him formulating envisage a defense of a biblical view of the antiquity of the world.

"PREUVES DE JESUS-CHRIST": THE OBSCURITY OF THE HISTORICAL JESUS

From the perspective of modern Christian apologetics, Pascal's "Preuves de Jésus-Christ" may appear to be the weakest link in the entire *Apology*. Whereas the modern apologist is primarily concerned with establishing the historical reliability of those texts that make up the New Testament,[43] Pascal's emphasis is elsewhere. He does not seem to anticipate the unbeliever's challenging the historicity of the Gospels. Whereas modern Christian apologetics focus on the historicity of Jesus of Nazareth, Pascal's emphasis is on Christ's historical obscurity, which he takes to be a function of God's hidden nature in the Incarnation.

Only two arguments, both relatively incidental to the major focus of the chapter, seem to envisage a textual proof of the historicity of the New Testament. Fragment 349/318 notes the "discordance apparente des évangiles." Like the "faiblesses très apparentes" considered in fragment 268/236, the fact that the four Gospels do not present a picture of the life of Christ that is uniform in its historical detail suggests that "cela n'a pas été fait de concert." In other words, the Gospels are genuine historical records. The fact that they disagree on the level of historical detail rules out the possibility of a conspiracy to present an edited or biased view of the life of Christ. It also rules out the possibility that the whole story of the life of Christ was the invention of "un particulier" (cf. 688/436).

A second argument relative to the textual status of the Gospels concerns their style, which, Pascal argues, sets them apart from all other literary creations. "Qui a appris aux évangélistes les qualités d'une âme parfaitement héroïque pour la peindre si parfaitement en Jésus-Christ?" (347/316) The words of Christ himself in the Gospels betray a fusion of clarity and complexity that is simply not possible on a human literary level:

> Jésus-Christ a dit les choses grandes si simplement qu'il semble qu'il ne les a pas pensées, et si nettement néanmoins qu'on voit bien ce qu'il en pensait. Cette clarté jointe à cette naïveté est admirable. (340/309)[44]

Pascal's major emphasis in the "Preuves de Jésus-Christ," however, concerns Christ's historical obscurity. The ultimate proof of the *Apology*, for which this dossier is the final preparation, rests on the assumption that the "manière" of the coming of the Messiah must be figuratively interpreted (cf. 287/255). The prophecies of a temporal Messiah had the purpose of blinding those whose hearts were set on earthly things. The Messiah who actually came was recognized only by the pure of heart. Before proceeding to an exposition of the prophecies and their accomplishment, Pascal therefore stresses the temporal obscurity of the historical Jesus: "Jésus-Christ dans une obscurité (selon ce que le monde appelle obscurité), telle que les historiens n'écrivant que les importantes choses des États l'ont à peine aperçu" (331/300).

Traditionally, Christian apologists had attempted to make the best of the rare references to Christ in Josephus and the Roman historians. Pascal, however, departs completely from this tradition. He makes Jesus' historical obscurity stand as the principal sign that he was indeed the Messiah. For what comparatively obscure historical figure, he argues, ever wrought such dramatic changes in the history of the world? A description of the facts about the life of Jesus

> De trente-trois ans il en vit trente sans paraître. Dans trois ans, *il passe pour un imposteur*,[45] les prêtres et les principaux le rejettent, ses amis et ses plus proches le méprisent, enfin il meurt trahi par un des siens, renié par l'autre et abandonné par tous. (736/499; italics mine)

stands in inexpliciable contrast with the events that followed his death and resulted in the foundation of the Church. "Les princes quittent leurs grandeurs, les filles souffrent le martyre. D'où vient cette force? C'est que le Messie est arrivé. Voilà l'effet et les marques de sa venue" (332/301).

In the larger context of the *Apology*, Jesus' historical obscurity takes its place as a corollary of the fundamental principle *le Dieu caché*. The purpose of this "obscurité" was not only to blind those not meant to recognize the Messiah when he arrived but to be as well a stumbling block to those "charnels" who would follow. Yet Christ in the Incarnation was obscure only to those whose hearts were fixed on temporal things. To the pure of heart, Jesus was clearly not only the Messiah but God himself in human vesture:

> Jésus-Christ sans biens, sans aucune production au-dehors de science, est dans son ordre de sainteté. Il n'a point donné d'inventions, il n'a point régné, mais il a été humble, patient, saint, saint, saint à Dieu, terrible aux démons, sans aucun péché. *Ô qu'il est venu en grande pompe et en une prodigieuse magnificence aux yeux du coeur et qui voient la sagesse!* (339/308; italics mine)

"Saint, saint, saint à Dieu" recalls not only Isaiah's vision of God Himself enthroned in glory (Isaiah 6:1–3) but as well that moment in the Mass when the tolling of the bell at the thrice-holy of the Sanctus heralds God's descent into the elements of bread and wine during the approaching Prayer of Consecration. Here too only those whose hearts are fixed on heavenly things perceive Christ "en grande pompe et en une prodigieuse magnificence." The *charnels* perceive only the external trappings of the bread and wine. "Comme Jésus-Christ est demeuré inconnu parmi les hommes . . . ainsi l'Eucharistie parmi le pain commun" (258/225).

In order to provide a theological rationale for Christ's historical and sacramental obscurity, Pascal develops the theory of the three orders: "corps," "esprits," and "charité." Material "grandeurs" hold no attraction for men intent on "les recherches de l'esprit." Intellectual "grandeur" is, on the other hand, "invisible aux rois, aux riches, aux capitaines, à tous ces grands de chair." "La grandeur de la sagesse," i.e., knowledge of God, is likewise "invisible aux charnels et aux gens d'esprit." "Ce sont trois ordres différents" (339/308). These three orders are so self-contained that human effort can never achieve a transition from one to the next. From all the matter of the universe, man cannot extract even "une petite pensée." "De tous les corps et esprits on n'en saurait tirer un mouvement de vraie charité, cela est impossible et d'un autre ordre, surnaturel" (339/308).

Given the fact that the order proper to heavenly things is "charité," "il est bien ridicule de se scandaliser de la bassesse de Jésus-Christ, comme si cette bassesse était du même ordre duquel est la grandeur qu'il venait faire paraître." "Il eût été inutile à Archimède de faire le prince dans ses livres de géométrie." "Il eût été inutile à Notre Seigneur Jésus-Christ, pour éclater dans son règne de *sainteté*," to have come as a temporal king. His temporal obscurity, on the contrary, is the sign of his spiritual "grandeur," at least for those who have the eyes to see it:

> Qu'on considère cette grandeur-là dans sa vie, dans sa passion, dans son obscurité, dans sa mort, dans l'élection des siens, dans leur abandonnement, dans sa secrète résurrection et dans le reste. . . . Mais il y en a qui ne peuvent admirer que les grandeurs charnelles. . . . (339/308)

In fragment 329/298, Pascal invokes the notion of the three "ordres" in a response to those who object that Scripture "n'a pas d'ordre." Because it is addressed, not to the intellect, but to the heart, Scripture does not proceed by way of "principe et démonstration." The heart has an order of its own. "On ne prouve pas qu'on doit être aimé en exposant d'ordre les causes de l'amour, cela serait ridicule." By the same token, one cannot expect Christ and the apostles, who address men's hearts, to follow principles of demonstration proper to the intellect. "Jésus-Christ, saint Paul ont l'ordre de la charité, non de l'esprit, car ils voulaient échauffer, non instruire" (329/298).

For Pascal, where there is "obscurité" there is also "clarté." Having emphasized Jesus' historical obscurity, he turns to what for him is the dazzling clarity of the single most important proof of Christianity, the Resurrection. Sacy, we recall, argues that had the Resurrection not happened, it would be impossible to explain the foundation of the Christian Church. The followers of Jesus were frightened and scattered as a result of his death. Had the risen Christ not appeared to them, the disciples would have had no motivation to found the Church.[46] Pascal takes up exactly the same argument: "Tandis que Jésus-Christ était avec eux [les apôtres], il les pouvait soutenir. *Mais après cela, s'il ne leur est apparu, qui les a fait agir?*" (353/322; italics mine.)

In order not to accept the Resurrection, Pascal argues, one must reach one of two conclusions. Either Christ's followers were sincerely deceived in believing that he rose from the dead, or else they fabricated the entire story. The apostles were either "trompés" or "trompeurs." Neither of these explanations, Pascal insists, is acceptable. The apostles can hardly have been the victims of self-deception. "Car il n'est pas possible de prendre un homme pour être ressuscité"[47] (353/322). Nor is the hypothesis of a conspiracy on the part of the apostles believable:

> L'hypothèse des apôtres fourbes est bien absurde. Qu'on la suive tout au long, qu'on s'imagine ces douzes hommes assemblés après la mort de Jésus-Christ faisant le complot de dire qu'il est ressuscité! Ils attaquent par là toutes les puissances. Le coeur des hommes est étrangement penchant à la légèreté, au changement, aux promesses, aux biens. Si peu que l'un de ceux-là se fût

démenti par tous ces attraits, et qui plus est par les prisons, par les tortures et par la mort, ils étaient perdus.
Qu'on suive cela! (341/310)

Pascal's faith in the Resurrection is based upon the same principle as his acceptance of the historicity of the Old Testament, that of *témoignage*. Just as the Jews are living witnesses of their ancestors' exodus out of Egypt, so the apostles and their successors are the *témoins* of this new passover from death to life. Their testimony is sealed by the blood of the martyrs. "Je ne crois que les histoires dont les témoins se feraient égorger" (663/822).

Like the chapters that have preceded it, "Preuves de Jésus Christ" looks forward to the definitive argument of "Prophéties." "Jésus-Christ prédit quant au temps et à l'état du monde. . . . Qu'on est heureux d'avoir cette lumière dans cette obscurité" (348/317). Though containing arguments that are valid in their own right, this chapter has principally served to focus the interlocutor's attention on the person of Christ. It may seem surprising that the *Apology* has taken so long to get around to presenting such a central figure. This is a key element in Pascal's overall apologetic strategy. He only introduces the historical figure of Jesus when he is ready to bring on his definitive argument, that Christ was the Messiah predicted and prefigured by the whole of the Old Testament.

"PROPHETIES": THE DEFINITIVE ARGUMENT OF THE *APOLOGY* RECONSTRUCTED WITH THE AID OF THE SACY BIBLE

"La plus grande des preuves de Jésus-Christ sont les prophéties" (368/335). Given its role as the definitive proof in Pascal's *Apology*, "Prophéties" (XXV/XXIV) merits an attention that has rarely been accorded it by commentators on the *Pensées*.[48] The reason for such neglect of the chapter lies largely in its documentary nature. Pascal only occasionally provides indications of how he planned to use the long lists of scriptural citations assembled in the chapter and amplified almost a hundredfold by dossiers LIV–LX (*séries* XII–XVIII). Reconstructing the broad outlines of Pascal's proof means first of all examining the content and context of those biblical citations that form his documentation of "la plus grande des preuves."

As often as not, simply looking up a passage cited by Pascal in a modern translation of the Bible fails to clarify what use he intended to make of it. Modern biblical commentaries are of equally little help. Biblical studies have been so thoroughly revolutionized since the advent of textual criticism that most passages that Pascal interprets as prophetic are passed over in silence by modern commentaries. The distance between the world of biblical scholarship upon which Pascal relied and that of modern textual criticism can be easily illustrated. Pascal will place a major emphasis on the prophecy found in Daniel 9. A comparison of his translation of Daniel 9:26 (based upon the Vulgate) and that of the Jerusalem Bible (based upon the Hebrew) is extremely revealing:

> Pascal: "Après ces 62 semaines, le Christ sera tué et un peuple viendra avec son prince, qui détruira la ville et le sanctuaire." (720/485)
>
> Jerusalem Bible: "Et après les soixante-deux semaines, un messie supprimé —et . . . ne sera pas à lui—la ville et le sanctuaire détruits par un prince qui viendra."

Whereas Pascal obviously intends to interpret the passage as predicting the death of Christ and the destruction of Jerusalem at the hands of the Romans, the Jersualem Bible totally ignores this traditional reading. It identifies the "anointed one" ("un messie") as the high priest Onias of 2 Machabees 4 and attaches no figurative meaning to the passage at all.[49] In order to analyze Pascal's use of scriptural citations, we must consult a text based upon the Vulgate. For English translations we will make use of the Douay translation.[50] In cases where commentary is needed to reconstruct Pascal's interpretation of a passage, we shall make use of the Sacy Bible.

It is significant that in his commentaries on the Books of the Prophets, Sacy emphasizes that the prophecies are the most powerful proof of Christianity:

> Il y a eu en tout temps et il y aura jusques à la fin du monde des impies et des libertins, ennemis . . . de la religion de Jésus-Christ, dont toute la joye est d'en détruire, s'ils le pouvoient, *les fondemens*. Or, nous n'avons rien de plus fort pour prouver la vérité de cette religion que les prophéties, qui ont marqué si longtemps devant, et d'une manière si précise l'Incarnation du Fils de Dieu, sa mort, sa résurrection, le salut des nations, la réprobation des juifs, la destruction de leur Ville et l'établissement de l'Eglise sur les ruines du paganisme.[51]
>
> Les ouvrages des Prophètes sont . . . une des preuves les plus constantes de la certitude de notre Religion. C'est ce que Dieu nous apprend de sa propre bouche. . . .[52]
>
> Il n'y a rien de si puissant pour établir . . . *la véritable religion* que l'autorité des divines prophéties. . . . Ce qu'on peut encore établir par ces prophéties est la divinité des livres saints de l'Ecriture.[53]

Such texts suggest that Pascal's very choice of the prophecies as "la plus grande des preuves" reflects his consultation with Sacy and the other theologians of Port-Royal concerning the historical focus of his *Apology*. Nor should we fail to note Sacy's use of certain key phrases that constantly recur in the *Pensées*: "fondemens," "la véritable religion," "preuves convaincantes." In fact, a whole series of parallels between Sacy's treatment of the prophecies and ideas developed in the *Pensées* merit our attention.

Pascal insists that "la plus grande des preuves" originates with God him-

L'ECRITURE ET LE RESTE 195

Figure 12. The divine inspiration of Isaiah; illuminated chapter title, *Isaïe*, Sacy Bible, 1702 (Service photographique, Bibliothèque Nationale)

self: "c'est aussi à quoi Dieu a le plus pourvu." (368/335) Sacy likewise stresses God's design in providing such a proof:

> Dieu ayant résolu de sauver le monde quatre mille ans après sa création et de le sauver par la mort et par la résurrection de son Fils . . . a voulu fonder cette foy sur des *preuves si convaincantes* qu'elles pussent distinguer *la véritable religion* de toutes les sociétez sacrilèges que le démon avoit déjà inventés ou qu'il pourrait inventer dans la suite de tous les siècles.[54]

Pascal's decision to found his *Apology* on the prophecies rather than on miracles is clarified by an argument that Sacy formulates in his preface to *Les douzes petits prophètes*. In fragment 211/180, we saw Pascal distinguishing between "miracles," proper to the life of Christ ("parce que les prophéties n'étant pas encore accomplies"), and the "miracle subsistant" constituted by "les prophéties accomplies." Sacy makes a similar distinction. During his earthly ministry, Christ gave "des preuves claires de qui il était par un nombre infini de miracles." Afterward, however, the pagans, when presented with these miracles, attributed them to magic. Knowing that this would happen, God had prepared in advance the proof constituted by the prophecies:

> La Sagesse éternelle, à l'égard de laquelle les choses futures sont déjà présentes, prévoyoit que le démon, qui avoit rendu quelques magiciens très célèbres dans le monde, s'efforceroit de mettre Jésus-Christ en ce rang et d'attribuer ses miracles à la magie.

> C'est en effet ce qui est arrivé à la naissance de l'Eglise. Car lorsque l'on a représenté aux Payens les merveilles de la vie de Jésus-Christ, ils ont répondu que des magiciens en avoient fait d'aussi grands. . . .
> Dieu donc, voulant étouffer d'une manière convaincante l'extravagance de ces impostures . . . a voulu que la prophétie précédât les miracles et que la certitude de cette première preuve rendît témoignage à la sainteté de la seconde.[55]

In "Excellence de cette manière de prouver Dieu" (XV/XIV), we saw Pascal ruling out metaphysical proofs of God's existence in favor of the "preuves solides et palpables" of the prophecies. In his preface to the book of Daniel, Sacy explains why the prophecies are a superior proof to an argument founded upon "raisons naturelles":

> Si un homme par exemple entreprend de faire voir l'existence du vray Dieu par la création de l'univers et par cet ordre admirable qui paroît dans toute la nature; un impie s'élèvera contre luy, en luy soutenant que le ciel et la terre sont de toute éternité sans aucun principe qui les ait produits;[56] et il n'est pas si aisé de le réduire au silence.
> Mais si l'on convient d'une prophétie qu'on ne puisse raisonablement la contester; si l'on demeure d'accord qu'elle a esté proposée à tout un peuple plusieurs siècles avant que les choses qui y sont prédites se soient accomplies; et si enfin l'accomplissement de ces choses n'est pas moins incontestable; nul impie qui ne voudra pas renoncer à la raison ne pourra se dispenser de reconnoître qu'il y a nécessairement quelque Estre supérieur . . . qui gouverne toutes choses.[57]

Sacy's explanation of why the prophecies "ont dû être obscures" recalls Pascal's theory that had the Jews been able to understand the "sens spirituel" of the Law, "leur témoignage n'eût point eu de force, puisqu'ils en eussent été amis" (738/502). Like Pascal, Sacy conceives of the Jews as the zealous guardians of a "livre scellé." "Le Saint Esprit, qui parloit par [la bouche des prophètes], devoit s'accommoder aux Juifs qui ne comprenoient que ce qui tomboit sous les sens." The prophets promise the Jews "une riche abondance de toutes choses dans leurs villes, dans leurs champs et dans leurs maisons" in order to ensure their conservation of the prophecies. This is necessary because the Jews have a special mission of "témoignage."[58]

The pagans, when confronted with the prophecies and their accomplishment, were so struck by the clarity of this proof that they assumed that the prophecies must have been a forgery. They argued that these documents must have been composed by the apostles, so clear was their prediction of specific events in the life of Christ. "Les chrétiens renvoyoient alors les Payens aux Juifs, pour apprendre d'eux quel jugement on devoit faire de ces livres prophétiques." The pagans learned from the Jews that the prophecies were genuine historical documents dating from long before the time of Christ. The fact that these same Jews were "ennemis mortels" of Christianity "rendoit le témoignage qu'ils portaient en . . . faveur [de ces livres prophétiques] entièrement irréprochable."[59]

Sacy's observations clarify the relationship of the argument of "Prophéties" to those dossiers in which Pascal develops the notion of the "témoignage" of the Jews. In Pascal's mind, the historicity of the prophecies is guaranteed by the historicity of the Jews themselves. "Prophéties" repeatedly emphasizes that the whole of the Jewish tradition looks forward to the Messiah:

> Quand un seul homme aurait fait un livre des prédictions de Jésus-Christ pour le temps et pour la manière et que Jésus-Christ serait venu conformément à ces prophéties, ce serait une force infinie.
> Mais il y a bien plus ici. C'est une suite d'hommes durant quatre mille ans qui constamment et sans variations viennent l'un ensuite de l'autre prédire ce même avènement. *C'est un peuple tout entier qui l'annonce et qui subsiste depuis quatre mille années pour rendre en corps témoignage* des assurances qu'ils en ont et dont ils ne peuvent être divertis par quelques menaces et persécutions qu'on leur fasse. (364/332; italics mine)

Pascal's documentation of the 4,000-year "témoignage" of this "peuple tout entier" aims to transcend the traditionally accepted prophetic books of the Old Testament. "Le Messie a toujours été cru" (314/282). "Moïse d'abord enseigne la Trinité, le péché originel, le Messie." "David grand témoin" (346/315). Fragment 504/609, "qu'il devait venir un Libérateur qui écraserait la tête au démon," even seems to anticipate seeing a prophecy of the Messiah in God's words to the serpent in Genesis 3:15.[60] Pascal's aim is indeed to document "le Christ promis *dès le commencement du monde*" (313/281; italics mine).

Pascal may have intended to organize his proof in a kind of chronological order, beginning with the "témoignage" of the Patriarchs and leading up to the more specific prophecies of Daniel, Isaiah, and those other prophets whom he says God raised up "durant mille six cents ans." (368/335) Pascal would then have turned to another argument. During the 400 years preceding the birth of Christ, God dispersed the Jews, and with them the prophecies, "dans tous les lieux du monde":

> Voilà quelle a été la préparation à la naissance de Jésus-Christ, dont l'Evangile devant être cru de tout le monde il a fallu non seulement qu'il y ait eu des prophéties pour le faire croire, mais que ces prophéties fussent par tout le monde pour le faire embrasser par tout le monde. (368/335)

Up until this point in the *Apology*, Pascal's discussion of the prophecies has focused almost exclusively on their figurative nature and emphasized their veiled character. "Prophéties" and the subsequent dossiers associated with it, however, stress the literal realization of the prophecies on the plane of history. Père Dubarle took this radical shift in emphasis to represent a fundamental inconsistency in Pascal's argument.[61] This is not, however, necessarily the case. According to Pascal's scheme, the prophecies are figurative only insofar as they concern "la manière du Messie" (cf. 287/255). Such an interpretation is necessary to explain the contradiction between the temporal Messiah predicted by the letter of the prophecies and the state of lowliness and historical obscurity in which Christ actually came (cf. 305/274). Having explained in the "Preuves de Jésus-Christ" how Christ's historical obscurity bears out a figurative interpretation of those prophecies relating to "la manière du Messie," Pascal then turns to the literal realization of other aspects of the same prophecies.

Taken together, the documentation assembled in "Prophéties" and in the subsequent dossiers LIV–LX (*séries* XXI–XVIII) suggests four categories of prophecies whose literal realization Pascal plans to demonstrate: (1) the conversion of the Gentiles; (2) the reprobation of the Jews; (3) particular events in the life of Christ; and (4) the time of the coming of the Messiah. Pascal's documentation takes three forms: passages of Scripture copied out and/or translated; biblical citations indicated by chapter and verse; and a relatively small number of citations accompanied by explanatory notes.

The category most clearly envisaged by the chapter "Prophéties" itself concerns those Old Testament texts that predict the conversion of the Gentiles to the God of Israel. Since God's revelation of Himself to Moses, the apologist argues, and until the coming of Christ, "aucun païen n'avait adoré le Dieu des Juifs." Yet from the time of Christ onward, "la foule des païens adore cet unique Dieu, les temples sont détruits, les rois mêmes se soumettent à la croix" (370/338).

That monotheism to which Plato was able to convert only "quelque peu d'hommes choisis et si instruits" remained for two thousand years the unique possession of the Jews. Then suddenly, "une force secrète le persuade à cent milliers d'hommes ignorants par la vertu de peu de paroles." The history of the early Church documents the dramatic nature of this conversion. "Les filles consacrent à Dieu leur virginité et leur vie, les hommes renoncent à tous plaisirs." "Les riches quittent leurs biens, les enfants quittent la maison délicate de leurs pères pour aller dans l'austérité d'un désert, etc." (370/338).

Pascal seeks to provide ample documentation that this dramatic conversion of the "foule de païens" to the God of Israel was predicted throughout the Old Testament. Fragment 354/323 contains several citations destined to document the "vocation des gentils": "*Omnes Gentes venient et adorabunt eum*";[62] "*Parum est ut, etc. Isaïe*";[63] "*Adorabunt eum omnes reges.*"[64] Fragment 355/324, summarizing Ezekiel 30:13 and Malachi 1:11, documents the prophets' prediction of the ruin of the pagan religions:

> Qu'alors l'idolâtrie serait renversée, que ce Messie abattrait toutes les idoles et ferait entrer les hommes dans le culte du vrai Dieu.

Que les temples des idoles seraient abattus et que parmi toutes les nations et en tous les lieux du monde lui serait offerte une hostie pure, non point des animaux.[65]

In dossier LIX (*série* XVII), Pascal copies out and translates several long passages from the book of Isaiah that he interprets as anticipating the "conversion des gentils": Isaiah 65:1–19: "*Ceux-là m'ont trouvé qui ne me cherchaient point. J'ai dit: 'Me voici, me voici,' au peuple qui n'invoquait point mon nom. . . .*"; Isaiah 66:18: " *. . . Je viendrai pour les assembler avec toutes les nations et les peuples . . . de ceux qui seront sauvés j'en enverrai aux nations: en Afrique, en Lydie, en Italie, en Grèce, et aux peuples qui n'ont point ouï parler de moi . . .* " (735/489). Fragment 736/498 (dossier LX/*série* XVIII) gathers an additional series of references under the rubric "vocation des gentils": Joel 2:28; Hosea 2:24; Deuteronomy 32:21; Malachi 1:11.[66]

Of particular interest is dossier LIV (*série* XII), in which Pascal assembles a series of texts predicting the conversion of the Gentiles, which he notes that the Talmud recognizes as prophetic. From the *Pugio fidei*, his unique guide to the rabbinic tradition, he transcribes and translates long passages from Isaiah 49, Isaiah 51, and Haggai 2.[67] In taking these passages from the Talmud, Pascal seems to anticipate making the same argument that we have seen Sacy formulating. The historicity of the prophecies is guaranteed by the "témoignage" of the Jews. The rabbis themselves, Pascal would have gone on to point out, deem prophetic those very texts on which he founds his proof.

In fragment 362/330, a particularly obscure reference to "*Isaïe*, 19, 19" notes a prophecy of "*un autel en Égypte* au vrai Dieu." Sacy's explication of this passage clarifies the use to which Pascal intended to put this reference. Sacy explains that the passage predicts that "multitude de solitaires" who would establish themselves in the deserts of Egypt during the first centuries of Christianity. "Dieu a fait de ces anciens ennemis de son peuple un peuple de saints."[68] The reference, therefore, serves to document a prophecy of the historical event Pascal notes in fragment 370/338: "les enfants quittent la maison délicate de leurs pères pour aller dans l'austérité d'un désert."

Fragment 375/343 finds Pascal noting a prophecy of the ruin of paganism drawn, not from the Old Testament, but from the writings of the pagans themselves: "Le grand Pan est mort." Plutarch, in his *De defectu oraculorum*, recounts that during the reign of Tiberius a voice was heard proclaiming the death of the god Pan. Pascal, like a number of apologists before him, takes Pan to represent polytheism and the oracle reported by Plutarch to be a prophecy of the cessation of the pagan religions. Guez de Balzac, who may well be Pascal's source for the citation, explicates the oracle as follows: "Le grand Pan est mort par la naissance du Fils de Dieu, ou plustost par celle de sa doctrine; il ne faut pas le ressusciter. Au levé de cette lumière, tous les phantasmes du paganisme s'en sont enfuis; il ne les faut pas faire revenir."[69]

A second category of prophetic texts envisaged by "Prophéties" concerns the "réprobation des Juifs." "Que les Juifs réprouveraient Jésus-Christ et qu'ils seraient réprouvés de Dieu par cette raison. Que la vigne élue ne donnerait que du verjus"[70] (379/347). In the fragment "Sincérité des Juifs" (692/452), Pascal points to a paradox. The Jews "portent avec amour et fidélité" a book in which it is repeatedly written that they will be deprived of their promised inheritance and of their status as God's chosen people. Moses predicts the "réprobation des Juifs" in Deuteronomy 32:21[71] (736/493). The Pentateuch in another passage declares "que Dieu les frappera d'aveuglement et qu'ils tâtonneraient en plein midi comme les aveugles"[72] (379/347). This paradox should be a sign to the *libertin* of the supernatural character of the prophecies: "Sincères contre leur honneur, et mourant pour cela, cela n'a point d'exemple dans le monde ni sa racine dans la nature" (736/492) (see figure 13; the notation is the last of those at the righthand center of the page).

Pascal's documentation of those prophecies concerning the fate of the Jews is scattered throughout dossiers LIV–LX (*séries* XII–XVIII). Under the rubric "Captivité des Juifs sans retour," he files a citation from Jeremiah 11:11: "*Je ferai venir sur Juda des maux desquels ils ne pourront être délivrés.*" Another series of citations filed in the same dossier serve to document the prophets' prediction of the "réprobation du temple" and the abrogation of the old ceremonial convenant (735/489). Pascal's translation of Isaiah 65:16 makes his interpretation of the prophetic character of the passage particularly clear: "*Votre nom sera en exécration à mes élus, et je leur donnerai un autre nom*" (736/497). Fragment 734/487 notes Hosea 1:9: "*Vous ne serez plus mon peuple et je ne serai plus votre Dieu.*"

Dossier LIV/*série* XII, Pascal's collection of texts recognized as prophetic by the Talmud, contains the apologist's translation of Deuteronomy 18:16:

> *Et le Seigneur me dit: "Leur prière est juste. Je leur susciterai un prophète . . . dans la bouche duquel je mettrai mes paroles, et il leur dira toutes les choses que je lui aurai ordonnées. Et il arrivera que quiconque n'obéira point aux paroles qu'il leur portera en mon nom, j'en ferai moi-même le jugement."*
> (718/483)

The apologist would have used this passage to document not only the Pentateuch's anticipation of the Messiah but as well a prophecy of the "réprobation des Juifs."

Pascal, in a number of fragments, notes that other biblical texts seem to contradict the prophecy of the reprobation of the Jews. 2 Chronicles (7:18) speaks of the "règne éternel de la race de David" (380/348). In Amos 3:2,

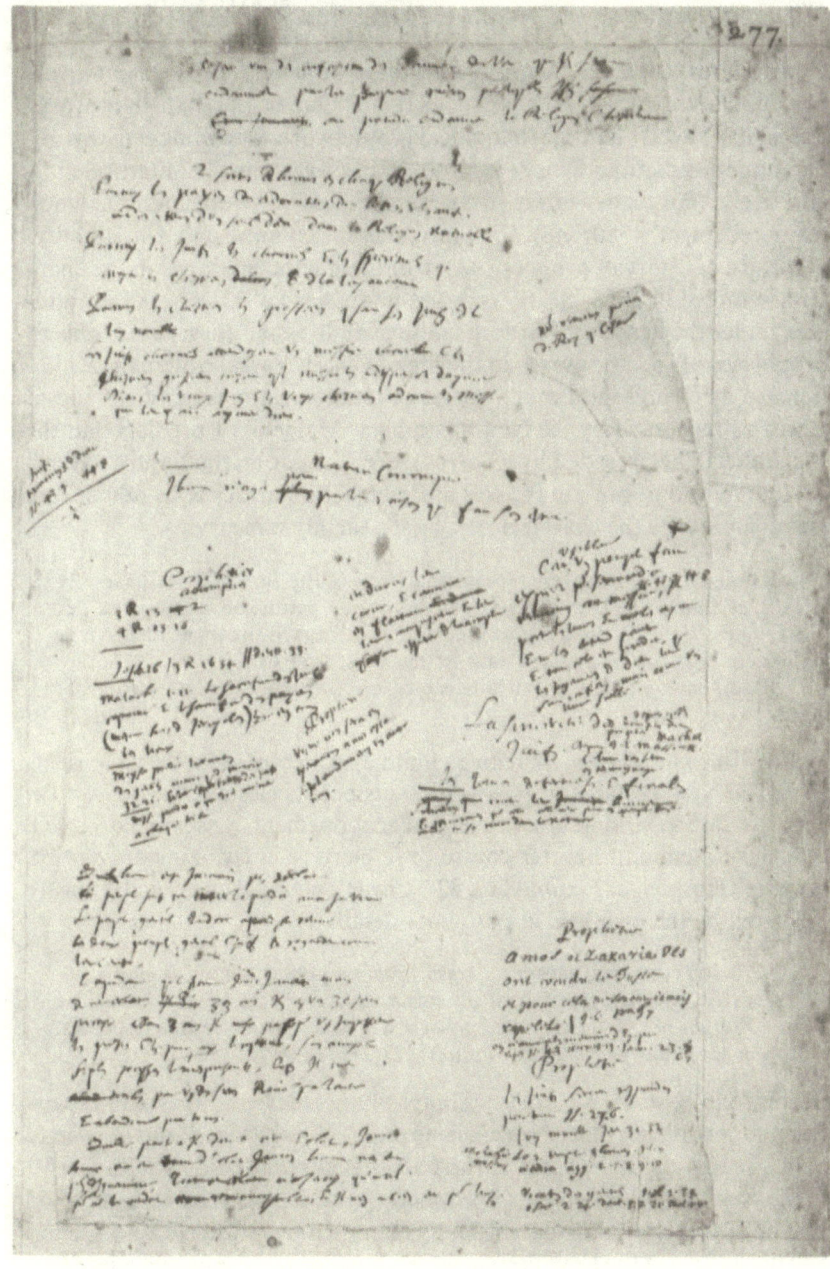

Figure 13. Page documenting a projected argument of "Prophéties": "La sincérité des Juifs," in the *Recueil original* (Bibliothèque Nationale, MS français 9202, folio 277) (Service photographique, Bibliothèque Nationale)

God declares to Israel: "*De toutes les nations de la terre, je n'ai reconnu que vous pour être mon peuple*" (718/483). In "Que la Loi était figurative," Pascal has already laid the theoretical groundwork for reconciling this apparent contradiction. This second set of passages must be interpreted figuratively. "Le règne éternel de la race de David" "n'est point accompli temporellement" (380/348). In reality, these texts anticipate Christianity.

A third category of prophetic texts, although not envisaged in the chapter assembled in 1658, clearly emerges in dossier LVIII/*série* XVI. Gathered under the heading "Pendant la durée du Messie," these texts concern prophecies of specific events in the life of Christ. Pascal orders these citations so as to present a more or less chronological mosaic of the life of Christ as recounted by the New Testament. Malachi 2:1 predicts that the Messiah will be preceded by a "précurseur," i.e., John the Baptist; Micah 5:2 that he will be born in the city of Bethlehem. Various texts taken from Isaiah announce the character of Christ's earthly ministry:

> Il doit aveugler les sages et les savants: *Isaïe* 6 [10]; *Isaïe* 8 [14–15]; *Isaïe* 29 [10]; et annoncer l'Evangile aux pauvres et aux petits, ouvrir les yeux des aveugles: *Isaïe* 29; *Isaïe* 61; et rendre la santé aux infirmes et mener à la lumière ceux qui languissent dans les ténèbres: *Isaïe* 61 [3].
>
> Il doit enseigner la voie parfaite et être le précepteur des gentils: *Isaïe* 55; 42, 1–7. (734/487)

Still using Old Testament texts to build up a picture of the Jesus presented by the New Testament, Pascal presents prophecies of Christ's conflict with the elders: "Il doit être la pierre d'achoppement, de scandale: *Isaïe* 8 [14]. Jerusalem doit heurter contre cette pierre. Les édifiants doivent réprouver cette pierre: *Psaume* 117, 22." Christ's betrayal and crucifixion are predicted by the prophets in particular detail:

> . . . Il doit être rejeté, méconnu, trahi: [*Psaume*] 108, 8; vendu: *Zacharie*, 11, 12; craché, souffleté, moqué, affligé en une infinité de manières; abreuvé de fiel: *Psaume* 68, 22; transpercé: *Zacharie*, 12, 10; les pieds et les mains percés, tué, et ses habits jetés au sort: *Psaume* [22].[73] (734/487)

Psalm 15:[10] predicts Christ's rising from the dead, and Hosea 6:3 specifies that it will take place "le troisième jour." His ascension into heaven to take a seat at the right hand of the Father is announced by Psalm 110.[74]

In assembling this collage of prophetic texts, Pascal gives no indication that he appreciates a textual difficulty identified by modern biblical scholars: the writers of the New Testament made conscious use of such messianic texts in constructing their accounts of the life of Christ. Nor does the apologist appear to see any need to demonstrate that his texts were intended as prophetic by those who wrote them. His choice of Old Testament texts is in no way original. He follows the example of the Fathers and that of the New Testament itself.[75] "Acceptant, les yeux fermés, ce que disent à Port-Royal les théologiens et les spécialistes de l'Ecriture sainte," Henri Gouhier observes, "Pascal retrouve dans l'argumentation les habitudes que l'exercice des mathématiques, la pratique de la méthode expérimentale et l'observation des hommes ont imposées à sa pensée: rigueur logique, souplesse dialectique, art du dilemne, finesse psychologique, sens du relatif."[76] In effect, Pascal's method in fragment 734/487 takes its model from geometrical reasoning. He attempts to square the evidence of the Old Testament prophecies with the life of Christ as reported by the New Testament. Historical research and textual criticism play no part whatsoever in his proof.

Pascal would have assigned particular importance in his proof to a fourth category of prophetic texts: those predicting the time of the arrival of the Messiah. He alludes to these texts in "Que la Loi était figurative," where he distinguishes between the "temps" ("prédit clairement") and the "manière" ("prédit obscurément") of the arrival of the Messiah (287/255): "Jésus-Christ est venu *dans le temps prédit*, mais non pas dans l'état attendu" (301/270; italics mine). In "Prophéties," Pascal spells out his argument:

> Les prophètes ayant donné diverses marques qui devaient toutes arriver à l'avènement du Messie, il fallait que toutes ces marques arrivassent en même temps. Ainsi il fallait que la quatrième monarchie fût venue lorsque les septante semaines de *Daniel* seraient accomplies et que le sceptre fût alors ôté de Juda. Et tout cela est arrivé sans aucune difficulté. Et qu'alors il arrivât le Messie. Et Jésus-Christ est arrivé alors, qui s'est dit le Messie. Et tout cela est encore sans difficulté. Et cela marque bien la vérité des prophéties. (371/339)[77]

Pascal's documentation of the prophecies predicting the time of the arrival of the Messiah is contained in dossier LVI/*série* XIV, in which he copies out and translates extensive passages from Daniel 2, 8, 9, and 11. Nowhere in the dossier, however, does Pascal explain how he means to explicate these passages. Sacy's commentaries on the eighth and ninth books of Daniel greatly clarify Pascal's references to the "quatre monarchies" and the "septante semaines" in fragments 371/339, 367/336, and 370/338. Sacy explains that the four monarchies referred to by the archangel Gabriel in his explication of Daniel's dream (Daniel 8:20-25) are those of the Chaldeans, the Medes and the Persians, the Greeks, and the Romans.[78] The "septante semaines" refer to Daniel's prediction of the time of "la mort du Messie . . . prédite plus de 500 ans auparavant" in Daniel 9:24-27:[79]

> Dieu a abrégé et fixé les temps à soixante-dix semaines, en faveur de votre peuple, et de votre ville sainte, afin que ses prévarications soient abolies . . . et que le Saint des saints soit oint de l'huile sacrée.
> Sçachez donc cecy. . . . Depuis l'ordre qui sera donné pour rebâtir Jérusalem, jusqu'au Christ chef de mon peuple, il y aura sept semaines et soixante-deux semaines. . . .
> Et après soixante-deux semaines le Christ sera mis à mort; et le peuple qui le doit renoncer ne sera point son peuple. . . .

> Il confirmera son alliance avec plusieurs dans une semaine, et à la moitié de la semaine les hosties et les sacrifices seront abolis. . . . (Sacy's translation)

Sacy explains that the weeks referred to in this prophecy are not ordinary weeks but rather "des semaines d'années comme dans le *Lévitique*." "Ainsi les *soixante et dix semaines* dont l'ange parle à Daniel font le nombre de 490 ans" (7 × 70). This number must be subsequently adjusted, since verse twenty-seven indicates that the Messiah will be put to death "vers le milieu de cette dernière semaine." Sacy therefore arrives at the number 486.[80] According to the prophecy, this number was to have been added to the date when the order would go out for the rebuilding of the city of Jersualem. Consulting the *Abrégé de la Chronologie Sainte*,[81] Sacy finds that Artaxerxes gave out such an order in "l'an du monde" 3550. Adding 486 to 3550, he comes up with the year 4036 "l'an du monde."[82] According to the same chronology, Christ was born in "l'an du monde" 4000. Translating Sacy's figures into modern notation, we find him interpreting Daniel 9:24–27 as predicting that the Messiah was to have been put to death in the year 36 A.D.

Whereas Sacy's calculations work out almost to the year, Pascal is more cautious. "Les soixante-dix semaines de *Daniel* sont équivoques pour le terme du commencement . . . à cause des diversités des chronologistes. Mais toute cette différence ne va qu'à deux cents ans" (373/341). Whereas Sacy only consults the *Abrégé de la Chronologie Sainte*, Pascal takes into account the fact that the chronologists vary in their reckonings concerning the date of the order to rebuild Jerusalem.[83] Pascal would appear to have a more critical eye for empirical data than Sacy. As in the case of his response to the *Sinicae Historiae*, we again find biblical chronologies representing an unresolved problem in Pascal's notes for the *Apology*.

On the whole, solid parallels exist between Sacy's arguments and those anticipated by Pascal's notes. Pascal obviously intends to reckon the "soixante-dix semaines" in terms of Sacy's "semaines d'années." Like Sacy's, his emphasis will be on the convergence of three separate prophecies concerning the time of the arrival of the Messiah. We may reconstruct Pascal's argument as follows. The prophets had predicted the arrival of the Messiah in the fourth of four great monarchies, after the seat of power had been removed from Jerusalem and in the fifth century following the return from Exile. Christ arrived in the fourth of four successive monarchies, during the Roman occupation of Jerusalem, and in the fifth century following Daniel's prophecy.

Viewed from the perspective of the prophecies, Pascal concludes, the whole of secular history takes on new meaning. "Qu'il est beau de voir par les yeux de la foi Darius et Cyrus, Alexandre, les Romains, Pompée et Hérode agir sans le savoir pour la gloire de l'Evangile"[84] (348/317). Like God himself, the history of salvation is hidden from human reason and may

Figure 14. The exaltation of the Divine Name; illuminated title, Préface, Sacy Bible, 1702 (Service photographique, Bibliothèque Nationale)

be perceived only "par les yeux de la foi." The prophecies, however, enable "ceux qui cherchent de tout leur coeur" to penetrate the veil of secular history and recognize "la véritable religion."

1. Pascal's description, in the *Entretien avec M. de Saci*, of Montaigne's critique of reason in the *Essais*. Cf. Bédier, p. 69.
2. Dossier XLVI/*série* III, in which this fragment is found, consists of Pascal's subsequent elaboration of the principal ideas of "Commencement" into a more finished argument.
3. Seminar, "Les Limites de la raison chez Pascal," University of Paris IV, 12 May 1977.
4. "[The Jews of Berea] received the word with all eagerness, daily searching the scriptures whether these things were so" (Douay translation).
5. Gouhier presents a convincing case that this project was an outgrowth of the "miracle de la Sainte-Epine." See *Blaise Pascal: commentaires*, chap. 3, pp. 149–62.
6. *Pensées*, p. 118 n. 7.
7. Isaiah 45:15: "Verily thou art a hidden God, the God of Israel the Saviour." Isaiah 53:5: "His look was as it were hidden and despised, whereupon we esteemed him not." Isaiah 8:14: "And he shall be . . . a stone of stumbling and . . . a rock of offence to the two houses of Israel . . . a snare and a ruin to the inhabitants of Jerusalem." (Douay translation.)
8. *Les Pensées de Pascal*, p. 255.
9. *Blaise Pascal: Commentaires*, p. 206.
10. *La Sainte Bible* (1702), Préface, p. xliv (italics mine).
11. *La Sainte Bible* (1702), Préface, p. xlvi.
12. *La Sainte Bible* (1702), Préface, p. xlvi.
13. *La Sainte Bible* (1702), Préface, p. lxiv.
14. *La Sainte Bible* (1702), Préface, p. xlvi.
15. *Les Pseaumes de David*, Préface, pp. vii–viii.

16. *Les Pseaumes de David*, Préface, pp. v–vi.
17. *Les Pseaumes de David*, Préface, p. xii.
18. *Les Pseaumes de David*, Préface, p. xiii.
19. "The Lord said to my Lord: *Sit thou at my right hand*" (Douay translation).
20. Isaiah 5:25: "*Therefore is the wrath of the Lord kindled* against his people." Exodus 20:5: "I am the Lord thy God, mighty, *jealous*." (Douay translation.)
21. See J. Mesnard, "La théorie des figuratifs," p. 232 n. 70.
22. Boucher, p. 182.
23. Genesis 49:10: "till he come that is to be sent" (Douay translation).
24. Hosea 3:4: "The children of Israel shall sit many days without king and without prince, and without sacrifice and without altar" (Douay translation).
25. Leviticus 7:34.
26. In fragment 693/453 Pascal assembles a whole dossier of texts to this effect. Among them: "Que les anciennes choses seront oubliées: *Isaïe*, 43, 18–19. Qu'on ne se souviendra plus de l'arche: *Jérémie*, 3, 15–16. Que le temple serait rejeté: *Jérémie* 7, 12–13–14. Que les sacrifices seraient rejetés, et d'autres sacrifices purs établis: *Malachie*, 1, 11."
27. Genesis 17:7–9. Cited by Pascal in fragment 651/799.
28. Jeremiah 31:31: "Behold the days shall come, saith the Lord, and I will make a new covenant with the house of Israel" (Douay translation).
29. Ezechiel 20:25: "Therefore I also gave them statutes which were not good, and judgments, in which they shall not live" (Douay translation).
30. John 1:47: "Jésus, voyant Nathanaël qui le venait trouver, dit de lui: "Voici *un vrai Israélite* sans déguisement." John 8:36: "Si donc le Fils vous met en liberté, vous serez *véritablement libres*." John 6:32: "Moïse ne vous a point donné le pain du ciel; mais c'est mon Père qui vous donne *le véritable pain du ciel*." (Sacy's transations.) Cf. fragment 299/268: "vrai jeûne, vrai sacrifice, vrai temple."
31. Cf. fragment 301/270: "Mais Dieu n'ayant pas voulu découvrir ces choses à ce peuple qui en était indigné et ayant voulu néanmoins les produire afin qu'elles fussent crues, il en a prédit le temps clairement et les a quelquefois exprimées clairement, mais abondamment en figures, afin que ceux qui aimaient les choses figurantes s'y arrêtassent . . . et que ceux qui aimaient les figurées les y vissent."
32. *La Sainte Bible* (1702), Préface, p. xliv.
33. *La Genèse*, Préface, Seconde Partie, partie ii.
34. *L'Exode*, Préface, p. xv.
35. *La Genèse*, Préface, Première Partie, partie v.
36. Brunschvicg, 12:ccvii.
37. *L'Exode*, Préface, p. xxxiv.
38. Sacy's vision of the Old Testament "saints" coincides precisely with that of Pascal: "Moyse a vécu pendant le Vieux Testament sans être néanmoins du Vieux Testament. . . . Il a crû très-certainement que Jésus-Christ naîtroit et mourroit pour les hommes" (*L'Exode*, Préface, p. xxxiv).
39. This fragment does not figure in Lafuma's edition. For its history, see Sellier, *Pensées*, p. 431 n. 1. Cf. *La Bible de Royaumont*, p. 546: "Il est visible que Moyse n'a rien écrit qui ne fust encore dans la mémoire de tous les hommes, puisqu'il n'estoit éloigné d'Adam que de quatre ou cinq générations."
40. Cf. fragment 489/590: "*Adam forma futuri*. Les six jours pour former [l']un, les six âges pour former l'autre. Les six jours que Moïse représente pour la formation d'Adam ne sont que la peinture des six âges pour former Jésus-Christ et l'Eglise."
Pascal would appear to interpret Saint Augustine's six ages as follows: (1) from Adam to Noah; (2) from Noah to Abraham; (3) from Abraham through the bondage in Egypt; (4) from Moses to David; (5) from the foundation of the Temple by Solomon to the Captivity in

Babylon; (6) from the end of the Babylonian Exile to the birth of Christ. The seventh age, ushered in by the Incarnation and prefigured by Adam's creation on the seventh day, will last until the end of time.

Philippe Sellier, pointing to another fragment (315/283: "Les six âges, les six pères des six âges, les six merveilles à l'entrée des six âges, les six orients à l'entrée des six âges"), identifies the source of Saint Augustine's theory of the six ages as *De Genesi contra Manichaeos*, I, 23: "l'histoire du monde se divise en six périodes, semblables aux six jours de la Création, qui ont eu chacun un soir et un matin (un orient), et furent marqués par une merveille. Adam-Déluge, Noé-Babel, Abraham-Saül, David-déportation de Babylone, Purification par l'exil-Refus du Messie, Jésus humble-Jésus glorieux. Le septième âge sera le repos sans fin de ceux qui ont aimé Dieu. Les "pères" sont Adam, Noé . . ." (*Pensées*, p. 170 n. 6).

In fragment 489/590 ("six âges pour former Jésus-Christ") Pascal appears to modify the details of Augustine's scheme. Significantly enough, however, his model mirrors that of the *Bible de Royaumont*.

41. *Pensées*, p. 393 n. 12.

42. Cf. fragment 716/481, 'Contre l'*Histoire de la Chine*": "Différence d'un livre reçu d'un peuple ou qui forme un peuple."

43. See, for example, Bishop John Robinson's *Can We Trust the New Testament* (Oxford: Mowbrays, 1977).

44. See fragment 658/812: "Le style de l'Evangile est admirable en tant de manières. . . ."

45. Georges Couton points to the words "il passe pour un *imposteur*" as evidence that Pascal is familiar with the libertine doctrine of the *Trois Imposteurs* (Couton, p. 193).

46. *La Genèse*, Préface, Première Partie, partie iv.

47. Pascal has in mind the New Testament writers' emphasis on the physical resurrection of Jesus. Cf. Luke 24:39–42 and John 20:24–28.

48. Studies of the role of the prophecies in the *Pensées* are few: P. Lagrange's "Pascal et les prophéties messianiques," *Revue biblique*, October 1906; R. Jolivet's "Pascal et l'argument prophétique," *Revue Apologétique*, 15 July and 1 August 1923; E. Tauzin's "Les Notes de Pascal sur les prophéties messianiques," *Revue Apologétique*, October 1924. The most useful study is to be found in Henri Gouhier's *Commentaires*, pp. 212–20.

49. Modern scholarship reckons that Daniel was composed in its present form in about 164 B.C., not, as Pascal supposes, 400 years earlier during the Babylonian Exile. The references that Pascal takes to be prophetic, modern scholarship takes to be contemporary: the "messie" refers to Onias III, assassinated in about 175 B.C.; the desecration of the temple refers to the Great Persecution of 167–164 B.C. and the establishment of the cult of the Olympian Zeus in the Temple in Jerusalem (*La Sainte Bible . . . de Jérusalem*, p. 1203).

50. Whose rendering of Daniel 9:26 perfectly reflects that of Pascal: "After sixty-two weeks Christ shall be slain . . . and a people with their leader shall destroy the city and the sanctuary."

51. *Daniel: traduit en françois avec une explication tirée des saint pères . . . par Le Maistre de Sacy*, Prestre, p. 196 (italics mine).

52. *Isaïe: traduit en françois avec une explication tirée des saints pères . . . par Le Maistre de Sacy*, Prestre, Préface, p. 1.

53. *Daniel*, Préface, pp. xii–xiii (italics mine). Cf. fragment 305/274: "Pour prouver tout d'un coup les deux [Testaments] il ne faut que voir si les prophéties de l'un sont accomplies en l'autre."

54. *Les douzes petits prophètes: traduits en françois . . .*, Préface, p. iv (italics mine).

55. *Les douzes petits prophètes*, Préface, pp. v–vi.

56. The position of the neo-Epicureans. See pp. 56–57, above.

57. *Daniel*, Préface, p. xi.

58. *Les douzes petits prophètes*, Préface, pp. xx–xxi.

59. *Les douzes petits prophètes*, Préface, p. xvi.

60. "I will put enmities between thee and the woman, and thy seed and her seed: she shall crush thy head, and thou shalt lie in wait for her heel" (Douay). Traditional exegesis sees in this passage a figure of the Blessed Virgin.

61. A. M. Dubarle, "Pascal et l'interprétation de l'Ecriture," pp. 359–61.

62. Psalm 21:28: "All the ends of the earth shall remember and shall be converted to the Lord; *All the kindreds of the Gentiles shall adore in his sight.*"

63. Isaiah 49:6: "*It is a small thing* that thou shouldst . . . raise up the tribes of Jacob. . . . Behold I have given thee to be a light of the Gentiles."

64. Psalm 71:11: "And *all the kings of the earth shall adore him*: all nations shall serve him."

65. In noting this prophecy, Pascal is thinking of the Mass, the new and universal rite that would replace the temple sacrifices of the Old Covenant. "Une hostie pure" recalls the canon of the Mass: "*Hostiam puram*, Hostiam sanctam, Hostiam immaculatam."

66. Joel 2:28: "And it shall come to pass after this, that I will pour out my spirit upon all flesh: and your sons and your daughters shall prophesy: your old men shall dream dreams, and your young men shall see visions." Cf. fragment 360/328: "Vos FILS PROPHÉTISERONT." Cf. also, the struck citation in "Contrariétés": "*Omnis caro foenum*" (164/131). Hosea 2:24: "And I will say to that which was not my people: Thou art my people." Deuteronomy 32:21: "Je les irriterai en substituant à leur place une nation insensée" (Sacy's translation). Malachi 1:11: see Pascal's summary in fragment 355/324.

67. Isaiah 49:6: ". . . *C'est peu de chose que tu convertisses les tribus de Jacob, je t'ai suscité pour être la lumière des gentils.* . . ." Isaiah 51:4: ". . . *car une loi sortira de moi et un jugement qui sera la lumière des gentils.*" Haggai 2:4: ". . . *La gloire de ce nouveau temple sera bien plus grande que la gloire du premier.* . . ."

68. *Isaïe*, p. 142.

69. *Oeuvres* (Paris: 1665), 2:533. Cited by Pintard, *Le Libertinage érudit dans la première moitié du XVIIe siècle*, p. 64. Sellier cites Charron's *Trois vérités* (ii, 8): "A la belle arrivée de Jésus-Christ, les oracles sont demeurés muets. . . . Plutarque en a fait un traité exprès, ou il se morfond pour en trouver la cause" (*Pensées*, p. 190 n. 21).

70. Isaiah 5:4–5: "Qu'ai-je dû faire de plus à ma vigne que je n'y point fait? Est-ce que je lui ai fait tort d'attendre qu'elle portât de bons raisins, au lieu qu'elle n'en produit que de mauvais? Mais je vous montrerai ce que je m'en vais faire à ma vigne: . . . je détruirai tous les murs qui la défendent, et elle sera foulée aux pieds" (Sacy's translation).

71. "Je leur cacherai mon visage, et je considérerai leur fin malheureuse, car ce peuple est une race corrompue. . . . Ils m'ont voulu comme piquer de jalousie, en adorant ceux qui n'étaient point dieux . . . et moi je les piquerai aussi de jalousie, en aimant ceux qui n'étaient point mon peuple . . ." (Sacy's translation).

72. Deuteronomy 28:28–29.

73. Psalm 108:8: "May his days be few . . ."; Zacharias 11:12: "and they weighed for my wages thirty pieces of silver" (cf. Matthew 27:9); Psalm 68:22: ". . . in my thirst they gave me vinegar to drink" (cf. *Matthew* 27:48); Zacharias 12:10: " . . . and they shall look upon me, whom they have pierced" (cf. John 19:37); Psalm 22 (21 in Vulgate):18: "they parted my garments amongst them; and upon my vesture they cast lots" (cf. Matthew 27:35).

74. Psalm 15 (Vulgate):10: "Because thou wilt not leave my soul in hell; nor wilt thou give thy holy one to see corruption." Hosea 6:3: "He will revive us after two days: on the third day he will raise us up and we shall live in his sight." Psalm 110: "The Lord said to my Lord: Sit thou at my right hand."

75. In relying upon the writers of the New Testament to identify which Old Testament texts are prophetic, Pascal shows himself a faithful follower of Port-Royal. Sacy insists that the ultimate tribunal in interpreting the Old Testament is the New Testament. See Chapter 3.

76. *Blaise Pascal: Commentaires*, p. 226.

77. Cf. fragments 367/336 and 370/338.

78. *Daniel*, Préface, p. vi.
79. *Daniel*, Préface, p. vii.
80. *Daniel*, pp. 191–92, 194.
81. Compiled by Lancelot, the *Abrégé de la Chronologie Sainte* is appended to the *Bible de Royaumont* and to the 1702 edition of the Sacy Bible.
82. *Daniel*, pp. 194–95.
83. A great number of sacred chronologies were composed during the seventeenth century. *La Sainte Chronologie* of J. d'Auzoles presents 79 opinions, arrived at by 122 different scholars, concerning the date of the creation of the world. See Delassault pp. 210–12.
84. Darius, Cyrus, Alexander, and the Romans represent the "quatre monarchies." Pompey, the conqueror of Jerusalem, and Herod acted without knowing it to accomplish the prophecy concerning the removal of the "sceptre" from Judah.

Conclusion

GOD "AU-DEHORS": PASCAL'S EMPIRICISM AND THE
MODERN RELIGIOUS SENSIBILITY

In the *Entretien avec M. de Saci*, Pascal proposes an alternative to the "lumières imparfaites" of profane philosophy. The rival theories of Epictetus and Montaigne, because they fail to resolve the central enigma of the human condition, must "se brisent et s'anéantissent pour faire place à la vérité de l'Evangile."[1] No formula penetrates quite so well to the heart of the apologetic strategy sketched by the *Pensées*. According to the plan revealed by the dossiers of 1658, Pascal programs profane philosophy for its own self-destruction. The conflicting theories of the Stoics and the Skeptics serve to cancel each other out in order to "faire place" for an examination of Christian Revelation as contained in Scripture.

The whole aim of Pascal's *Apology* would have been to prove "la vérité de l'Evangile." "La plus grande des preuves" of the veracity of the Gospel was to have been the argument proposed in "Prophéties" and elaborated in the dossiers subsequent to the *liasses* of 1658. Almost every other major theological and historical development in the *Pensées* anticipates, and in some way lays the groundwork for, this definitive proof. The chapters concerning the authenticity of the Pentateuch, the *témoignage* of the Jews, *figures*, and the obscurity of the historical Jesus all find their place in a chain of investigations designed to persuade the unbeliever to accept the testimony of the Bible.

Pascal's whole apologetic endeavor, Etienne Périer reminds us in the preface to the Edition de Port-Royal of the *Pensées*, was to demonstrate that "la religion chrétienne avait autant de marques de certitude et d'évidence que les choses qui sont reçues dans le monde pour les plus indubitables."[2] The arguments of the historical *liasses*, and in particular those that would have constituted "la plus grande des preuves," serve to underscore the essentially empirical character that Pascal intended to give to his defense of Christianity. In Pascal's view, God's hidden nature means that human reason can never hope to penetrate the veil of Revelation. Yet in his infinite mercy, God has appended "marques visibles" to Revelation so that those who search with all their heart may believe. The most important of these outward and visible signs are the Old Testament prophecies and their accomplishment in the New Testament. Because they are "solides et palpables" (221/189), the prophecies are subject to empirical analysis. Man's fallen reason may act upon their evidence without exceeding its inherent limits.

Henri Gouhier is surely correct when he attributes the empirical character of Pascal's definitive argument to "les habitudes que l'exercice des mathématiques, la pratique de la méthode expérimentale et l'observation des hommes ont imposées à sa pensée."[3] Pascal's model in squaring the Old Testament prophecies with the evidence of the New Testament certainly takes its inspiration from geometrical reasoning. We have not failed to note, however, that the Pascal who meditates on the mysteries of the prophecies no longer strictly adheres to those epistemological principles we found him setting down in the preface to *Sur le Traité du vide*. No longer does he insist that the "droits séparés" of empirical and religious truth must never be confused.

In the preface to *Sur le Traité du vide*, Pascal had argued that no "autorité," theological or secular, should be allowed to interfere with the objective demonstration of empirical fact. In his exposition in the *Apology* of "la plus grande des preuves," however, the empirical facts themselves are selected and ordered on the basis of an unmistakable authority. It is the Bible itself, along with the exegetical tradition, that determines which Old Testament texts are to be examined in the first place. Pascal's model is no longer the strict scientific method proposed in the preface to *Sur le Traité du vide*. It cannot be because the evidence to be examined is not ordinary empirical evidence. Rather, it is those "marques visibles" that God has attached to Revelation. Scriptural exegesis cannot be numbered among those sciences that Pascal had described as requiring augmentation "pour devenir parfaites."[4] There can be no innovation or augmentation in a science whose authority is that of Revelation itself.

In the eighteenth *Provinciale*, Pascal had set down the principle that since "le rapport des sens est unique," the Bible must always be interpreted in a way "qui convient au rapport fidèle des sens."[5] In the course of the *Pensées*, he never consciously violates this principle or bends empirical data to make his proofs more convincing. In the case of the temporal prophecy of Daniel 9, we find him a good deal more careful with the facts than Sacy.[6] However, at several points in his notes we do find the apologist excluding any data that might cast doubt on the strict veracity of the Bible's account of sacred history. He dismisses the theories of Isaac de la Peyrère as "extravagances" (478/575) and relegates the evidence of the *Sinicae historiae* to the status of "roman" (688/436). The examples of La Peyrère and the *Sinicae historiae* are admittedly marginal to the larger concerns of the *Apology*. But so, too, Pascal insists in fragment 196/164, is the most burn-

CONCLUSION

ing scientific issue of the age. "Je trouve bon qu'on n'approfondisse pas l'opinion de Copernic, mais ceci—Il importe à toute la vie de savoir si l'âme est mortelle ou immortelle."

Pascal's position could not be more clear. Even the question of the shape of the physical universe pales into insignificance when set up against the fate of a single human soul. Once awakened from the torpor of "divertissement," the unbeliever has more important issues to ponder than those that pertain to the purely physical universe. Pascal's refusal to grant a fair hearing to libertine, or even scientific,[7] challenges to the infallibility of Bible history is at least comprehensible in the context of his larger apologetic strategy. As in his suppression of a literal exposition of Genesis in "A.P.R.," the apologist seeks to avoid constellating opposing arguments in the mind of his interlocutor. Yet the student of the history of ideas is not wrong to be troubled by the fact that Pascal's personal notes consistently rule out even the slightest alteration in the traditional biblical understanding of human history.

As misconceived as it was, La Peyrère's theory of the "préAdamites" represented a growing awareness that man's history had to be more complex, and more ancient, than the Christian chronologists had ever imagined. Pascal's total lack of sensitivity to this new awareness is obvious from his reaction to the *Sinicae Historiae*. His only concern is to refute any potential challenge to biblical chronologies. Completely caught up in a defense of the Bible's infallibility, the apologist does not pause for one moment to wonder if the chronologies of the Chinese might represent genuine empirical evidence. The way in which he states the question betrays the fact that the epistemological perspective of *Sur le Traité du vide* no longer holds: "Lequel est le plus croyable des deux: Moïse ou la Chine?" (663/822).

Even given the influence of the theology and theologians of Port-Royal, it still seems troubling that so critical and analytical a thinker as Pascal unquestioningly endorsed Sacy's theory that only five generations of Patriarchs stood between Moses and the Creation. Sacy's position is easier to understand. His training was entirely theological, his point of view intensely monastic. Pascal, on the other hand, had moved in scientific circles from childhood. Early in his scientific career, he had seen the necessity of distinguishing between empirical and religious truth, taking Père Noel to task for invoking the doctrine of the Eucharist against the results of his "expériences sur le vide."[8] Why is it then that the Pascal of the *Apology* does not hesitate to invoke the authority of Moses and the Pentateuch against the evidence of the *Sinicae historiae*? What change in his epistemological perspective was wrought by his great conversion to the "Dieu d'Abraham, Dieu d'Isaac, Dieu de Jacob, non des philosophes et des savants"?

The Pascal who arrived at Port-Royal-des-Champs in 1655 already had a considerable psychological investment in a passion for orthodoxy of doctrine. That much is clear from Mme Périer's account of the "affaire Saint-Ange." Pierre Courcelle establishes the fact that Sacy "a orienté Pascal, à cette date, vers la lecture des *Confessions*."[9] Given everything we know about Monsieur de Sacy, it seems likely that he also sought to orient the future apologist toward the study of the Bible. It does not seem unreasonable to think that Sacy's vision of the unity, inviolability, and infallibility of the Bible could have served as a catalyst, focusing Pascal's fervor for dogmatic orthodoxy onto the sphere of sacred history.

It has not been possible to document the hypothesis that Pascal actually consulted Sacy concerning the historical focus of his *Apology*. Our study of the *Pensées*, however, has elucidated in Pascal's arguments the same sense of urgency regarding the need to prove the historical inerrancy of the Bible that animates Sacy's scriptural commentaries. Pascal's extreme hostility to any challenge to the historical authority of the Bible might well be the result of Sacy's influence. But it is just as much the result of his having fallen into a biblical vision of human history. The product of 1,700 years of typological exegesis, this vision must have so captured Pascal's imagination that he was rendered insensitive to the more complex understanding of human history that was germinating in the minds of his contemporaries.

However fascinating we find Pascal's exposition of the biblical drama of salvation, we still come away from the *Pensées* with the feeling that the historical proofs would constitute a major stumbling block for the modern *chercheur*. The whole force of what was to have been the definitive argument of the *Apology* seems to lack the enduring power of those other arguments designed to shock an agnostic temperament out of the folly of "divertissement." The predicament of "un homme dans un cachot, ne sachant si son arrêt est donné" (195/163) appeals to us in a way that "la plus grande des preuves" does not. The inaccessibility of Pascal's historical proofs may of course be attributed to the progress of biblical studies. Yet the modern reader's failure to be drawn into Pascal's line of reasoning may not be totally the product of the fact that he has read Bultmann or Tillich.

Since the time of the writing of the *Pensées*, there have been a number of fundamental shifts in the whole Western religious sensibility. The myth of "man's first disobedience," for instance, no longer holds a real grip on the popular religious imagination. A long tradition of humanistic and scientific ideas concerning the perfectibility of man and human society has diluted its essential pessimism. Even official Christianity has tended to seat the vision of the Heavenly Jerusalem a little closer to *terra firma* and to stress God's transcendence more than man's corruption.

CONCLUSION 215

Pascal's use of the Fall in the first stage of his apologetic itinerary still makes for a thought-provoking argument. His perception that man's universal search for happiness suggests "qu'il y a eu autrefois dans l'homme un véritable bonheur" (181/148) still seems at least plausible. The idea has a distinct affinity with the myth of a Golden Age and occurs in transmuted forms in both Marxist theories of history and in psychoanalytic theories concerning the origin of the psyche. On the other hand, what seems so alien to us in Pascal's argument is his notion that a historical Fall of all men in Adam can explain the central paradox of the human dilemma. Because it is rooted in a literal view of Genesis and wedded to a creationist theory that few still believe, Pascal's argument loses its coherence when taken as metaphor. It cannot easily be divorced from the Augustinian doctrine of Original Sin, from which it draws its emotional and psychological power.

Another idea that runs completely against the grain of Pascal's thought has emerged with particular force in the contemporary religious imagination. Long latent in the Christian *mythos* and perhaps resurfacing under the influence of Eastern thought, this notion holds that if God is to be found, He must be found within man himself. The modern Christian theologian might argue that the idea by no means contradicts the real meaning of the doctrine of the Incarnation. The fact remains, however, that this same principle was held in abhorrence by the entire Augustinian tradition. It is a commonplace of the popular spirituality of our age to speak of the human soul (or spirit) as containing "a spark of the divine." Pascal could not have taken a more contrary point of view. In the *Entretien avec M. de Saci*, he severely censures Epictetus for maintaining "que l'âme est une portion de la substance divine."[10]

Given their insistence on the total corruption of the human heart, the neo-Augustinian theologians of Port-Royal could provide no rationale for any such search for God inside man. One may search the *Mémoires* of Fontaine in vain for the slightest hint that the Solitaires ever intended to retire to Port-Royal-des-Champs in order to search for God in the depths of their own souls. Their entire purpose in fleeing the corruption of the world, Fontaine tells us over and over again, was to "faire pénitence." Pascal is equally emphatic concerning the corruption and emptiness of man's interior self: "Que le coeur de l'homme est creux et plein d'ordure" (171/139). His whole criticism of profane philosophy is that it urges men to seek "le souverain bien" (and hence God) within themselves:

> Nous sommes pleins de choses qui nous jettent au-dehors.
> Notre instinct nous fait sentir qu'il faut chercher notre bonheur hors de nous. Nos passions nous poussent au-dehors, quand même les objets ne s'offriraient pas pour les exciter. Les objets du dehors nous tentent d'eux-mêmes

et nous appellent, quand même nous n'y pensons pas. Et ainsi les philosophes ont beau dire: "Rentrez-vous en vous-mêmes, vous y trouverez votre bien;" on ne les croit pas. Et ceux qui les croient sont les plus vides et les plus sots. (176/143)

In a note in his edition of the *Pensées*, Philippe Sellier seizes upon a perspective that is critical to understanding Pascal's position. Man's search for God must take place *outside* the human heart:

> Lorsqu'il imagine son espace intérieur, Pascal se le représente comme une citerne ténébreuse et suintante, dont le fond est un *"cloaque,"* un lieu de souillures et de boue, où croupit une végétation mauvaise, solidement enracinée, et dont l'arrachement est douloureux (fr. 457). Ces *"racines"* sont comme de fines griffes, un réseau de lianes, de *"liens."* Tel est le *"vilain fond de l'homme"* (fr. 244). Quand il se penche sur la margelle de son coeur, Pascal voit son *"abîme d'orgueil, de curiosité, de concupiscence"* (fr. 751).—Alors que saint Augustin rencontrait Dieu dans les espaces féeriques de son âme, Pascal insiste sur la haine de soi et rencontre presque toujours Dieu en quelque sorte "au-dehors": dans la nature, dans le Christ, dans l'Eucharistie, dans l'Ecriture, dans les pauvres (*Lettre 4 à Charlotte de Roannez*).[11]

Pascal accords a special privilege to the faculty of intuition. It is "notre instinct" that contradicts the philosophers' admonition that the true search is an interior one. Pascal appeals to this same faculty in "Contrariétés," "Le Souverain Bien," and "A.P.R." in order to awaken his interlocutor's recognition that man is no longer in the state of his creation. This "instinct impuissant du bonheur de [sa] première nature" is the pitiful residue of man's former state of communication with God. A "lumière confuse de son auteur" (182/149), this instinct is itself the reason why men so paradoxically seek "le souverain bien" in "divertissement" and in created things:

> Qu'est-ce donc que nous crie cette avidité et cette impuissance, sinon qu'il y a eu autrefois dans l'homme un véritable bonheur, dont il ne lui reste maintenant que la marque et la trace toute vide, et qu'il essaie inutilement de remplir de tout ce qui l'environne, recherchant des choses absentes le secours qu'il n'obtient pas des présentes, mais qui en sont toutes incapables, parce que ce gouffre infini ne peut être rempli que par un objet infini et immuable, c'est-à-dire que par Dieu même. (181/148)

The search for God in the *Pensées* winds its way through an ascending hierarchy of categories, from the "marque . . . toute vide" that the Fall has left in the human heart to those "marques visibles" that God has appended to Revelation. Intuitively, man recognizes that God must be sought "au-dehors." Ironically, the inward search advocated by the philosophers is even more misdirected than the folly of "divertissement." For at least in coveting created things, men follow the prompting of an instinct that is the "trace toute vide" of their "première nature." All men search for God without knowing it—"jusqu'à ceux qui vont se pendre" (181/148). The most depraved sinners follow the same initial impulse as the holiest saints. "La vie ordinaire des hommes est semblable à celle des saints. Ils recherchent tous leur satisfaction et ne diffèrent qu'en l'objet où ils la placent" (306/275).

Though Pascal shares Sacy's notion that God made the world in the first place "pour donner une grande idée de lui-[même],"[12] the *Pensées* consistently rule out searching for God in the design of the universe. God's having hidden himself in nature is a function of the corruption of human reason in the Fall. Those who have "la foi vive dedans le coeur" do not fail to recognize the truth that "tout ce qui est n'est autre chose que l'ouvrage du Dieu qu'ils adorent" (644/781). But the salvation of those whose hearts have yet to be filled with grace will in no way be advanced by natural proofs of God's existence. At most, reason can only deduce the God of the deists. The Christian God is not simply the author of geometrical truths. Nor does he simply exercise his Providence over human affairs. He is the God of Abraham and Isaac and Jacob, the God of love and consolation. "C'est un Dieu qui remplit l'âme et le coeur de ceux qu'il possède" (690/449).

In Pascal's view, God is paradoxically even more hidden in the Incarnation of Jesus than beneath the veil of nature. "Il s'est encore plus caché en se couvrant de l'humanité."[13] Just as the Risen Christ is veiled in the Eucharist by the species of bread and wine, so too God was veiled in human flesh by the person of Jesus of Nazareth. Pascal pushes this traditional analogy one step further. Just as the historical Jesus is for the modern unbeliever veiled in the mists of historical obscurity, so too is the unique message of the Gospel obscured by the letter of Scripture. "Comme Jésus-Christ est demeuré inconnu parmi les hommes, ainsi sa vérité parmi les opinions communes, sans différence à l'extérieur. Ainsi l'Eucharistie parmi le pain commun" (258/225). Yet for those who have the eyes to see Him, both the Eucharist and the person of Jesus are "saint, saint, saint à Dieu" (339/308).

The believing Christian whose heart is filled with God himself need go no further. By faith, he glimpses God's hidden presence not in himself but in the Eucharist, the Bible, and the person of Jesus. The unbeliever, however, must ascend to another level if he hopes to be permitted to share in the same perception. He must examine those "marques visibles" that God has attached to sacred history so that he too may believe. In the last analysis, those "marques divines" of which Divine Wisdom speaks in "A.P.R." are the only exception to the rule that God has hidden himself from the sight of men. Given the apologist's conviction that God must be sought outside man, Pascal's *Apology* must have a historical focus. The historical proofs are not marginal to some larger apologetic concern. Nor were they meant simply to buttress Pascal's so-called philosophical arguments. They are the core of Pascal's projected *Apology* and the ultimate argument upon which he intended to rest his case.

"LA FOLIE DE LA CROIX": THE LIMITS OF APOLOGETIC DIALOGUE

At the end of part one of Sacy's *Préface à la Genèse* stands an idea of capital relevance to the meaning of the *Pensées*. Christian apologetics, Sacy asserts, is in the last analysis of limited utility. Many of the greatest of the saints and martyrs lacked sufficient "lumière d'esprit" to appreciate historical or rational proofs of Christianity. In "Conclusion," the final chapter of the dossiers of 1658, Pascal adopts precisely the same position. "Ne vous étonnez pas," he admonishes his *libertin*, "de voir des personnes simples croire sans raisonnement" (412/380). "Ceux que nous voyons chrétiens sans la connaissance des prophéties et des preuves ne laissent pas d'en juger aussi bien que ceux qui ont cette connaissance" (414/382).

Pascal's position perhaps takes us entirely by surprise. The whole force of the *Apology* is based upon the premise that Christianity is historically demonstrable. The prophecies, empirical evidence on which reason can act without exceeding its inherent limitations, serve as the final proof in an argument designed to bring about reason's abdication in the face of Revelation. Yet most Christians, Pascal is the first to point out, have no knowledge of the prophecies. The ultimate source of "la véritable religion" is the Bible. Yet the great majority of believers adhere to Christianity "sans avoir lu les *Testaments*" (413/381).

In the course of this study, I have attempted to demonstrate that Pascal's final position is far removed from the fideism of the *Essais* of Montaigne. The ultimate proofs of Christianity are empirical. Not only is "la véritable religion" reasonable. Not to believe the testimony of Holy Writ is profoundly unreasonable. "Ce sera une des confusions des damnés de voir qu'ils seront condamnés par leur propre raison par laquelle ils ont prétendu condamner la religion chrétienne" (206/175). Yet ordinary Christians believe "'sans raisonnement." God grants to "des personnes simples" what he so often denies to those of high estate. "Il incline leur coeur à croire" (412/380).

Pascal admits that the Christian who believes "sans preuve n'aura peut-être pas de quoi convaincre un infidèle." Therein lies the true raison d'être of Christian apology. "Ceux qui savent les preuves de la religion prouveront sans difficulté que ce fidèle est véritablement inspiré de Dieu, quoiqu'il ne peut le prouver lui-même" (414/382). The true aim of apologetics is to vindicate the faith of those who already believe. Those empirical proofs that constitute a historical demonstration of Christianity are but figures of

CONCLUSION 219

more profound spiritual realities. Those who believe "sans avoir lu les *Testaments*" have instinctively seized these truths through the mechanism of the heart. "Ils en jugent par le coeur comme les autres en jugent par l'esprit" (414/382).

In the last analysis, an intellectual submission to the doctrines of Christianity is insufficient. "Qu'il y a loin de la connaissance de Dieu à l'aimer" (409/377). Apology cannot attempt to force God's hand. It can only hope to awaken a grace that God has already dispensed. From the perspective of Augustinian theology, in which all things are preordained by God, apology is but another vehicle for the working out of predestination and election.

Those who stand outside Christianity misunderstand the meaning of conversion. They imagine that it consists of a two-way contract between an individual and God. " 'Si j'avais vu un miracle,' disent-ils, 'je me convertirais.' " "Comment assurent-ils," Pascal can only reply, "qu'ils feraient ce qu'ils ignorent?"

> Ils s'imaginent que cette conversion consiste en une adoration qui se fait de Dieu comme un commerce et une conversation telle qu'ils se la figurent. La conversion véritable consiste à s'anéantir devant cet être universel qu'on a irrité tant de fois et qui peut vous perdre légitimement à toute heure, à reconnaître qu'on ne peut rien sans lui et qu'on n'a rien mérité de lui que sa disgrâce. Elle consiste à connaître qu'il y a une opposition invincible entre Dieu et nous et que sans un médiateur il ne peut y avoir de commerce. (410/378)

In the "prosopopée" of "A.P.R.," Divine Wisdom reassures the *libertin* that accepting Revelation will not mean abandoning reason. "Je n'entends pas que vous soumettiez votre créance à moi sans raison, et ne prétends point vous assujettir avec tyrannie" (182/149). At the end of the *Apology*, we find Pascal defining conversion to Christianity in a way that seems to exclude not only the exercise of reason but the very utility of apologetic dialogue. God is no longer portrayed as Divine Wisdom, who gently guides the unbeliever to the light of Revelation. He is "cet être universel . . . qui peut vous perdre légitimement à toute heure" (410/378). The *libertin*, who has presumably accepted the historical arguments in favor of Christianity, must now "s'anéantir" in order to experience a genuine conversion of the heart.

When he concludes his defense of Christianity by insisting that conversion is an essentially irrational act, Pascal recapitulates a paradox fundamental to the meaning of the *Pensées*. Pascal's whole enterprise rests on the premise that the unbelief of his interlocutor may be altered through rational argument. Augustinian theology, however, holds that belief or unbelief, like salvation or damnation, is preordained and unalterable. Pascal is writing an apology within a theological tradition that, if its fundamental positions are taken to their logical conclusion, does not admit the utility of apologetic dialogue. The unique character and enduring fascination of the *Pensées* are in large measure the product of this fundamental paradox.

Pascal's understanding of the nature of Scripture reflects an antirationalism inherent in neo-Augustinian theology. At Port-Royal, no scriptural injunction received greater emphasis than Saint Paul's warning that the wisdom of this world can only serve to empty the cross of Christ.[14] Reason, Pascal observes in the fragment titled "Préface de la seconde partie," misleads those seeking God. Assuming that God is made in its own image, reason prompts men to search for evidence of God's presence in the visible universe. "Ce n'est pas de cette sorte que l'Ecriture, qui connaît mieux les choses qui sont de Dieu, en parle. Elle dit au contraire que Dieu est un Dieu caché; et que, depuis la corruption de la nature, il les a laissés dans un aveuglement dont ils ne peuvent sortir que par Jésus-Christ, hors duquel toute communication avec Dieu est ôtée: *Nemo novit Patrem, nisi Filius, et cui Filius voluerit revelare*"[15] (644/781).

Pascal is acutely aware that the doctrine of the Incarnation, the assertion that God is knowable only in the person of Jesus, is in every way a scandal to reason. Yet nowhere in the *Apology* does he ever attempt to mitigate its irrationality. To the contrary, he rejoices that Christ came to "aveugler les sages et les savants" and to "annoncer l'Évangile aux pauvres et aux petits" (734/487). With Saint Paul, he gives thanks that God has "made foolish the wisdom of this world."[16] The whole of Revelation, he reminds the *libertin*, ultimately points toward "la folie de la croix":

> Cette religion si grande en miracles; saints, purs, irréprochables, savants et grands témoins; martyrs; rois—David—établis, Isaïe prince du sang; si grande en science; après avoir étalé tous ses miracles et toute sa sagesse, elle réprouve tout cela et dit qu'elle n'a ni sagesse ni signe, mais la croix et la folie.
>
> Car ceux qui par ces signes et cette sagesse ont mérité votre créance et qui vous ont prouvé leur caractère vous déclarent que rien de tout cela ne peut nous changer et nous rendre capable de connaître et aimer Dieu que la vertu de la folie de la croix, sans sagesse ni signe. (323/291)

According to the theologians of Port-Royal, reason's inability to penetrate the mysteries of Revelation is a function of the Incarnation. "Cet étrange secret," Pascal explains in a letter to Mlle de Roannez, "dans lequel Dieu s'est retiré, impénétrable à la vue des hommes, est une grande leçon":

> [Dieu] est demeuré caché sous le voile de la nature qui nous le couvre jusqu'à l'Incarnation; et quand il a fallu qu'il ait paru, il s'est encore plus caché en se couvrant de l'humanité. Il était bien plus reconnaissable quand il était invisible, que non pas quand il s'est rendu visible. Et enfin quand il a voulu accomplir la promesse qu'il fit à ses Apôtres de demeurer avec les hommes jusqu'à son dernier avènement, il a choisi d'y demeurer dans le plus étrange et le plus obscur secret de tous, qui sont les espèces de l'Eucharistie. . . . On peut ajouter à ces considérations le secret de l'Esprit de Dieu caché encore dans l'Ecriture.[17]

CONCLUSION   221

Reason is incapable of perceiving the Real Presence of Christ in the Eucharist (258/225). Nor was it reason that led the Apostles and the early Church to acknowledge the divinity of Jesus. The Bible, because it participates in the mystery of the Word Incarnate, is not subject to rational analysis. The wisdom of this world can only serve to empty the cross of Christ, to divest Scripture of its power to save. "Qui doute," writes Sacy, "qu'une sainteté rustique et ignorante . . . ne soit préférable sans comparaison à une science stérile et superbe?"[18]

Exegesis, at least when it takes its models from Scripture itself, is not a science of human invention. Its authority is that of Revelation. Yet, in order to truly understand the meaning of the Bible, one must look beyond the principles of exegesis to their ultimate source. "Ne dites pas que vous ne pouvez pas comprendre l'Ecriture," Sacy advises the readers of the *Nouveau Testament de Mons*, "aimez Dieu et il n'y aura rien que vous n'entendiez. . . . Celuy qui aime sçait tout: parce qu'il possède la fin à laquelle tout se rapporte."[19] The same principle stands at the heart of Pascal's epistemology. "Jésus-Christ est l'objet de tout et le centre où tout tend. Qui le connaît connaît la raison de toutes choses" (690/449).

1. Bédier, pp. 74–75.
2. Lafuma, p. 495.
3. *Blaise Pascal: Commentaires*, p. 226.
4. Lafuma, pp. 230–31.
5. Lafuma, p. 467.
6. See p. 204, above.
7. The Copernican theory of the solar system called into question, among other things, the strict veracity of the Bible's account that Joshua stopped the sun in the sky for a whole day (Joshua 10:13).
8. See pp. 19–20, above.
9. "De Saint Augustin à Pascal, par Sacy," in *Pascal présent*, pp. 133–46.
10. Bédier, p. 56.
11. *Pensées*, p. 100 n. 10.
12. Fontaine, 2:53.
13. Letter to Charlotte de Roannez (IV), Lafuma, p. 267.
14. I Corinthians 1:17–18: "For Christ did not send me to baptize but to preach the gospel, and not with worldly wisdom, *lest the cross of Christ be emptied of its power*. For the word of the cross is folly to those who are perishing, but to us who are being saved it is the power of God" (Revised Standard translation). Cf. fragment 655/808: "*Ne evacuetur crux Christi.*" See also Colossians 2:8, where Saint Paul restates the same idea with even greater force: "Make sure that no one traps you . . . by some secondhand, empty, rational philosophy based on the principles of this world instead of on Christ" (Jerusalem Bible translation).
15. Matthew 11:27: ". . . No one knows the Father except the Son and those to whom the Son chooses to reveal him" (Jerusalem Bible translation).
16. I Corinthians 1:20–21: ". . . If it was God's wisdom that human wisdom should not know God, it was because God wanted to save those who have faith through the foolishness of

the message that we preach" (Jerusalem Bible translation). Cf. fragment 221/189: "*Quia non cognovit per sapientiam, placuit Deo per stultitiam praedicationis salvos facere.*"

17. Lafuma, p. 267. Letter of October 1656.
18. *Daniel*, p. 244.
19. *Nouveau Testament de Mons*, Préface, Première Partie.

Bibliography

1. Works of Pascal

Oeuvres complètes
Brunschvicg, ed. 14 vols. Collection des Grands Ecrivains de la France. Paris: Hachette, 1904–14. *Pensées* in vols. 12–14.
Lafuma, ed. Collection l'Intégrale. Paris: Seuil, 1963.
Mesnard, J., ed. 3 vols. published to date. Bibliothèque Européenne. Paris: Desclée de Brouwer, 1964–. *Pensées* will figure in vol. 5.

Pensées
Havet, E., ed. 2d edition. Paris: Delagrave, 1866.
Sellier, P., ed. Paris: Mercure de France, 1976. Edition based upon the *Seconde Copie*.

2. Works of Louis-Isaac Le Maistre de Sacy

Lettres chrestiennes et spirituelles. Paris: Desprez, 1690.
Lettres inédites: 1650–1683. G. Delassault, ed. Paris: Nizet, 1959.
Le Nouveau Testament de Nostre Seigneur Jésus-Christ traduit en françois selon l'édition vulgate avec les différences du Grec. (Nouveau Testament de Mons). Mons: chez Gaspard Migeot, 1668.
La Sainte Bible . . . traduite en françois . . . avec de courtes notes tirées des Saints Pères. Liège: chez Broncart, 1702.
La Genèse: traduite en françois avec l'explication du sens littéral et du sens spirituel. Paris: Lambert Roulland, 1683.
L'Exode et Le Lévitique: traduits en françois. . . . Lyon: Leonard Plaignard, 1683.
Les Nombres. . . . 2d edition. Paris: G. Desprez, 1685.
Le Deutéronome. . . . 2d edition. Paris: G. Desprez, 1686.
Les Pseaumes de David. 3 vols. Paris: G. Desprez, 1699.
Les Proverbes de Salomon. . . . Paris: chez la Veuve Sareux, 1672.
L'Ecclésiaste de Salomon. . . . Bruxelles: chez Fricx, 1699.
Isaïe: traduit en françois . . . par Le Maistre de Sacy, Prestre. Bruxelles: chez Fricx, 1700.
Daniel: traduit . . . par Le Maistre de Sacy, Prestre. Bruxelles: chez Fricx, 1700.
Les douze petits prophètes. . . . Bruxelles: chez Fricx, 1698.
Les Machabées. . . . Paris: G. Desprez, 1691.

3. Manuscripts Cited

Archives Nationales
  Minutier Général, Etude LXXX, "vente du 9 mars 1684"
Bibliothèque de la Société de Port-Royal
  MS. P.R. 22, 23, 24. (*Mémoires* of Fontaine).
  MS. P.R. 128 bis. (*Recueil de dissertations sur divers sujets théologiques et de morale*).
Bibliothèque de l'Histoire du Protestantisme
  MS. 113 (*Mémoires* of Fontaine).
Bibliothèque Mazarine
  MS. 2465, 2466 (*Mémoires* of Fontaine).
  MS. 4555 (*Mémoires* of Fontaine).
Bibliothèque Nationale
  MS. 4333, nouvelles acquisitions françaises.
  MS. 1702, f. fr., n.a. f° 270–74.

4. Other Works Cited

Adam, Antoine. *Les Libertins au XVIIe siècle*. Paris: Buchet/Chastel, 1964.

Arnauld, Antoine. *Défense de la traduction imprimée à Mons: contre les sermons du Père Meinbourg, Jésuite*. Cologne: Jean du Buisson, 1668.

———. *Défense des versions de l'Ecriture Sainte, des offices de l'Eglise et des ouvrages des Pères et en particulier de la nouvelle traduction du Bréviaire*. Cologne: Nicolas Schouten, 1688.

———. *Oeuvres de Messire Antoine Arnauld*. 43 vols. Paris: Gabriel de Bellegarde, 1775–83.

Bédier, Joseph. "Etablissement d'un texte critique de 'L'Entretien de Pascal avec M. de Saci.'" In *Etudes critiques*. Paris: A. Collin, 1903.

Bogan, Z. *Homerus sive comparatio Homeri cum scriptoribus sacris quoad norman loquendi*. Oxoniae: 1658.

Bossuet, J.-B. *Discours sur l'histoire universelle*. Paris: Garnier-Flammarion, 1966.

Boucher, J. *Les Triomphes de la religion chrestienne contenans les résolutions de trois cens soixante et six questions*. Paris: L. Sonnius, 1628.

Clémencet, Dom. *Histoire générale de Port-Royal depuis la réforme de l'abbaie jusqu'à son entière destruction*. Amsterdam: chez Jean Vanduren, 1755–57.

Cognet, Louis. "Le jugement de Port-Royal sur Pascal." In *Blaise Pascal: l'homme et l'oeuvre*. Cahiers de Royaumont. Paris: Editions de Minuit, 1956.

Couchoud, P.-L. "L'Entretien de Pascal avec M. de Saci a-t-il eu lieu?" *Mercure de France* 311 (February 1951): 216–28.

Courcelle, Pierre. *L'Entretien de Pascal et Sacy: ses sources et ses énigmes*. Paris: Vrin, 1960

———. "De Saint Augustin à Pascal par Sacy." In *Pascal présent*. 2d edition. Clermont-Ferrand: G. de Bussac, 1962.

Couton, Georges. "Libertinage et Apologétique: les Pensées de Pascal contre la thèse des Trois Imposteurs." *XVIIe Siècle*, April-June 1980, pp. 181–95.

Dedieu, Joseph. "Survivances et influences de l'apologétique traditionnelle dans les *Pensées.*" *Revue d'histoire littéraire de la France,* October-December 1930 and January 1931, pp. 481–513 and 1–39.

Delassault, Geneviève. *Le Maistre de Sacy et son temps.* Paris: Nizet, 1957.

Desmarests de Saint-Sorlin. *Les Délices de l'Esprit: dialogues dédiez aux beaux esprits du monde.* Paris: A. Courbé, 1658.

Dubarle, A.-M. "Pascal et l'interprétation de l'Ecriture." In *Les Sciences philosophiques et théologiques,* 1941–42, 2:346–79.

Filleau de la Chaise. *Discours sur les Pensées de Pascal.* In Brunschvicg, vol. 12.

Fontaine, Nicolas. *Mémoires pour servir à l'histoire de Port-Royal.* Utrecht: 1736.

――――. *L'Histoire du Vieux et du Nouveau Testament, avec des explications édifiantes, tirées des Saints Pères . . . par le Sieur de Royaumont.* (*Bible de Royaumont*). Attributed to Sacy by the catalogue of the Bibliothèque Nationale.

Garasse, Père. *La Doctrine curieuse des beaux esprits de ce tems ou prétendus tels. . . .* Paris: chez Chapplet, 1624.

Gazier, A. "Un nouveau manuscrit de l'Entretien de Pascal avec M. de Saci." *Revue d'histoire littéraire de la France,* July 1895 (reprint).

Goldmann, Lucien. *Le Dieu caché: étude sur la vision tragique dans les Pensées de Pascal et dans le théâtre de Racine.* Paris: Gallimard, 1955.

――――. "Le Pari est-il écrit 'pour le libertin'?" In *Blaise Pascal: l'homme et l'oeuvre.* Cahiers de Royaumont. Paris: Editions de Minuit, 1956.

Gouhier, Henri. *Blaise Pascal: commentaires.* Paris: Vrin, 1971.

――――. *Pascal et les humanistes chrétiens: l'affaire Saint-Ange.* Paris: Vrin, 1974.

Gounelle, André. *"L'Entretien de Pascal avec M. de Sacy": étude et commentaire.* Paris: Presses Universitaires de France. 1966.

Hermant, Godefroy. *Mémoires.* A. Gazier, ed. Paris: Plon, 1905.

Hubert, Marie-Louise. *Pascal's Unfinished Apology: A Study of His Plan.* New Haven, Conn.: Yale University Press, 1952.

Jansenius, C. *Pentateuchus sive Commentarius in V Libros Moysis.* Lovanii: J. Zegeri, 1641.

Jolivet, R. "Pascal et l'argument prophétique." *Revue Apologétique* 36 (15 July and 1 August 1923): 486–94 and 513–22.

Julien-Eymard d'Angers, O.F.M. "Le Stoïcisme d'après l' 'Humanitas theologica' de Pierre Lescalopier, S.J." *Bulletin de littérature écclésiastique* 56 (1955): 23–36, 147–61.

Lagrange, M.-J. "Pascal et les prophéties messianiques." *Revue Biblique,* October 1906, pp. 533–60.

La Mothe Le Vayer. "*Rapports de l'Histoire Profane à la Sainte.*" In *Oeuvres de La Mothe Le Vayer.* Dresde: Michel Groell, 1758. Vol. 6, "lettre xciii."

――――. *Parallèles historiques.* In *Oeuvres. . . .* Vol. 7, "lettre cxvi."

La Peyrère, Isaac de. *Systema theologicum ex Praeadamitarum hypothesi.* Paris: 1655.

Lefebvre, Henri. *Pascal.* Paris: Nagel, 1954.

Lhermet, J. *Pascal et la Bible.* Paris: Vrin, 1930.

Mesnard, Jean. *Les Pensées de Pascal.* Paris: Société d'Edition d'Enseignement Supérieur, 1976.

———. *Pascal*. Paris: Hatier, 1967.

———. "Aux origines de l'édition des *Pensées*: les deux Copies." In *Les "Pensées" de Pascal ont trois cents ans*. Clermont-Ferrand: G. de Bussac, 1971.

———. "La Théorie des figuratifs dans les *Pensées* de Pascal." *Revue d'histoire de la philosophie et d'histoire générale de la civilisation*, July-September 1943, pp. 219–53.

Naudé, G. *Apologie pour tous les grands hommes qui ont esté faussement soupçonnez de Magie*. Paris: F. Targa, 1625.

Orcibal, Jean. *La Spiritualité de Saint-Cyran avec ses écrits de piété inédits*. Paris: Vrin, 1962.

———. *Les Origines du Jansénisme*. Paris: Vrin, 1947. Vol. 2.

———. "Les Jansénistes face à Spinoza." *Revue de littérature comparée*, October 1949, pp. 441–68.

Périer, Etienne. *Préface de l'Edition de Port-Royal*. In Lafuma, pp. 494–501.

Périer, Mme (Gilberte). *Vie de Blaise Pascal*. In Lafuma, pp. 17–33.

Périer, Marguerite. *Additions au Nécrologe de Port-Royal*. In Mesnard (*Oeuvres Complètes*), 1:1139–40.

Pintard, René. *Le Libertinage érudit dans la première moitié du XVIIe siècle*. Paris: Boivin, 1943.

———. "Pascal et les libertins." In *Pascal Présent*. Clermont-Ferrand: G. de Bussac, 1962.

Racine, Jean. *Abrégé de l'Histoire de Port-Royal*. In *Oeuvres complètes*. Collection Les Grands Ecrivains de la France. Paris: Hachette, 1886.

Saint-Cyran (Jean Duvergier de Hauranne, Abbé de). *Oeuvres chrestiennes et spirituelles*. Lyon: chez L. Aubin, 1679.

———. *Lettres chrestiennes et spirituelles*. Paris: J. Lemire, 1645.

Sainte-Beuve. *Port-Royal*. Bibliothèque de la Pléiade. Paris: Gallimard, 1952.

Sellier, Philippe. *Pascal et Saint Augustin*. Paris: A. Colin, 1970.

———. *Pascal et la liturgie*. Paris: Presses Universitaires de France, 1966.

Simon, Richard. *Critique de la bibliothèque des auteurs ecclésiastiques*. Paris: chez Etienne Ganeau, 1729.

Steinmann, Jean. *Richard Simon et les origines de l'exégèse biblique*. Paris: Desclée de Brouwer, 1960.

Stillingfleet, E. *Origines Sacrae or rational account of the grounds of Christian Faith as to the truth and divine authority of the Scriptures*. London: 1666.

Strowski, F. *Pascal et son temps*. Paris: Plon, 1907–8. Vol. 2.

Tauzin, E. "Les Notes de Pascal sur les prophéties messianiques." *Revue Apologétique*, October 1924.

Vossius, G.-J. *De theologia Gentili et physiologia christiana sive de origine de progressu idolatriae*. Amsterdam: C. Blaen, 1642.

General Index

Abelard, 35
Abraham, 107, 176, 184, 213, 217
Abrégé de la Chronologie Sainte (Lancelot), 204
"Académiciens", 28
Actes des Apôtres (Sacy), v. 1:8, 54, 76; v. 17:11, 168
Adam, 31, 58, 61, 63, 85, 87, 99, 100, 101, 103, 104–7, 108, 110, 111, 119, 121, 133, 149–50, 156, 162, 172, 176, 186–87, 215
Adam, Antoine, 157
Agar, 86
Amos 3:2, 200
Amram, 85
Andilly, Robert d', 45
Apologie de Raymond de Sebonde (Montaigne), 27–28
Apologie de la religion chrétienne (Pascal). See *Pensées* (Pascal)
Apostles, 77, 78, 192–93, 196, 221
A.P.R., 37, 80, 213, 217, 219
"A.P.R.", 135, 139–45, 146, 147, 148, 149, 151, 152, 156, 158, 159–61, 167, 172, 216
Aristotle, 22, 56, 82, 104, 111
Arnauld, Agnès, 21, 45
Arnauld, Angélique, 7, 45
Arnauld, Antoine, 23, 26, 35, 36, 45, 46, 50–52, 62, 64, 67 n. 14, 173
Arnauld, Catherine, 45, 46
Athées (*athéisme*), 113, 152, 157, 167
Augustine, Saint, 15, 22, 28, 29, 35, 59, 66, 74, 76, 77, 78, 79, 82, 83, 86, 87, 89, 94 nn. 20 and 28, 95 n. 36, 104, 111, 117, 119, 158, 171, 177, 188, 206 n. 40, 216
Automatisme des bêtes, 23
Auzoles, J. d', 62, 209 n. 83
Aztecs, 188

Babel, 65

Balzac, Guez de, 199
Barcos, Martin de, 36, 46
Beaubrun, Henri-Charles de, 54
Bédier, J., 10–14
Bénichou, Paul, 154
Beurrier, Père, 35, 152, 153; portraits of *libertins* by, 155–57
Bèze, Théodore de, 36
Bible, 19, 32, 35, 38, 47, 61–67, 92–93, 99, 102, 105–8, 119–21, 146–47, 149–50, 155, 156, 193–94, 212–14, 221; and "les deux sens de l'Ecriture," 173–84; and *libertins*, 56–61; at Port-Royal, 20–24; in spiritual life of Sacy, 21–24; Sacy's translation of New Testament, 48–53
Bogan, 64
Bossuet, Jacques Bénigne, 51, 52, 53, 62
Boucher, J., 60–61, 66, 156, 178

Cain, 59, 79
Calvinists, 50–51, 111
Campanella, 152
Cantique des Cantiques (Sacy), 54
Champaigne, Philippe de, 21, 24
Cicero, 82, 104, 158
Clémencet, Dom, 21, 36, 48, 49
Clement IX (pope), 51
Clement XI (pope), 67 n. 14
Cognet, Louis, 11, 38
"Commencement," 145, 166–67
Comparaison des chrétiens des premiers temps avec ceux d'aujourd'hui (Pascal), 123 n. 43.
Comparatism: between Bible and pagan myths, 63–65
"Conclusion," 218–19
Confessions (Augustine), 15, 29, 35, 117
"Contrariétés," 131–39, 140, 143, 147, 156, 158, 159, 163 n. 27, 216

"Contre la fable d'Esdras," 162
Copernicus, 213
Copies (of *Pensées*): 126–29, 151
Corinthians (I): vv. 1:17–18, 221 n. 14; vv. 1:20–21, 221 n. 16; v. 10:6, 86; v. 10:11, 181; v. 14:20, 177
Corneille, P., 46
Couchoud, P.-L., 9, 39 nn. 20–21
Counter Reformation, 47, 51
Courcelle, Pierre, 9, 14–17, 25, 30, 31, 33, 34, 35, 214
Couton, Georges, 157
Creation, the, 62, 63, 66, 85, 87, 102, 153, 156, 187, 188, 213
Cross, the, 74, 77, 89, 218–20
Cumiranus, Séraphin, 57
Cyprian, Saint, 83
Cyrano de Bergerac, 57, 58

D'Angers, Père Julien-Eymard, 26, 41 n. 93
Daniel: vv. 8:20–25, 9:24–27, 203; vv. 9:24–27, 204; v. 9:26, 194
David, 92, 171, 197, 220
Défense de la traduction imprimée à Mons (Arnauld), 50–51
Deism, 113, 153, 157, 217
Delassault, Genevieve, 3, 9, 36, 46, 48, 63, 67 n. 2
Descartes, 22–23
Desmarests de Saint-Sorlin, 61, 64, 65, 66, 156
Desmolets, Père Pierre-Nicolas, 8, 10
Deuteronomy: vv. 6:13, 6:16, 8:3, 122 n. 32; vv. 18:16, 32:21, 200; vv. 28:28–29, 208 n. 72; v. 32:31, 179, 199
Dialectical oppositions in the *Pensées*, 109
Dieu caché (*Deus absconditus*), 92, 143, 161, 166, 170–72, 181, 191
Discours sur les Pensées de M. Pascal (Filleau de la Chaise), 148–51
Discours sur les preuves du livre de Moïse (Filleau de la Chaise), 62
Discours sur l'histoire universelle (Bossuet), 62
"Divertissement," 140, 167, 213, 216
Doctrine curieuse (Garasse), 57–58, 60
Dogmatistes, 132–33
Douze petits prophètes (Sacy), 54, 195
Dubarle, Père, 197
Du Fossé, Thomas, 54, 68 n. 43

Ecclésiaste (Sacy), 54; v. 3:18, 138
Ecrits sur la grâce (Pascal), 110, 111, 119, 123 n. 62

Ecriture. See Bible
Egyptians, 185, 189
Elus, 172
Emmaus, 75, 178
Entretien avec M. de Saci (Fontaine), 4–5, 7–17, 24–35, 37, 79, 80, 132, 133, 205 n. 1, 211, 215
Epictetus, 9, 15, 24, 25–26, 30, 31, 33, 132, 211, 215
Epicureanism, 56, 156
Esdras, 57, 187
Essais (Montaigne), 27–28, 218
Etémare, l'abbé d', 8, 10
Eucharist, 18, 19, 33, 49, 75, 88, 93, 171, 191, 216, 217, 221
Evangile, l', 31, 32, 35, 36, 48–53, 189–90, 204, 211
Eve, 23, 106, 121, 123 n. 62
"Excellence," 165, 169, 196
Exegesis, 20, 76, 187, 173–82, 193–204, 221; Sacy on, 84–92
Exode (Sacy), 54, 88–91
Exodus, 89, 118; vv. 17:11–12, 94 n. 35; v. 20:5, 206 n. 20; v. 33:20, 58
Expérience, 20, 81, 104, 114–19, 125, 192–30, 133, 142, 145, 166
Ezechiel, 198; v. 20:25, 179, 206 n. 29
Ezra, Rabbi Aben, 57

Fall, the, 31, 32, 37, 58, 87, 99–102, 125–26, 130–45, 147–48, 149–52, 155, 158–59, 161, 163 n. 15, 172, 215, 217; absence of scriptural exposition of, in *Pensées*, 119–21; in argument of *Pensées*, 108–14; Sacy's presentation of, 102–8
Faugère, Prosper, 11, 37
"Fausseté des autres religions," 83, 157
Fideism, 57, 129, 218
Figuratifs, 71, 73, 86, 88, 91, 170, 173–82
Figures, 74, 75, 86–91, 92, 109, 170, 172, 173–82, 211
Filleau de la Chaise, 62, 115–16, 120, 145, 148–51, 182, 183
Flood, the, 59, 61, 85, 153, 176, 187
"Fondements," 166, 170–72, 194
Fontaine, Nicolas, 4, 7–17, 21–22, 34–35, 53, 54, 55, 56, 122 n. 24, 215; *Entretien avec M. de Saci*, 24–33
Fréquente Communion, La (Arnauld), 46, 50

Galatians 4:21–31, 86
Galileo, 19
Garasse, Père François, 57–58, 60, 64, 65, 66, 156

INDEX

Gassendi, Pierre, 152
Gazier, André, 11 n. 28
Gazier, Auguste, 10–11
Genèse (Sacy), 54, 58, 71–88, 102–8
Genesis, 61, 64, 73, 79, 85, 86, 87, 100, 101, 110, 112, 113, 115, 119–21, 122 n. 17, 133, 139, 143, 156, 213, 215; in Filleau's account, 149–50; in E. Périer's account, 146–47; and Sacy's exposition of the Fall, 102–8; vv. 2:17, 3:5, 123 n. 62; v. 3:15, 197; vv. 5:27, 32:30, 58; v. 6:14, 88; vv. 8:20 and 27–28, 178; vv. 17:7–9, 179; v. 49:10, 206 n. 23
Gentiles, 76, 77; conversion of, 198–200
Goldmann, Lucien, 154
Gouhier, Henri, 9, 25, 154, 175, 203, 205 n. 5, 207 n. 48, 212
Goulu, Jean de Saint-François, 9, 15, 41 n. 92
Gounelle, André, 3, 34
"Grandeur," 130–31
Grotius, H., 64, 66, 83

Haggai, 199; v. 2:4, 208
Hamon, Jean, 24
Harlay, M. de, 51
Havet, Ernest, 8
Heracles, 64
Hilarius, Saint, 83
Histoire critique de l'Ancien Testament (Richard Simon), 62
"*Histoire de la Chine*," 188–89, 213
Hobbes, Thomas, 57, 152
Homer, 73, 189
Hosea: v. 1:9, 200; v. 2:24, 199, 208 n. 66; v. 3:4, 179, 206 n. 24; v. 6:3, 202
Hubert, Marie-Louise, 121 n. 1, 162 n. 1
Huré, Charles, 64, 68 n. 43

Iliad (Homer), 64, 122 n. 17, 189
Imitation de Jésus-Christ (Sacy, tr.), 47
Incarnation, the, 32, 33, 55, 56, 91, 99, 104, 105, 106, 111, 113, 114, 172, 175, 189, 191, 194, 215, 217, 220
Isaac, 85, 213, 217
Isaiah, 54, 197, 198; ch. 29, 61, 55, 202; v. 5:25, 206 n. 20; vv. 6:10, 8:14–15, 29:10, 61:3, 42:1–7, 202; vv. 6:1–3, 191; vv. 19:19, 65:1–19, 66:18, 199; v. 40:6, 138; vv. 43:18–19, 206 n. 26; vv. 45:15, 53:5, 8:14, 205 n. 7; v. 49:6, 208 n. 63; vv. 59:9–11, 37; v. 65:16, 200
Islam, 71, 83–84, 157, 175, 186

Jacob, 176, 179, 187, 213, 217
Jansenius, 53, 61, 66, 94 n. 28, 109, 117, 119
Jeremiah, 21, 187; vv. 3:15–16, 206 n. 26; v. 31:31, 179, 206 n. 28
Jerusalem, 194, 202; destruction of, 77
Jesuits, 110–11, 188
Jesus Christ, 157, 169, 171–72, 173, 176, 180, 181, 182, 194, 202, 220–21; and Adam, 106; attacked by *libertins*, 155; and Mohammed, 83–84; and Moses, 73–76; "Preuves de Jesus-Christ," 189–93
Job, 130
Joel: v. 2:28, 138, 199, 208 n. 66
John: vv. 3:14–15, 74; vv. 5:39, 6:32, 75; v. 5:46, 94 n. 5; vv. 8:36, 6:32, 1:47, 206 n. 30
Jonah, 58
Josephus, 77, 187, 190
Joshua, 61 n. 71, 92
Juifs (Jews), 78–79, 91–92, 107, 146, 149, 156, 166, 178, 179, 182–89, 193, 196, 197, 198, 211; and rabbinical tradition, 173–74; *réprobation des*, 200–202
Justin, 83

Kings (I): vv. 28:8–21, 61 n. 72
Koran, 83–84, 180

La Fontaine, Jean de, 46
Lafuma, Louis, 126–27
La Mothe le Vayer, François de, 26, 59, 111, 152, 153, 156
Lancelot, Claude, 209 n. 8
La Peyrère, Isaac de, 58, 61, 152, 156, 212, 213
Le Maitre, Antoine, 7, 8, 9 n. 21, 36, 46, 67 n. 14
Le Pailleur, 152
"Lettre pour porter à rechercher Dieu," 158
"Lettre sur la mort de son père" (Pascal), 117
Levi, 85
Leviathan (Hobbes), 57
Lévitique (Sacy), 54, 204; v. 6:9, 65; v. 7:34, 179
Lhermet, J., 3, 17, 20, 27, 93
Liasse-table, 127–29, 151
Libertin, 33, 38, 56–61, 76, 82, 83, 120, 133, 138, 139, 146, 147, 149, 151, 152–59, 160, 166, 167, 170, 180, 184, 185, 194, 200, 218, 219, 220
"Loi figurative," 173, 175, 176, 178–81, 202
Longueville, Mme de, 53
Louvain Bible, 47–48, 52
Luke: v. 2:14,·50; v. 10:42, 181; v. 21:24, 77; vv. 24:13–32, 178; vv. 24:44–45, 177

Luynes, Charles-Louis, duc de, 7, 36, 175

Maccabees (I): v. 3:48, 65; (II) ch. 2, 187; ch. 4, 194
Malachi: v. 1:11, 198, 199, 206 n. 26; v. 2:1, 202
Manichean heresy, 29, 82
Marot, 51
Martini, Raymond, 173–74, 188
Matthew: vv. 4:1–10, 122 n. 31; v. 8:11, 76–77; v. 11:27, 221 n. 15; v. 12:40, 58; v. 11:27, 221 n. 15
Meinbourg, Père, 50
Mémorial (Pascal), 5–6
Mercury, 64
Méré, Antoine Gombault, chevalier de, 154–55
Mersenne, Père Martin, 152–53, 157
Mesnard, Jean, 8–9, 11–12, 15–16, 25, 34, 37–38, 87, 118, 126–29, 139, 150–51, 154, 160, 161, 162 n. 2, 175, 206 n. 21
Messie (Messiah): 76, 91, 169, 171–72, 173, 176, 181, 182, 183, 197, 198, 203–5; "Preuves de Jesus-Christ," 190–91
Metaphysical proofs, 112, 114, 148, 169, 196
Methuselah, 58, 85
Micah: v. 5:2, 202
Miracles, 57, 61, 73, 78, 169, 184; of Jesus, 77
"Misère"/"Grandeur," 37, 109, 121, 130–39, 140–42, 146–47, 148, 149, 150, 151, 158
Miton, Damien, 154–55, 158
Mohammed, 83–84, 148, 157, 180
Molière, 46
Mons, Nouveau Testament de, 48–53, 67 n. 14, 221
Montaigne, 15, 24, 25, 27–31, 33, 129, 130, 131, 132, 153, 188, 205 n. 1, 211, 218
Moses, 57, 58, 59, 61, 63, 64, 71, 82, 83, 85, 89, 92, 93, 104, 107, 108, 150, 157, 176, 179, 182, 185–87, 197, 198, 200, 213; and the New Testament, 73–76
Mystère de Jésus (Pascal), 123 n. 62, 172

Naudé, Gabriel, 59
Neo-Stoics, 26
New Testament, 77, 86, 106, 168, 173, 177, 178, 180, 202, 203, 212; and "Preuves de Jesus-Christ," 189–90
Nicodemus, 74
Nicole, Pierre, 23, 35, 36, 67 n. 14
Nierembergius, 64
Noah, 58, 65, 88, 176, 183
Noël, Père, 19–20, 213
Nouet, Père Jacques, 50

Numbers: ch. 21, 111; v. 21:89, 74

Obscurité, 190–191
Odyssey (Homer), 64, 122 n. 17
Old Testament, 53–54, 60–61, 75, 76, 81, 83–84, 86, 87, 88, 89, 102, 106, 107, 108, 122 n. 17, 151, 165, 168, 173, 175, 176, 177, 179, 180, 181, 182, 183, 184, 185, 187, 188, 193, 202, 203, 211, 212
Orcibal, Jean, 69 n. 79
"Ordre," 99, 192
Origen, 34 n. 121
Original Sin, 18, 76, 99–102, 174, 197, 215; atheists' critique of doctrine of, 155; Sacy's exposition of, 102–8; treatment of, in *Pensees*, 108–21

Païens sages, 111
"Paix de l'Eglise," 51, 53
Pan, le grand, 199
"Pari, le," 154, 162
Pascal, Blaise: apologetic uses of Fall by, 130–45; and "A.P.R.," 145–52; "conversion" and first retreat of, at Port-Royal, 14–17; defense of Moses by, 62; empirical character of *Apology* of, 211–17; "entretien" of, with M. de Sacy, 24–35; evolution of apologetic vocation of, 17–20; exposition of doctrine of Fall by, 108–21; and "fable d'Esdras," 187; on hidden character of Revelation, 158–62; on Jewish people, 182–85; on "la plus grande des preuves," 193–205; on *libertins*, 152–58; on limits of apologetic dialogue, 218–21; and order of *Pensées*, 125–30; other meetings of, with Sacy, 36–37; and "Preuves de Jésus-Christ," 189–93; on proof of figurative character of Old Testament, 178–82; on proof of Pentateuch, 185–86; and rabbinical tradition, 173–75; role of Bible in *Pensées* of, 99–101; and *Sinicae Historiae*, 188–89; on uses of reason, 166–70
Pascal, Jacqueline, 4–5, 7, 16, 37
Patriarches, 85, 92, 186–87, 197, 213
Paul, Saint, 74, 86, 88, 102, 119, 123 n. 60, 176, 177, 181, 192, 220
Pelagian heresy, 26, 104, 111
Pentateuch, 57, 58, 61, 62, 66, 71, 75, 85, 107, 119, 151, 162, 183, 185, 186–87, 189, 200, 211, 213
Périer, Etienne, 37, 38, 62, 120, 126, 145–48, 149, 150, 151, 211
Périer, Gilberte Pascal, 4–5, 7, 17, 18, 38, 152, 153, 158, 214

INDEX 231

Périer, Louis, 126
Périer, Marguerite, 4, 8, 10, 36–37
"Perpétuité," 162, 183, 184
"Petites Ecoles," 47
Petrarch, 35
Phaedrus, 47
Philo, 122, n. 17, 187
Philosophes, 33, 61, 79–81, 83, 104, 117, 139–40, 146, 149
Pintard, René, 152–53, 154–55
Plato, 82, 198
Platonists, 83
Pliny, 104
Plutarch, 199
Polytheism, 91
Pomponne, 54
Port-Royal (Paris), 20–21, 45, 46
Port-Royal-des-Champs, 4–5, 7, 24, 35, 36, 37, 46, 53, 214, 215
Préadamites. See La Peyrère, Isaac de
Préface à la Genèse (Sacy), 56, 57, 58, 60, 63, 66–67, 71–93, 157, 182, 186, 218
Préface sur le traité du vide (Pascal), 19, 212, 213
"Preuves de Jésus-Christ," 76, 157, 165, 189–93, 198
"Preuves de Moïse," 157, 162, 165, 183, 187
"Preuve des miracles par la prophétie et de la prophétie par les Juifs" (Sacy), 78
Prophéties, 71, 78, 165–66, 168, 169, 170–71, 172, 176, 177, 178, 179, 180, 181, 182, 211, 212, 218; as "la plus grande des preuves," 193–205
"Prosopopée," 135, 140, 142, 159, 219
Protestant exegesis, 74
Protestant heresies, 76
Protestant translations of Bible, 22, 27, 47, 50
Proverbs, 140; v. 8:31, 138
Provinciales, Les (Pascal), 20, 36, 110, 212
Psalms: v. 21:28, 208 n. 62; v. 48:12, 163 n. 15; v. 71:11, 208 n. 64; v. 77:2, 177; v. 81:6, 138; v. 109:1, 178; vv. 117–22, 108:8, 68:22, 15:10, 202
Pugio fidei (Raymond Martini), 173–74, 199
Pyrrhoniens, 132–33

Quesnel, Père, 67 n. 14

"Rabbinage," 163 n. 27, 173–75
Rabelais, 123 n. 59
Racine, Jean, 21, 36, 46
Raison (reason): 20, 28, 81, 102, 106, 107, 112, 113, 114, 125–126, 136, 166, 171, 181, 204, 212, 217, 218, 219, 220, 221; *soumission et usage de*, 166–70
Rebours, Antoine de, 17, 18–19, 39 n. 21
Recueil original (Pensées), 126
Réflexions morales (Quesnel), 67 n. 14
Réprobation des juifs, 77, 198, 200–202
Réprouvés, 92, 172
Resurrection: 73, 74, 77, 78, 192–93
Revelation: 28, 30, 31, 60, 75, 85, 99, 102, 104, 106, 107, 108–14, 119, 120, 125–26, 129–30, 133, 136, 140, 142, 143, 145, 159, 160–62, 166, 167, 168, 169, 171, 172, 173, 211, 216, 218, 219, 220; proofs of Christianity drawn from outside, 79–84
Roannez, Charlotte de, 111, 216, 220
Rois (Sacy), 54
Romans (Book of): v. 5:12, 102
Romans, 185, 194
Royaumont, Bible de, 105, 112, 121, 122 n. 24, 206 n. 39, 207 n. 40, 209 n. 81

Sacy, Isaac-Louis Le Maistre de, 3, 7, 54–56, 57, 58, 109, 110, 111, 119, 133, 136, 157, 161, 163 n. 15, 181, 183, 199, 203, 204, 214, 217, 218, 221; analysis of Old Testament prophecies by, 194–97; Bossuet on, 52–53; on Cartesian philosophy, 22–23; cites *Pensées*, 108; defense of Bible by, 61–67; devotion of, to Scripture, 21–24; "entretien" of, with Pascal, 45–46; exposition of doctrine of Original Sin by, 101–7; exposition of exegetical principles by, 84–92; on figurative character of Old Testament, 175–78; life of, to 1650, 45–46; literary works of, 46–47; method of spiritual direction of, 24; and *Préface à la Genèse*, 71–93; as translator of *Nouveau Testament de Mons*, 48–50; as translator of Old Testament, 53–54
Sagesse (Sacy), 54
Sagesse de Dieu, 135, 140–45, 158, 160–61, 167, 217, 219
Saint-Cyran, Jean Duvergier de Hauranne, abbé de, 17, 23, 32, 35, 39 n. 21, 45, 46, 55, 62, 66, 88, 112
Sainte-Ange, Jacques Forton, 18, 214
Sainte-Beuve, 8, 12, 20, 27, 45, 46, 47; on style of Sacy, 53
Sainte Chronologie (d'Auzoles), 62
Saints, 184; Old Testament, 92
Salomon, 130
Samson, 64
Saturn, 65
Sellier, Philippe, 16, 37, 38, 111, 117,

Sellier, Philippe (*continued*)
  126, 139, 151, 158–59, 168, 169, 188, 207, 216
Sem, 85, 187
Sens littéral, 102
Sens spirituel, 86, 176–82, 183, 196
Septuagint, 58, 187
Séricourt, Simon Le Maistre de, 46, 67 n. 2
Serpent d'airain, 74–75
Simon, Richard, 56, 62, 65–66, 87, 180
Singlin, Antoine, 4–5, 7, 24, 39 n. 21, 46
Sinicae Historiae, 188–89, 213
Sirmond, Père Jacques, 62
Skepticism (Skeptics), 28, 29, 31, 33, 132–33, 153, 211
Socrates, 111
Solitaires (of Port-Royal), 7, 46, 62, 80, 145, 152, 215
"Soumission et usage de la raison," 165, 167
"Souverain Bien," 117–18, 131, 139–40, 216
Spinoza, 62, 180
Stillingfleet, E., 64
Stoics, 31, 33, 211
Strowski, Fortunat, 9

Talmud, 174, 199, 200
Témoignage, 166, 193, 196, 197, 199, 211
Tertullian, 32, 42 n. 121, 65, 83
Touret, 54, 68 n. 43
"Transition," 169
Trent, Council of, 52, 76
Tribus Impostoribus (theory of), 157
Trinité (la Sainte), 76, 197
Triomphes de la religion chrestienne (Boucher), 60
Tronchai, Michel, 8, 10–11

Unigenitus: 67 n. 14

Vallemont, Le Maistre de, 67 n. 2
Vanino, Lucilio, 58
Vaumurier, 7, 36, 48, 49, 175
Véritable religion, 139–42, 175, 185, 194, 195, 205, 218
Voisin, Joseph de, 173
Vossius, 64

Zacharie: vv. 11:12, 12:10, 202

Index to "Pensees" Cited

Fragment numbers are those of the Lafuma *Oeuvres completes* (Collection l'Integrale, Editions du Seuil, 1963)

Fr.	Ref.	Fr.	Ref.
1	94 n. 22	175	218
4	164 n. 49	180	165, 169, 195
5	154	182	168
6	99, 121, 158	185	40 n. 64 168
44	176	188	41 n. 98
69	162 n. 12	189	100, 165, 169, 171, 212, 222 n. 16
110	159, 162 n. 12	190	112, 169
111	130	198	169–70
114	130	203	94 n. 22
117	130, 131	207	94 n. 22
122	37	209	83, 84, 94 n. 22, 170
126	123 n. 53	215	170
131	110, 115, 122 n. 37, 132, 133, 135, 136, 138, 139, 159, 163 n. 27, 164 n. 49	218	94 n. 22, 180
		223	170
		225	171, 191, 217, 221
139	215	226	101, 108, 119
143	140, 216	228	171, 172
148	116, 117, 118, 119, 121, 131, 140, 215, 216, 217	232	171
		233	171
149	37, 42 n. 112, 80, 140, 142, 143, 151, 158, 160, 161, 167, 172, 216, 219	235	172
		236	150, 171, 172, 190
		237	171
150	167	242	171
151	166	243	94 n. 22
154	166	251	67 n. 24
158	167	252	94 n. 28
160	154	253	94 nn. 6–7, 178, 180, 181
161	167	255	181, 190, 198, 203
163	167, 214	257	177, 179, 180
164	167, 212	260	177, 179, 181
165	166	263	179
170	168	267	180, 181
171	168	268	206 n. 30
172	168	270	89, 181, 203, 206 n. 31
174	168	272	178

Fr.	Ref.	Fr.	Ref.
274	71, 165, 173, 175, 198	431	109, 121
275	217	436	186, 189, 190, 212
276	179, 180	449	113, 114, 115, 119, 153, 217, 221
277	174	451	184, 185
278	163 n. 27, 174	452	200
281	101, 119, 183, 197	453	206 n. 26
282	197	454	94 n. 22, 184, 185
283	207 n. 40	456	184
287	173	463	114
290	186	471	108, 109
291	220	474	108, 185, 189
292	186	481	188, 207 n. 42
296	63, 187	483	200, 202
298	192	485	194
300	190	487	200, 202, 203, 220
301	111, 191	489	37, 199, 200
308	191, 192, 217	492	184, 200
309	190	493	200
310	94 n. 10, 193	497	200
315	76, 197	498	199
316	190	499	190
317	193, 204	501	86
318	189	502	182, 196
321	94 n. 22	575	156, 212
322	192	590	86–87, 206 n. 40, 207 n. 40
323	198	597	164 n. 52
324	94 n. 9, 198, 208 n. 66	609	197
327	94 n. 9	614	182
328	208 n. 66	642	158, 164 n. 52
330	199	695	109, 114
332	197	769	113
335	193, 195, 197	781	112, 217, 220
336	203, 208 n. 77	799	206 n. 27
338	94 n. 9, 198, 199, 203, 208 n. 77	808	221 n. 14
339	203	809	109
341	204	812	207 n. 44
343	199	818	94 n. 6
347	94 n. 9, 200	820	125, 139, 159
348	200, 202	822	188, 193, 213
377	219	853	164 n. 52
378	219	919	123 n. 62
380	218	929	172
381	218	959	123 n. 62
382	218, 219	960	111
403	130, 162 n. 10	970–72	57, 164 n. 78, 187
418	154, 162		
427	101, 119, 158, 167		

www.ingramcontent.com/pod-product-compliance
Lightning Source LLC
Chambersburg PA
CBHW030134240426
43672CB00005B/124